THIS ONE'S A REAL
MOTHERFUCKER...

"... dazzling art and an interesting psychological drama"

– Bloody-Disgusting.com

"This comic is a really great read, like the kind of stuff we used to get from *Preacher*, *Y: The Last Man*, and *Transmetropolitan*."

– IGN.com

"Kowalski's art continues to impress, using light and shadow as his weapons, just as much as the understated colour spectrum that has become a signature of the series so far. Sex is a slow-builder, and one that we suspect will ultimately reward a reader with stamina and longevity."

– Behind the Panels

"... the art, the color, the textures, or the writing, everything about this comic is good and when it all comes together it is something amazing."

– Speak Geeky To Me

"... a great read with great characters who are all a bit off and deeply complex. 5/5 stars."

– Unleash the Fanboy

"Do yourselves a favor and just give it a chance, better yet, read it with your significant other. Do it. Come on. You know you want to."

– Ket's Comics

"Joe Casey and Piotr Kowalski have created a stylish look at an often overlooked part of the superhero genre."

– Comic Book Resources

"... anyone who approaches Sex with an open mind and a willingness to take their time with it is much more likely to have a fulfilling experience than those who try to rush it."

– Comic Bastards

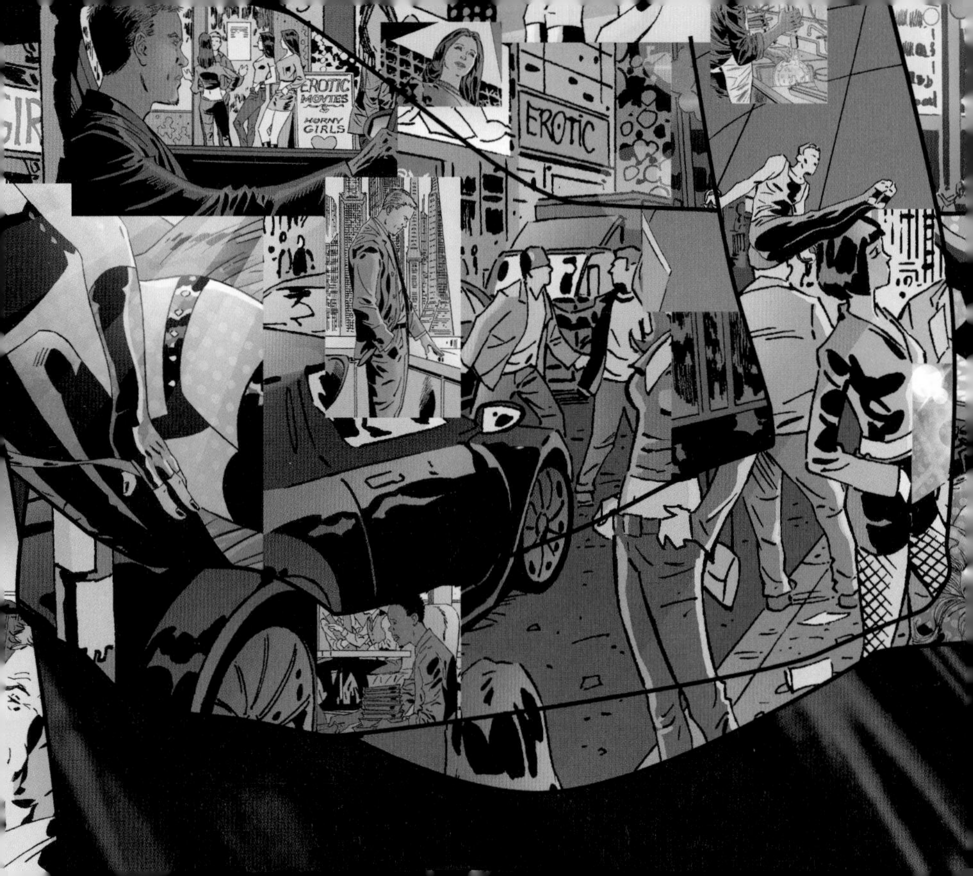

EROTIC MOVIES & HORNY GIRLS
EROTIC

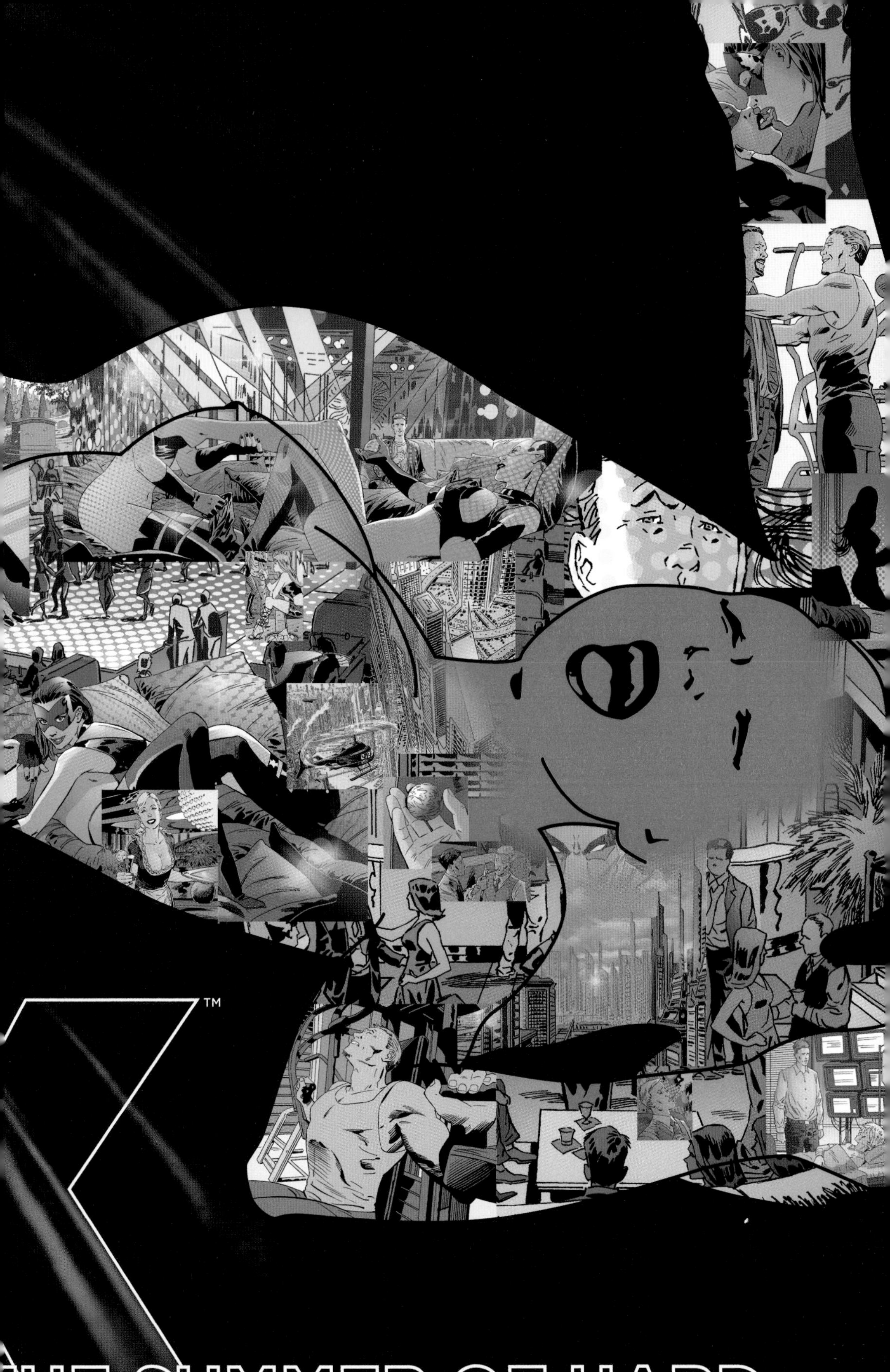

THE SUMMER OF HARD

www.manofaction.tv

IMAGE COMICS, INC.

ROBERT KIRKMAN
CHIEF OPERATING OFFICER
ERIK LARSEN
CHIEF FINANCIAL OFFICER
TODD MCFARLANE
PRESIDENT
MARC SILVESTRI
CHIEF EXECUTIVE OFFICER
JIM VALENTINO
VICE-PRESIDENT.
ERIC STEPHENSON
PUBLISHER
RON RICHARDS
DIRECTOR OF BUSINESS DEVELOPMENT
JENNIFER DE GUZMAN
PR & MARKETING DIRECTOR
BRANWYN BIGGLESTONE
ACCOUNTS MANAGER
EMILY MILLER
ACCOUNTING ASSISTANT
JAMIE PARRENO
MARKETING ASSISTANT
EMILIO BAUTISTA
SALES ASSISTANT
JAEMIE DUDAS
ADMINISTRATIVE ASSISTANT
JEREMY SULLIVAN
DIGITAL RIGHTS COORDINATOR
TYLER SHAINLINE
EVENTS COORDINATOR
DAVID BROTHERS
CONTENT MANAGER
JONATHAN CHAN
PRODUCTION MANAGER
DREW GILL
ART DIRECTOR
MEREDITH WALLACE
PRINT MANAGER
MONICA GARCIA
SENIOR PRODUCTION ARTIST
VINCENT KUKUA
JENNA SAVAGE
ADDISON DUKE
PRODUCTION ARTISTS

www.imagecomics.com

SEX Book One: The Summer of Hard.
First printing. November 2013.

ISBN: 978-1607067849

Published by Image Comics, Inc.

Office of publication:
2001 Center Street, Sixth Floor,
Berkeley, CA 94704.

Copyright © Joe Casey.
All rights reserved.

SEX, its logos, and all character likenesses
herein are trademarks of Joe Casey unless
expressly indicated. Contains material
originally published in single-magazine
form as SEX #1-8 by Image Comics. Image
Comics® and its logos are registered
trademarks and copyrights of Image Comics,
Inc. All rights reserved. No part of this
publication may be reproduced or transmitted,
in any form or by any means (except for short
excerpts for review purposes) without the
express written permission of Joe Casey or
Image Comics, Inc. All names, characters,
events, and locales in this publication,
except for satirical purposes, are entirely
fictional, and any resemblance to actual
persons (living or dead) or entities or events
or places is coincidental. PRINTED IN THE
USA. For information regarding the CPSIA on
this printed material call: 203-595-3636 and
provide reference # RICH – 523323.

For international licensing inquiries,
write to:
foreignlicensing@imagecomics.com

JOE CASEY WRITER
PIOTR KOWALSKI ARTIST
BRAD SIMPSON COLORIST
RUS WOOTON LETTERER
SONIA HARRIS GRAPHIC DESIGNER

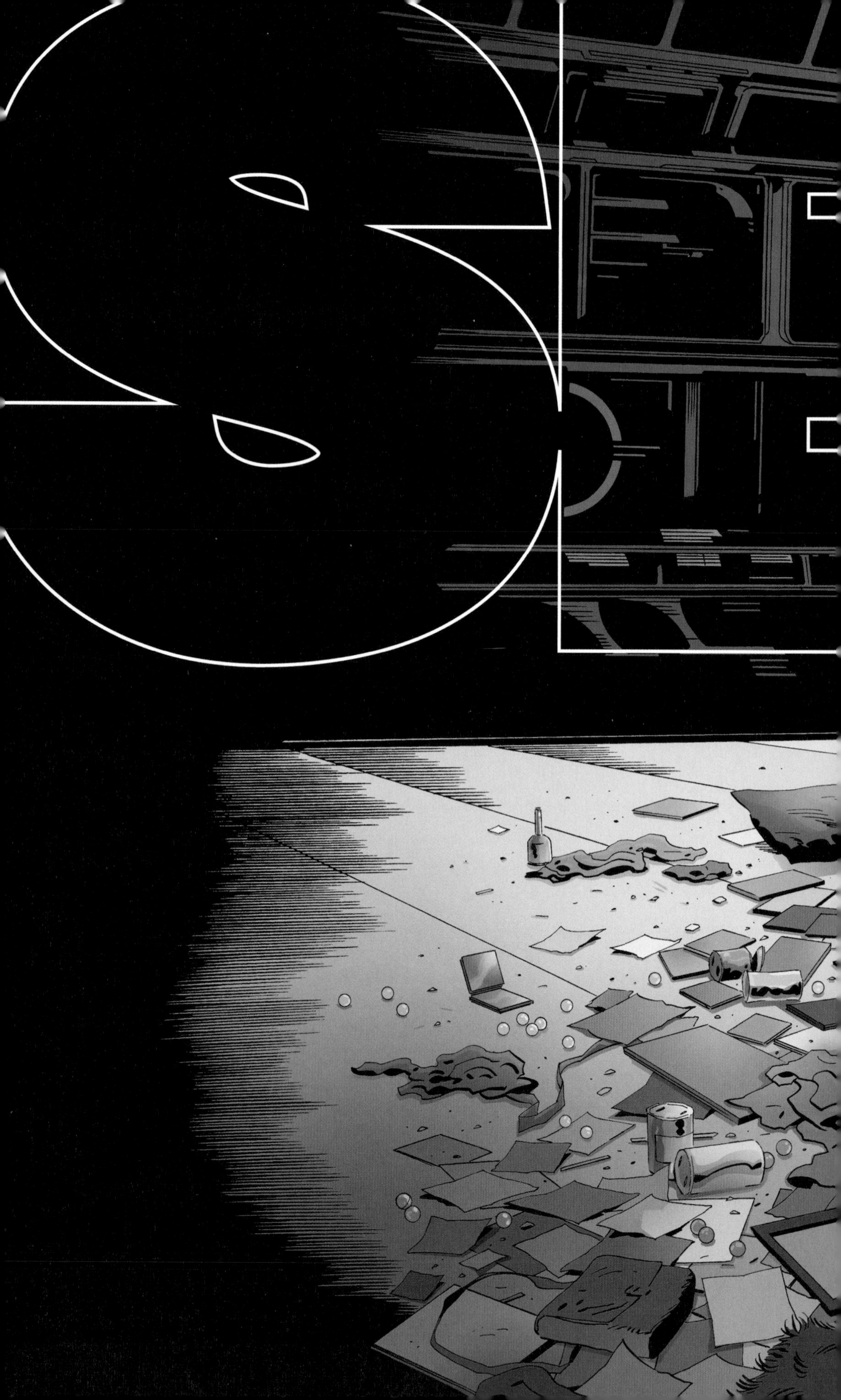

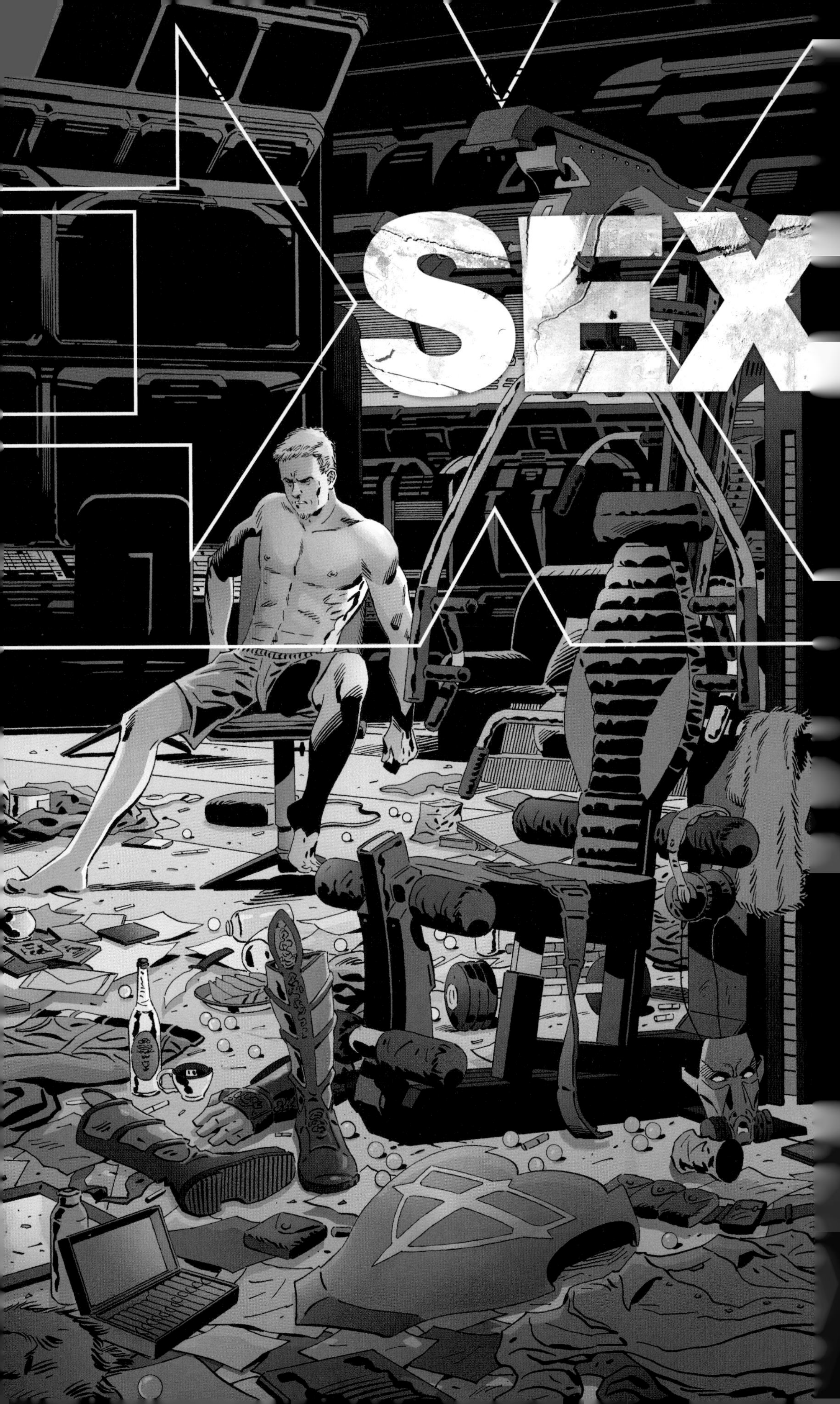
SEX

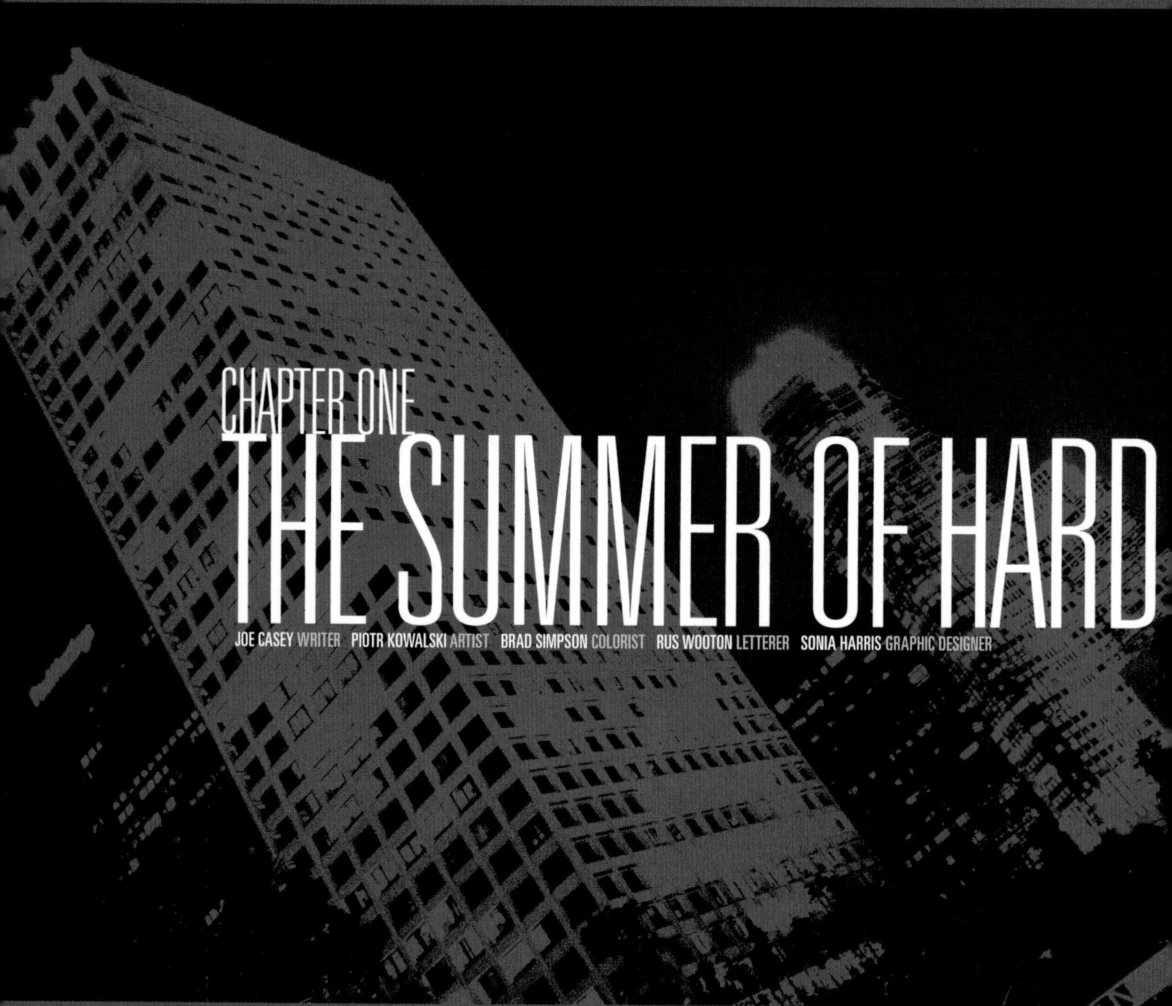

CHAPTER ONE

THE SUMMER OF HARD

JOE CASEY WRITER   PIOTR KOWALSKI ARTIST   BRAD SIMPSON COLORIST   RUS WOOTON LETTERER   SONIA HARRIS GRAPHIC DESIGNER

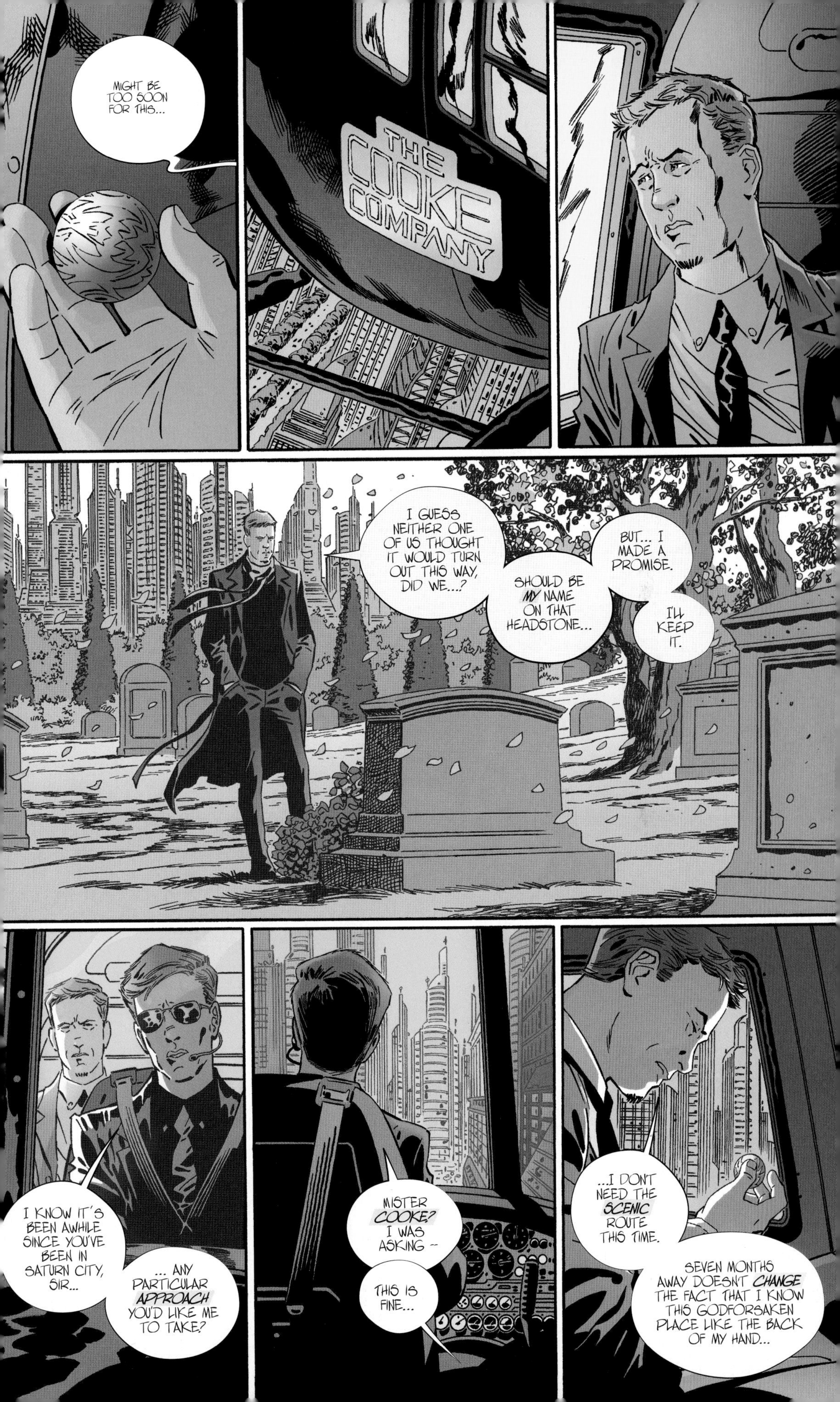
MIGHT BE TOO SOON FOR THIS...
THE COOKE COMPANY
I GUESS NEITHER ONE OF US THOUGHT IT WOULD TURN OUT THIS WAY, DID WE...?
SHOULD BE MY NAME ON THAT HEADSTONE...
BUT... I MADE A PROMISE.
I'LL KEEP IT.
I KNOW IT'S BEEN AWHILE SINCE YOU'VE BEEN IN SATURN CITY, SIR...
... ANY PARTICULAR APPROACH YOU'D LIKE ME TO TAKE?
MISTER COOKE? I WAS ASKING --
THIS IS FINE...
...I DON'T NEED THE SCENIC ROUTE THIS TIME.
SEVEN MONTHS AWAY DOESN'T CHANGE THE FACT THAT I KNOW THIS GODFORSAKEN PLACE LIKE THE BACK OF MY HAND...

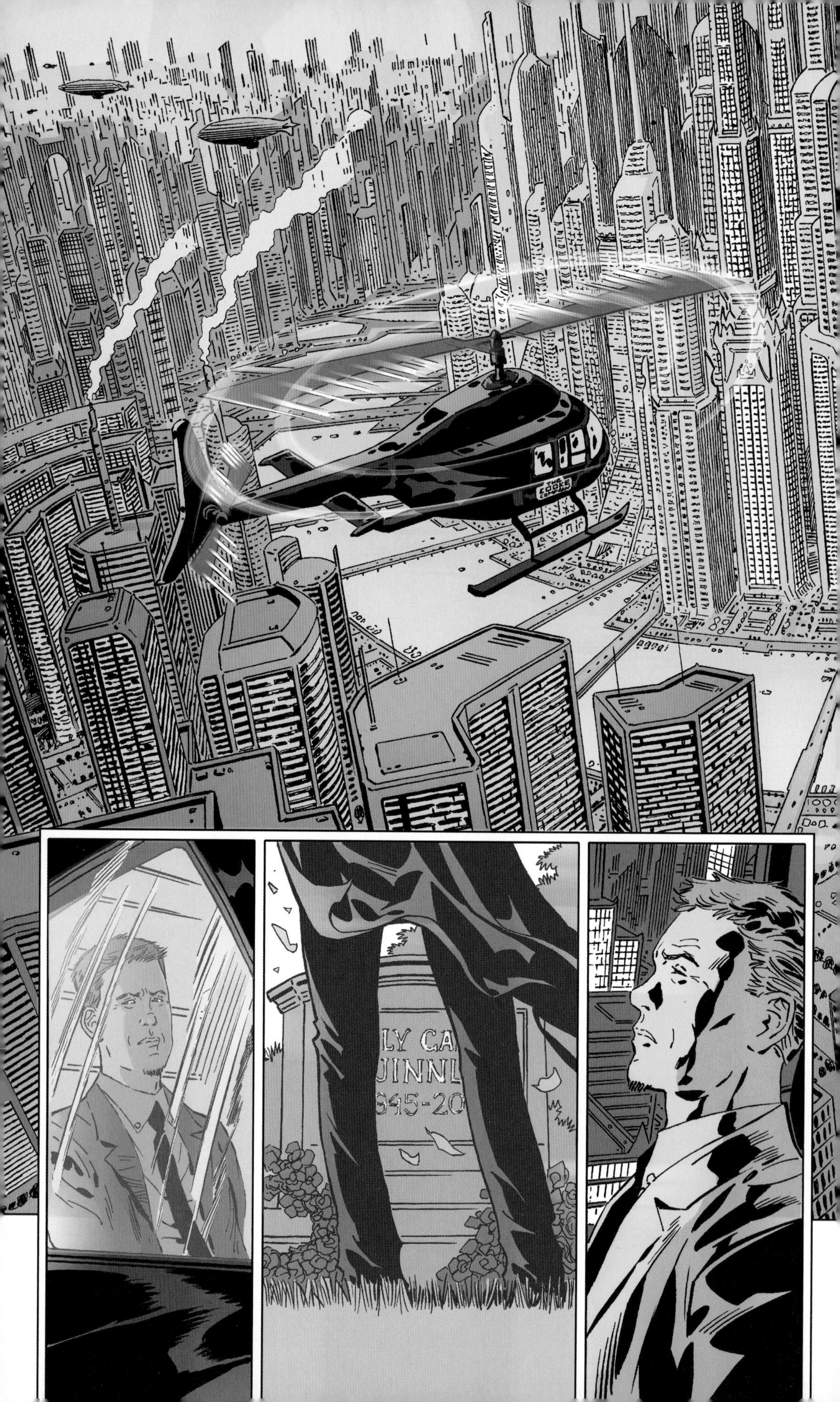
THE COOKE COMPANY
LY CA
JINNL
945-20

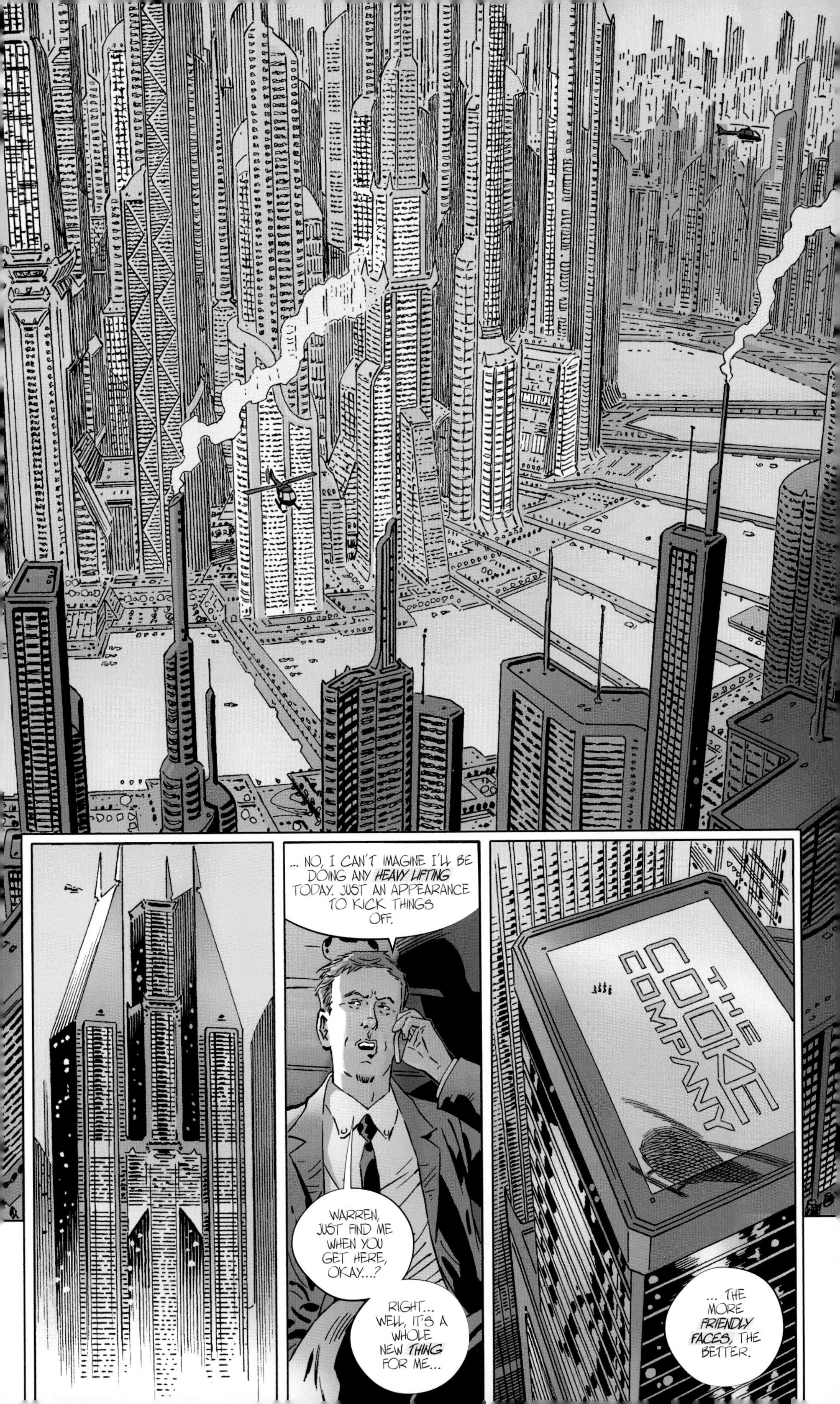
... NO, I CAN'T IMAGINE I'LL BE DOING ANY HEAVY LIFTING TODAY. JUST AN APPEARANCE TO KICK THINGS OFF.
WARREN, JUST FIND ME WHEN YOU GET HERE, OKAY...?
RIGHT... WELL, IT'S A WHOLE NEW THING FOR ME...
THE COOKE COMPANY
... THE MORE FRIENDLY FACES, THE BETTER.

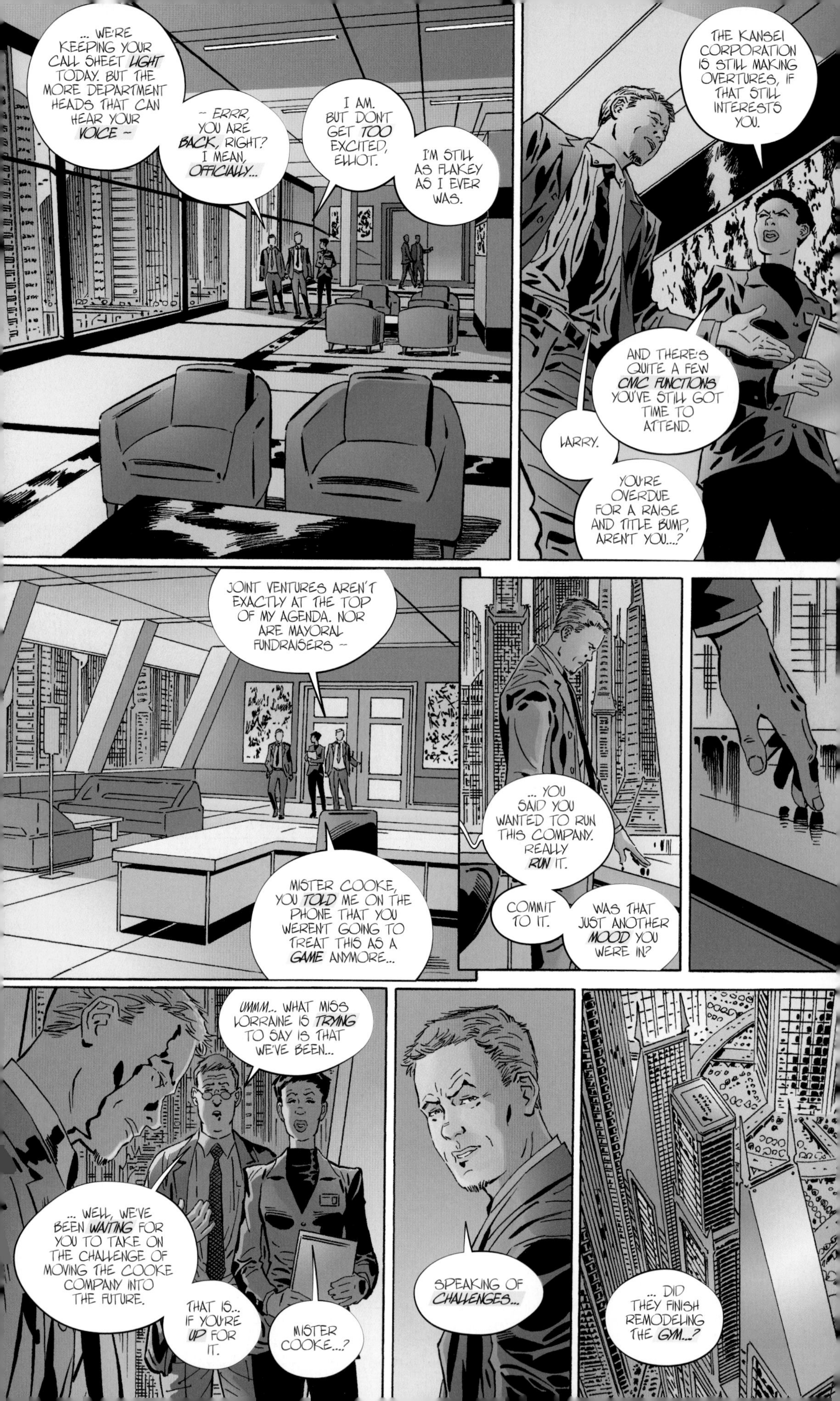
... WE'RE KEEPING YOUR CALL SHEET LIGHT TODAY. BUT THE MORE DEPARTMENT HEADS THAT CAN HEAR YOUR VOICE ~
~ ERRR, YOU ARE BACK, RIGHT? I MEAN, OFFICIALLY...
I AM. BUT DON'T GET TOO EXCITED, ELLIOT.
I'M STILL AS FLAKEY AS I EVER WAS.
THE KANSEI CORPORATION IS STILL MAKING OVERTURES, IF THAT STILL INTERESTS YOU.
AND THERE'S QUITE A FEW CIVIC FUNCTIONS YOU'VE STILL GOT TIME TO ATTEND.
LARRY.
YOU'RE OVERDUE FOR A RAISE AND TITLE BUMP, AREN'T YOU...?
JOINT VENTURES AREN'T EXACTLY AT THE TOP OF MY AGENDA. NOR ARE MAYORAL FUNDRAISERS ~
MISTER COOKE, YOU TOLD ME ON THE PHONE THAT YOU WEREN'T GOING TO TREAT THIS AS A GAME ANYMORE...
... YOU SAID YOU WANTED TO RUN THIS COMPANY. REALLY RUN IT.
COMMIT TO IT.
WAS THAT JUST ANOTHER MOOD YOU WERE IN?
UMMM... WHAT MISS LORRAINE IS TRYING TO SAY IS THAT WE'VE BEEN...
... WELL, WE'VE BEEN WAITING FOR YOU TO TAKE ON THE CHALLENGE OF MOVING THE COOKE COMPANY INTO THE FUTURE.
THAT IS... IF YOU'RE UP FOR IT.
MISTER COOKE...?
SPEAKING OF CHALLENGES...
... DID THEY FINISH REMODELING THE GYM...?

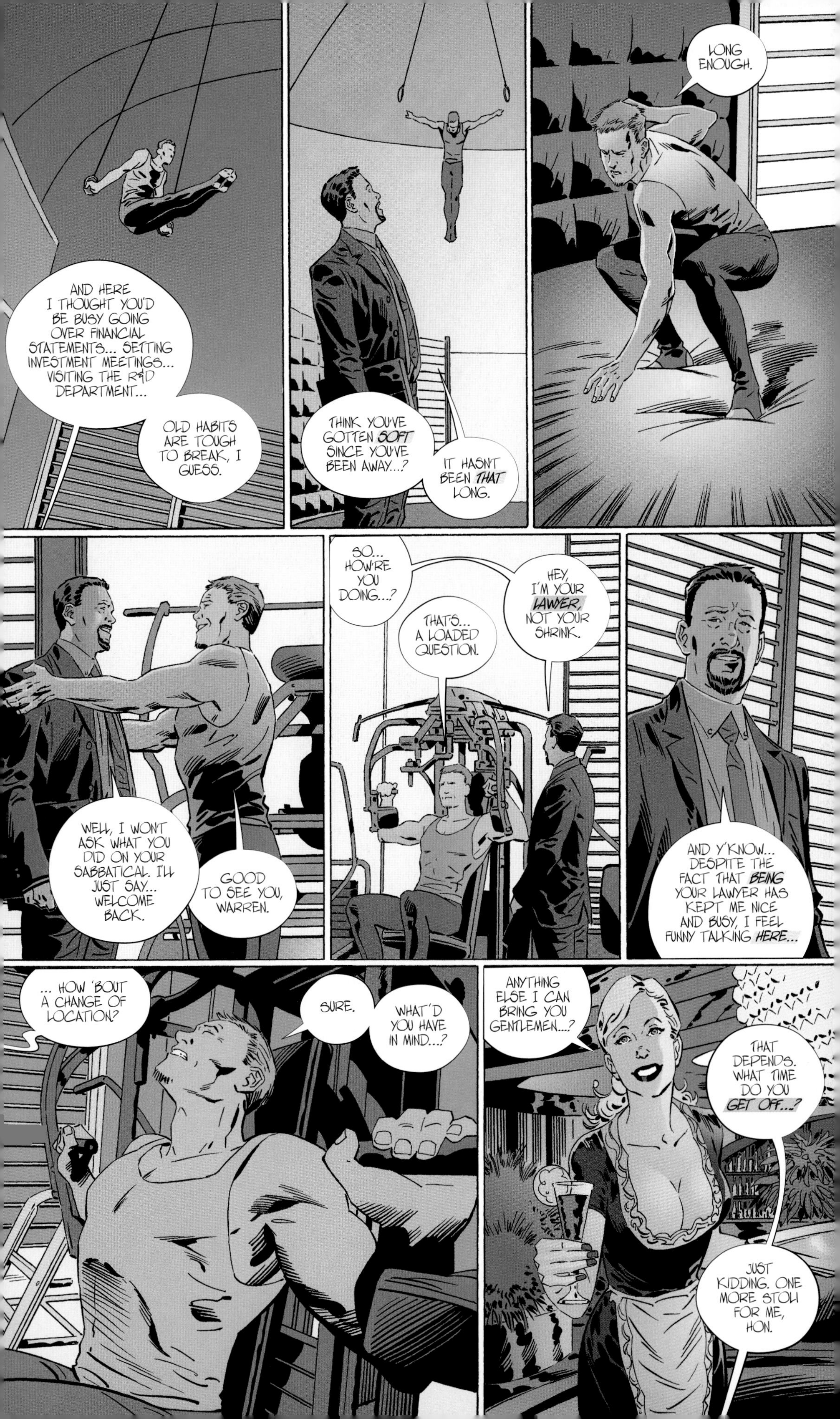
LONG ENOUGH.
AND HERE I THOUGHT YOU'D BE BUSY GOING OVER FINANCIAL STATEMENTS... SETTING INVESTMENT MEETINGS... VISITING THE R&D DEPARTMENT...
OLD HABITS ARE TOUGH TO BREAK, I GUESS.
THINK YOU'VE GOTTEN SOFT SINCE YOU'VE BEEN AWAY...?
IT HASN'T BEEN THAT LONG.
WELL, I WON'T ASK WHAT YOU DID ON YOUR SABBATICAL. I'LL JUST SAY... WELCOME BACK.
GOOD TO SEE YOU, WARREN.
SO... HOW'RE YOU DOING...?
THAT'S... A LOADED QUESTION.
HEY, I'M YOUR LAWYER, NOT YOUR SHRINK.
AND Y'KNOW... DESPITE THE FACT THAT BEING YOUR LAWYER HAS KEPT ME NICE AND BUSY, I FEEL FUNNY TALKING HERE...
... HOW 'BOUT A CHANGE OF LOCATION?
SURE.
WHAT'D YOU HAVE IN MIND...?
ANYTHING ELSE I CAN BRING YOU GENTLEMEN...?
THAT DEPENDS. WHAT TIME DO YOU GET OFF...?
JUST KIDDING. ONE MORE STOLI FOR ME, HON.

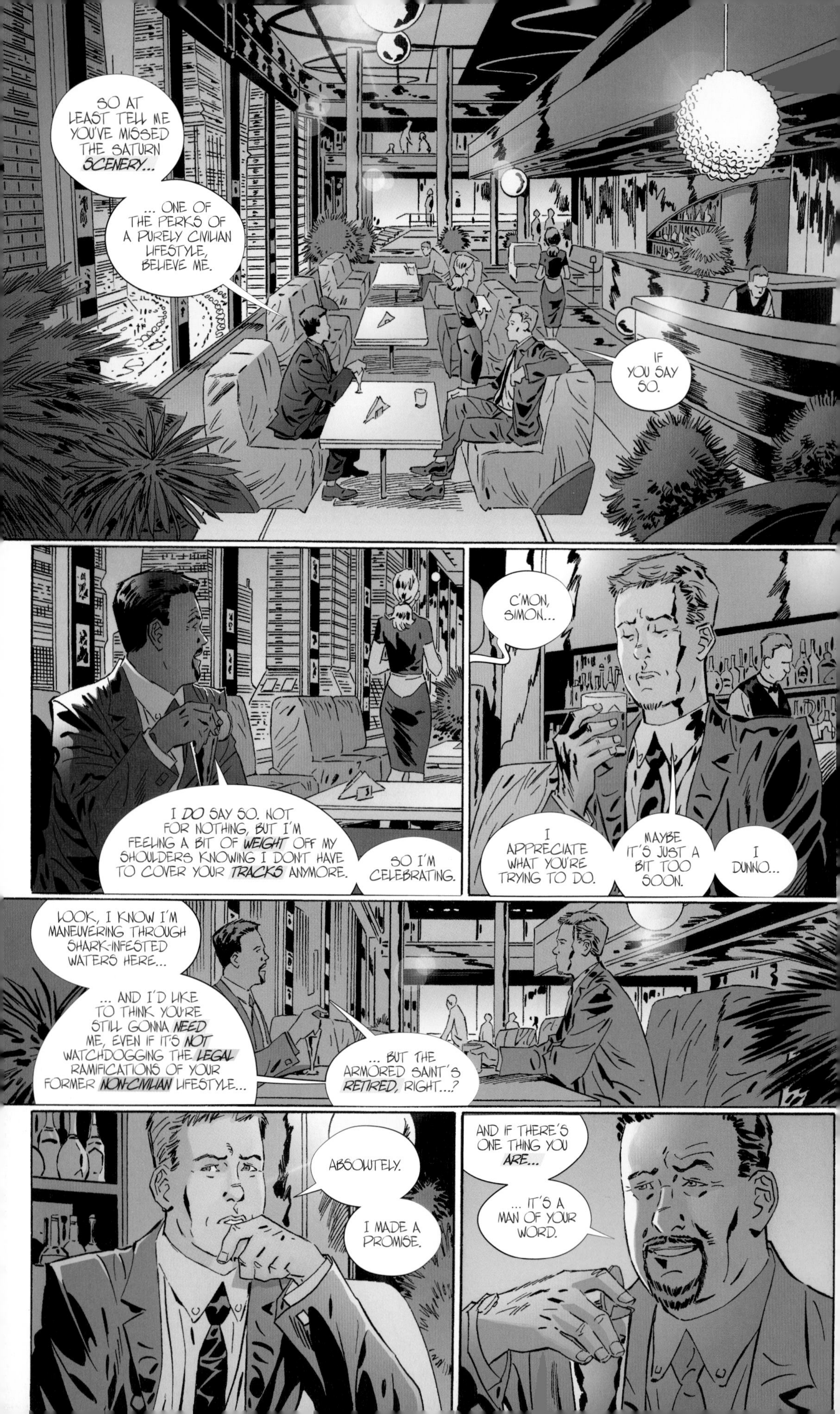
SO AT LEAST TELL ME YOU'VE MISSED THE SATURN SCENERY...
... ONE OF THE PERKS OF A PURELY CIVILIAN LIFESTYLE, BELIEVE ME.
IF YOU SAY SO.
I DO SAY SO. NOT FOR NOTHING, BUT I'M FEELING A BIT OF WEIGHT OFF MY SHOULDERS KNOWING I DON'T HAVE TO COVER YOUR TRACKS ANYMORE.
SO I'M CELEBRATING.
C'MON, SIMON...
I APPRECIATE WHAT YOU'RE TRYING TO DO.
MAYBE IT'S JUST A BIT TOO SOON.
I DUNNO...
LOOK, I KNOW I'M MANEUVERING THROUGH SHARK-INFESTED WATERS HERE...
... AND I'D LIKE TO THINK YOU'RE STILL GONNA NEED ME, EVEN IF IT'S NOT WATCHDOGGING THE LEGAL RAMIFICATIONS OF YOUR FORMER NON-CIVILIAN LIFESTYLE...
... BUT THE ARMORED SAINT'S RETIRED, RIGHT...?
ABSOLUTELY.
I MADE A PROMISE.
AND IF THERE'S ONE THING YOU ARE...
... IT'S A MAN OF YOUR WORD.

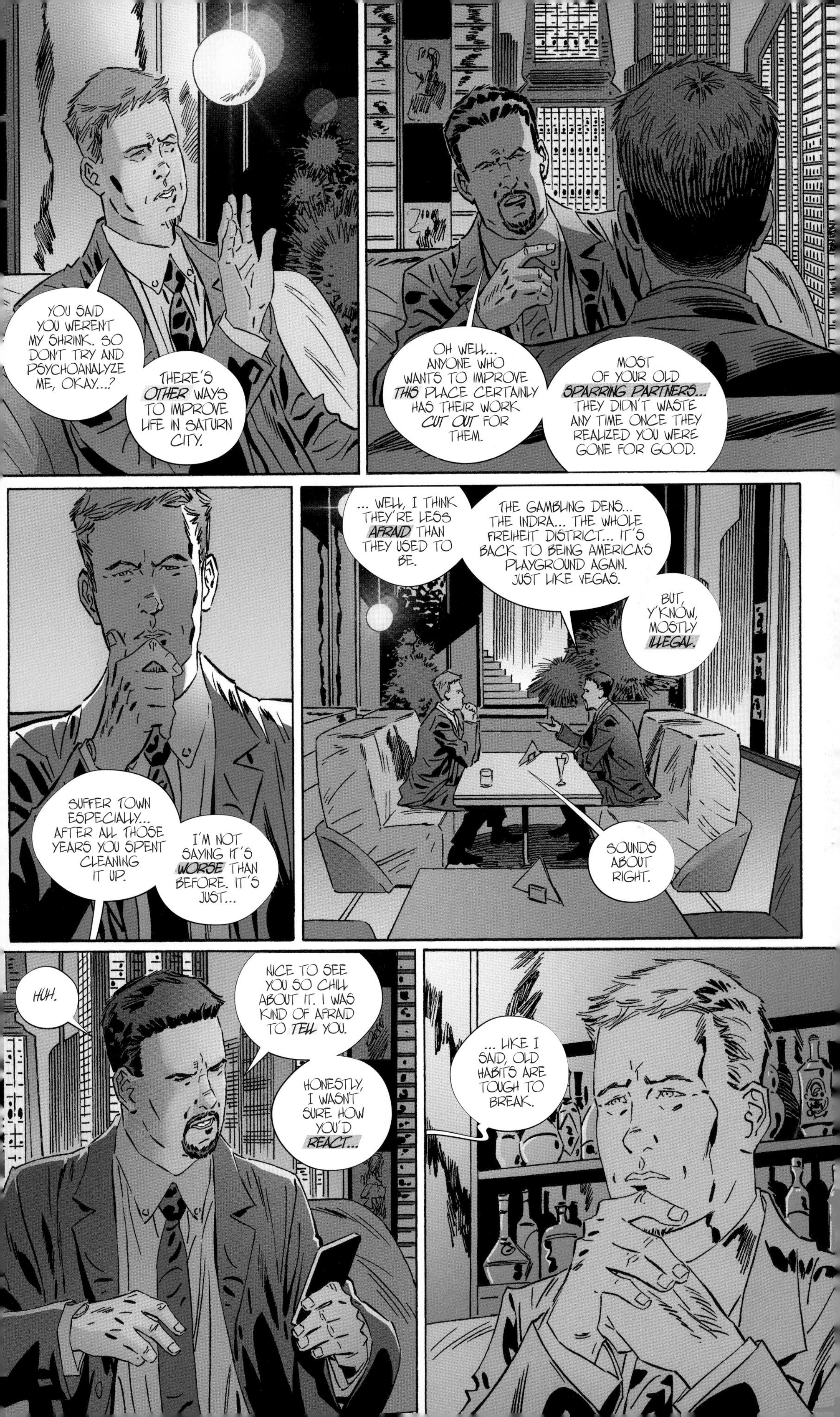
YOU SAID YOU WEREN'T MY SHRINK. SO DON'T TRY AND PSYCHOANALYZE ME, OKAY...?
THERE'S OTHER WAYS TO IMPROVE LIFE IN SATURN CITY.
OH WELL... ANYONE WHO WANTS TO IMPROVE THIS PLACE CERTAINLY HAS THEIR WORK CUT OUT FOR THEM.
MOST OF YOUR OLD SPARRING PARTNERS... THEY DIDN'T WASTE ANY TIME ONCE THEY REALIZED YOU WERE GONE FOR GOOD.
SUFFER TOWN ESPECIALLY... AFTER ALL THOSE YEARS YOU SPENT CLEANING IT UP.
I'M NOT SAYING IT'S WORSE THAN BEFORE. IT'S JUST...
... WELL, I THINK THEY'RE LESS AFRAID THAN THEY USED TO BE.
THE GAMBLING DENS... THE INDRA... THE WHOLE FREIHEIT DISTRICT... IT'S BACK TO BEING AMERICA'S PLAYGROUND AGAIN. JUST LIKE VEGAS.
BUT, Y'KNOW, MOSTLY ILLEGAL.
SOUNDS ABOUT RIGHT.
HUH.
NICE TO SEE YOU SO CHILL ABOUT IT. I WAS KIND OF AFRAID TO TELL YOU.
HONESTLY, I WASN'T SURE HOW YOU'D REACT...
... LIKE I SAID, OLD HABITS ARE TOUGH TO BREAK.

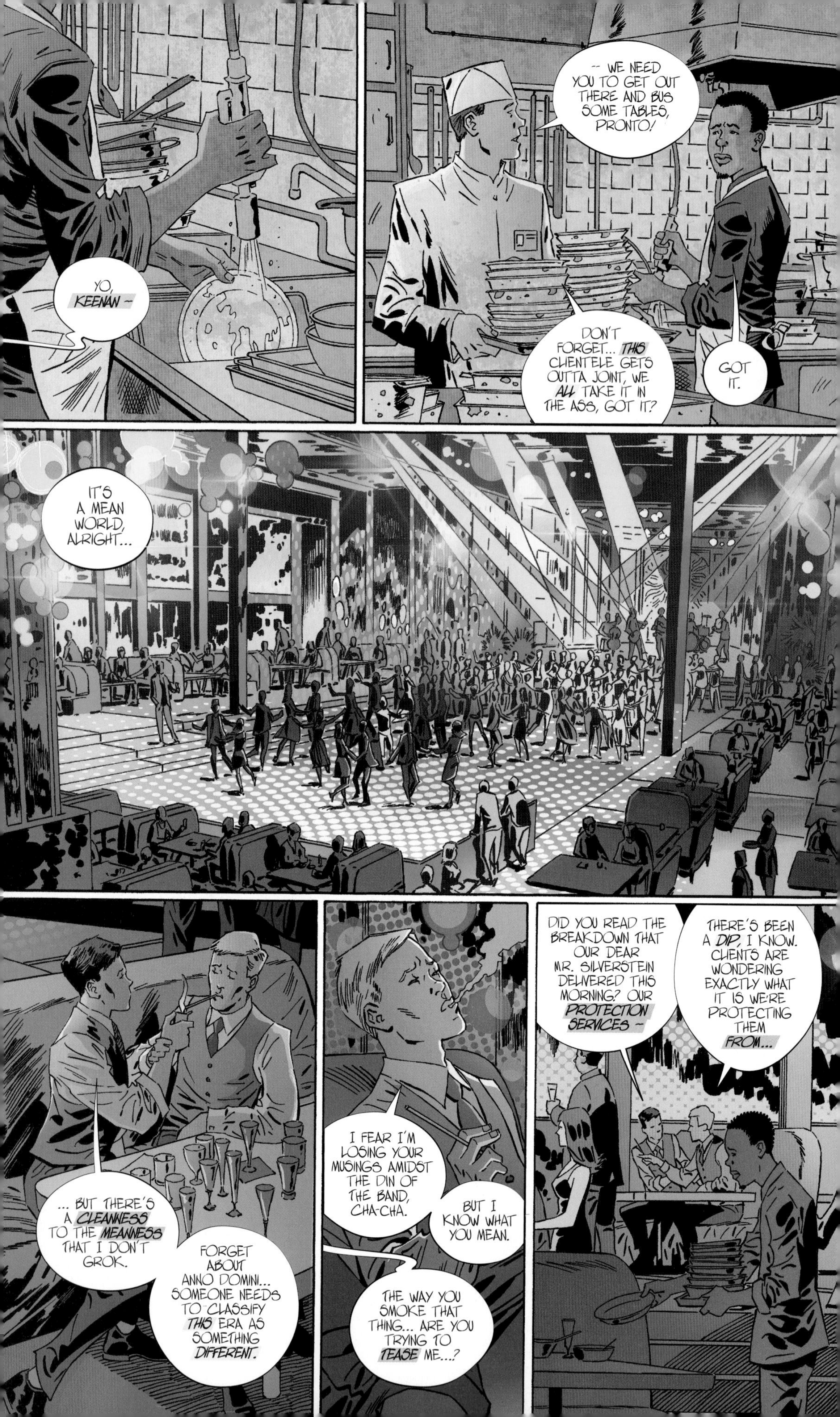
YO, KEENAN --
-- WE NEED YOU TO GET OUT THERE AND BUS SOME TABLES, PRONTO!
DON'T FORGET... THIS CLIENTELE GETS OUTTA JOINT, WE ALL TAKE IT IN THE ASS, GOT IT?
GOT IT.
IT'S A MEAN WORLD, ALRIGHT...
... BUT THERE'S A CLEANNESS TO THE MEANNESS THAT I DON'T GROK.
FORGET ABOUT ANNO DOMINI... SOMEONE NEEDS TO CLASSIFY THIS ERA AS SOMETHING DIFFERENT.
I FEAR I'M LOSING YOUR MUSINGS AMIDST THE DIN OF THE BAND, CHA-CHA.
BUT I KNOW WHAT YOU MEAN.
THE WAY YOU SMOKE THAT THING... ARE YOU TRYING TO TEASE ME...?
DID YOU READ THE BREAKDOWN THAT OUR DEAR MR. SILVERSTEIN DELIVERED THIS MORNING? OUR PROTECTION SERVICES --
THERE'S BEEN A DIP, I KNOW. CLIENTS ARE WONDERING EXACTLY WHAT IT IS WE'RE PROTECTING THEM FROM...

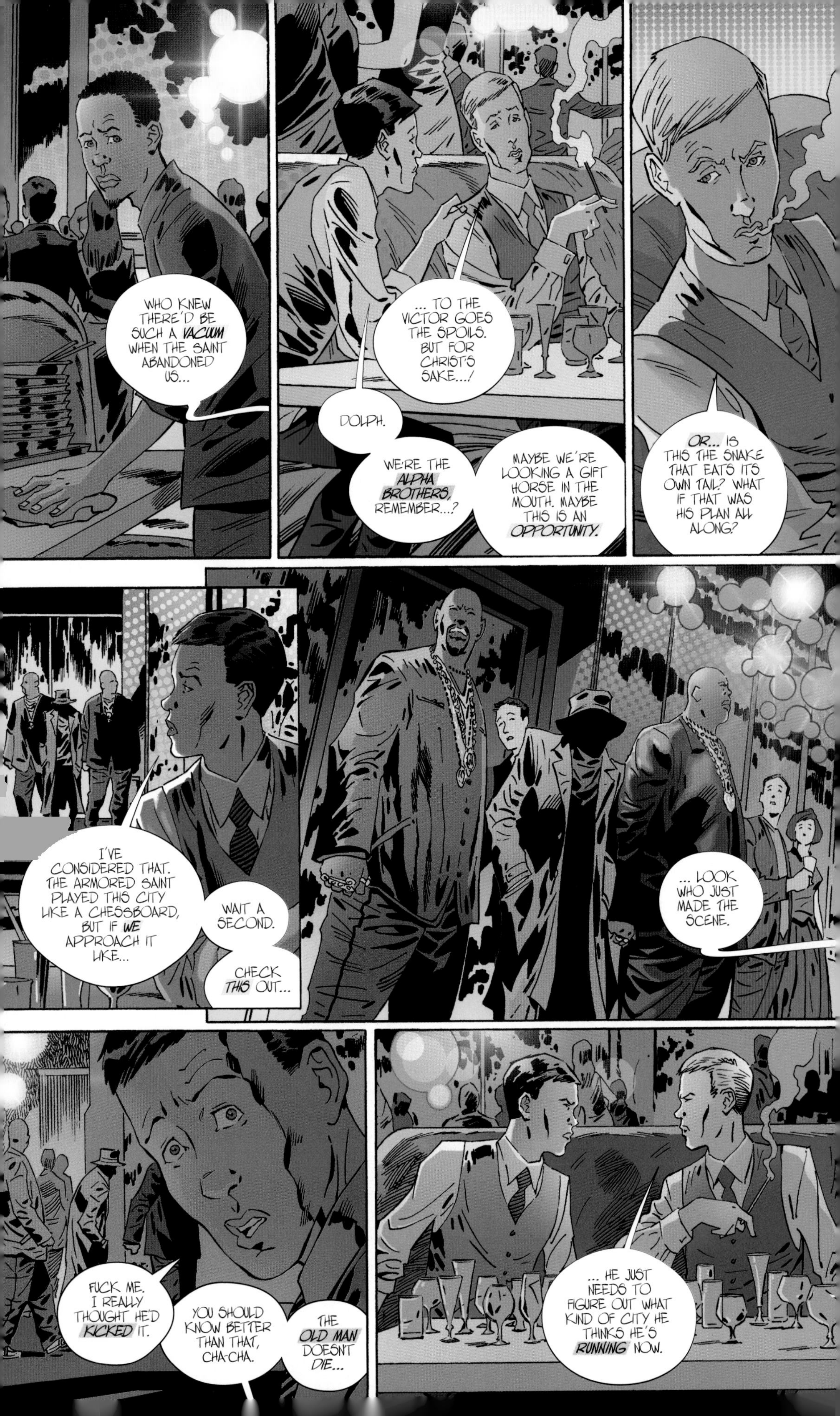
WHO KNEW THERE'D BE SUCH A VACUUM WHEN THE SAINT ABANDONED US...
... TO THE VICTOR GOES THE SPOILS. BUT FOR CHRIST'S SAKE...!
DOLPH.
WE'RE THE ALPHA BROTHERS, REMEMBER...?
MAYBE WE'RE LOOKING A GIFT HORSE IN THE MOUTH. MAYBE THIS IS AN OPPORTUNITY.
OR... IS THIS THE SNAKE THAT EATS ITS OWN TAIL? WHAT IF THAT WAS HIS PLAN ALL ALONG?
I'VE CONSIDERED THAT. THE ARMORED SAINT PLAYED THIS CITY LIKE A CHESSBOARD, BUT IF WE APPROACH IT LIKE...
WAIT A SECOND.
CHECK THIS OUT...
... LOOK WHO JUST MADE THE SCENE.
FUCK ME. I REALLY THOUGHT HE'D KICKED IT.
YOU SHOULD KNOW BETTER THAN THAT, CHA-CHA.
THE OLD MAN DOESN'T DIE...
... HE JUST NEEDS TO FIGURE OUT WHAT KIND OF CITY HE THINKS HE'S RUNNING NOW.

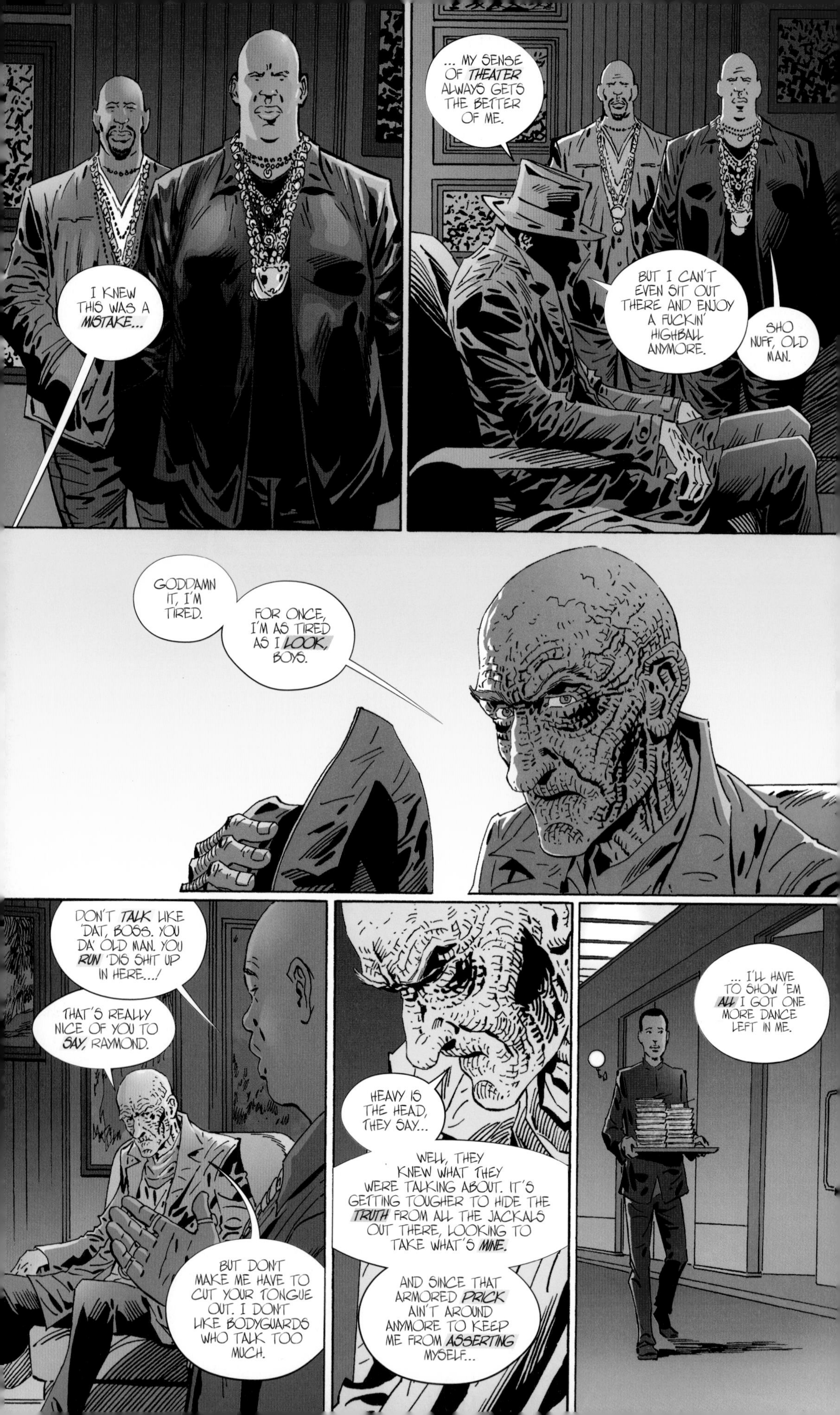
I KNEW THIS WAS A MISTAKE...
... MY SENSE OF THEATER ALWAYS GETS THE BETTER OF ME.
BUT I CAN'T EVEN SIT OUT THERE AND ENJOY A FUCKIN' HIGHBALL ANYMORE.
SHO NUFF, OLD MAN.
GODDAMN IT, I'M TIRED.
FOR ONCE, I'M AS TIRED AS I LOOK, BOYS.
DON'T TALK LIKE 'DAT, BOSS. YOU DA' OLD MAN. YOU RUN 'DIS SHIT UP IN HERE...!
THAT'S REALLY NICE OF YOU TO SAY, RAYMOND.
BUT DON'T MAKE ME HAVE TO CUT YOUR TONGUE OUT. I DON'T LIKE BODYGUARDS WHO TALK TOO MUCH.
HEAVY IS THE HEAD, THEY SAY...
WELL, THEY KNEW WHAT THEY WERE TALKING ABOUT. IT'S GETTING TOUGHER TO HIDE THE TRUTH FROM ALL THE JACKALS OUT THERE, LOOKING TO TAKE WHAT'S MINE.
AND SINCE THAT ARMORED PRICK AIN'T AROUND ANYMORE TO KEEP ME FROM ASSERTING MYSELF...
... I'LL HAVE TO SHOW 'EM ALL I GOT ONE MORE DANCE LEFT IN ME.

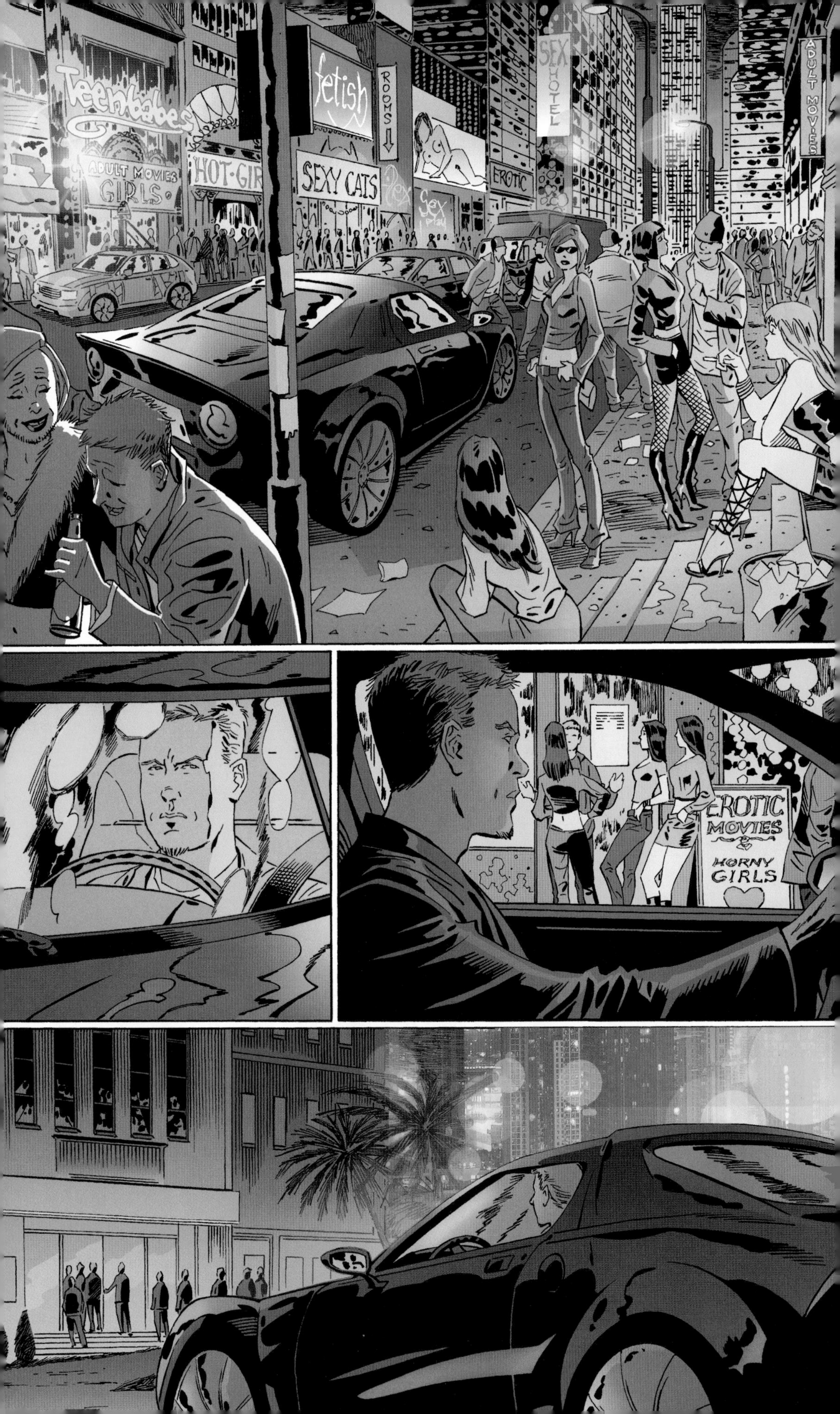
Teenbabes
ADULT MOVIES
GIRLS
HOT-GIRL
fetish
ROOMS
SEXY CATS
EROTIC
SEX HOTEL
ADULT MOVIES
EROTIC
MOVIES
HORNY
GIRLS

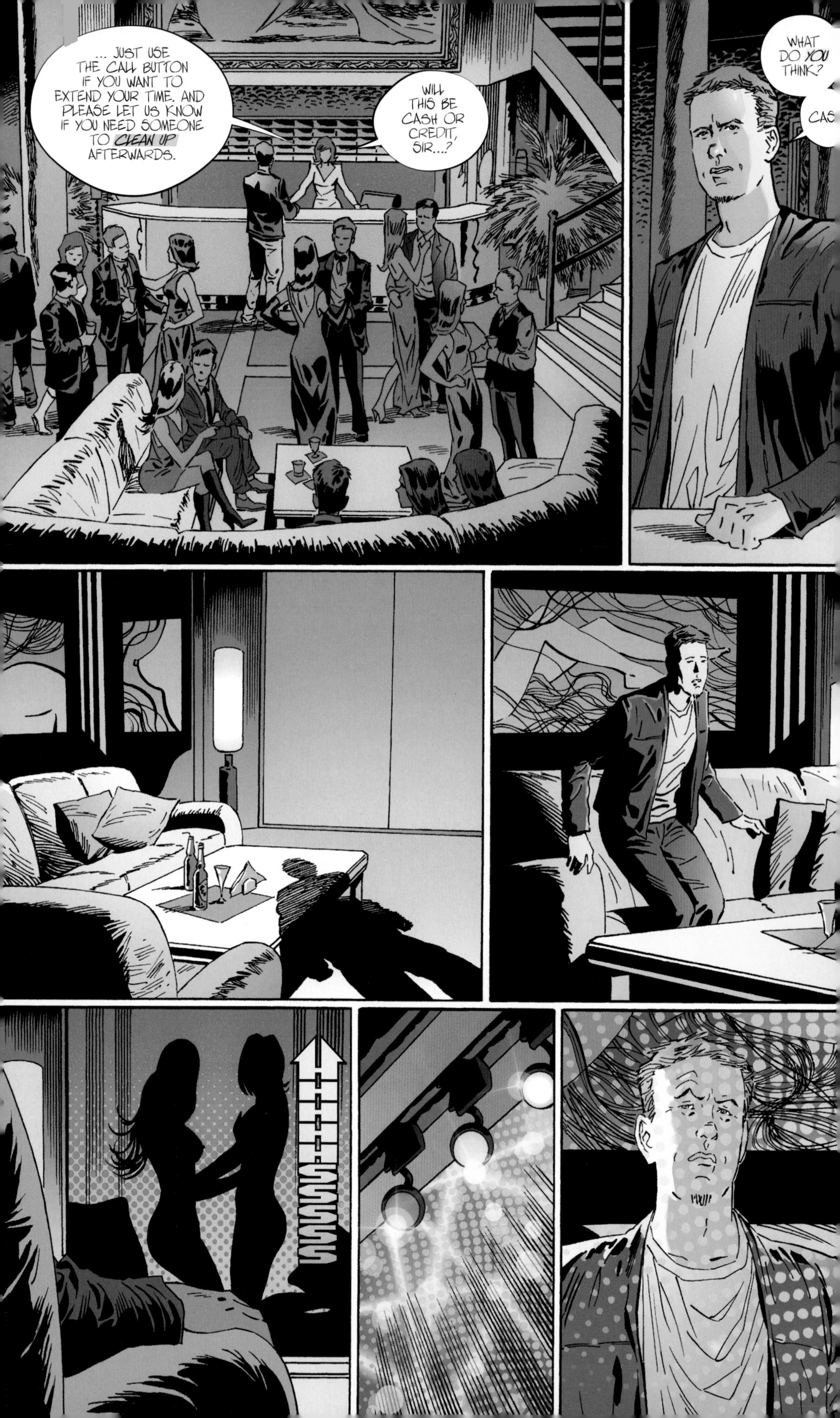
... JUST USE THE CALL BUTTON IF YOU WANT TO EXTEND YOUR TIME. AND PLEASE LET US KNOW IF YOU NEED SOMEONE TO CLEAN UP AFTERWARDS.
WILL THIS BE CASH OR CREDIT, SIR...?
WHAT DO YOU THINK?
HHHHSSSSS

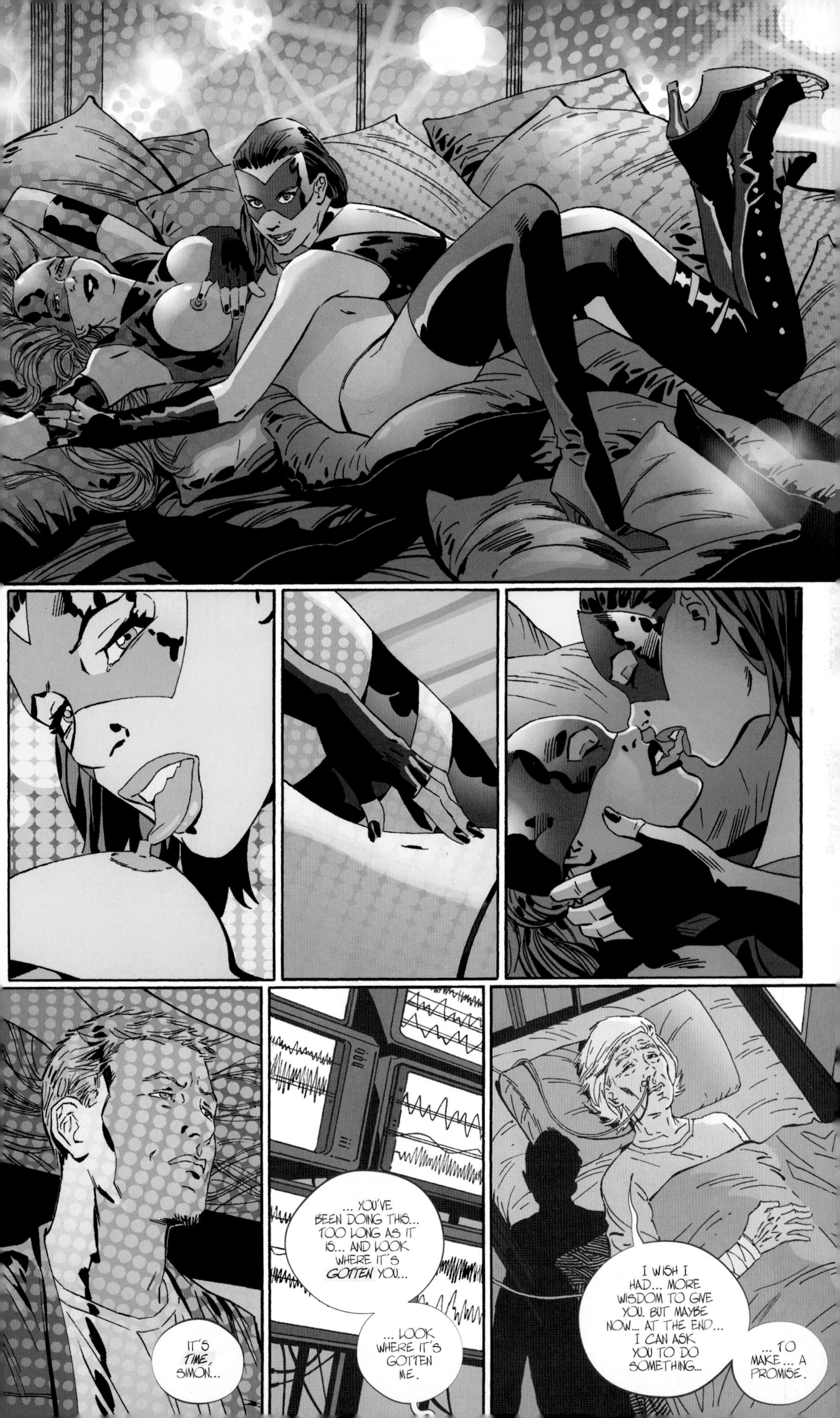
IT'S TIME, SIMON...
... YOU'VE BEEN DOING THIS... TOO LONG AS IT IS... AND LOOK WHERE IT'S GOTTEN YOU...
... LOOK WHERE IT'S GOTTEN ME.
I WISH I HAD... MORE WISDOM TO GIVE YOU. BUT MAYBE NOW... AT THE END... I CAN ASK YOU TO DO SOMETHING...
... TO MAKE... A PROMISE.

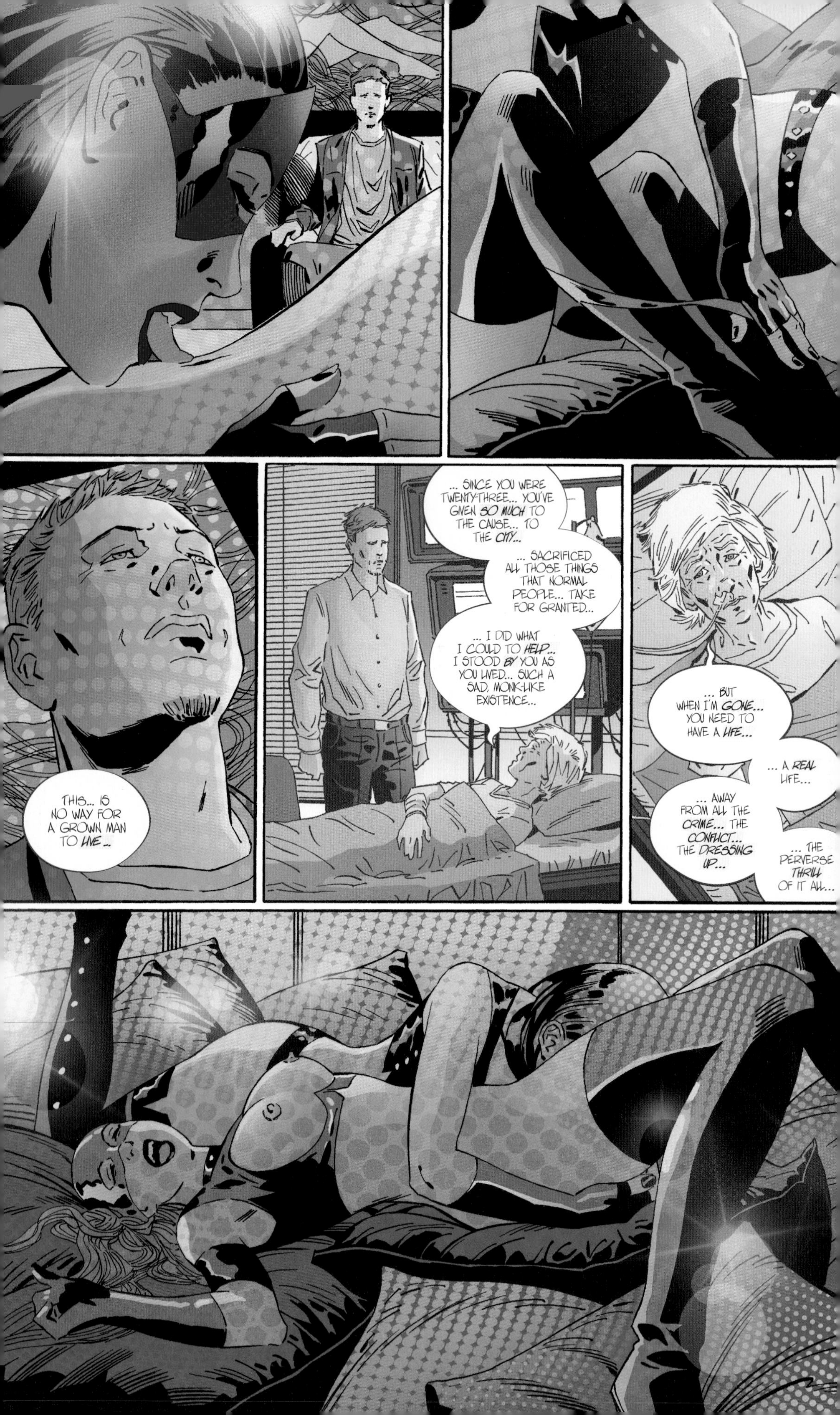
THIS... IS NO WAY FOR A GROWN MAN TO LIVE...
... SINCE YOU WERE TWENTY-THREE... YOU'VE GIVEN SO MUCH TO THE CAUSE... TO THE CITY...
... SACRIFICED ALL THOSE THINGS THAT NORMAL PEOPLE... TAKE FOR GRANTED...
... I DID WHAT I COULD TO HELP... I STOOD BY YOU AS YOU LIVED... SUCH A SAD, MONK-LIKE EXISTENCE...
... BUT WHEN I'M GONE... YOU NEED TO HAVE A LIFE...
... A REAL LIFE...
... AWAY FROM ALL THE CRIME... THE CONFLICT... THE DRESSING UP...
... THE PERVERSE THRILL OF IT ALL...

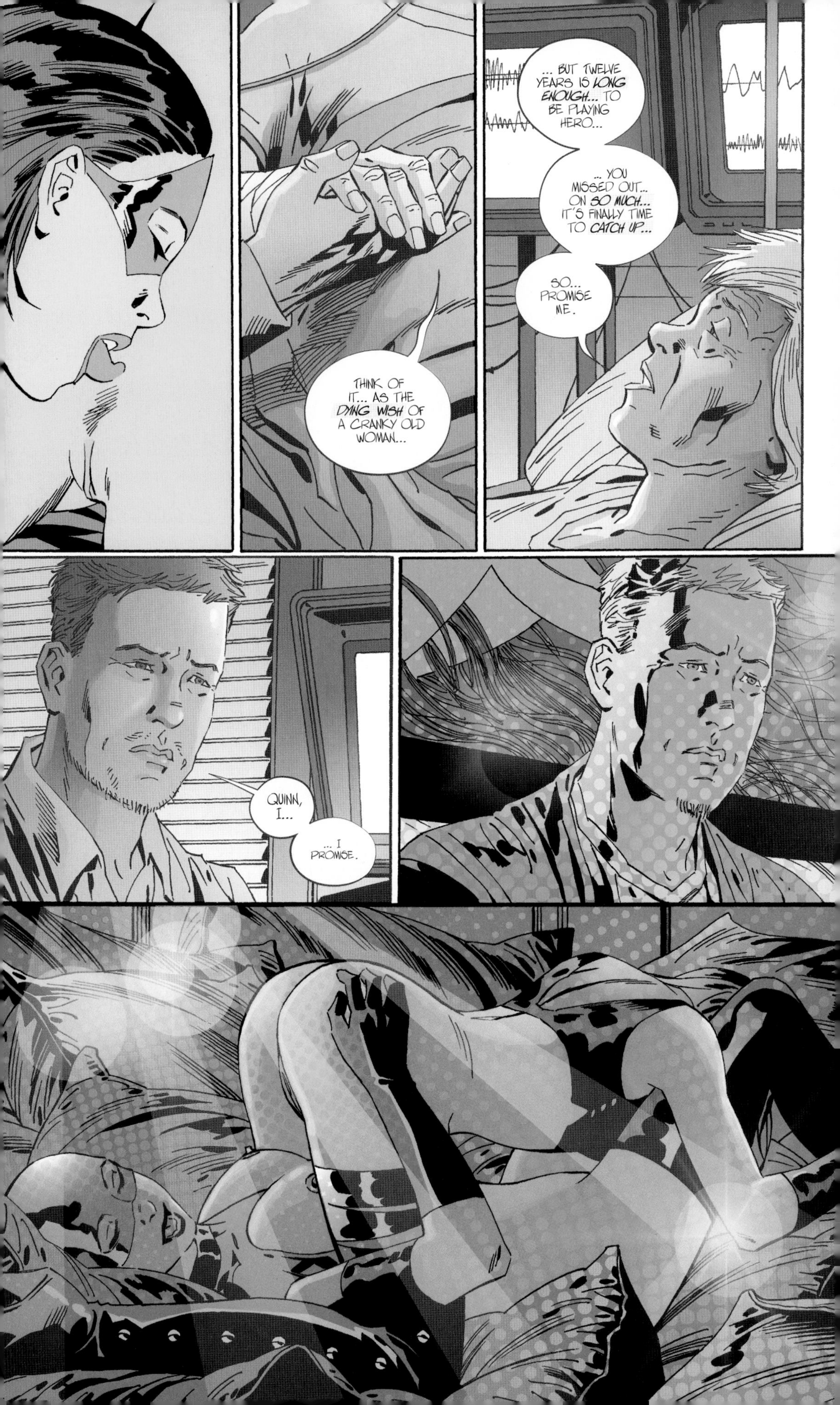
THINK OF IT... AS THE DYING WISH OF A CRANKY OLD WOMAN...
... BUT TWELVE YEARS IS LONG ENOUGH... TO BE PLAYING HERO...
... YOU MISSED OUT... ON SO MUCH... IT'S FINALLY TIME TO CATCH UP...
SO... PROMISE ME.
QUINN, I...
... I PROMISE.

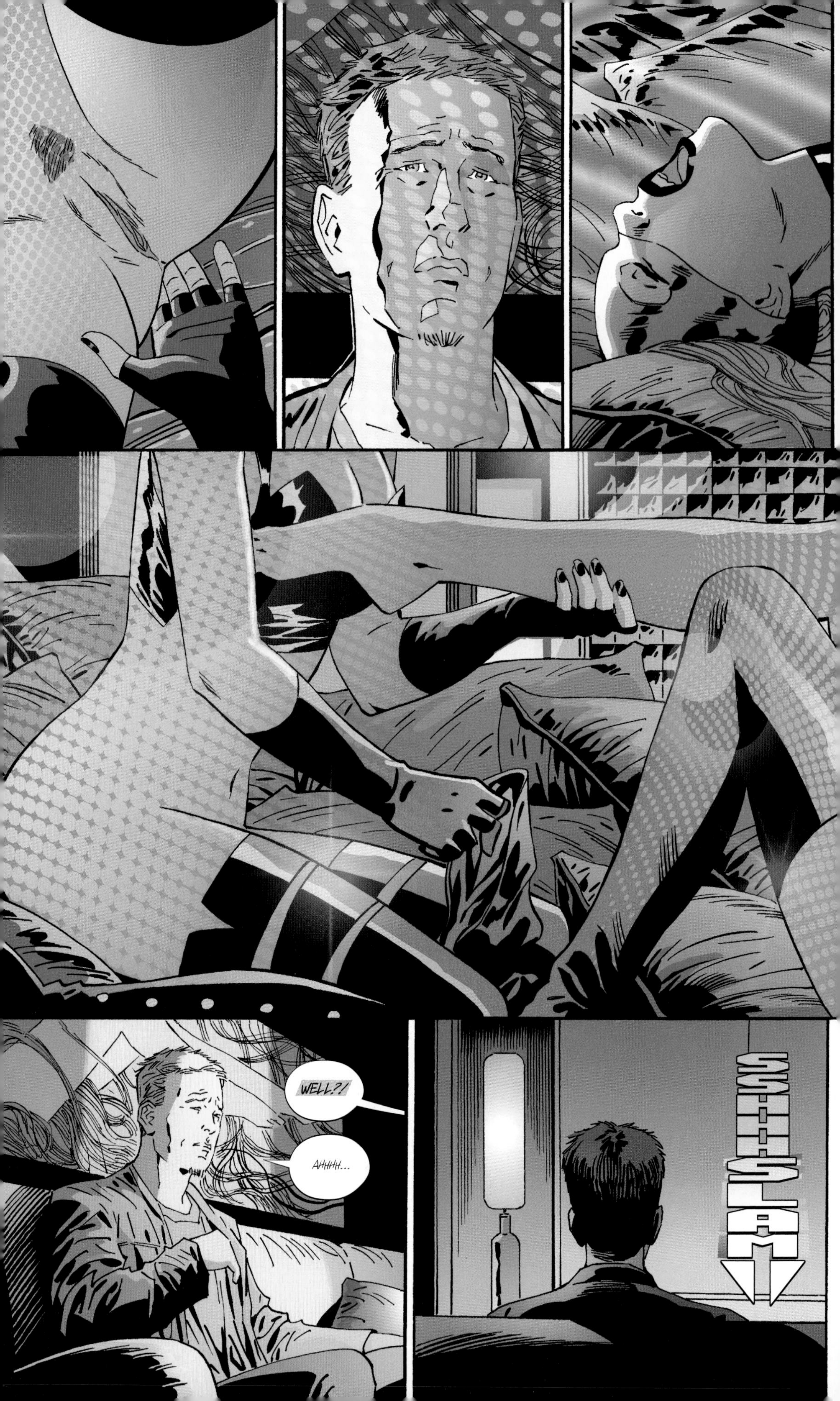
WELL?!
AHHHH...
SSHHSLAM

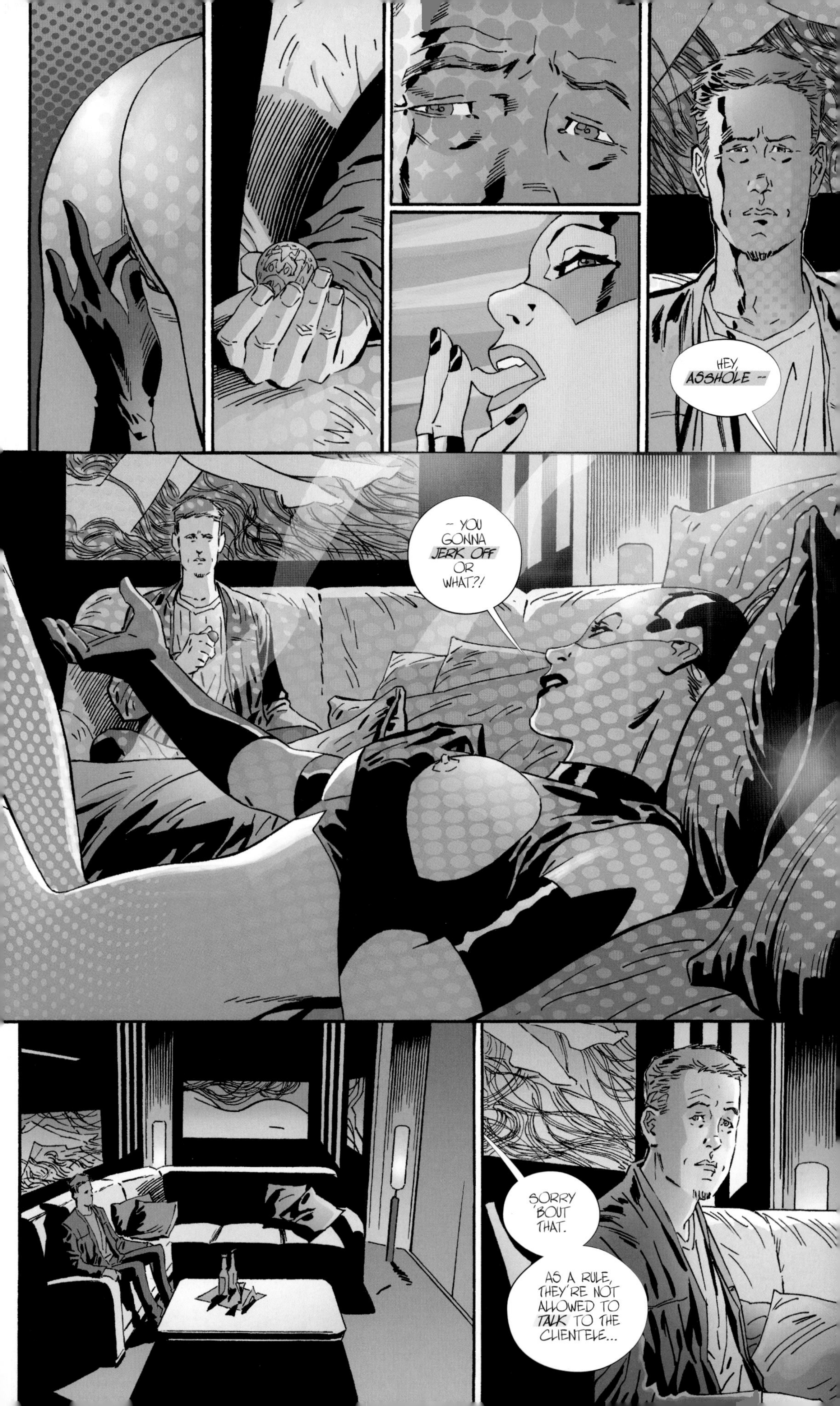
HEY, ASSHOLE --
-- YOU GONNA JERK OFF OR WHAT?!
SORRY 'BOUT THAT.
AS A RULE, THEY'RE NOT ALLOWED TO TALK TO THE CLIENTELE...

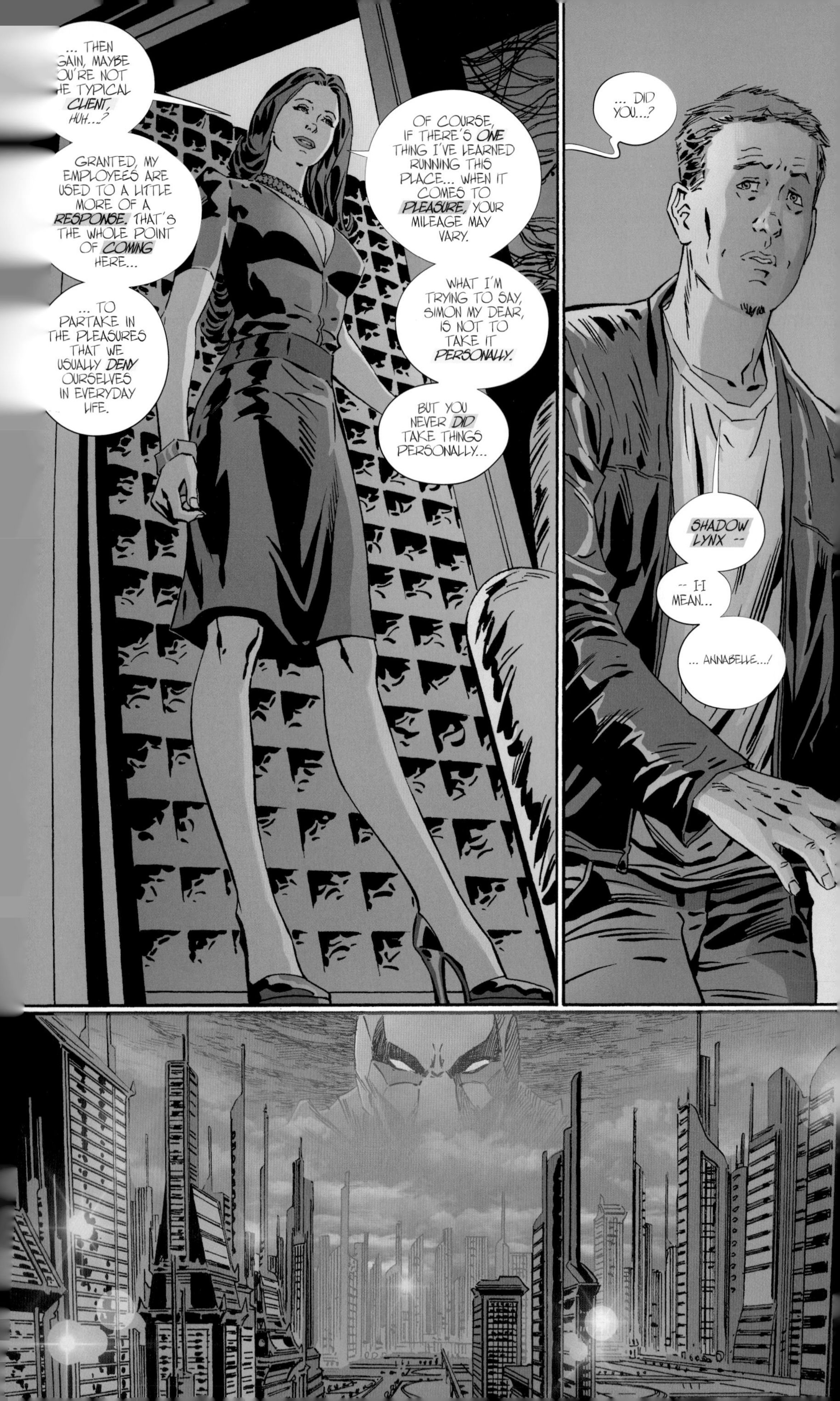
... THEN GAIN, MAYBE OU'RE NOT HE TYPICAL CLIENT, HUH...?
GRANTED, MY EMPLOYEES ARE USED TO A LITTLE MORE OF A RESPONSE. THAT'S THE WHOLE POINT OF COMING HERE...
... TO PARTAKE IN THE PLEASURES THAT WE USUALLY DENY OURSELVES IN EVERYDAY LIFE.
OF COURSE, IF THERE'S ONE THING I'VE LEARNED RUNNING THIS PLACE... WHEN IT COMES TO PLEASURE, YOUR MILEAGE MAY VARY.
WHAT I'M TRYING TO SAY, SIMON MY DEAR, IS NOT TO TAKE IT PERSONALLY.
BUT YOU NEVER DID TAKE THINGS PERSONALLY...
... DID YOU...?
SHADOW LYNX --
-- I-I MEAN...
... ANNABELLE...!

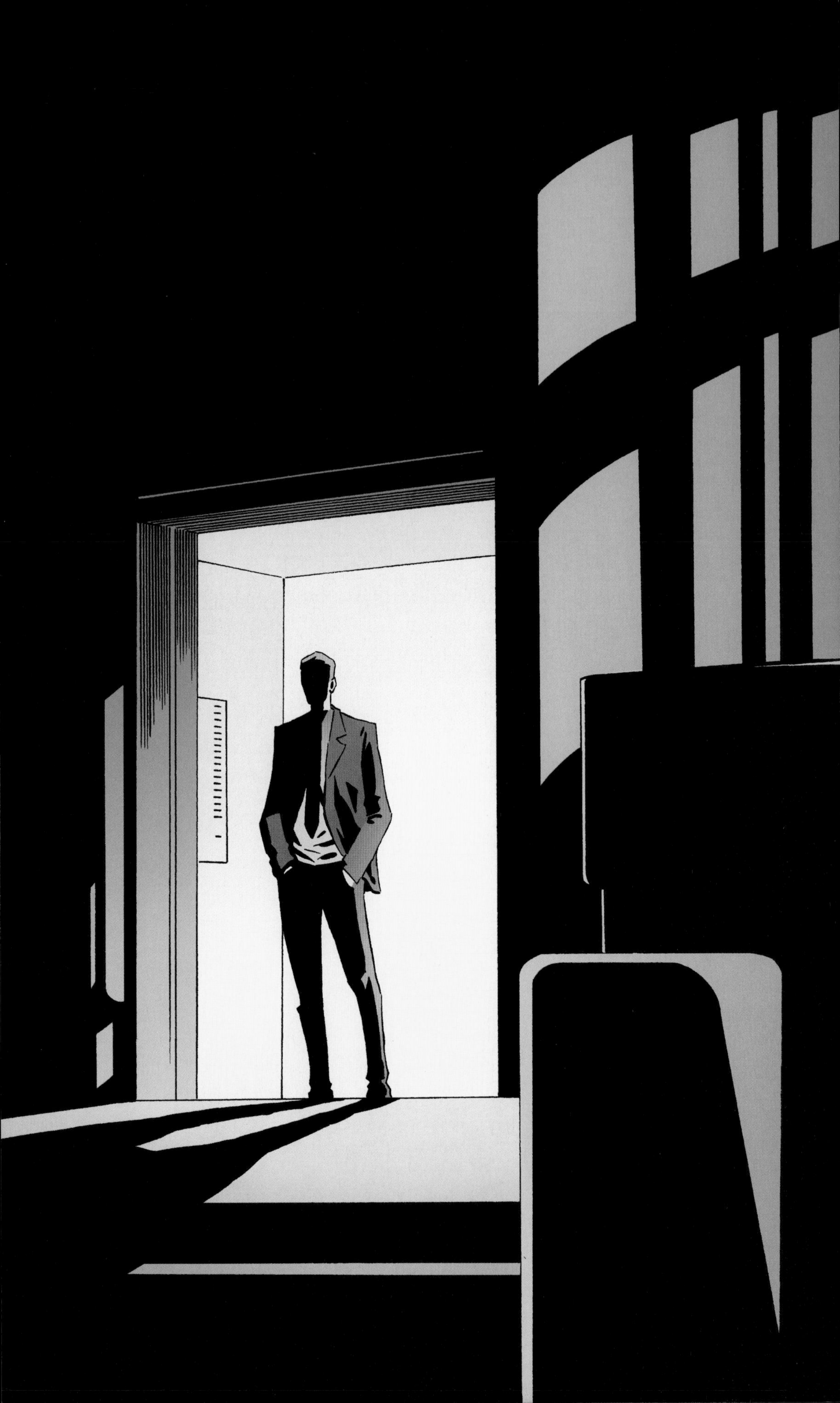

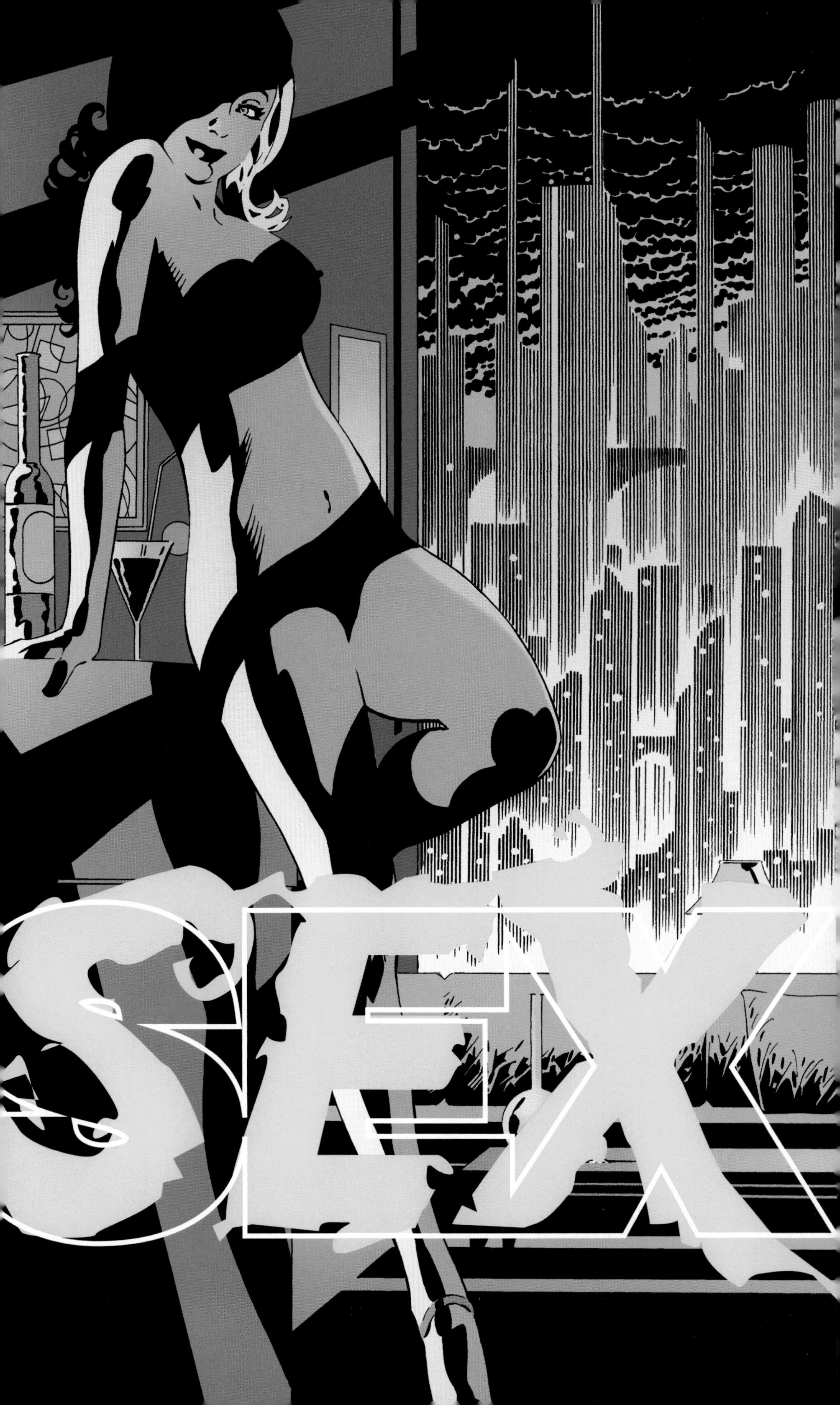
SEX

CHAPTER TWO
WUNDERBARE CHANCEN

JOE CASEY WRITER   PIOTR KOWALSKI ARTIST   BRAD SIMPSON COLORIST   RUS WOOTON LETTERER   SONIA HARRIS GRAPHIC DESIGNER

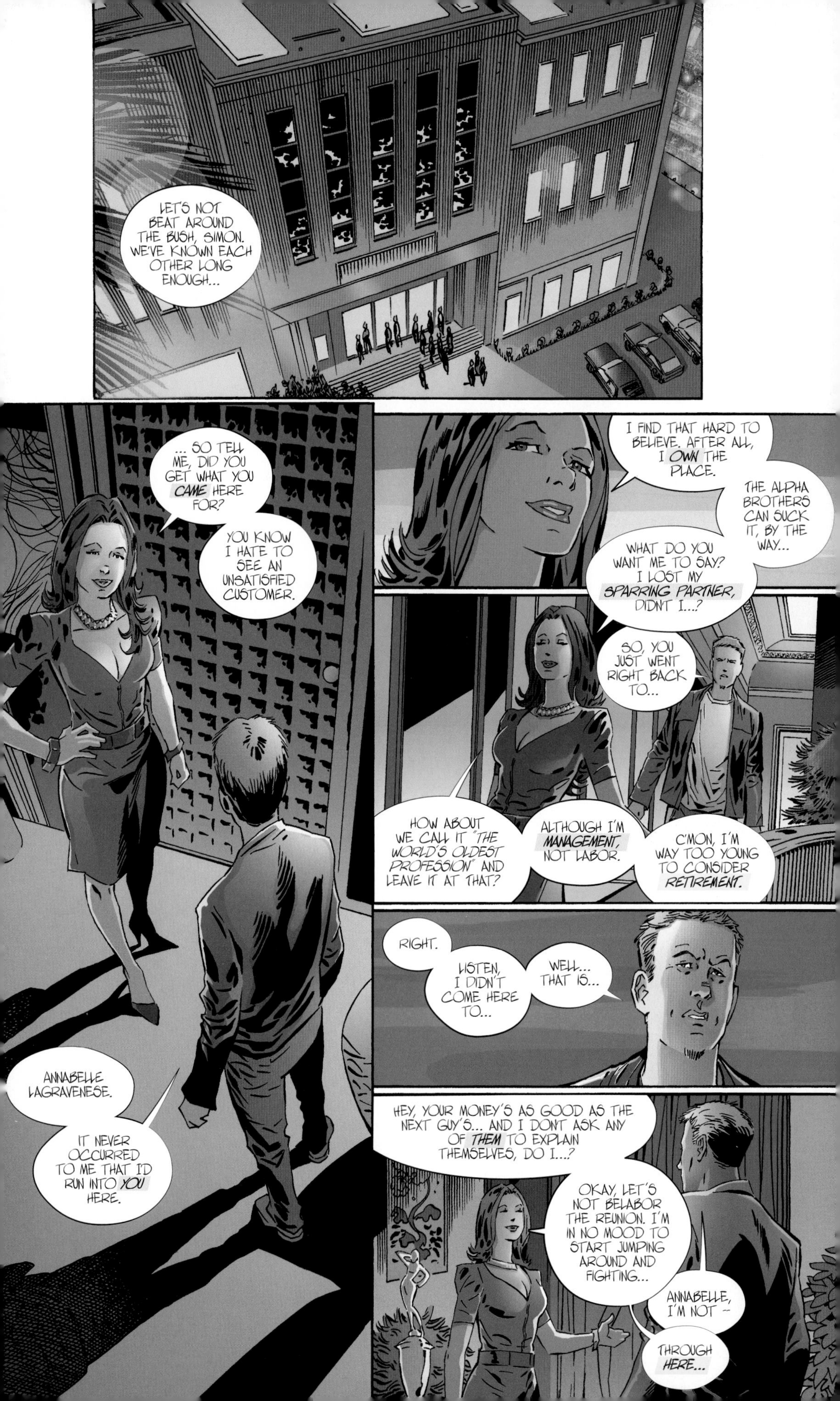

LET'S NOT BEAT AROUND THE BUSH, SIMON. WE'VE KNOWN EACH OTHER LONG ENOUGH...
... SO TELL ME, DID YOU GET WHAT YOU CAME HERE FOR?
YOU KNOW I HATE TO SEE AN UNSATISFIED CUSTOMER.
ANNABELLE LAGRAVENESE.
IT NEVER OCCURRED TO ME THAT I'D RUN INTO YOU HERE.
I FIND THAT HARD TO BELIEVE. AFTER ALL, I OWN THE PLACE.
THE ALPHA BROTHERS CAN SUCK IT, BY THE WAY...
WHAT DO YOU WANT ME TO SAY? I LOST MY SPARRING PARTNER, DIDN'T I...?
SO, YOU JUST WENT RIGHT BACK TO...
HOW ABOUT WE CALL IT "THE WORLD'S OLDEST PROFESSION" AND LEAVE IT AT THAT?
ALTHOUGH I'M MANAGEMENT, NOT LABOR.
C'MON, I'M WAY TOO YOUNG TO CONSIDER RETIREMENT.
RIGHT.
LISTEN, I DIDN'T COME HERE TO...
WELL... THAT IS...
HEY, YOUR MONEY'S AS GOOD AS THE NEXT GUY'S... AND I DON'T ASK ANY OF THEM TO EXPLAIN THEMSELVES, DO I...?
OKAY, LET'S NOT BELABOR THE REUNION. I'M IN NO MOOD TO START JUMPING AROUND AND FIGHTING...
ANNABELLE, I'M NOT --
THROUGH HERE...

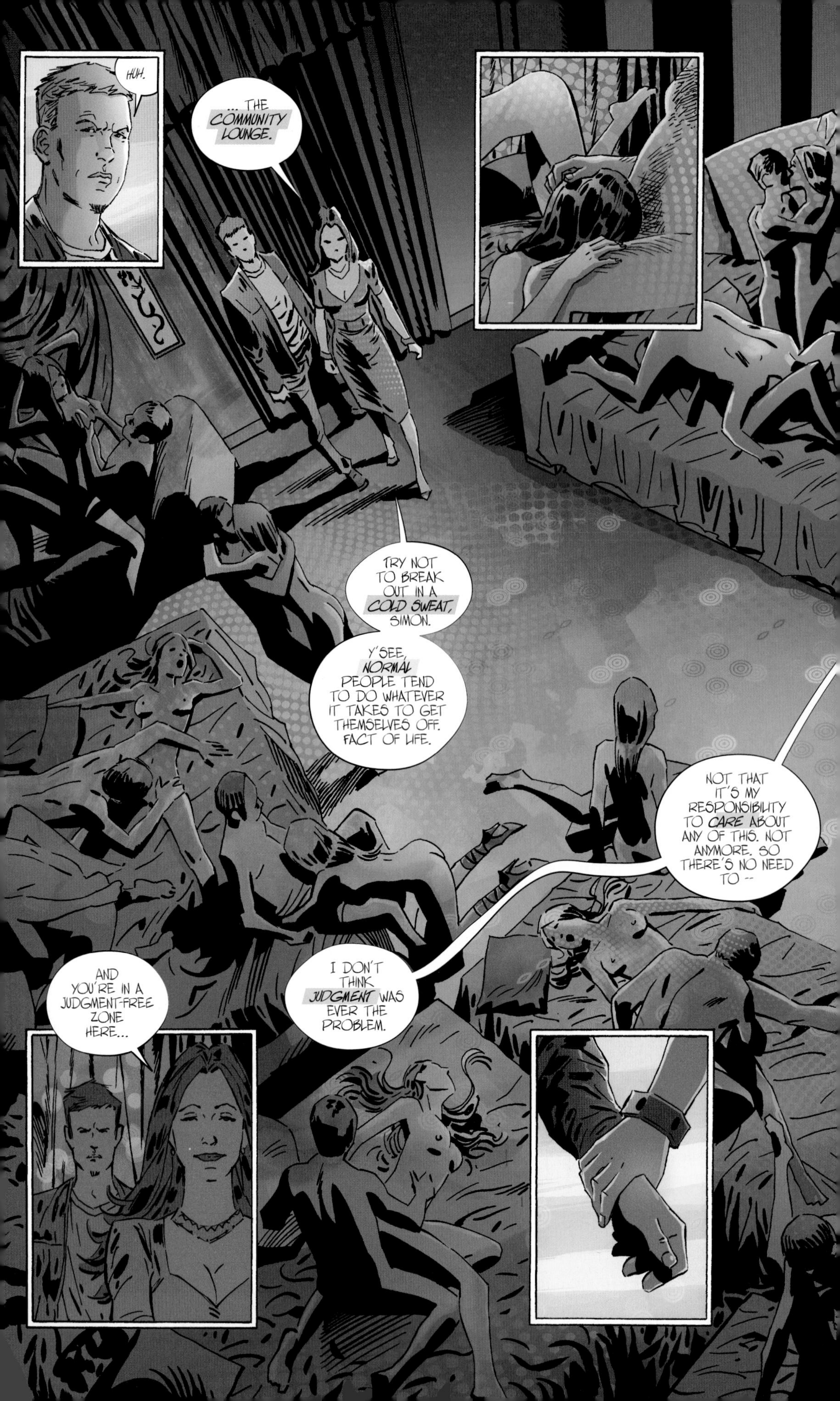
HUH.
... THE COMMUNITY LOUNGE.
TRY NOT TO BREAK OUT IN A COLD SWEAT, SIMON.
Y'SEE, NORMAL PEOPLE TEND TO DO WHATEVER IT TAKES TO GET THEMSELVES OFF. FACT OF LIFE.
NOT THAT IT'S MY RESPONSIBILITY TO CARE ABOUT ANY OF THIS. NOT ANYMORE. SO THERE'S NO NEED TO --
I DON'T THINK JUDGMENT WAS EVER THE PROBLEM.
AND YOU'RE IN A JUDGMENT-FREE ZONE HERE...

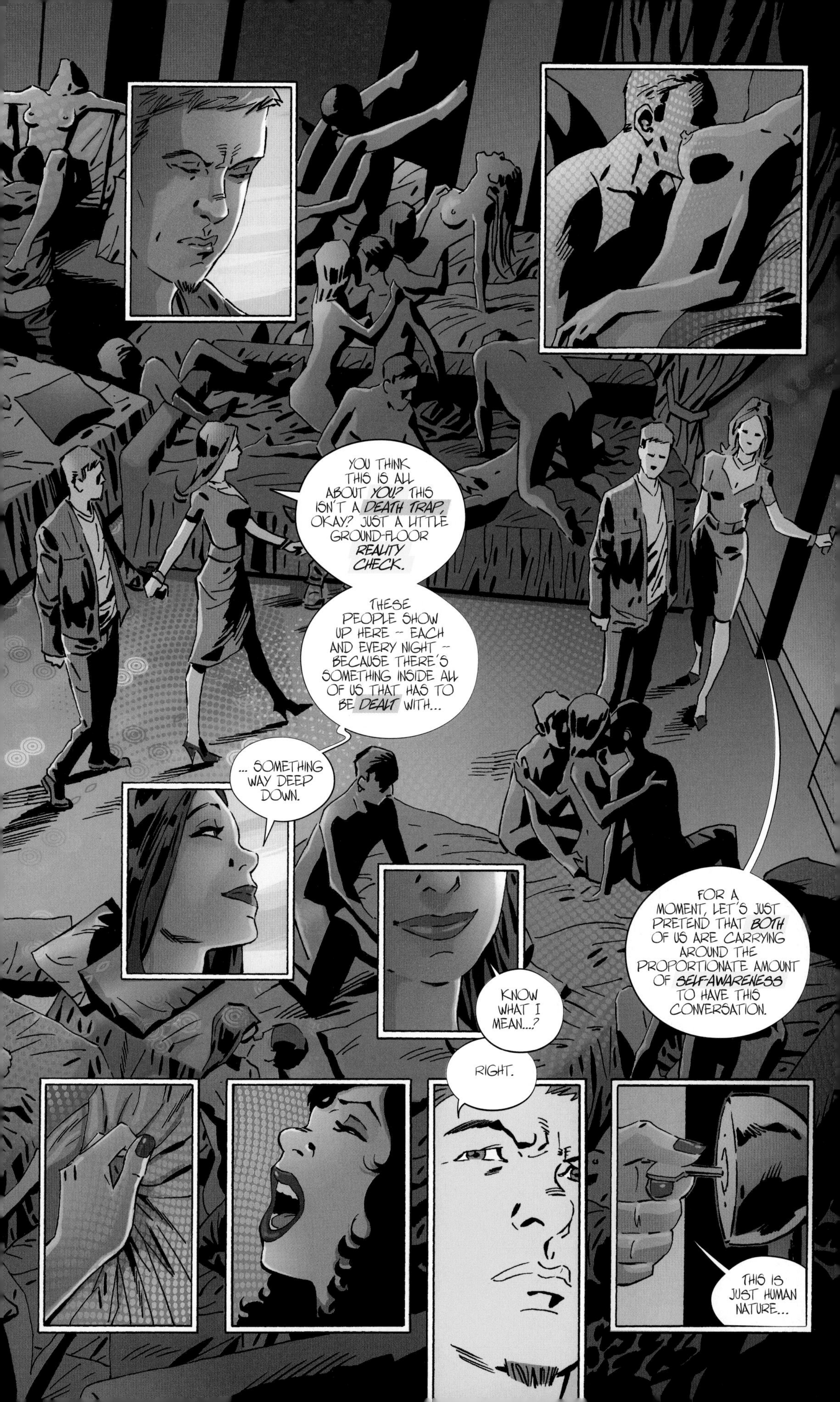

YOU THINK THIS IS ALL ABOUT YOU? THIS ISN'T A DEATH TRAP, OKAY? JUST A LITTLE GROUND-FLOOR REALITY CHECK.
THESE PEOPLE SHOW UP HERE -- EACH AND EVERY NIGHT -- BECAUSE THERE'S SOMETHING INSIDE ALL OF US THAT HAS TO BE DEALT WITH...
... SOMETHING WAY DEEP DOWN.
FOR A MOMENT, LET'S JUST PRETEND THAT BOTH OF US ARE CARRYING AROUND THE PROPORTIONATE AMOUNT OF SELF-AWARENESS TO HAVE THIS CONVERSATION.
KNOW WHAT I MEAN...?
RIGHT.
THIS IS JUST HUMAN NATURE...

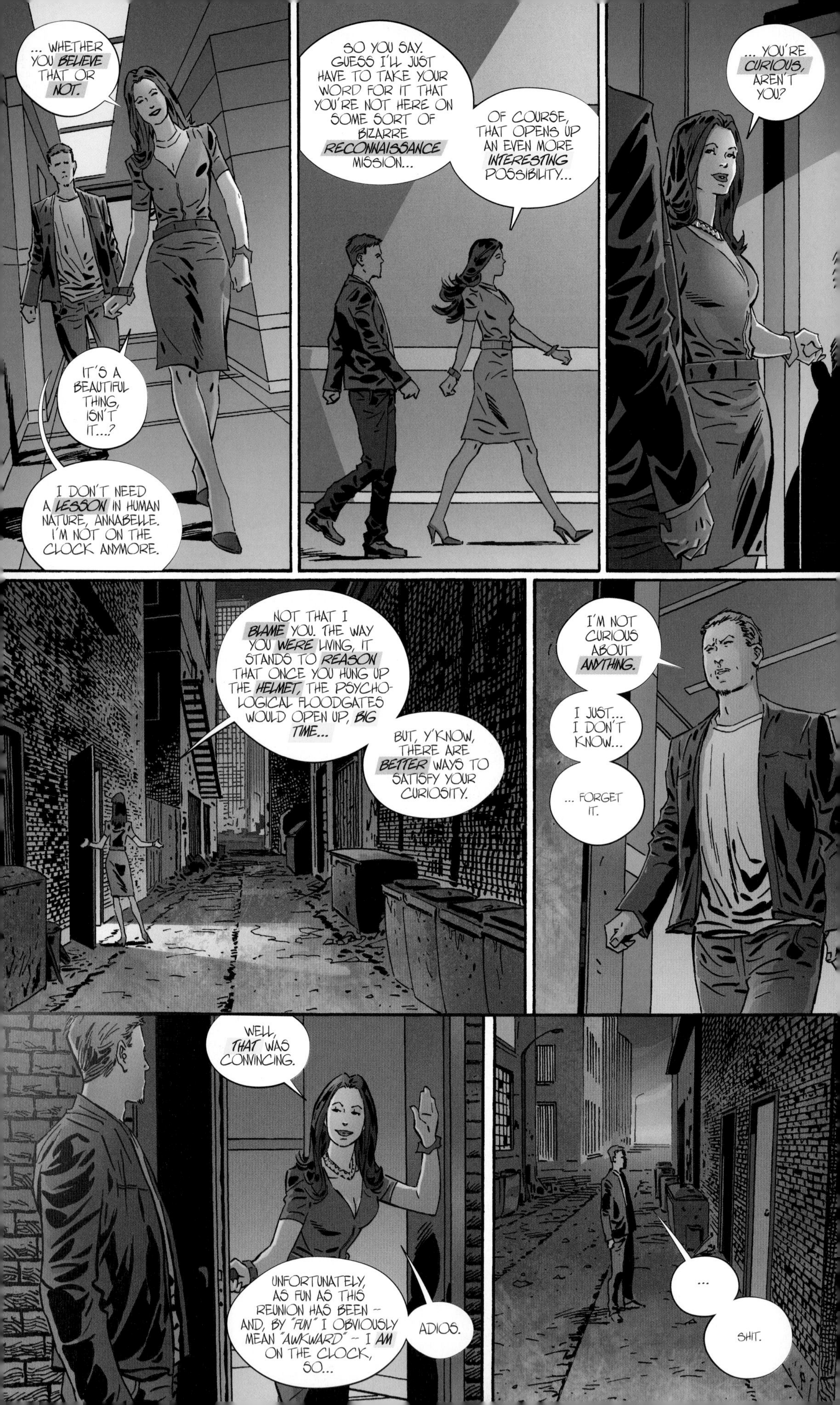
... WHETHER YOU BELIEVE THAT OR NOT.
IT'S A BEAUTIFUL THING, ISN'T IT...?
I DON'T NEED A LESSON IN HUMAN NATURE, ANNABELLE. I'M NOT ON THE CLOCK ANYMORE.
SO YOU SAY. GUESS I'LL JUST HAVE TO TAKE YOUR WORD FOR IT THAT YOU'RE NOT HERE ON SOME SORT OF BIZARRE RECONNAISSANCE MISSION...
OF COURSE, THAT OPENS UP AN EVEN MORE INTERESTING POSSIBILITY...
... YOU'RE CURIOUS, AREN'T YOU?
NOT THAT I BLAME YOU. THE WAY YOU WERE LIVING, IT STANDS TO REASON THAT ONCE YOU HUNG UP THE HELMET, THE PSYCHOLOGICAL FLOODGATES WOULD OPEN UP, BIG TIME...
BUT, Y'KNOW, THERE ARE BETTER WAYS TO SATISFY YOUR CURIOSITY.
I'M NOT CURIOUS ABOUT ANYTHING.
I JUST... I DON'T KNOW...
... FORGET IT.
WELL, THAT WAS CONVINCING.
UNFORTUNATELY, AS FUN AS THIS REUNION HAS BEEN -- AND, BY "FUN" I OBVIOUSLY MEAN "AWKWARD" -- I AM ON THE CLOCK, SO...
ADIOS.
...
SHIT.

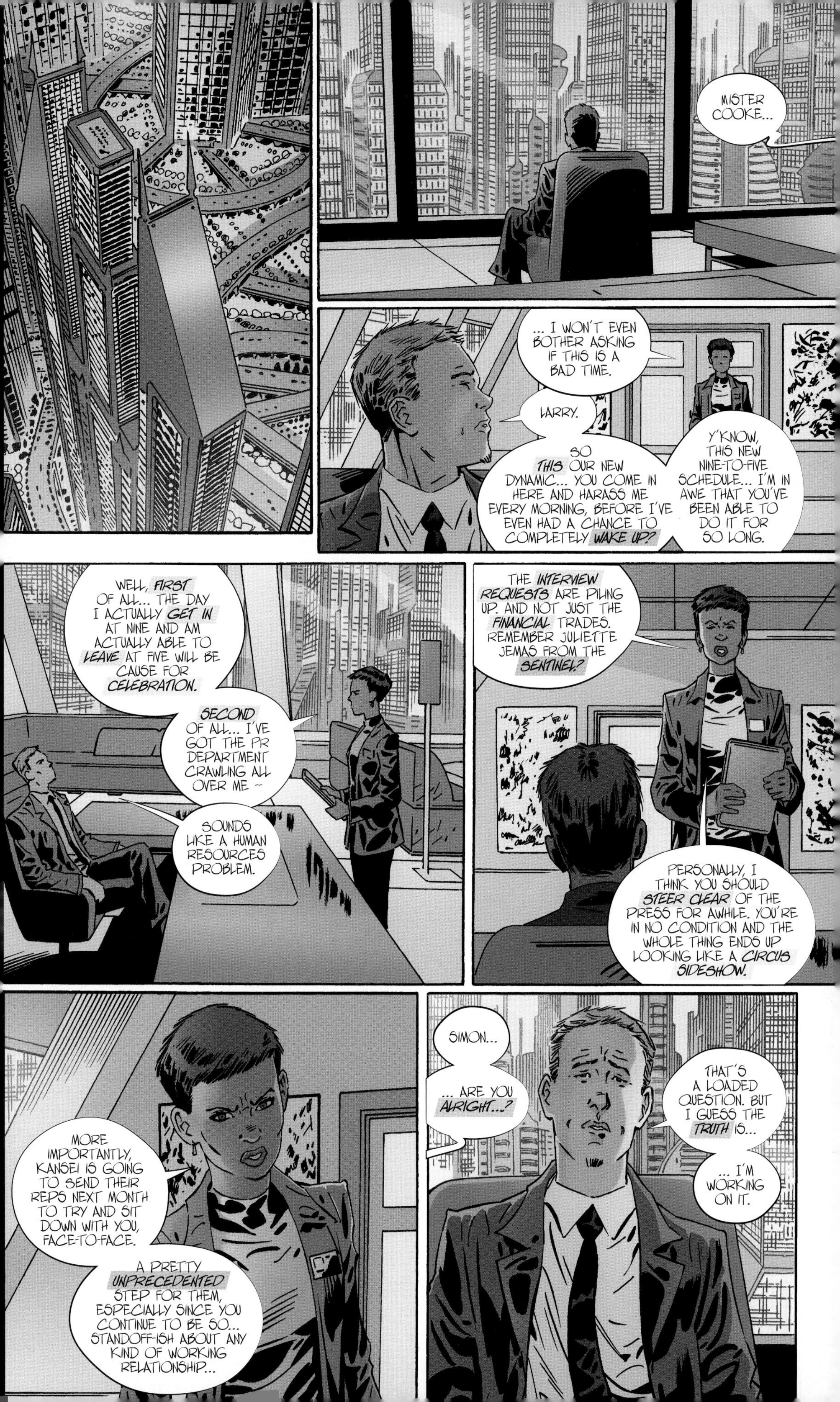

MISTER COOKE...
... I WON'T EVEN BOTHER ASKING IF THIS IS A BAD TIME.
LARRY.
SO THIS OUR NEW DYNAMIC... YOU COME IN HERE AND HARASS ME EVERY MORNING, BEFORE I'VE EVEN HAD A CHANCE TO COMPLETELY WAKE UP?
Y'KNOW, THIS NEW NINE-TO-FIVE SCHEDULE... I'M IN AWE THAT YOU'VE BEEN ABLE TO DO IT FOR SO LONG.
WELL, FIRST OF ALL... THE DAY I ACTUALLY GET IN AT NINE AND AM ACTUALLY ABLE TO LEAVE AT FIVE WILL BE CAUSE FOR CELEBRATION.
SECOND OF ALL... I'VE GOT THE PR DEPARTMENT CRAWLING ALL OVER ME --
SOUNDS LIKE A HUMAN RESOURCES PROBLEM.
THE INTERVIEW REQUESTS ARE PILING UP. AND NOT JUST THE FINANCIAL TRADES. REMEMBER JULIETTE JEMAS FROM THE SENTINEL?
PERSONALLY, I THINK YOU SHOULD STEER CLEAR OF THE PRESS FOR AWHILE. YOU'RE IN NO CONDITION AND THE WHOLE THING ENDS UP LOOKING LIKE A CIRCUS SIDESHOW.
MORE IMPORTANTLY, KANSEI IS GOING TO SEND THEIR REPS NEXT MONTH TO TRY AND SIT DOWN WITH YOU, FACE-TO-FACE.
A PRETTY UNPRECEDENTED STEP FOR THEM, ESPECIALLY SINCE YOU CONTINUE TO BE SO... STANDOFF-ISH ABOUT ANY KIND OF WORKING RELATIONSHIP...
SIMON...
... ARE YOU ALRIGHT...?
THAT'S A LOADED QUESTION. BUT I GUESS THE TRUTH IS...
... I'M WORKING ON IT.

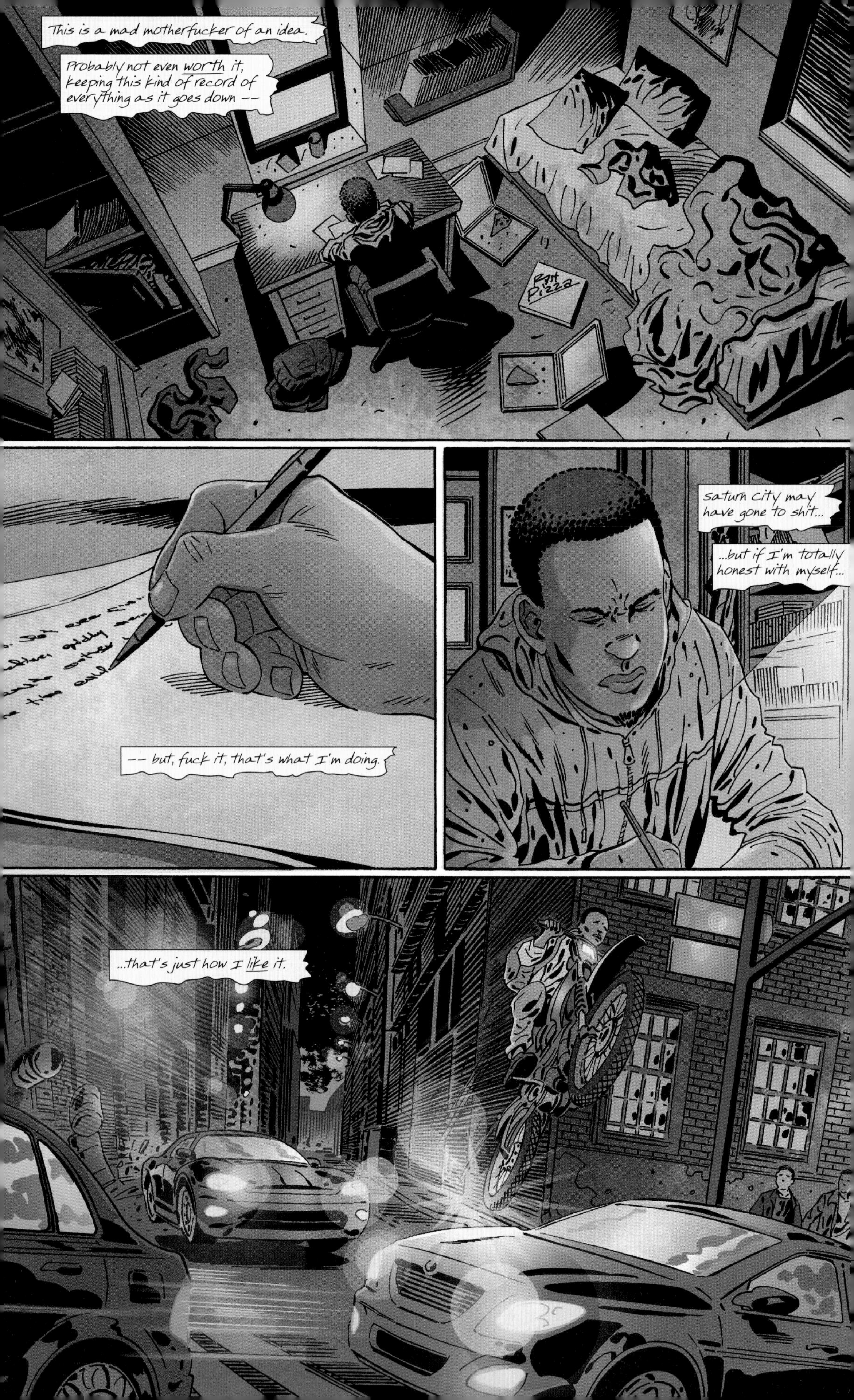
This is a mad motherfucker of an idea.
Probably not even worth it, keeping this kind of record of everything as it goes down --
-- but, fuck it, that's what I'm doing.
saturn city may have gone to shit...
...but if I'm totally honest with myself...
...that's just how I like it.

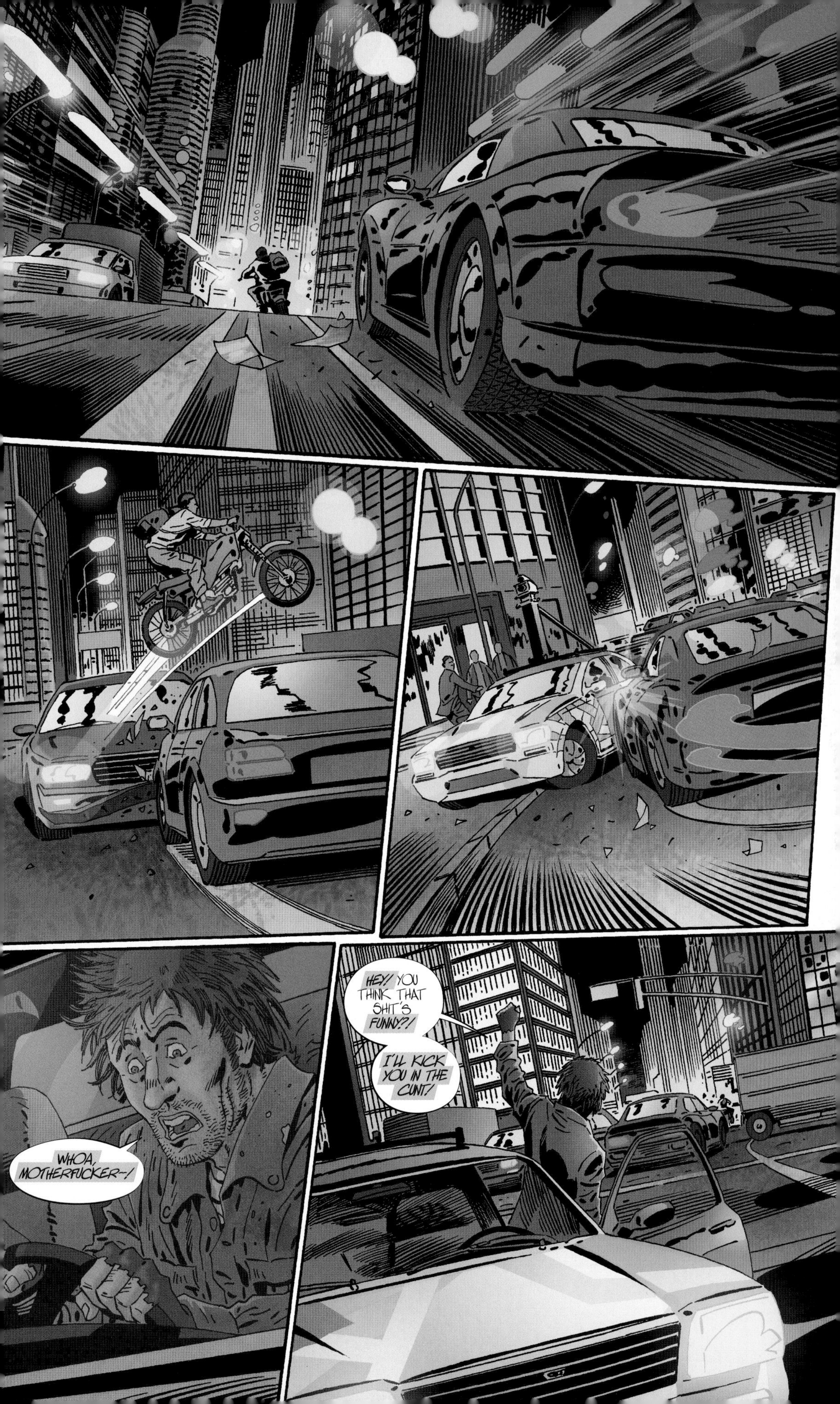
WHOA, MOTHERFUCKER--!
HEY! YOU THINK THAT SHIT'S FUNNY?!
I'LL KICK YOU IN THE CUNT!

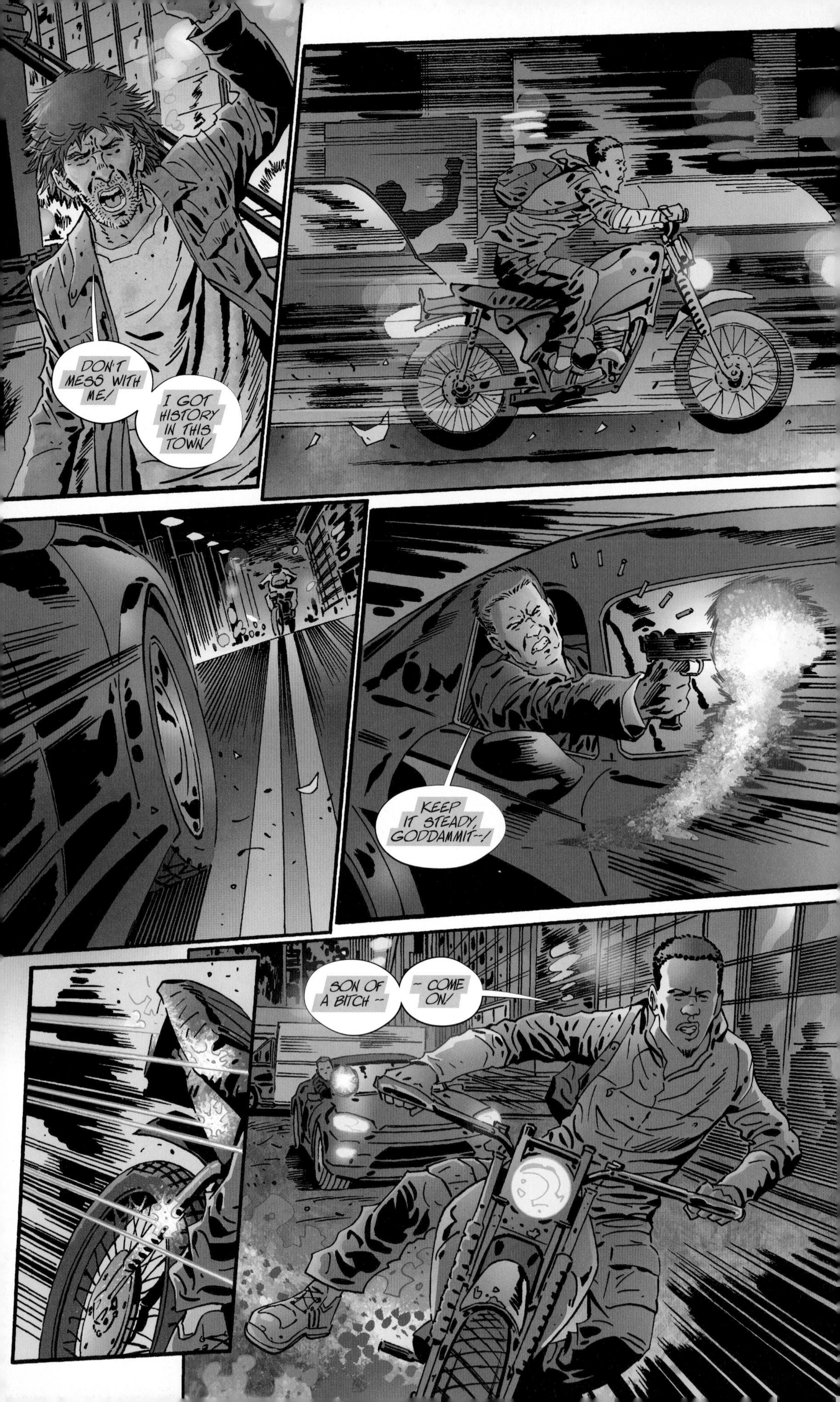
DON'T MESS WITH ME!
I GOT HISTORY IN THIS TOWN!
KEEP IT STEADY, GODDAMMIT--!
SON OF A BITCH --
-- COME ON!

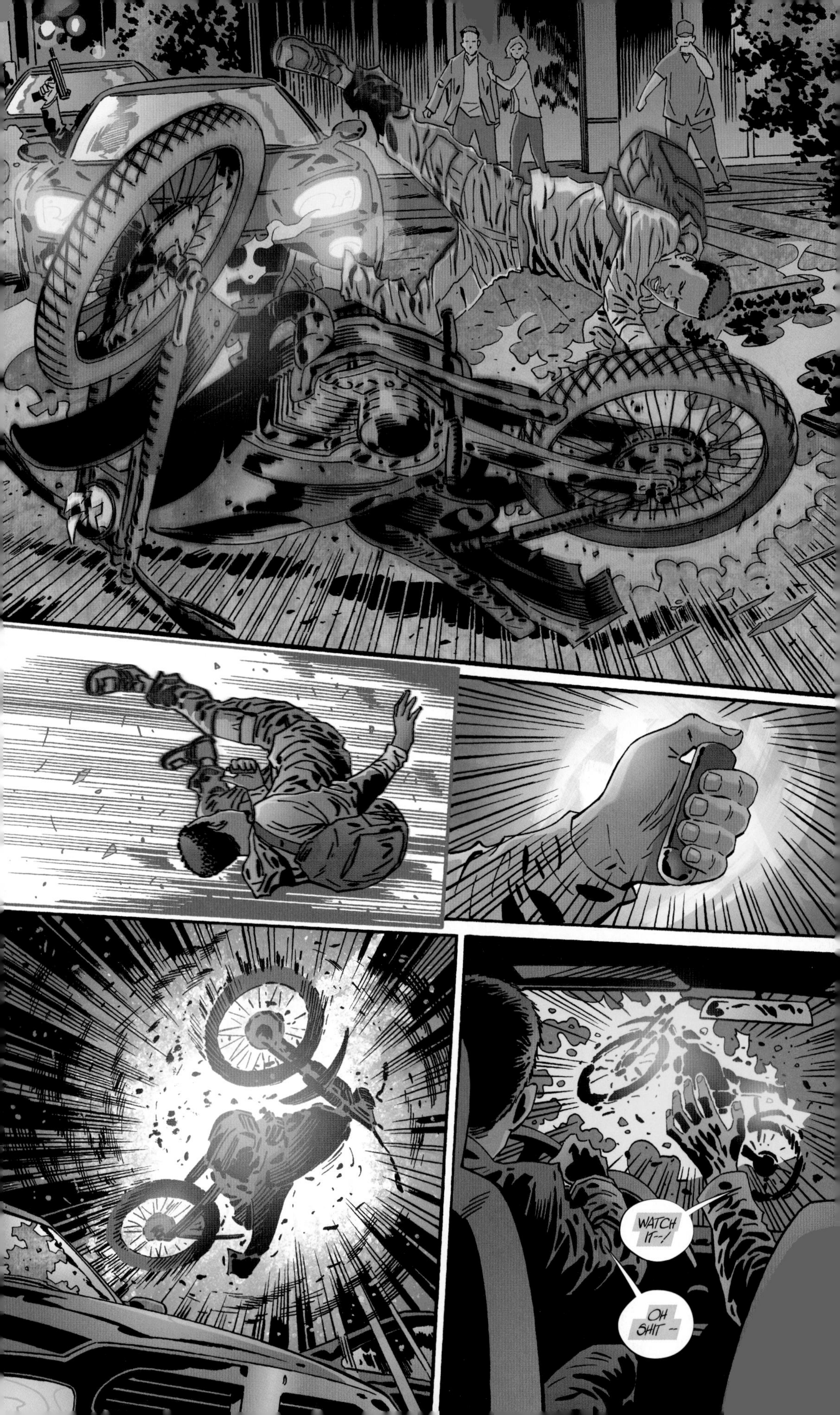
WATCH IT--!
OH SHIT--

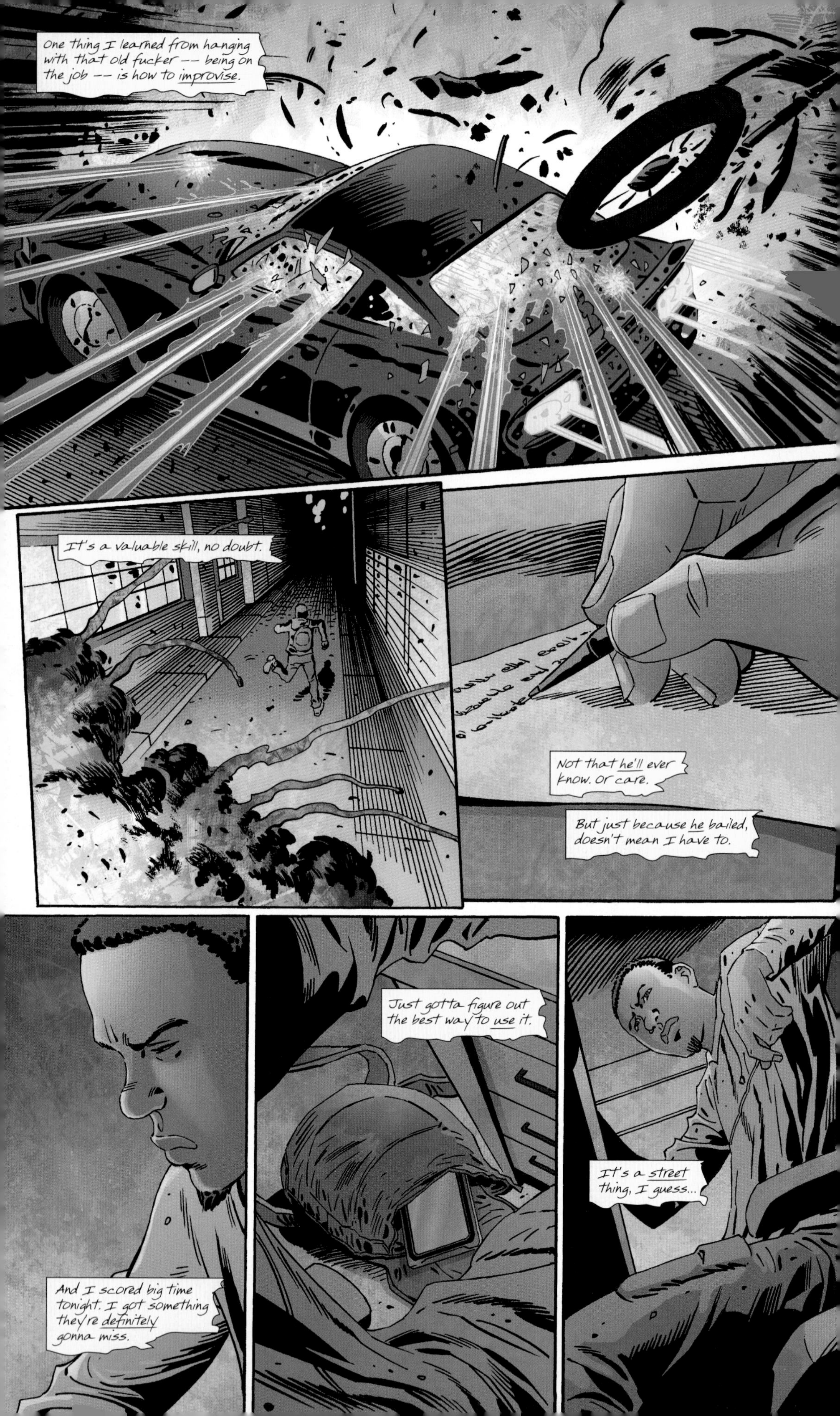

One thing I learned from hanging with that old fucker -- being on the job -- is how to improvise.
It's a valuable skill, no doubt.
Not that he'll ever know. Or care.
But just because he bailed, doesn't mean I have to.
And I scored big time tonight. I got something they're definitely gonna miss.
Just gotta figure out the best way to use it.
It's a street thing, I guess...

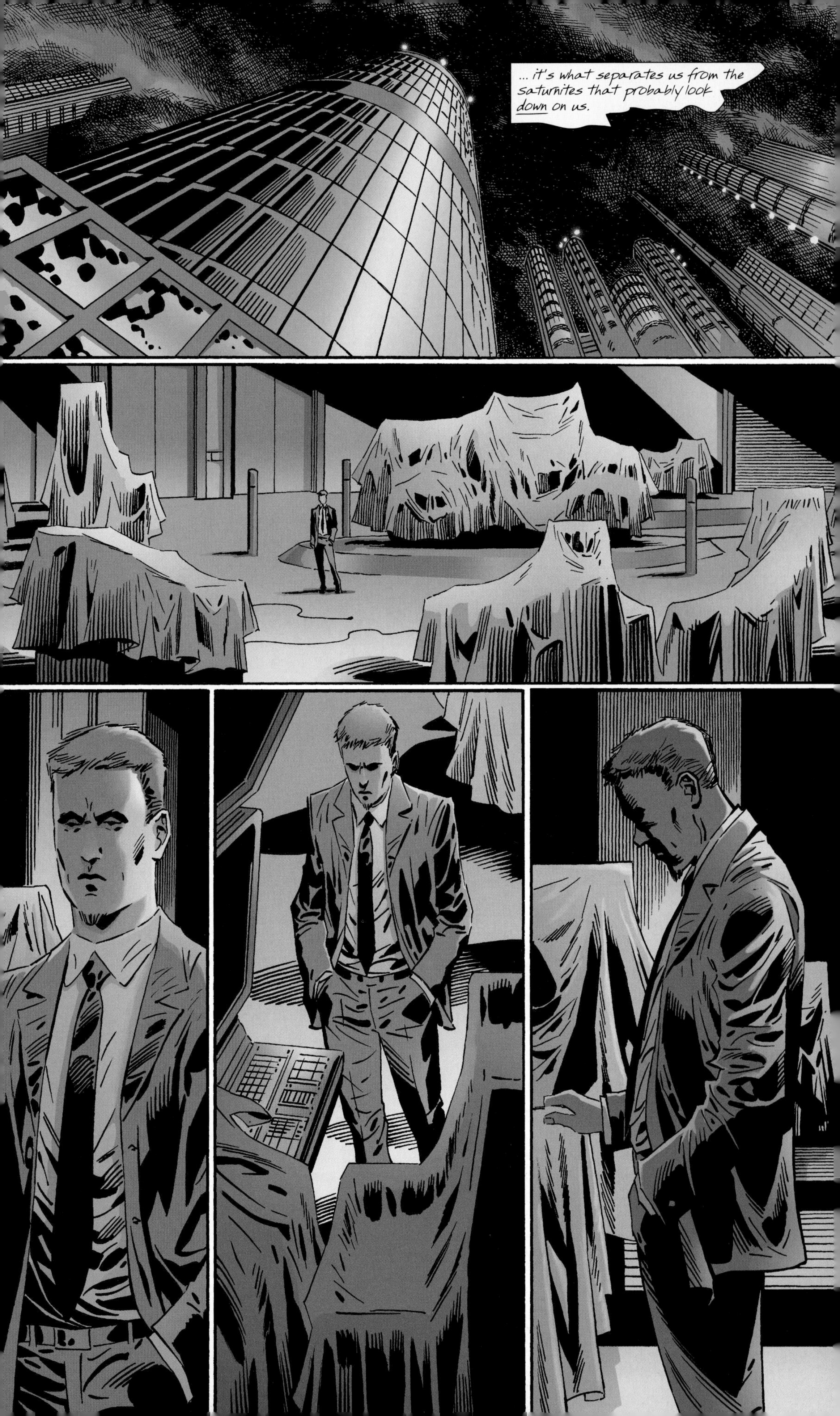
... it's what separates us from the saturnites that probably look down on us.

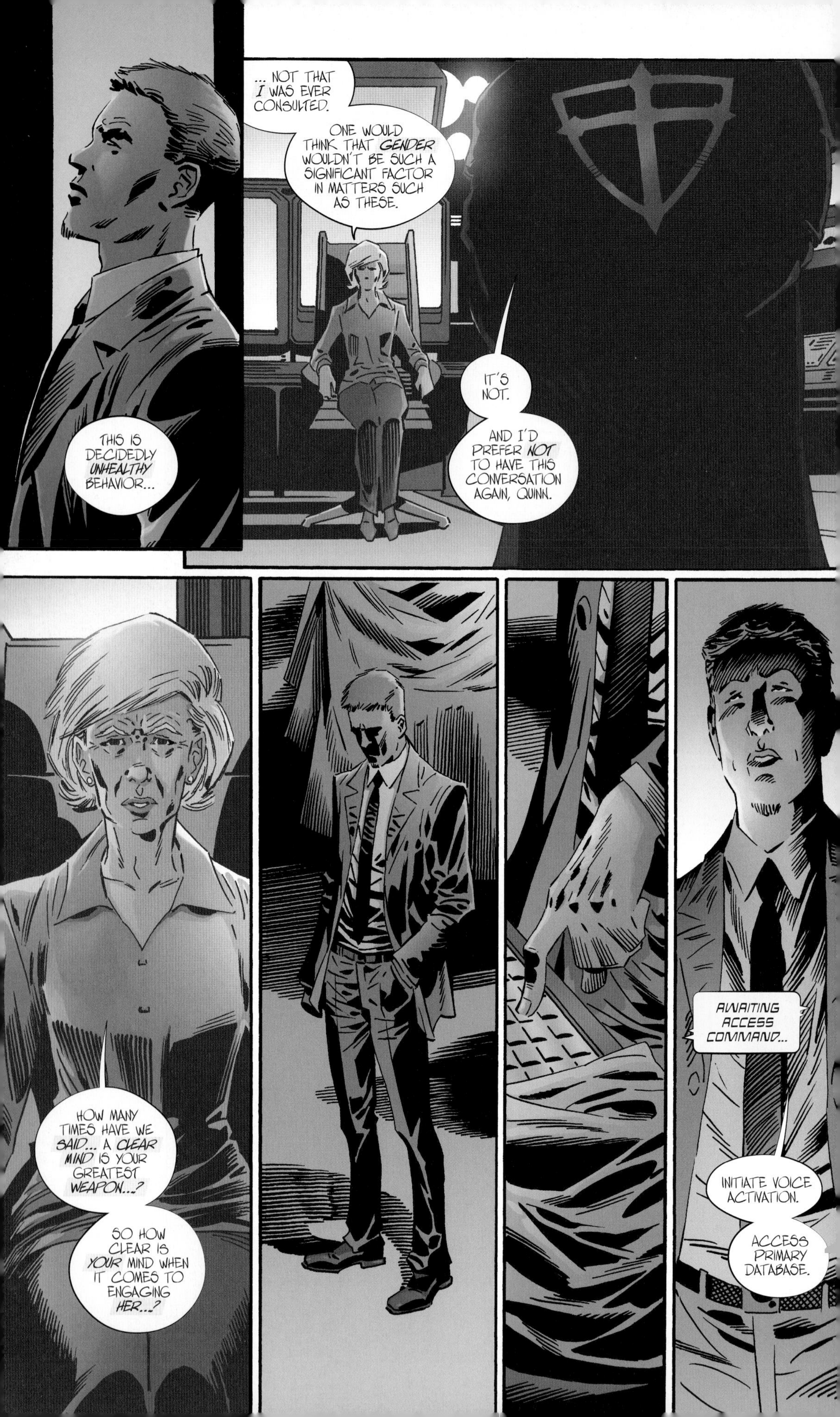
THIS IS DECIDEDLY UNHEALTHY BEHAVIOR...
... NOT THAT I WAS EVER CONSULTED.
ONE WOULD THINK THAT GENDER WOULDN'T BE SUCH A SIGNIFICANT FACTOR IN MATTERS SUCH AS THESE.
IT'S NOT.
AND I'D PREFER NOT TO HAVE THIS CONVERSATION AGAIN, QUINN.
HOW MANY TIMES HAVE WE SAID... A CLEAR MIND IS YOUR GREATEST WEAPON...?
SO HOW CLEAR IS YOUR MIND WHEN IT COMES TO ENGAGING HER...?
AWAITING ACCESS COMMAND...
INITIATE VOICE ACTIVATION.
ACCESS PRIMARY DATABASE.

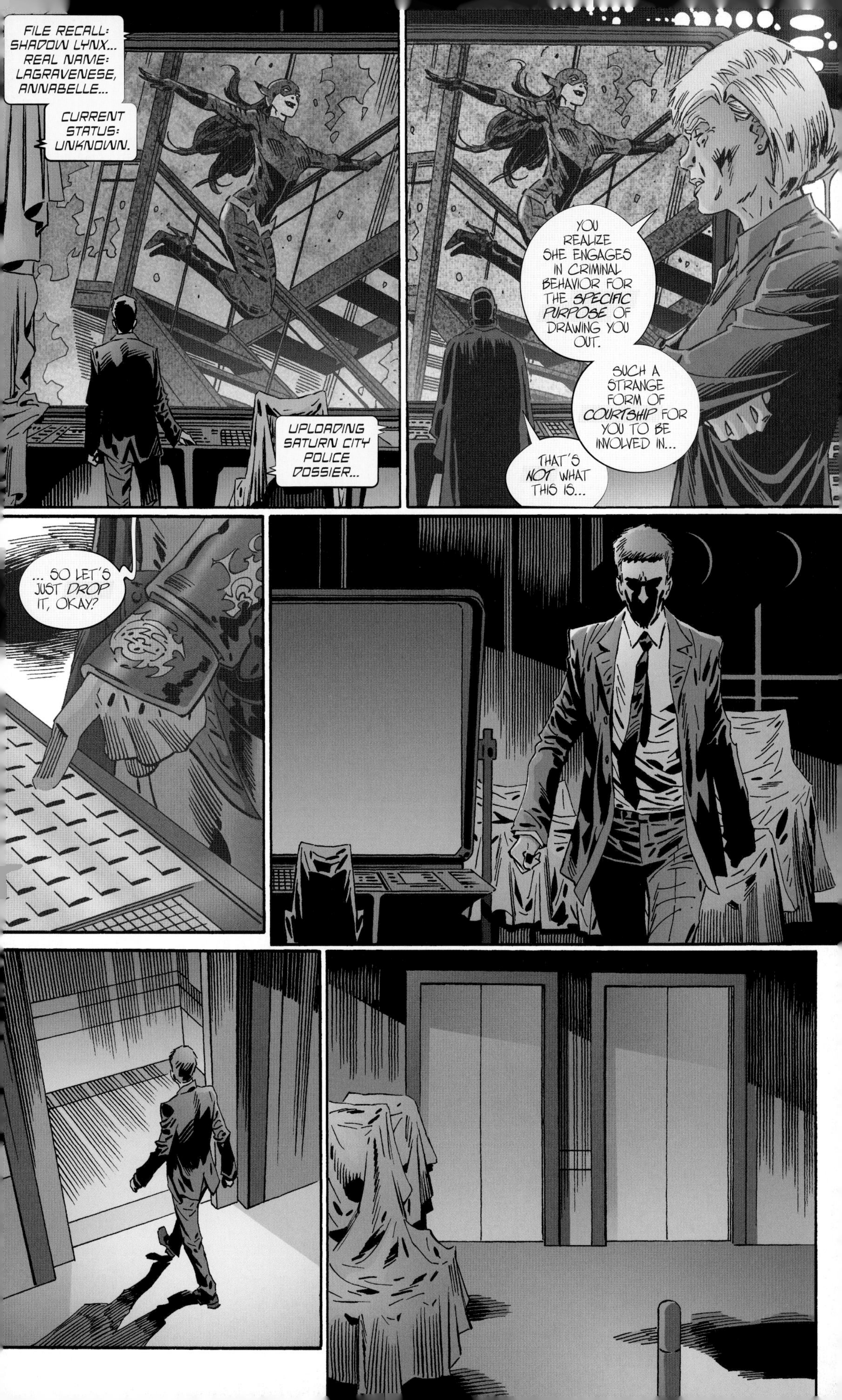
FILE RECALL: SHADOW LYNX... REAL NAME: LAGRAVENESE, ANNABELLE...
CURRENT STATUS: UNKNOWN.
UPLOADING SATURN CITY POLICE DOSSIER...
YOU REALIZE SHE ENGAGES IN CRIMINAL BEHAVIOR FOR THE SPECIFIC PURPOSE OF DRAWING YOU OUT.
SUCH A STRANGE FORM OF COURTSHIP FOR YOU TO BE INVOLVED IN...
THAT'S NOT WHAT THIS IS...
... SO LET'S JUST DROP IT, OKAY?

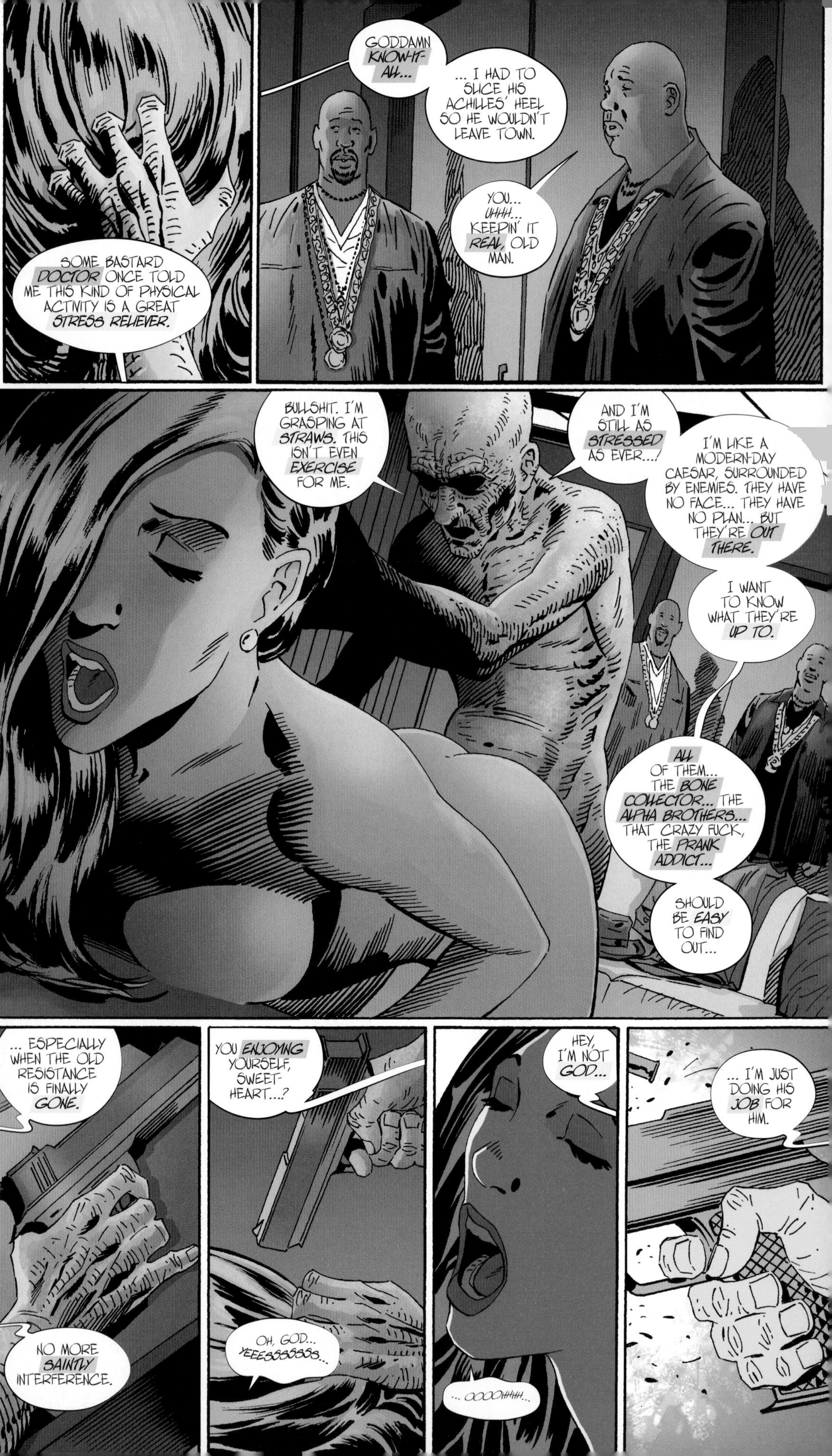
SOME BASTARD DOCTOR ONCE TOLD ME THIS KIND OF PHYSICAL ACTIVITY IS A GREAT STRESS RELIEVER.
GODDAMN KNOW-IT-ALL...
... I HAD TO SLICE HIS ACHILLES' HEEL SO HE WOULDN'T LEAVE TOWN.
YOU... UHHH... KEEPIN' IT REAL, OLD MAN.
BULLSHIT. I'M GRASPING AT STRAWS. THIS ISN'T EVEN EXERCISE FOR ME.
AND I'M STILL AS STRESSED AS EVER...!
I'M LIKE A MODERN-DAY CAESAR, SURROUNDED BY ENEMIES. THEY HAVE NO FACE... THEY HAVE NO PLAN... BUT THEY'RE OUT THERE.
I WANT TO KNOW WHAT THEY'RE UP TO.
ALL OF THEM... THE BONE COLLECTOR... THE ALPHA BROTHERS... THAT CRAZY FUCK, THE PRANK ADDICT...
SHOULD BE EASY TO FIND OUT...
... ESPECIALLY WHEN THE OLD RESISTANCE IS FINALLY GONE.
NO MORE SAINTLY INTERFERENCE.
YOU ENJOYING YOURSELF, SWEET-HEART...?
OH, GOD... YEEESSSSSSS...
HEY, I'M NOT GOD...
... OOOOHHHH...
... I'M JUST DOING HIS JOB FOR HIM.

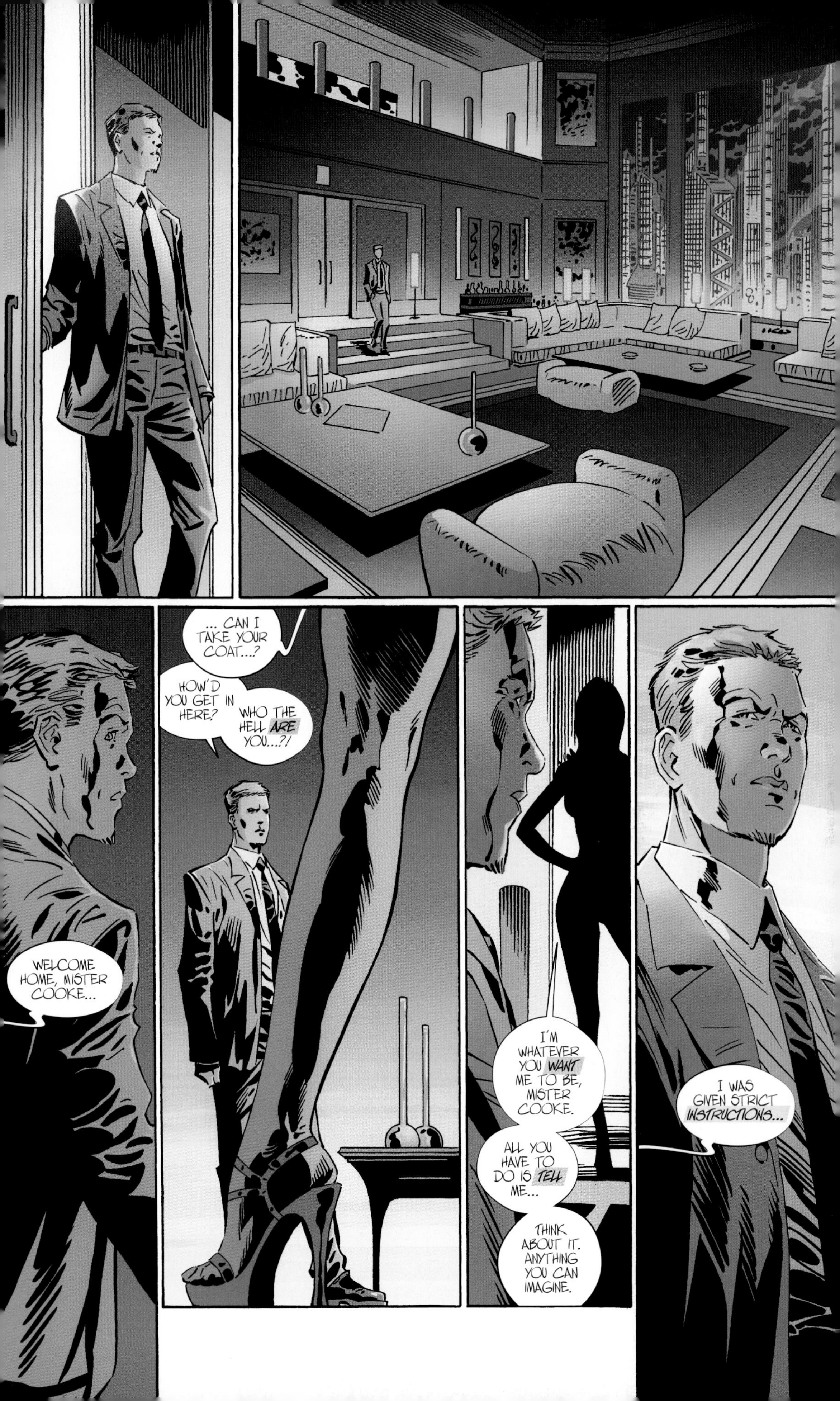
WELCOME HOME, MISTER COOKE...
... CAN I TAKE YOUR COAT...?
HOW'D YOU GET IN HERE?
WHO THE HELL ARE YOU...?!
I'M WHATEVER YOU WANT ME TO BE, MISTER COOKE.
ALL YOU HAVE TO DO IS TELL ME...
THINK ABOUT IT. ANYTHING YOU CAN IMAGINE.
I WAS GIVEN STRICT INSTRUCTIONS...

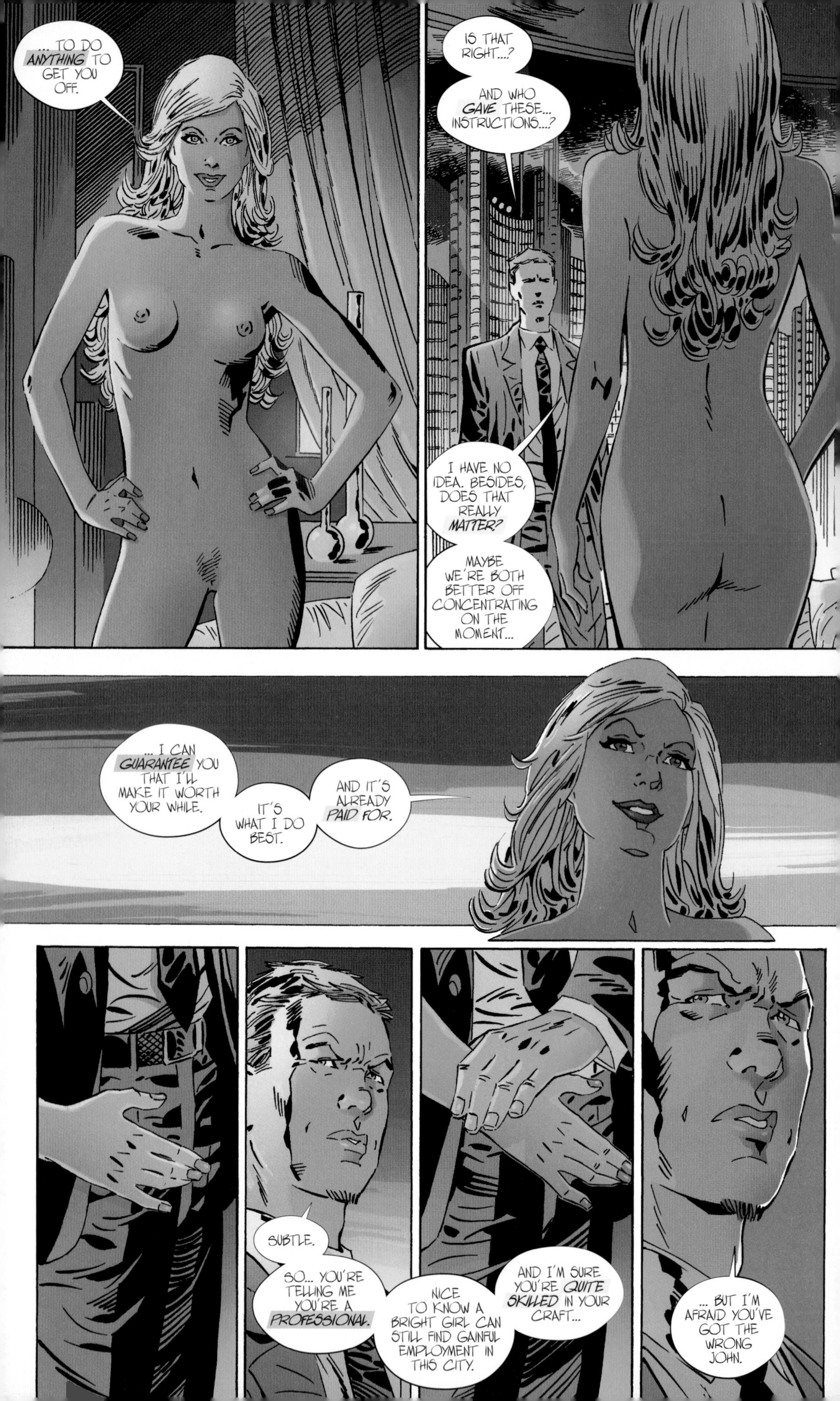

...TO DO ANYTHING TO GET YOU OFF.
IS THAT RIGHT...?
AND WHO GAVE THESE... INSTRUCTIONS...?
I HAVE NO IDEA. BESIDES, DOES THAT REALLY MATTER?
MAYBE WE'RE BOTH BETTER OFF CONCENTRATING ON THE MOMENT...
...I CAN GUARANTEE YOU THAT I'LL MAKE IT WORTH YOUR WHILE.
IT'S WHAT I DO BEST.
AND IT'S ALREADY PAID FOR.
SUBTLE.
SO... YOU'RE TELLING ME YOU'RE A PROFESSIONAL.
NICE TO KNOW A BRIGHT GIRL CAN STILL FIND GAINFUL EMPLOYMENT IN THIS CITY.
AND I'M SURE YOU'RE QUITE SKILLED IN YOUR CRAFT...
...BUT I'M AFRAID YOU'VE GOT THE WRONG JOHN.

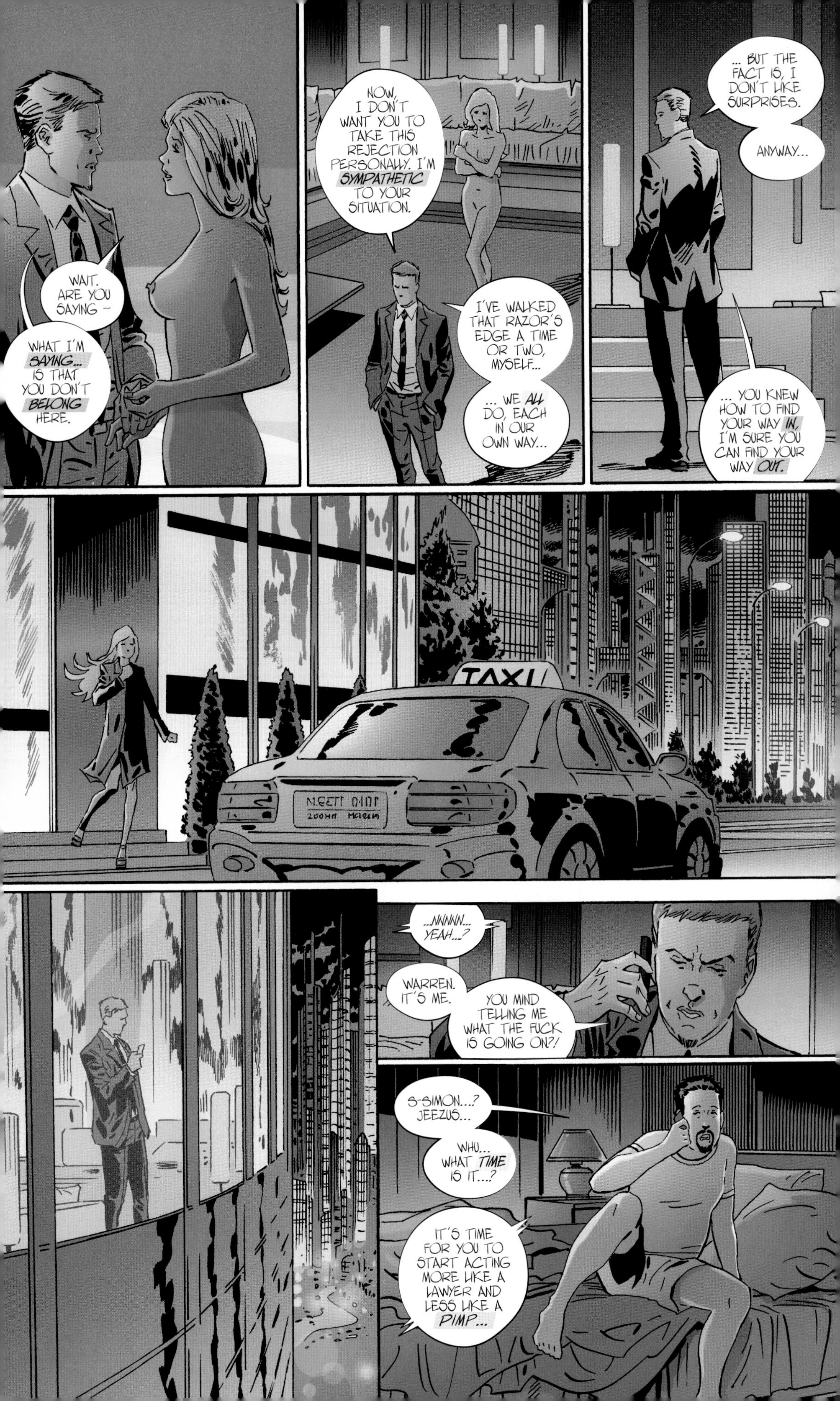

WAIT. ARE YOU SAYING --
WHAT I'M SAYING... IS THAT YOU DON'T BELONG HERE.
NOW, I DON'T WANT YOU TO TAKE THIS REJECTION PERSONALLY. I'M SYMPATHETIC TO YOUR SITUATION.
I'VE WALKED THAT RAZOR'S EDGE A TIME OR TWO, MYSELF...
... WE ALL DO, EACH IN OUR OWN WAY...
... BUT THE FACT IS, I DON'T LIKE SURPRISES.
ANYWAY...
... YOU KNEW HOW TO FIND YOUR WAY IN, I'M SURE YOU CAN FIND YOUR WAY OUT.
TAXI
...NNNNN... YEAH...?
WARREN. IT'S ME.
YOU MIND TELLING ME WHAT THE FUCK IS GOING ON?!
S-SIMON...? JEEZUS...
WHU... WHAT TIME IS IT...?
IT'S TIME FOR YOU TO START ACTING MORE LIKE A LAWYER AND LESS LIKE A PIMP...

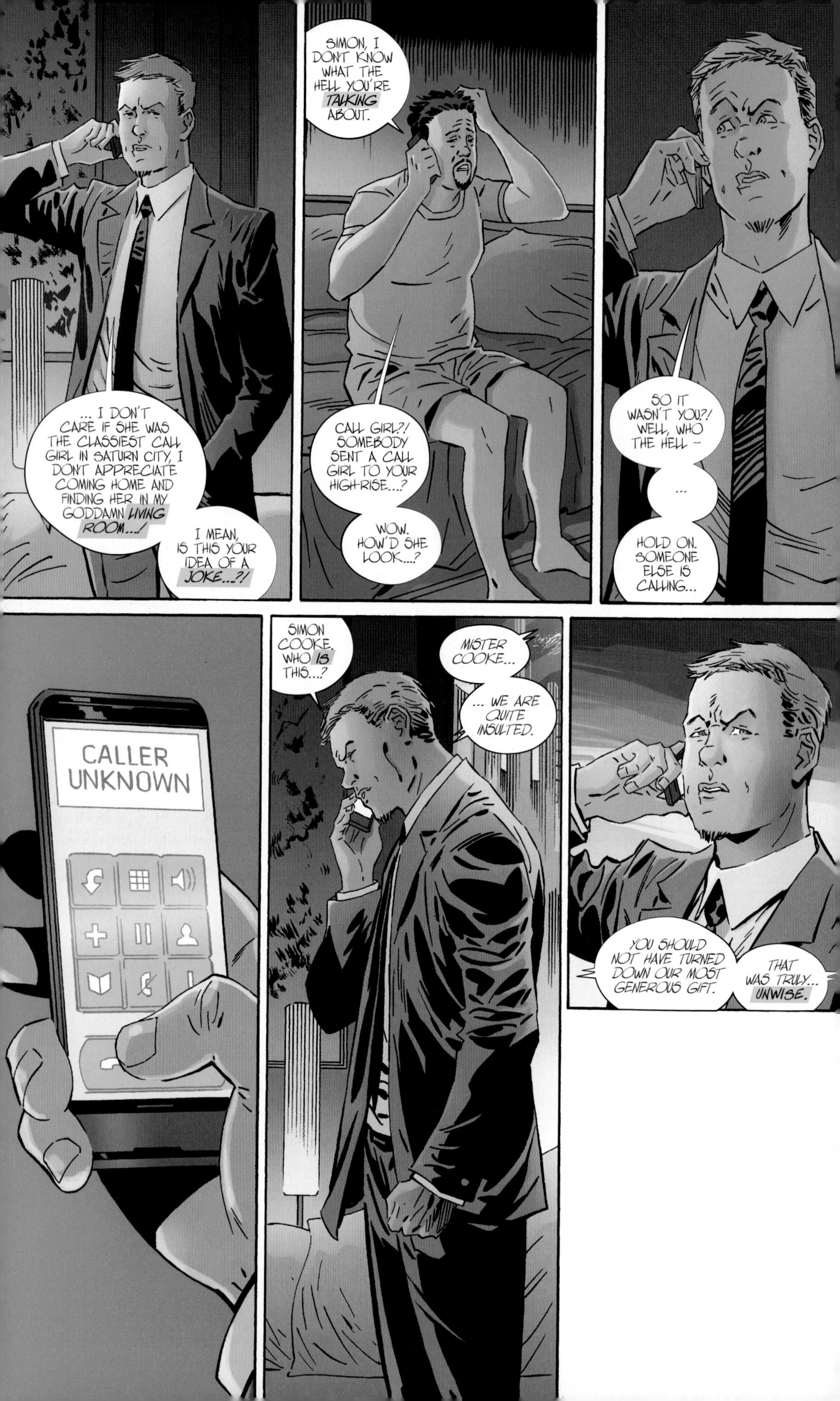
SIMON, I DON'T KNOW WHAT THE HELL YOU'RE TALKING ABOUT.
... I DON'T CARE IF SHE WAS THE CLASSIEST CALL GIRL IN SATURN CITY, I DON'T APPRECIATE COMING HOME AND FINDING HER IN MY GODDAMN LIVING ROOM...!
I MEAN, IS THIS YOUR IDEA OF A JOKE...?!
CALL GIRL?! SOMEBODY SENT A CALL GIRL TO YOUR HIGH-RISE...?
WOW. HOW'D SHE LOOK...?
SO IT WASN'T YOU?! WELL, WHO THE HELL --
...
HOLD ON. SOMEONE ELSE IS CALLING...
CALLER UNKNOWN
SIMON COOKE. WHO IS THIS...?
MISTER COOKE...
... WE ARE QUITE INSULTED.
YOU SHOULD NOT HAVE TURNED DOWN OUR MOST GENEROUS GIFT.
THAT WAS TRULY... UNWISE.

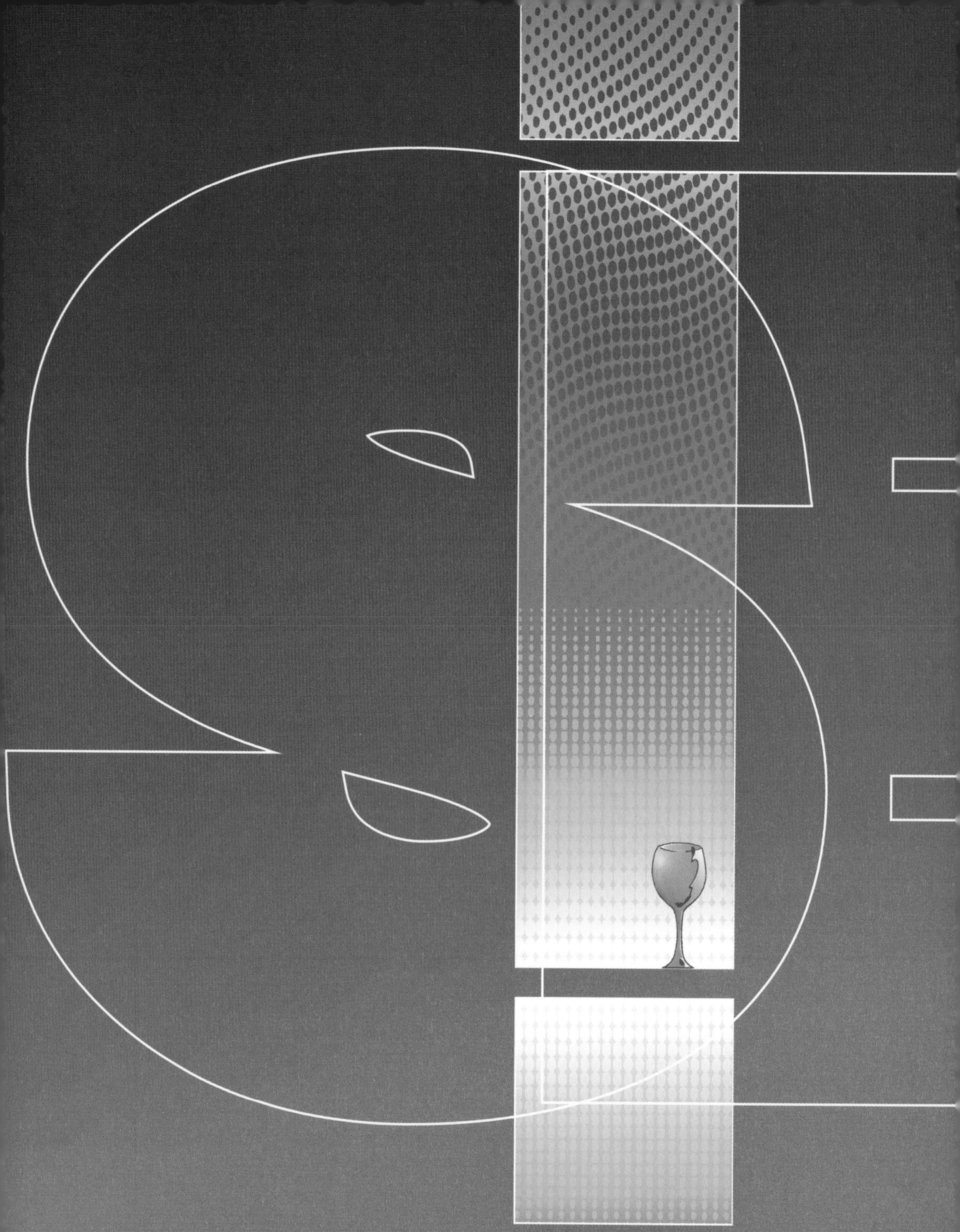

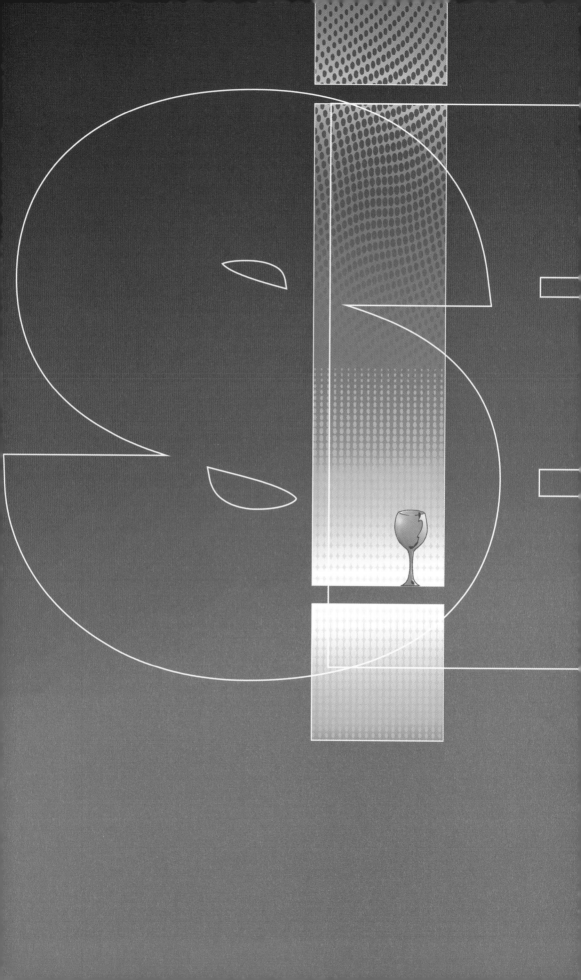

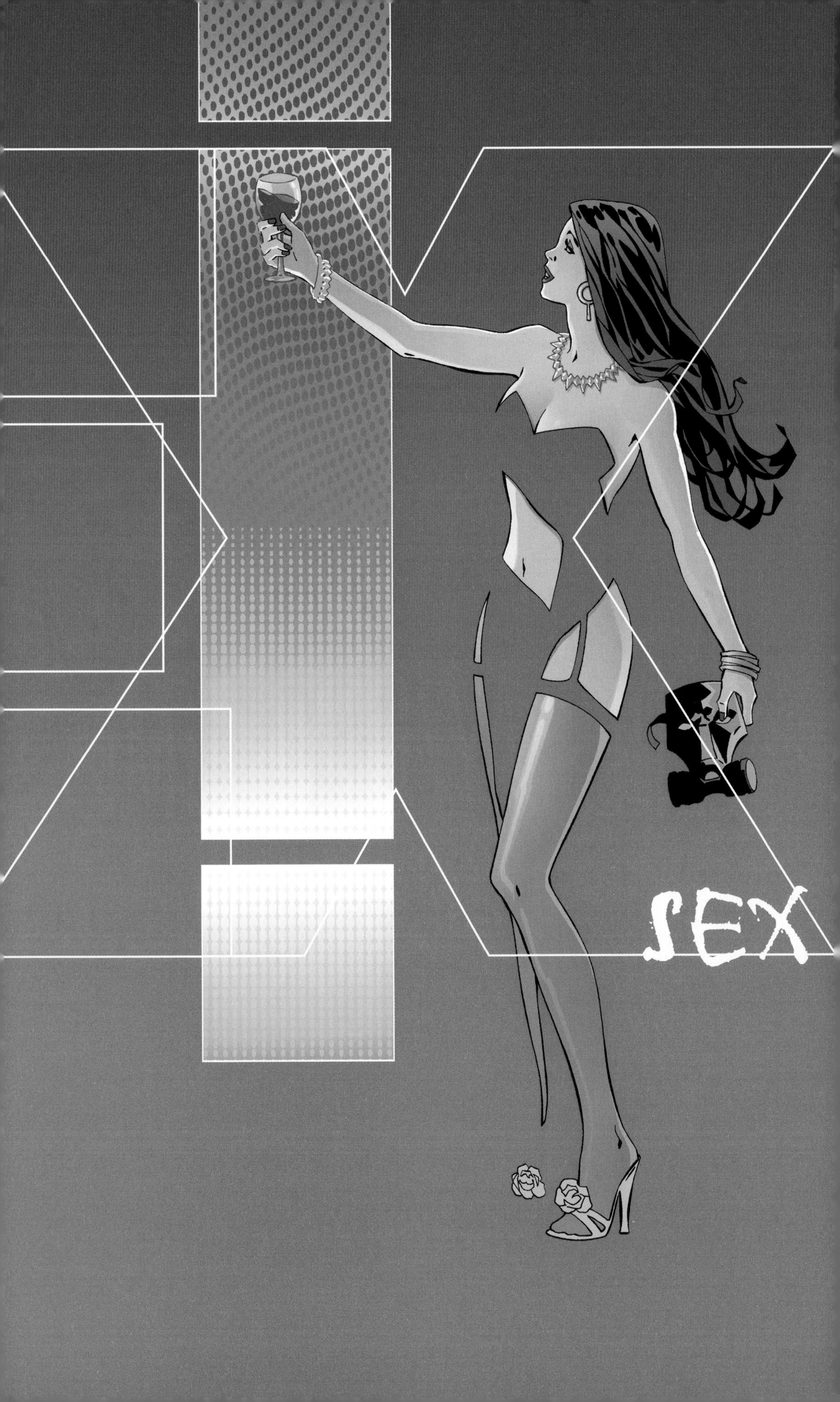
SEX

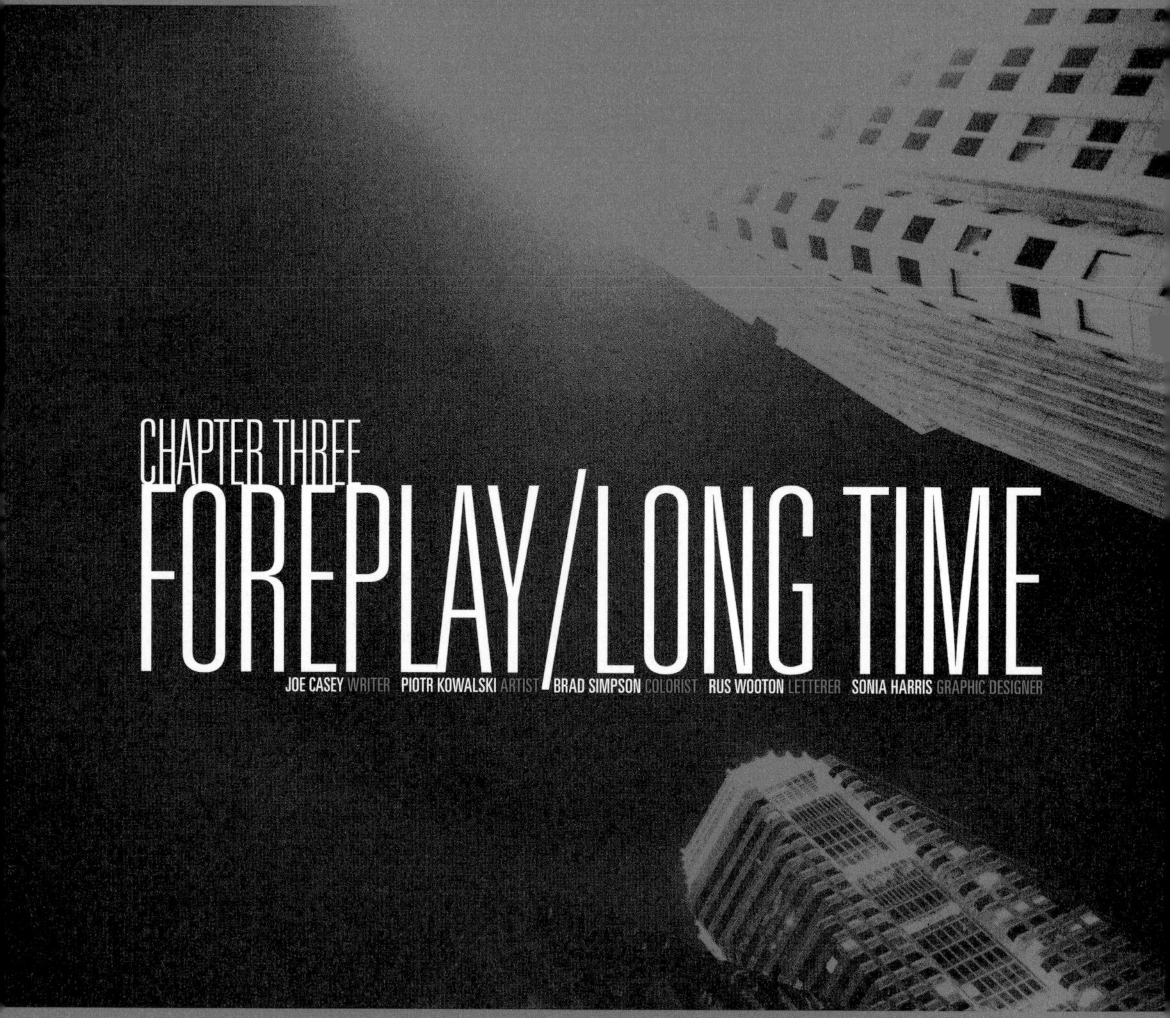

CHAPTER THREE

FOREPLAY/LONG TIME

JOE CASEY WRITER **PIOTR KOWALSKI** ARTIST **BRAD SIMPSON** COLORIST **RUS WOOTON** LETTERER **SONIA HARRIS** GRAPHIC DESIGNER

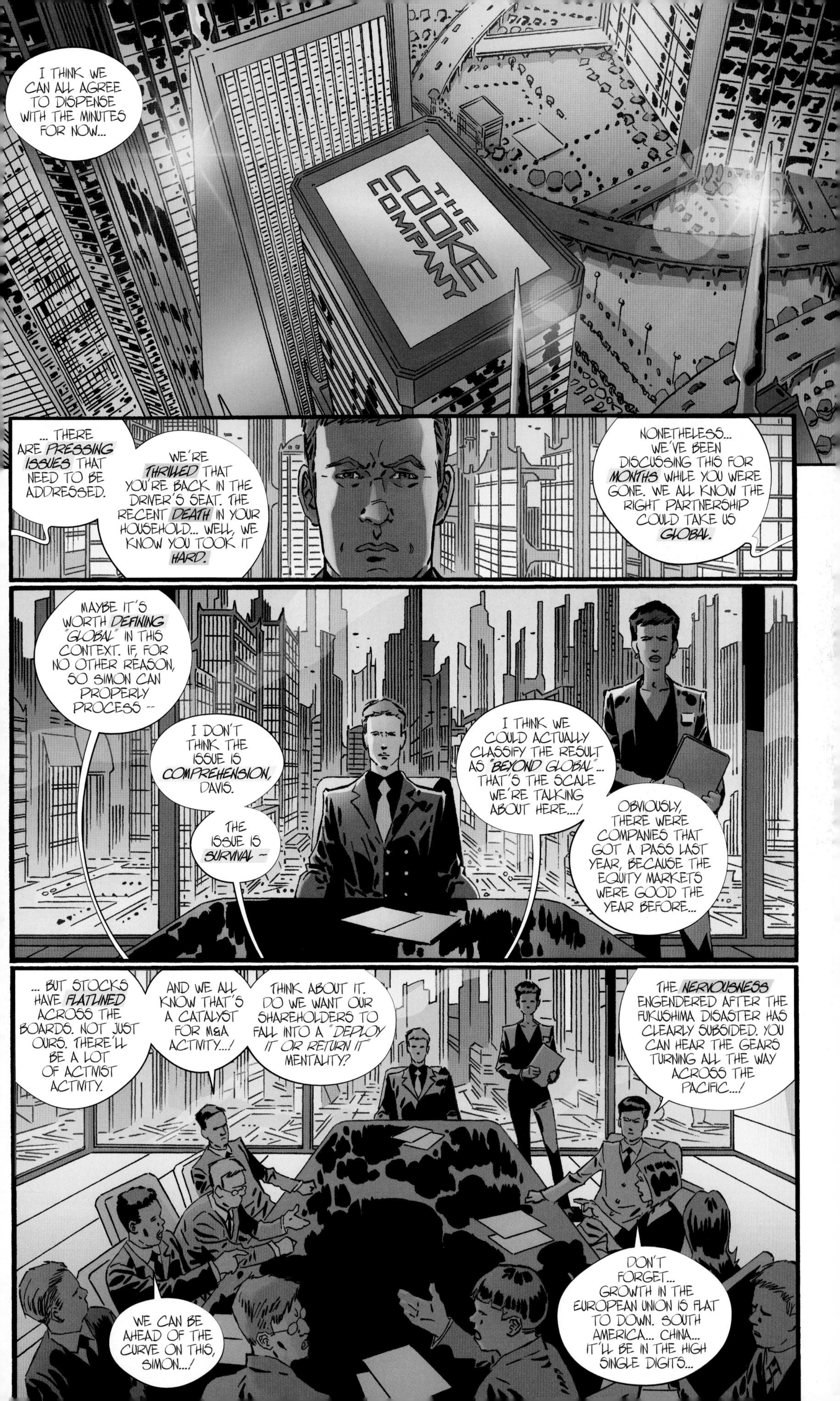

I THINK WE CAN ALL AGREE TO DISPENSE WITH THE MINUTES FOR NOW...
THE COOKE COMPANY
... THERE ARE PRESSING ISSUES THAT NEED TO BE ADDRESSED.
WE'RE THRILLED THAT YOU'RE BACK IN THE DRIVER'S SEAT. THE RECENT DEATH IN YOUR HOUSEHOLD... WELL, WE KNOW YOU TOOK IT HARD.
NONETHELESS... WE'VE BEEN DISCUSSING THIS FOR MONTHS WHILE YOU WERE GONE. WE ALL KNOW THE RIGHT PARTNERSHIP COULD TAKE US GLOBAL.
MAYBE IT'S WORTH DEFINING "GLOBAL" IN THIS CONTEXT. IF, FOR NO OTHER REASON, SO SIMON CAN PROPERLY PROCESS --
I DON'T THINK THE ISSUE IS COMPREHENSION, DAVIS.
THE ISSUE IS SURVIVAL --
I THINK WE COULD ACTUALLY CLASSIFY THE RESULT AS "BEYOND GLOBAL"... THAT'S THE SCALE WE'RE TALKING ABOUT HERE...!
OBVIOUSLY, THERE WERE COMPANIES THAT GOT A PASS LAST YEAR, BECAUSE THE EQUITY MARKETS WERE GOOD THE YEAR BEFORE...
... BUT STOCKS HAVE FLATLINED ACROSS THE BOARDS. NOT JUST OURS. THERE'LL BE A LOT OF ACTIVIST ACTIVITY.
AND WE ALL KNOW THAT'S A CATALYST FOR M&A ACTIVITY...!
THINK ABOUT IT. DO WE WANT OUR SHAREHOLDERS TO FALL INTO A "DEPLOY IT OR RETURN IT" MENTALITY?
THE NERVOUSNESS ENGENDERED AFTER THE FUKUSHIMA DISASTER HAS CLEARLY SUBSIDED. YOU CAN HEAR THE GEARS TURNING ALL THE WAY ACROSS THE PACIFIC...!
WE CAN BE AHEAD OF THE CURVE ON THIS, SIMON...!
DON'T FORGET... GROWTH IN THE EUROPEAN UNION IS FLAT TO DOWN. SOUTH AMERICA... CHINA... IT'LL BE IN THE HIGH SINGLE DIGITS...

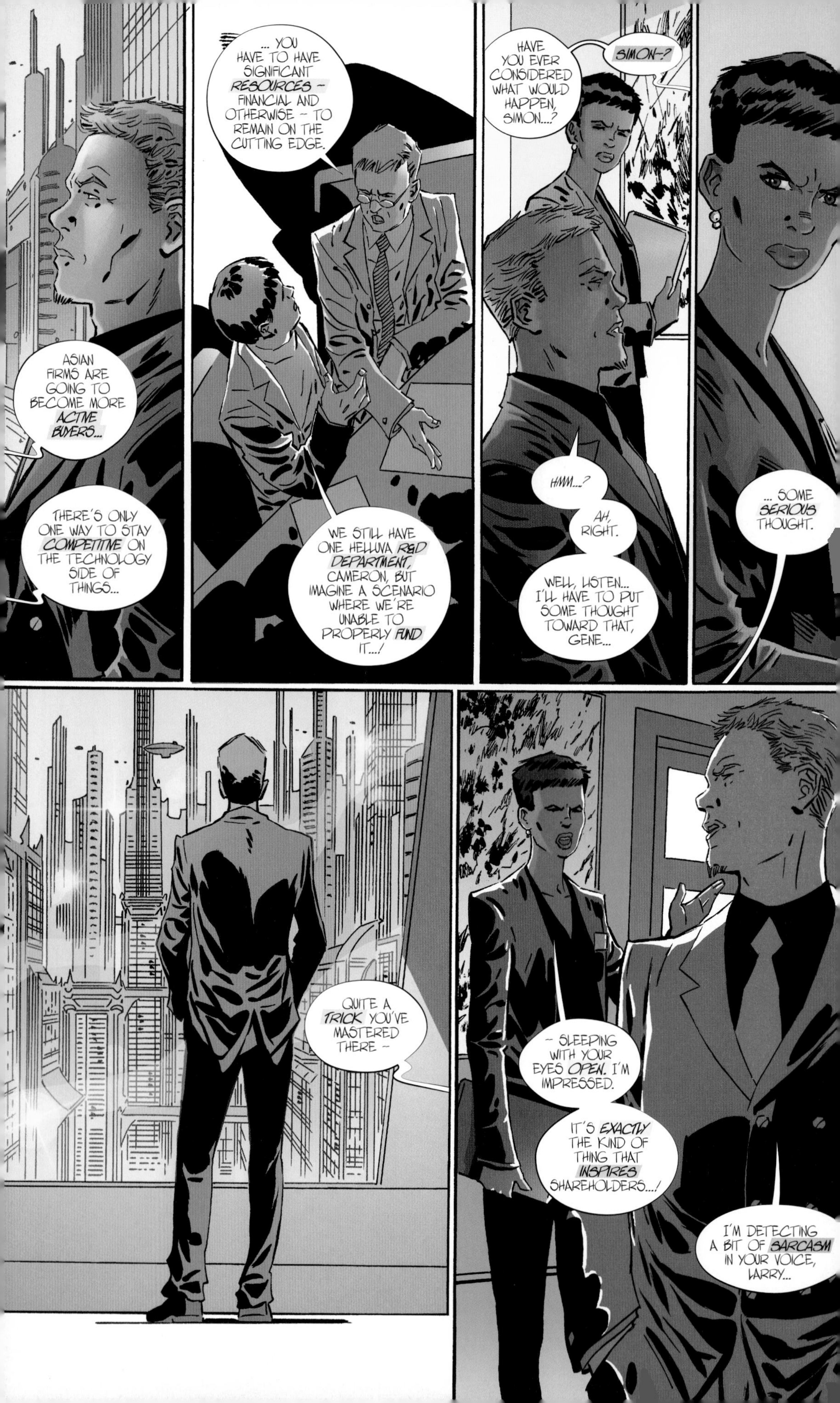
ASIAN FIRMS ARE GOING TO BECOME MORE ACTIVE BUYERS...
THERE'S ONLY ONE WAY TO STAY COMPETITIVE ON THE TECHNOLOGY SIDE OF THINGS...
... YOU HAVE TO HAVE SIGNIFICANT RESOURCES -- FINANCIAL AND OTHERWISE -- TO REMAIN ON THE CUTTING EDGE.
WE STILL HAVE ONE HELLUVA R&D DEPARTMENT, CAMERON, BUT IMAGINE A SCENARIO WHERE WE'RE UNABLE TO PROPERLY FUND IT...!
HAVE YOU EVER CONSIDERED WHAT WOULD HAPPEN, SIMON...?
SIMON--?
HMM...?
AH, RIGHT.
WELL, LISTEN... I'LL HAVE TO PUT SOME THOUGHT TOWARD THAT, GENE...
... SOME SERIOUS THOUGHT.
QUITE A TRICK YOU'VE MASTERED THERE --
-- SLEEPING WITH YOUR EYES OPEN. I'M IMPRESSED.
IT'S EXACTLY THE KIND OF THING THAT INSPIRES SHAREHOLDERS...!
I'M DETECTING A BIT OF SARCASM IN YOUR VOICE, LARRY...

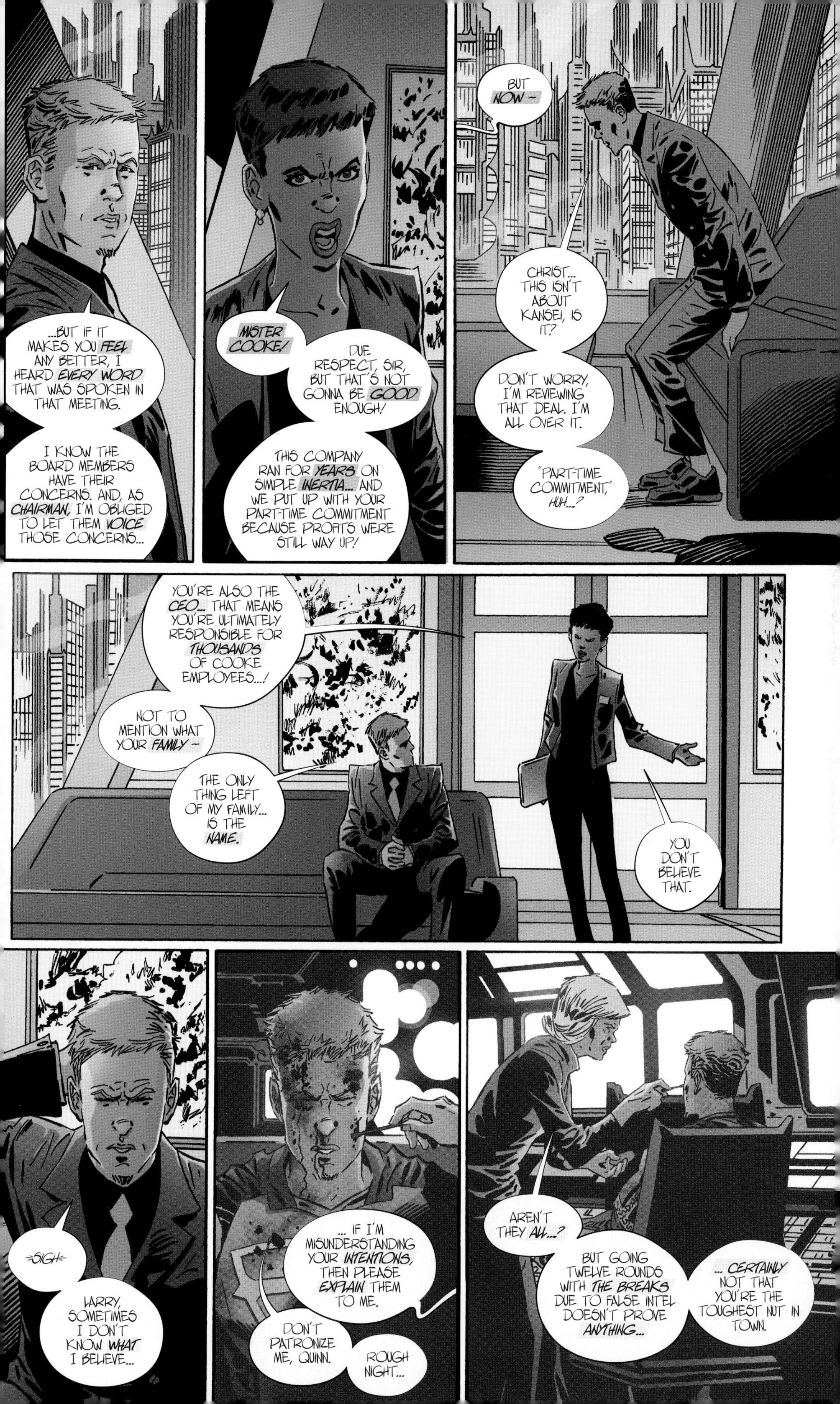
...BUT IF IT MAKES YOU FEEL ANY BETTER, I HEARD EVERY WORD THAT WAS SPOKEN IN THAT MEETING.
I KNOW THE BOARD MEMBERS HAVE THEIR CONCERNS. AND, AS CHAIRMAN, I'M OBLIGED TO LET THEM VOICE THOSE CONCERNS...
MISTER COOKE!
DUE RESPECT, SIR, BUT THAT'S NOT GONNA BE GOOD ENOUGH!
THIS COMPANY RAN FOR YEARS ON SIMPLE INERTIA... AND WE PUT UP WITH YOUR PART-TIME COMMITMENT BECAUSE PROFITS WERE STILL WAY UP!
BUT NOW --
CHRIST... THIS ISN'T ABOUT KANSEI, IS IT?
DON'T WORRY, I'M REVIEWING THAT DEAL. I'M ALL OVER IT.
"PART-TIME COMMITMENT," HUH...?
YOU'RE ALSO THE CEO... THAT MEANS YOU'RE ULTIMATELY RESPONSIBLE FOR THOUSANDS OF COOKE EMPLOYEES...!
NOT TO MENTION WHAT YOUR FAMILY --
THE ONLY THING LEFT OF MY FAMILY... IS THE NAME.
YOU DON'T BELIEVE THAT.
=SIGH=
LARRY, SOMETIMES I DON'T KNOW WHAT I BELIEVE...
... IF I'M MISUNDERSTANDING YOUR INTENTIONS, THEN PLEASE EXPLAIN THEM TO ME.
DON'T PATRONIZE ME, QUINN.
ROUGH NIGHT...
AREN'T THEY ALL...?
BUT GOING TWELVE ROUNDS WITH THE BREAKS DUE TO FALSE INTEL DOESN'T PROVE ANYTHING...
... CERTAINLY NOT THAT YOU'RE THE TOUGHEST NUT IN TOWN.

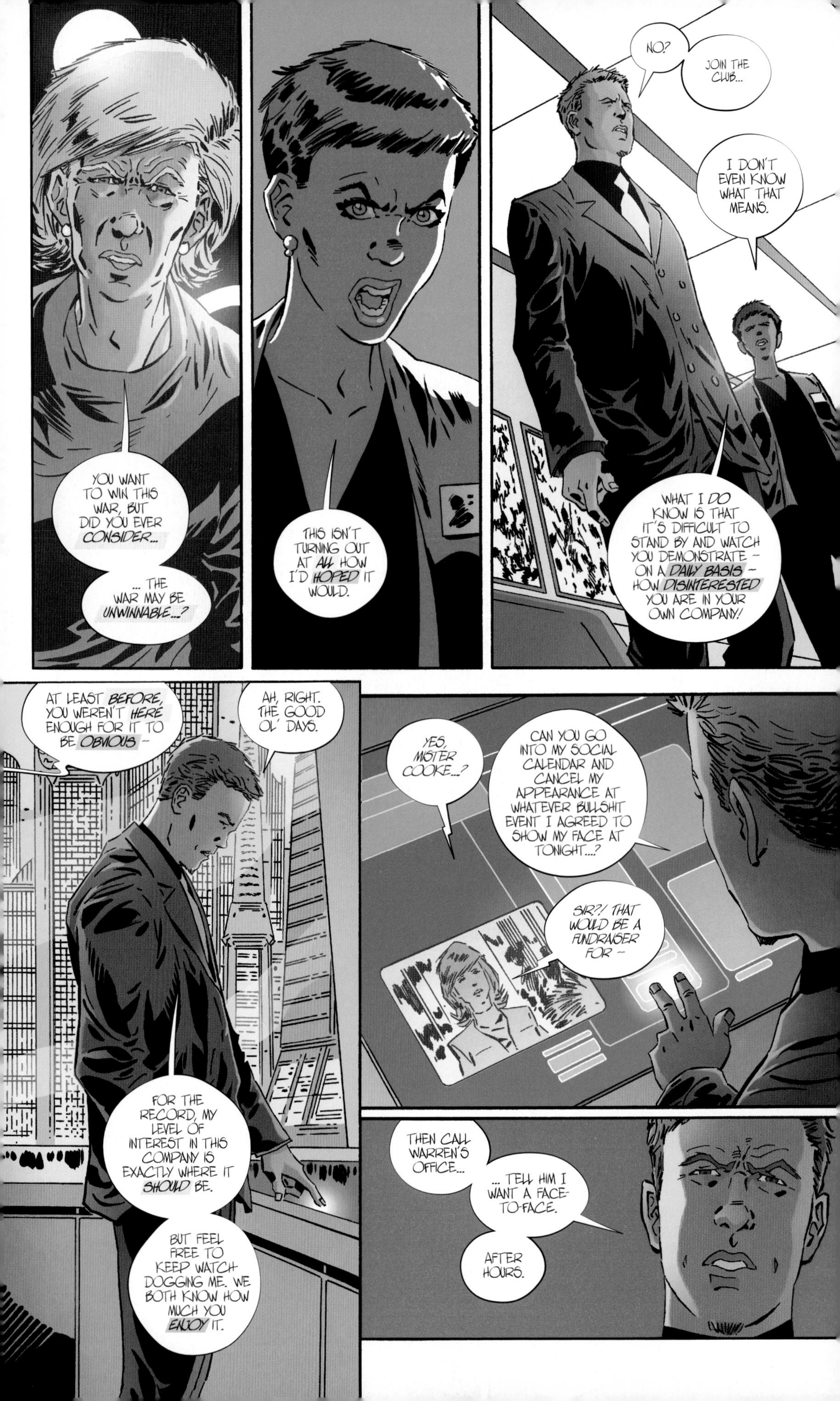
YOU WANT TO WIN THIS WAR, BUT DID YOU EVER CONSIDER...
... THE WAR MAY BE UNWINNABLE...?
THIS ISN'T TURNING OUT AT ALL HOW I'D HOPED IT WOULD.
NO?
JOIN THE CLUB...
I DON'T EVEN KNOW WHAT THAT MEANS.
WHAT I DO KNOW IS THAT IT'S DIFFICULT TO STAND BY AND WATCH YOU DEMONSTRATE -- ON A DAILY BASIS -- HOW DISINTERESTED YOU ARE IN YOUR OWN COMPANY!
AT LEAST BEFORE, YOU WEREN'T HERE ENOUGH FOR IT TO BE OBVIOUS --
AH, RIGHT. THE GOOD OL' DAYS.
FOR THE RECORD, MY LEVEL OF INTEREST IN THIS COMPANY IS EXACTLY WHERE IT SHOULD BE.
BUT FEEL FREE TO KEEP WATCH-DOGGING ME. WE BOTH KNOW HOW MUCH YOU ENJOY IT.
YES, MISTER COOKE...?
CAN YOU GO INTO MY SOCIAL CALENDAR AND CANCEL MY APPEARANCE AT WHATEVER BULLSHIT EVENT I AGREED TO SHOW MY FACE AT TONIGHT...?
SIR?! THAT WOULD BE A FUNDRAISER FOR --
THEN CALL WARREN'S OFFICE...
... TELL HIM I WANT A FACE-TO-FACE.
AFTER HOURS.

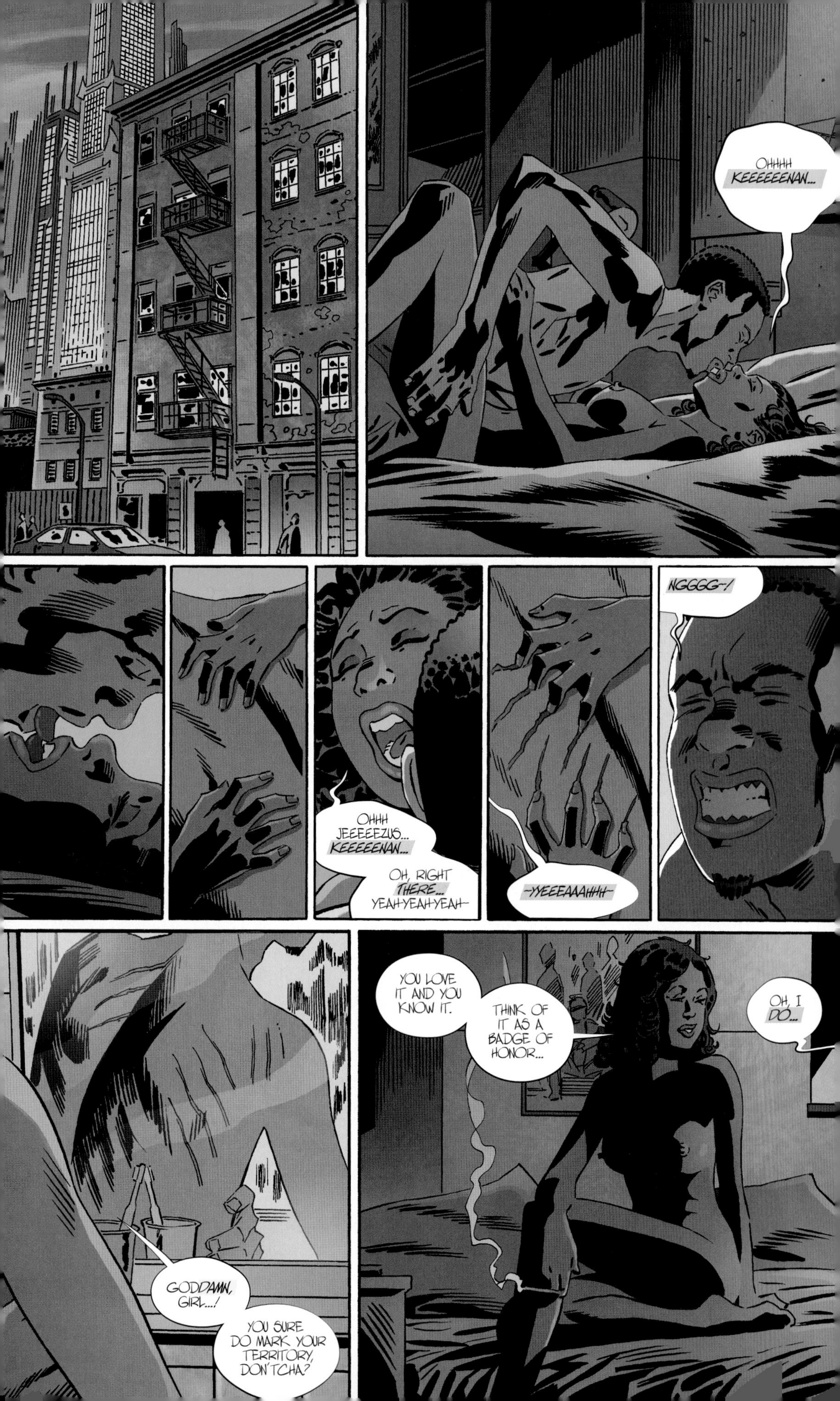

OHHHH KEEEEEENAN...
OHHH JEEEEEZUS... KEEEEEENAN...
OH, RIGHT THERE... YEAH-YEAH-YEAH-
~YYEEEAAAHHH~
NGGGG~!
GODDAMN, GIRL...!
YOU SURE DO MARK YOUR TERRITORY, DON'TCHA?
YOU LOVE IT AND YOU KNOW IT.
THINK OF IT AS A BADGE OF HONOR...
OH, I DO...

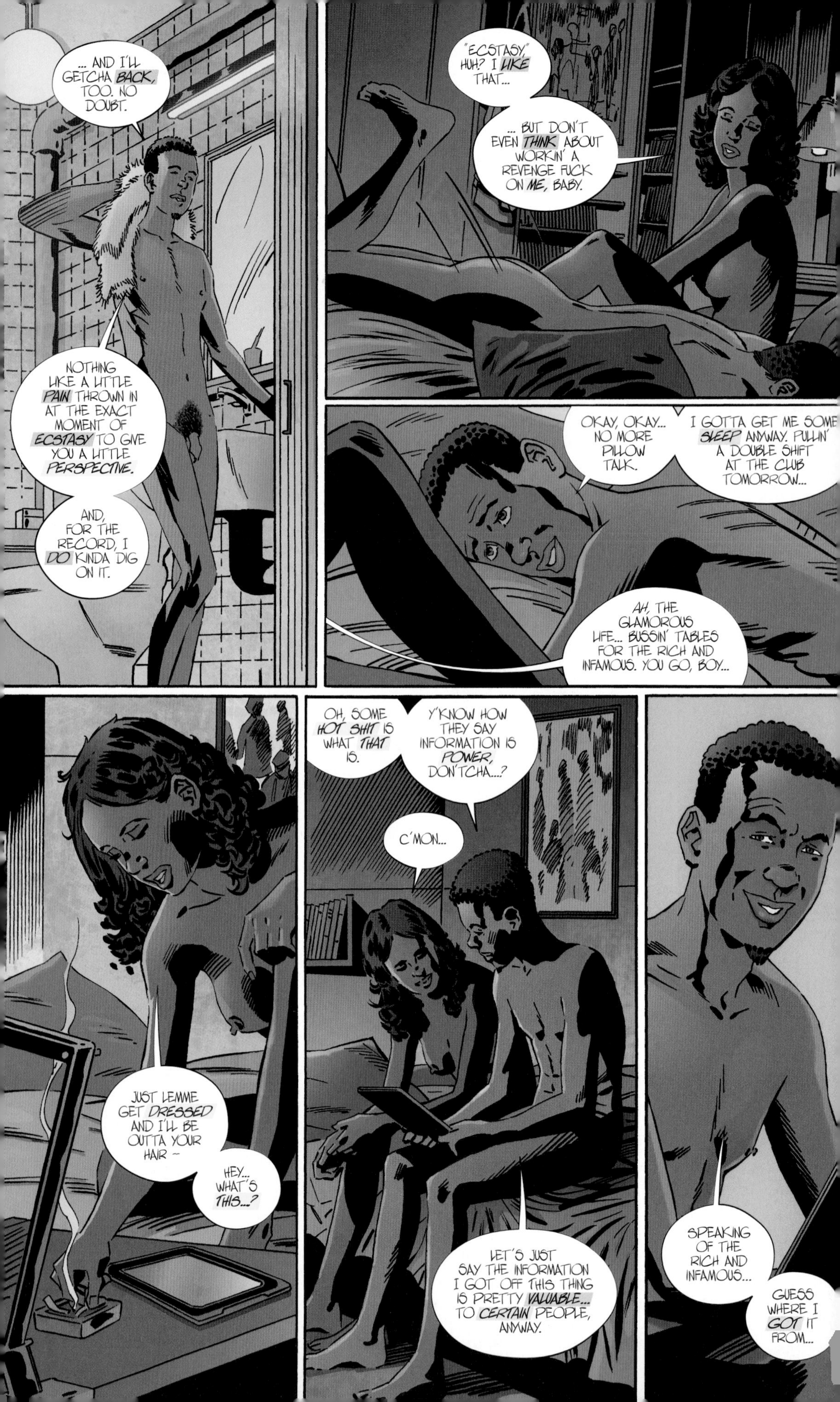

... AND I'LL GETCHA BACK, TOO. NO DOUBT.
"ECSTASY," HUH? I LIKE THAT...
... BUT DON'T EVEN THINK ABOUT WORKIN' A REVENGE FUCK ON ME, BABY.
NOTHING LIKE A LITTLE PAIN THROWN IN AT THE EXACT MOMENT OF ECSTASY TO GIVE YOU A LITTLE PERSPECTIVE.
AND, FOR THE RECORD, I DO KINDA DIG ON IT.
OKAY, OKAY... NO MORE PILLOW TALK.
I GOTTA GET ME SOME SLEEP ANYWAY. PULLIN' A DOUBLE SHIFT AT THE CLUB TOMORROW...
AH, THE GLAMOROUS LIFE... BUSSIN' TABLES FOR THE RICH AND INFAMOUS. YOU GO, BOY...
JUST LEMME GET DRESSED AND I'LL BE OUTTA YOUR HAIR ~
HEY... WHAT'S THIS...?
OH, SOME HOT SHIT IS WHAT THAT IS.
Y'KNOW HOW THEY SAY INFORMATION IS POWER, DON'TCHA...?
C'MON...
LET'S JUST SAY THE INFORMATION I GOT OFF THIS THING IS PRETTY VALUABLE... TO CERTAIN PEOPLE, ANYWAY.
SPEAKING OF THE RICH AND INFAMOUS...
GUESS WHERE I GOT IT FROM...

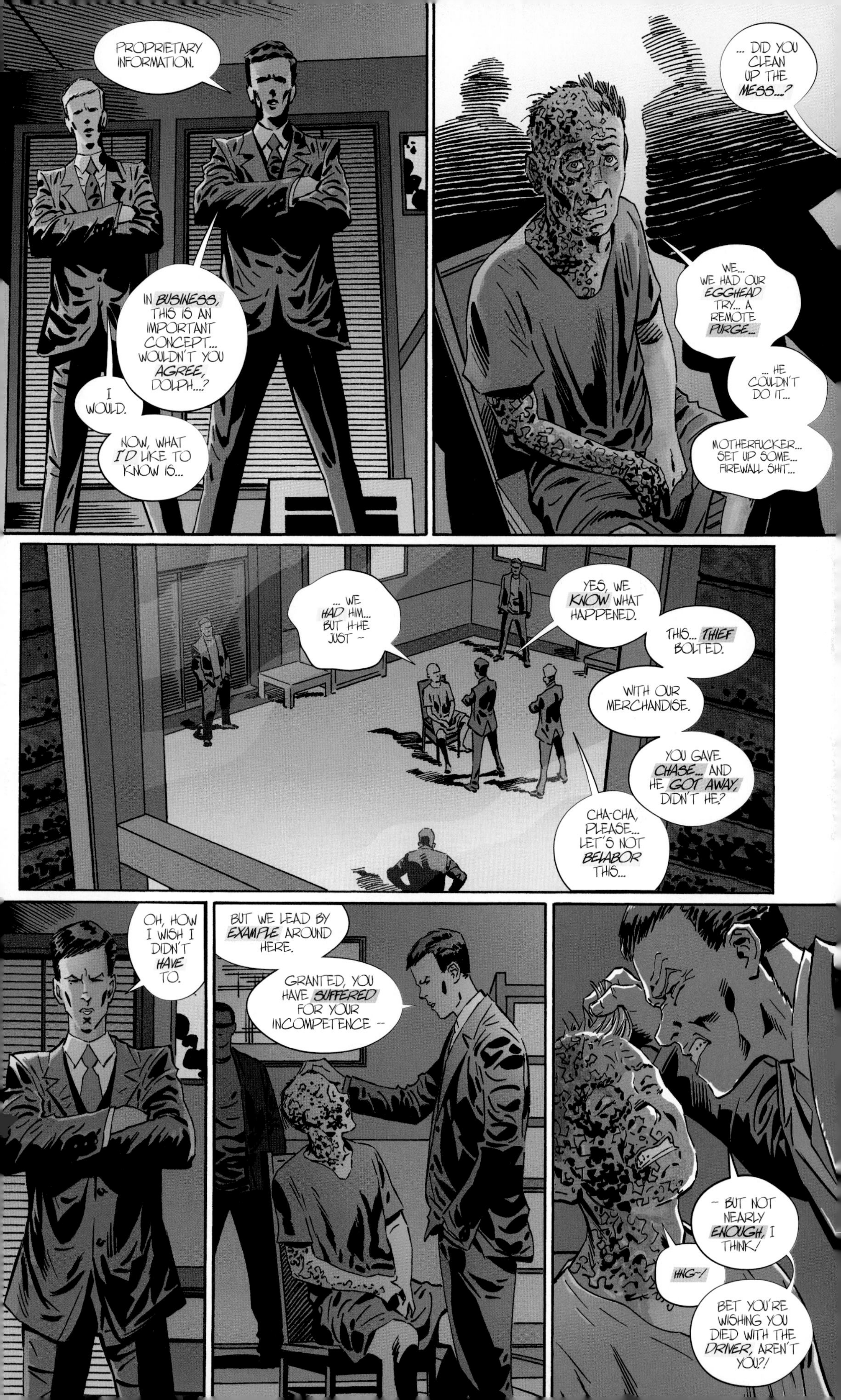
PROPRIETARY INFORMATION.
IN BUSINESS, THIS IS AN IMPORTANT CONCEPT... WOULDN'T YOU AGREE, DOLPH...?
I WOULD.
NOW, WHAT I'D LIKE TO KNOW IS...
... DID YOU CLEAN UP THE MESS...?
WE... WE HAD OUR EGGHEAD TRY... A REMOTE PURGE...
... HE COULDN'T DO IT...
MOTHERFUCKER... SET UP SOME... FIREWALL SHIT...
... WE HAD HIM... BUT H-HE JUST --
YES, WE KNOW WHAT HAPPENED.
THIS... THIEF BOLTED.
WITH OUR MERCHANDISE.
YOU GAVE CHASE... AND HE GOT AWAY, DIDN'T HE?
CHA-CHA, PLEASE... LET'S NOT BELABOR THIS...
OH, HOW I WISH I DIDN'T HAVE TO.
BUT WE LEAD BY EXAMPLE AROUND HERE.
GRANTED, YOU HAVE SUFFERED FOR YOUR INCOMPETENCE --
-- BUT NOT NEARLY ENOUGH, I THINK!
HNG--!
BET YOU'RE WISHING YOU DIED WITH THE DRIVER, AREN'T YOU?!

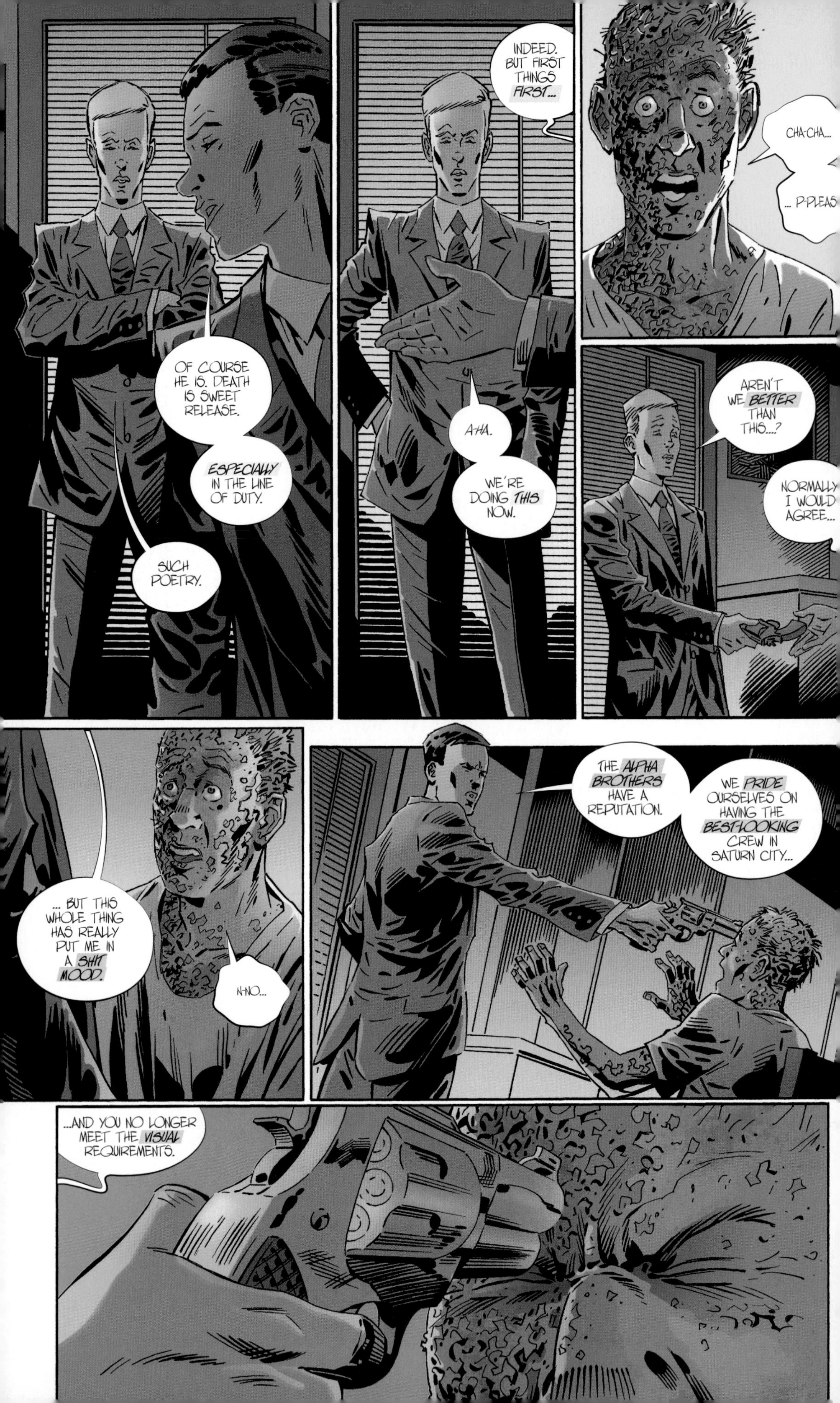

OF COURSE HE IS. DEATH IS SWEET RELEASE.
ESPECIALLY IN THE LINE OF DUTY.
SUCH POETRY.
INDEED. BUT FIRST THINGS FIRST...
A-HA.
WE'RE DOING THIS NOW.
CHA-CHA...
... P-PLEAS
AREN'T WE BETTER THAN THIS...?
NORMALLY I WOULD AGREE...
... BUT THIS WHOLE THING HAS REALLY PUT ME IN A SHIT MOOD.
N-NO...
THE ALPHA BROTHERS HAVE A REPUTATION.
WE PRIDE OURSELVES ON HAVING THE BEST-LOOKING CREW IN SATURN CITY...
...AND YOU NO LONGER MEET THE VISUAL REQUIREMENTS.

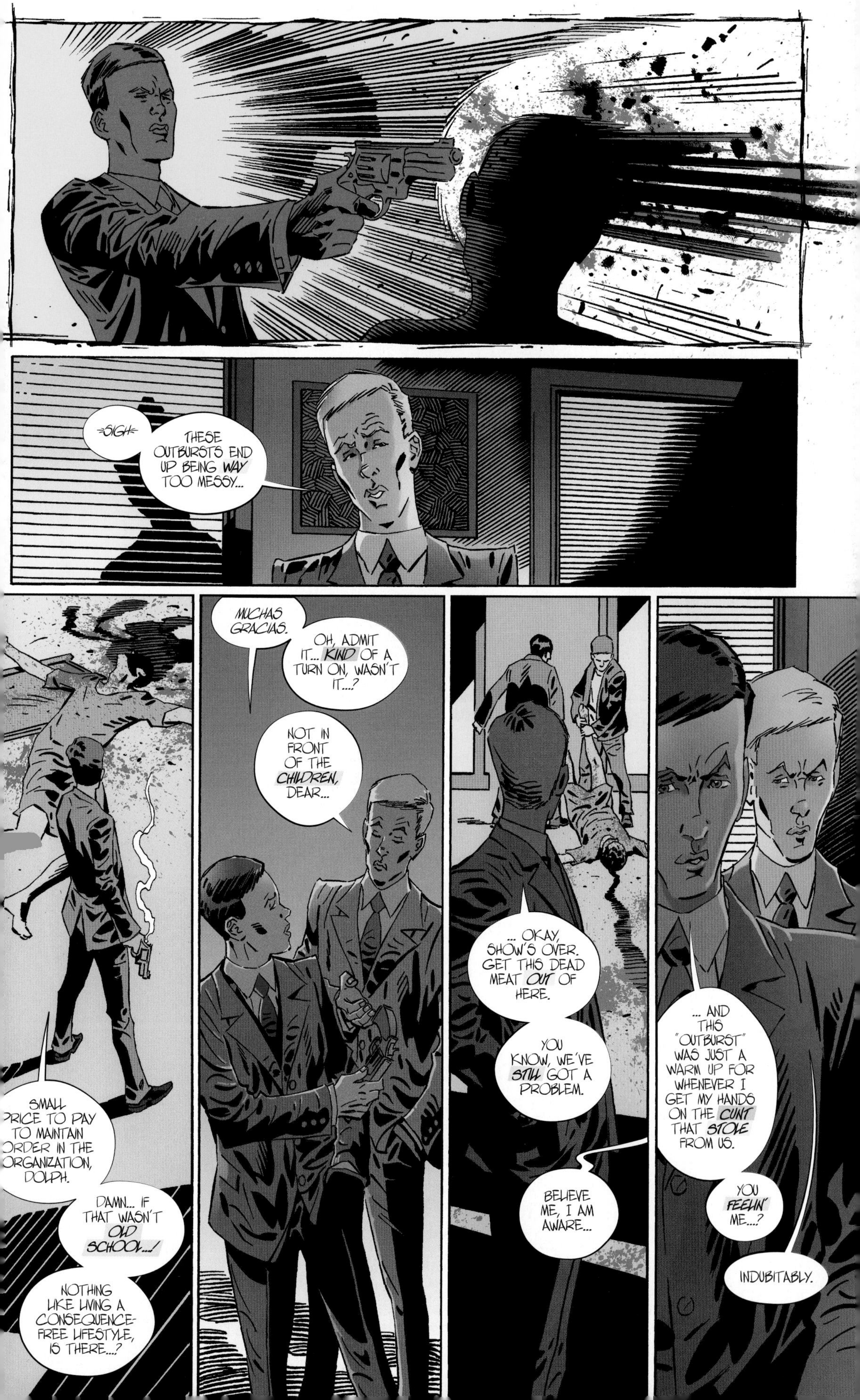
SIGH
THESE OUTBURSTS END UP BEING WAY TOO MESSY...
SMALL PRICE TO PAY TO MAINTAIN ORDER IN THE ORGANIZATION, DOLPH.
DAMN... IF THAT WASN'T OLD SCHOOL...!
NOTHING LIKE LIVING A CONSEQUENCE-FREE LIFESTYLE, IS THERE...?
MUCHAS GRACIAS.
OH, ADMIT IT... KIND OF A TURN ON, WASN'T IT...?
NOT IN FRONT OF THE CHILDREN, DEAR...
... OKAY, SHOW'S OVER. GET THIS DEAD MEAT OUT OF HERE.
YOU KNOW, WE'VE STILL GOT A PROBLEM.
BELIEVE ME, I AM AWARE...
... AND THIS "OUTBURST" WAS JUST A WARM UP FOR WHENEVER I GET MY HANDS ON THE CUNT THAT STOLE FROM US.
YOU FEELIN' ME...?
INDUBITABLY.

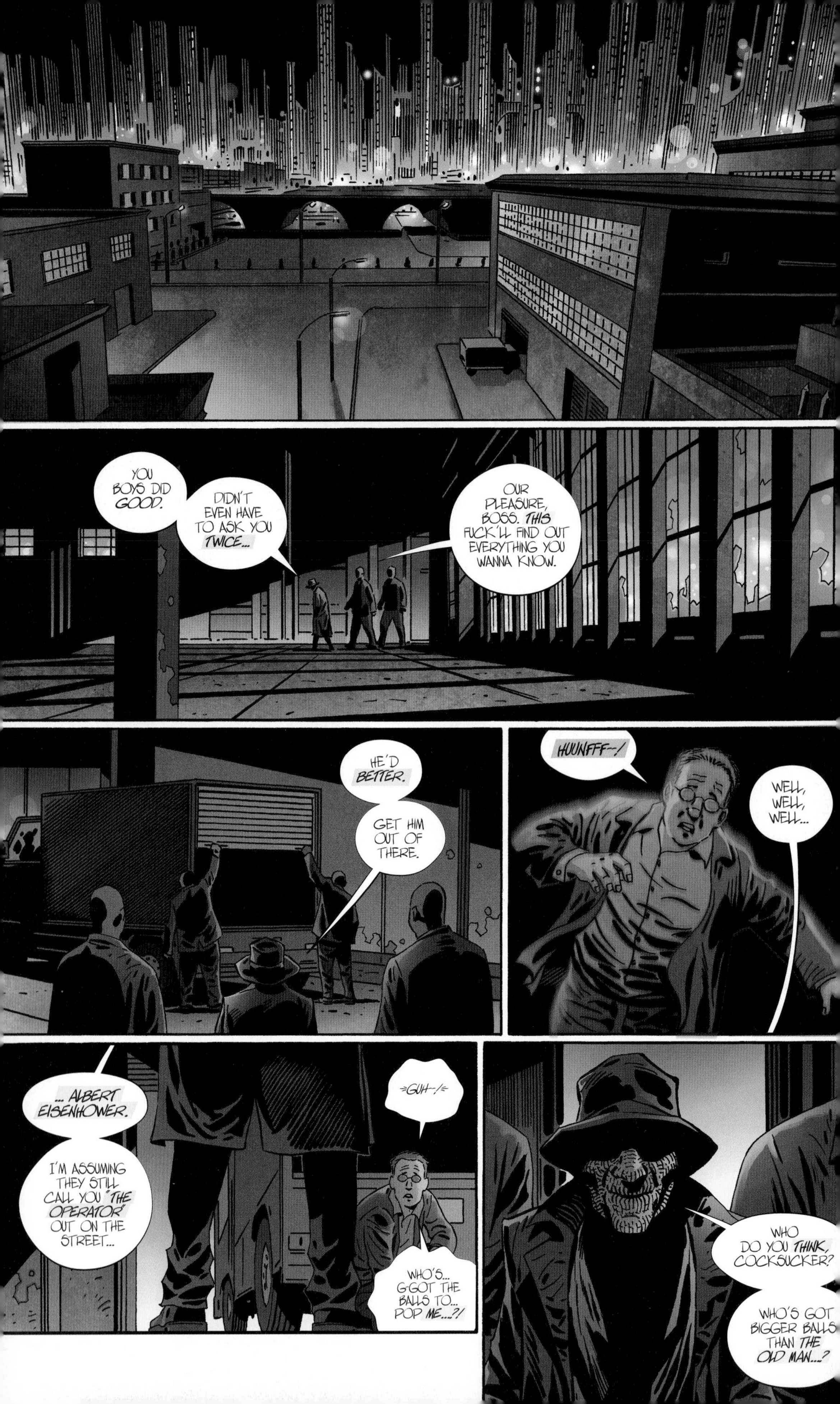

YOU BOYS DID GOOD.
DIDN'T EVEN HAVE TO ASK YOU TWICE...
OUR PLEASURE, BOSS. THIS FUCK'LL FIND OUT EVERYTHING YOU WANNA KNOW.
HE'D BETTER.
GET HIM OUT OF THERE.
HUUNFFF--!
WELL, WELL, WELL...
... ALBERT EISENHOWER.
I'M ASSUMING THEY STILL CALL YOU "THE OPERATOR" OUT ON THE STREET...
GUH--!
WHO'S... G-GOT THE BALLS TO... POP ME...?!
WHO DO YOU THINK, COCKSUCKER?
WHO'S GOT BIGGER BALLS THAN THE OLD MAN...?

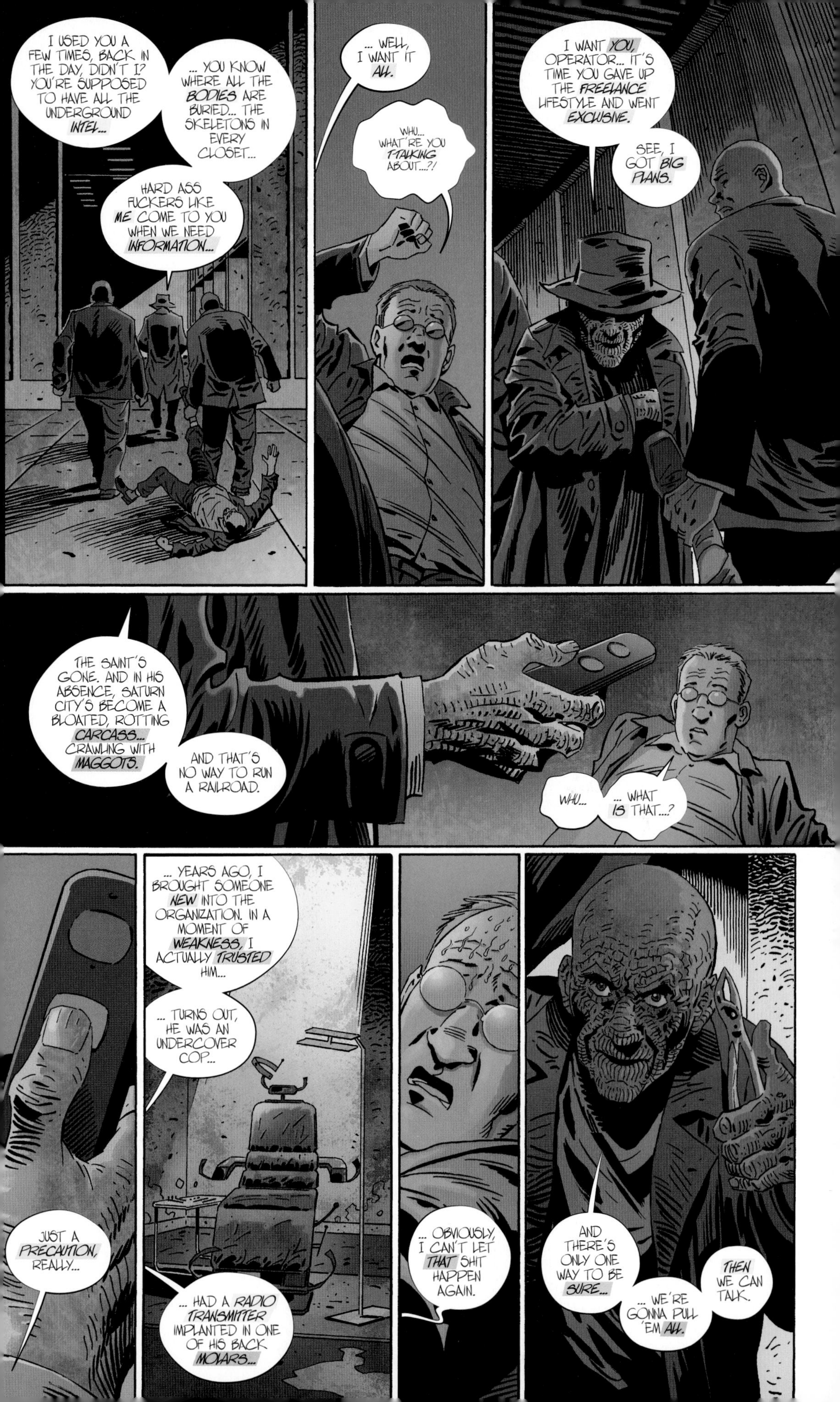

I USED YOU A FEW TIMES, BACK IN THE DAY, DIDN'T I? YOU'RE SUPPOSED TO HAVE ALL THE UNDERGROUND INTEL...
... YOU KNOW WHERE ALL THE BODIES ARE BURIED... THE SKELETONS IN EVERY CLOSET...
HARD ASS FUCKERS LIKE ME COME TO YOU WHEN WE NEED INFORMATION...
... WELL, I WANT IT ALL.
WHU... WHAT'RE YOU T-TALKING ABOUT...?!
I WANT YOU, OPERATOR... IT'S TIME YOU GAVE UP THE FREELANCE LIFESTYLE AND WENT EXCLUSIVE.
SEE, I GOT BIG PLANS.
THE SAINT'S GONE. AND IN HIS ABSENCE, SATURN CITY'S BECOME A BLOATED, ROTTING CARCASS... CRAWLING WITH MAGGOTS.
AND THAT'S NO WAY TO RUN A RAILROAD.
WHU...
... WHAT IS THAT...?
JUST A PRECAUTION, REALLY...
... YEARS AGO, I BROUGHT SOMEONE NEW INTO THE ORGANIZATION. IN A MOMENT OF WEAKNESS, I ACTUALLY TRUSTED HIM...
... TURNS OUT, HE WAS AN UNDERCOVER COP...
... HAD A RADIO TRANSMITTER IMPLANTED IN ONE OF HIS BACK MOLARS...
... OBVIOUSLY, I CAN'T LET THAT SHIT HAPPEN AGAIN.
AND THERE'S ONLY ONE WAY TO BE SURE...
... WE'RE GONNA PULL 'EM ALL.
THEN WE CAN TALK.

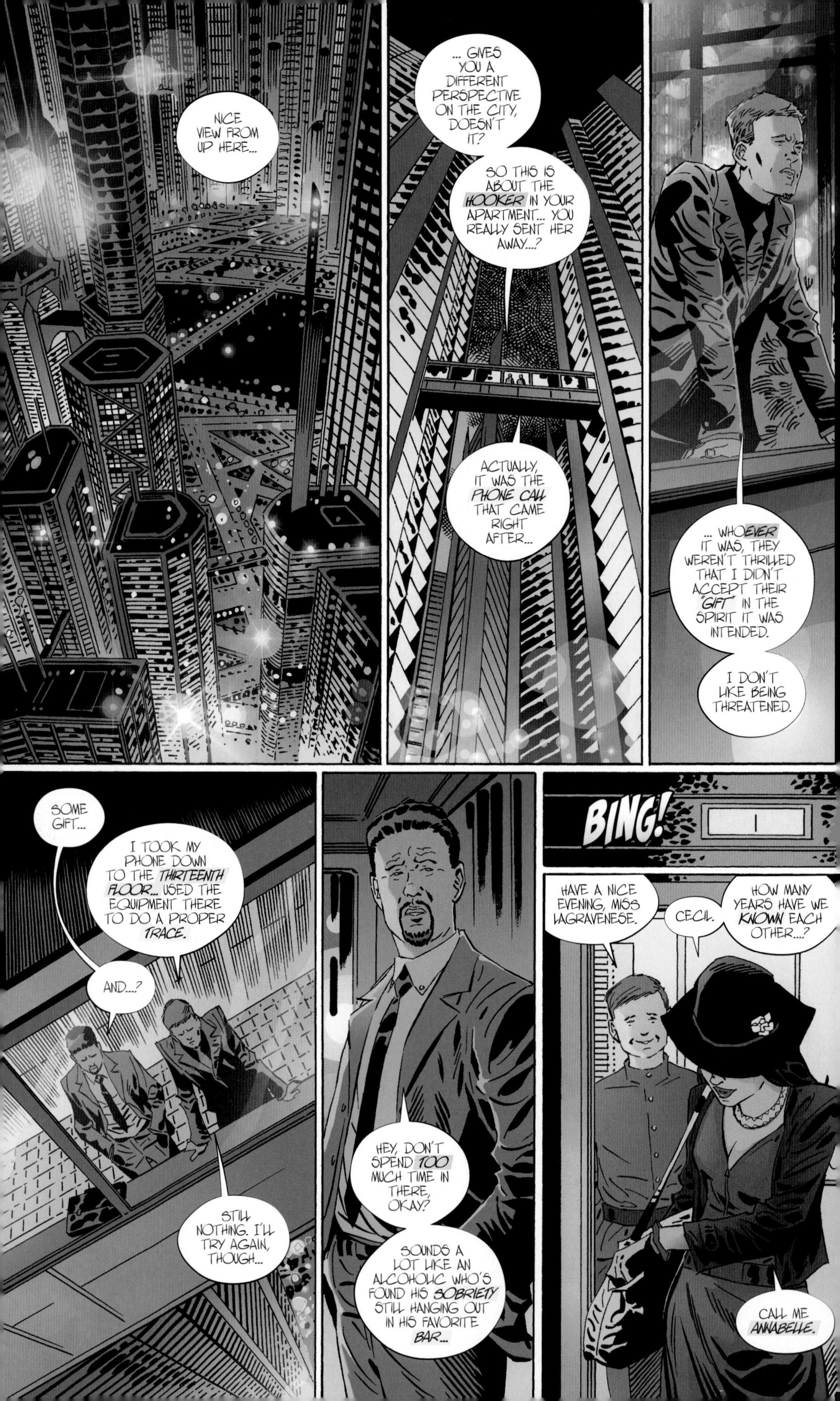

NICE VIEW FROM UP HERE...
... GIVES YOU A DIFFERENT PERSPECTIVE ON THE CITY, DOESN'T IT?
SO THIS IS ABOUT THE HOOKER IN YOUR APARTMENT... YOU REALLY SENT HER AWAY...?
ACTUALLY, IT WAS THE PHONE CALL THAT CAME RIGHT AFTER...
... WHOEVER IT WAS, THEY WEREN'T THRILLED THAT I DIDN'T ACCEPT THEIR "GIFT" IN THE SPIRIT IT WAS INTENDED.
I DON'T LIKE BEING THREATENED.
SOME GIFT...
I TOOK MY PHONE DOWN TO THE THIRTEENTH FLOOR... USED THE EQUIPMENT THERE TO DO A PROPER TRACE.
AND...?
STILL NOTHING. I'LL TRY AGAIN, THOUGH...
HEY, DON'T SPEND TOO MUCH TIME IN THERE, OKAY?
SOUNDS A LOT LIKE AN ALCOHOLIC WHO'S FOUND HIS SOBRIETY STILL HANGING OUT IN HIS FAVORITE BAR...
BING!
1
HAVE A NICE EVENING, MISS LAGRAVENESE.
CECIL.
HOW MANY YEARS HAVE WE KNOWN EACH OTHER...?
CALL ME ANNABELLE.

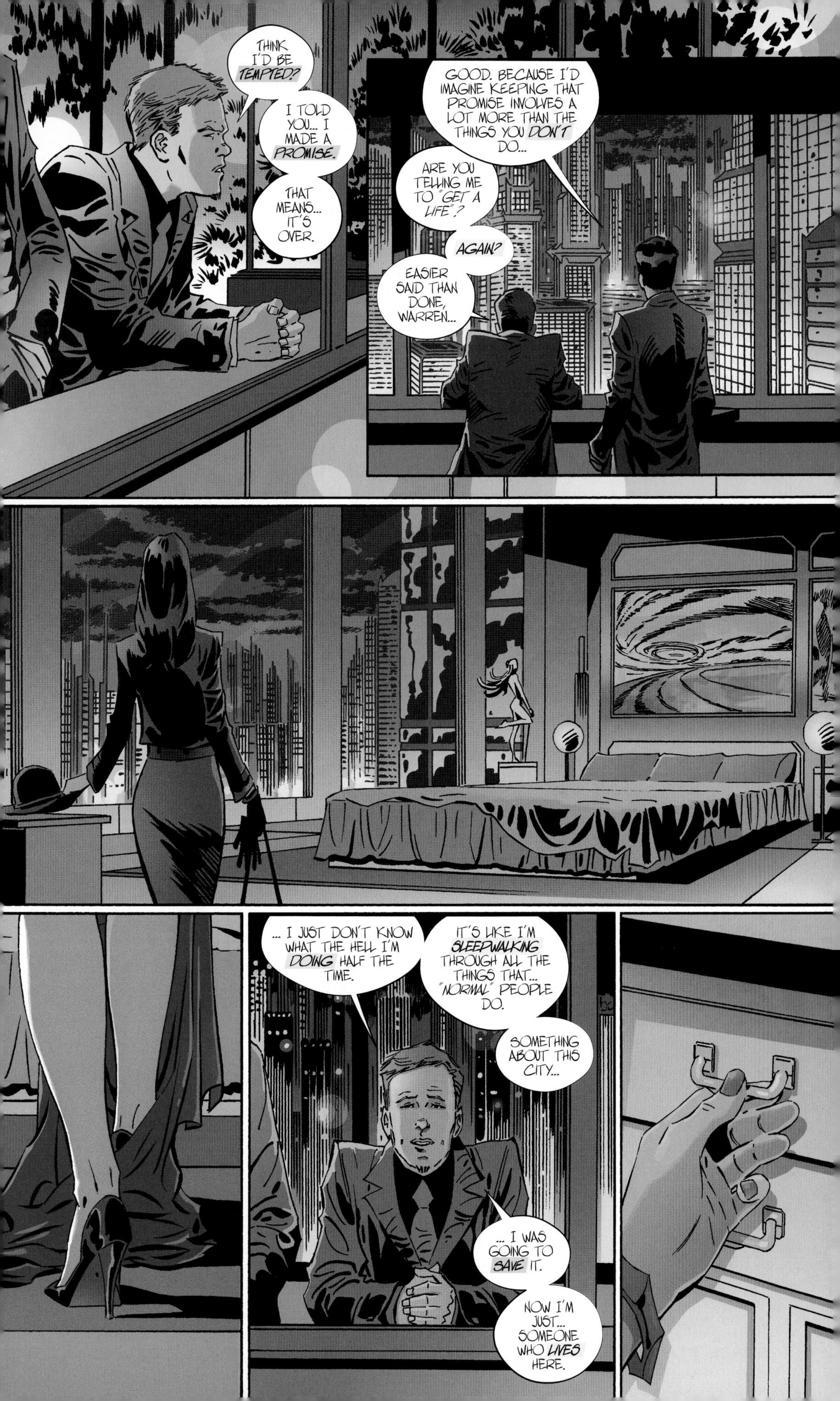
THINK I'D BE TEMPTED?
I TOLD YOU... I MADE A PROMISE.
THAT MEANS... IT'S OVER.
GOOD. BECAUSE I'D IMAGINE KEEPING THAT PROMISE INVOLVES A LOT MORE THAN THE THINGS YOU DON'T DO...
ARE YOU TELLING ME TO "GET A LIFE"?
AGAIN?
EASIER SAID THAN DONE, WARREN...
... I JUST DON'T KNOW WHAT THE HELL I'M DOING HALF THE TIME.
IT'S LIKE I'M SLEEPWALKING THROUGH ALL THE THINGS THAT... "NORMAL" PEOPLE DO.
SOMETHING ABOUT THIS CITY...
... I WAS GOING TO SAVE IT.
NOW I'M JUST... SOMEONE WHO LIVES HERE.

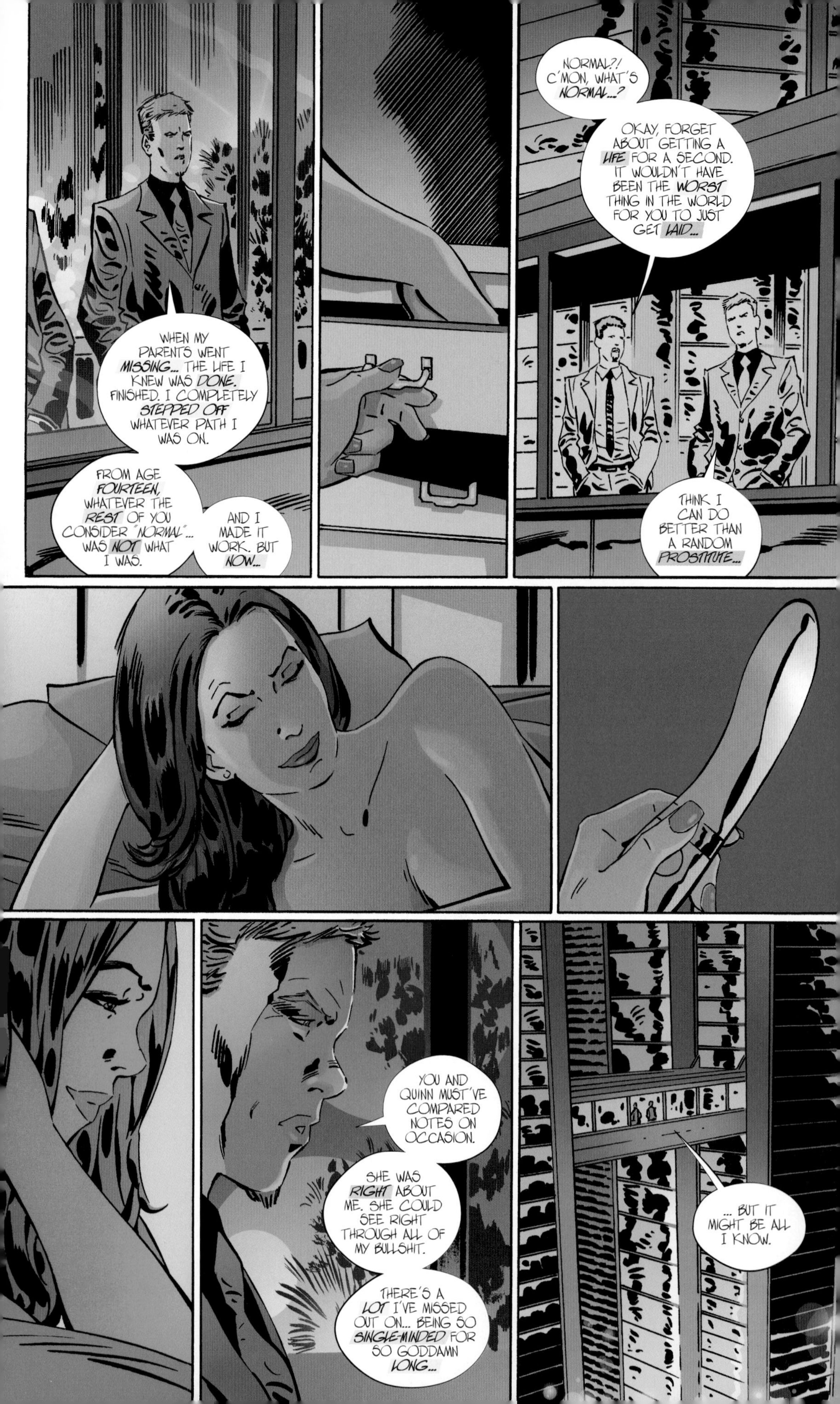

WHEN MY PARENTS WENT MISSING... THE LIFE I KNEW WAS DONE. FINISHED. I COMPLETELY STEPPED OFF WHATEVER PATH I WAS ON.
FROM AGE FOURTEEN, WHATEVER THE REST OF YOU CONSIDER "NORMAL"... WAS NOT WHAT I WAS.
AND I MADE IT WORK. BUT NOW...
NORMAL?! C'MON, WHAT'S NORMAL...?
OKAY, FORGET ABOUT GETTING A LIFE FOR A SECOND. IT WOULDN'T HAVE BEEN THE WORST THING IN THE WORLD FOR YOU TO JUST GET LAID...
THINK I CAN DO BETTER THAN A RANDOM PROSTITUTE...
YOU AND QUINN MUST'VE COMPARED NOTES ON OCCASION.
SHE WAS RIGHT ABOUT ME. SHE COULD SEE RIGHT THROUGH ALL OF MY BULLSHIT.
THERE'S A LOT I'VE MISSED OUT ON... BEING SO SINGLE-MINDED FOR SO GODDAMN LONG...
... BUT IT MIGHT BE ALL I KNOW.

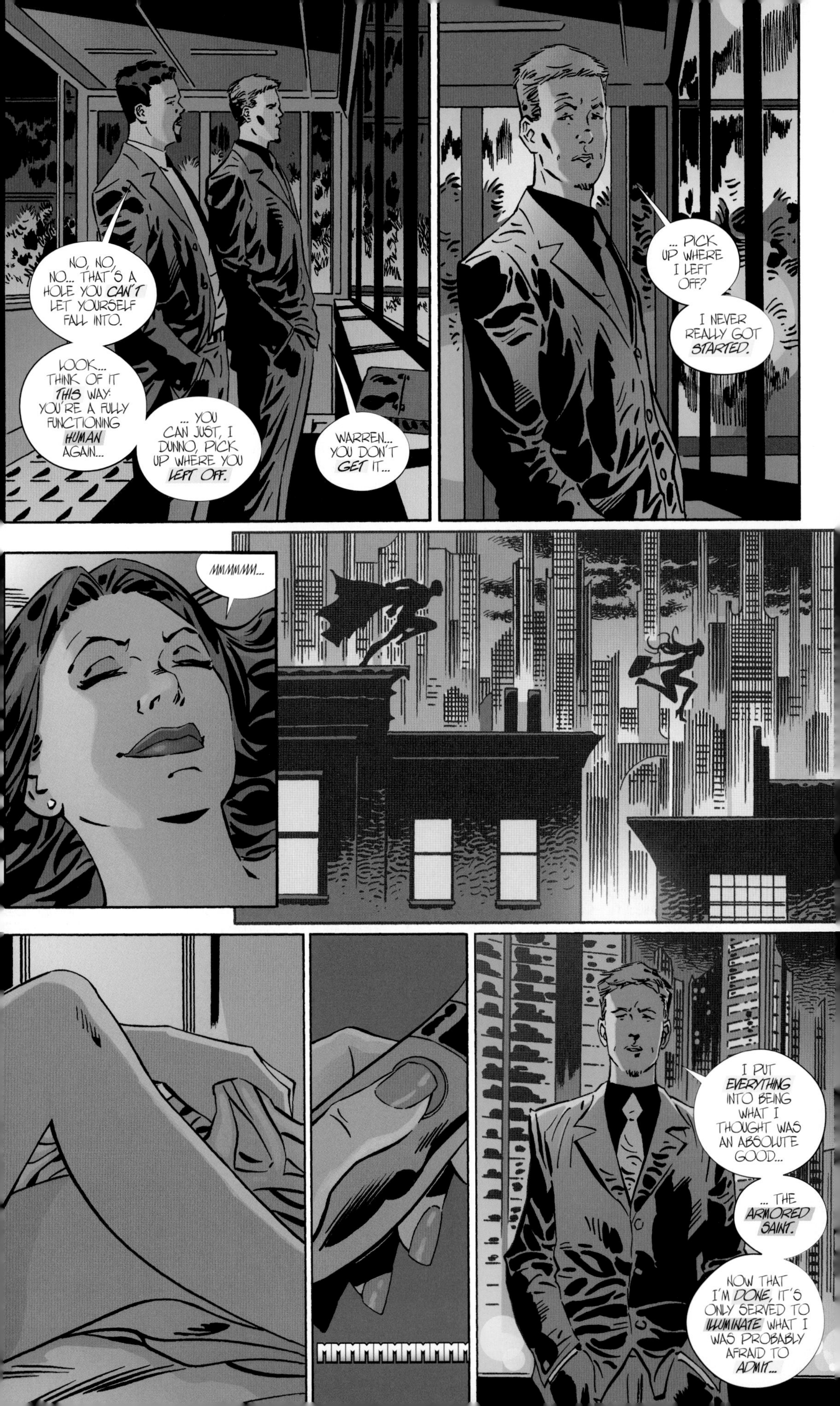

NO, NO, NO... THAT'S A HOLE YOU CAN'T LET YOURSELF FALL INTO.
LOOK... THINK OF IT THIS WAY: YOU'RE A FULLY FUNCTIONING HUMAN AGAIN...
... YOU CAN JUST, I DUNNO, PICK UP WHERE YOU LEFT OFF.
WARREN... YOU DON'T GET IT...
... PICK UP WHERE I LEFT OFF?
I NEVER REALLY GOT STARTED.
MMMMMM...
MMMMMMMMMMMM
I PUT EVERYTHING INTO BEING WHAT I THOUGHT WAS AN ABSOLUTE GOOD...
... THE ARMORED SAINT.
NOW THAT I'M DONE, IT'S ONLY SERVED TO ILLUMINATE WHAT I WAS PROBABLY AFRAID TO ADMIT...

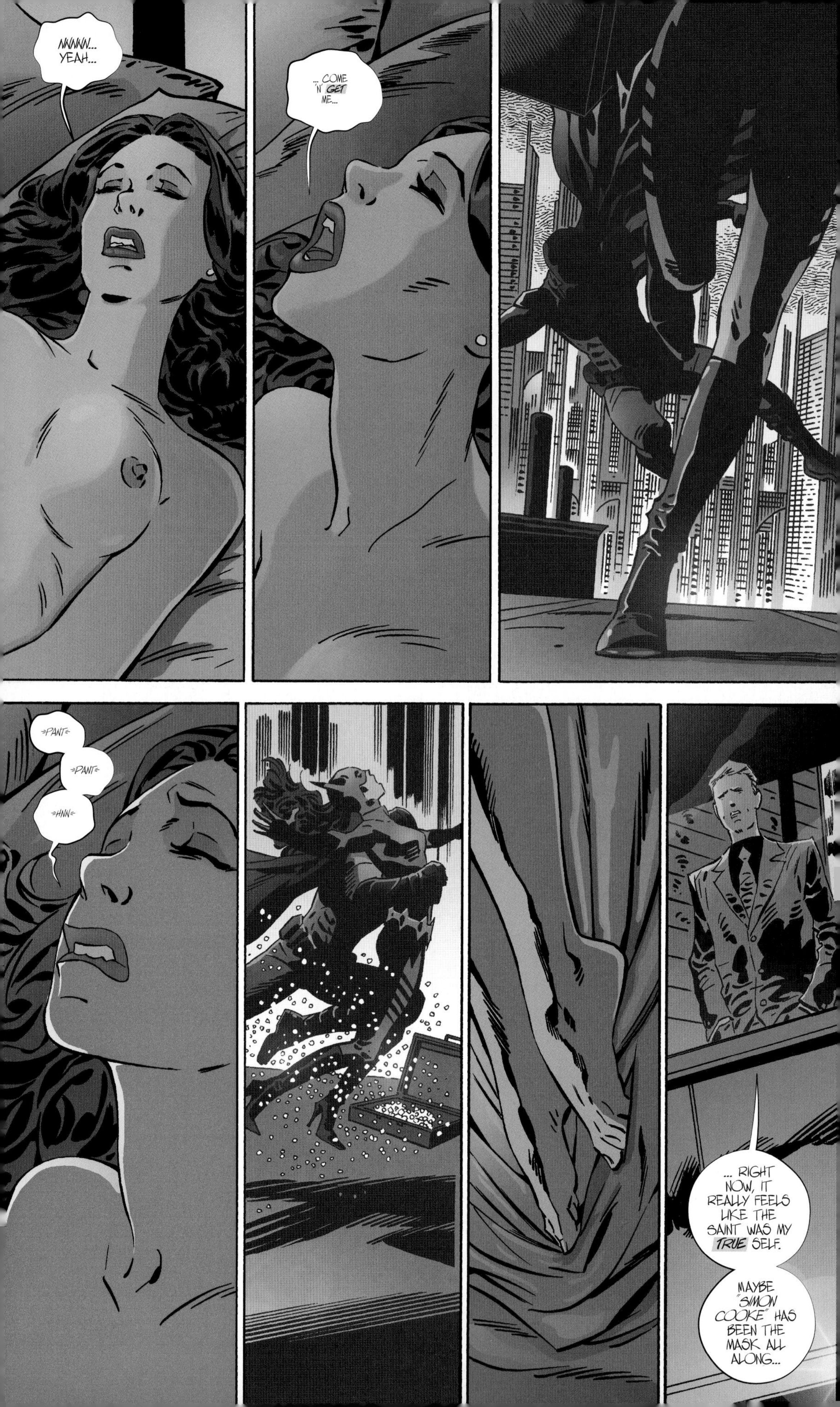
NNNNN... YEAH...
... COME 'N' GET ME...
PANT
PANT
HNN
... RIGHT NOW, IT REALLY FEELS LIKE THE SAINT WAS MY TRUE SELF.
MAYBE "SIMON COOKE" HAS BEEN THE MASK ALL ALONG...

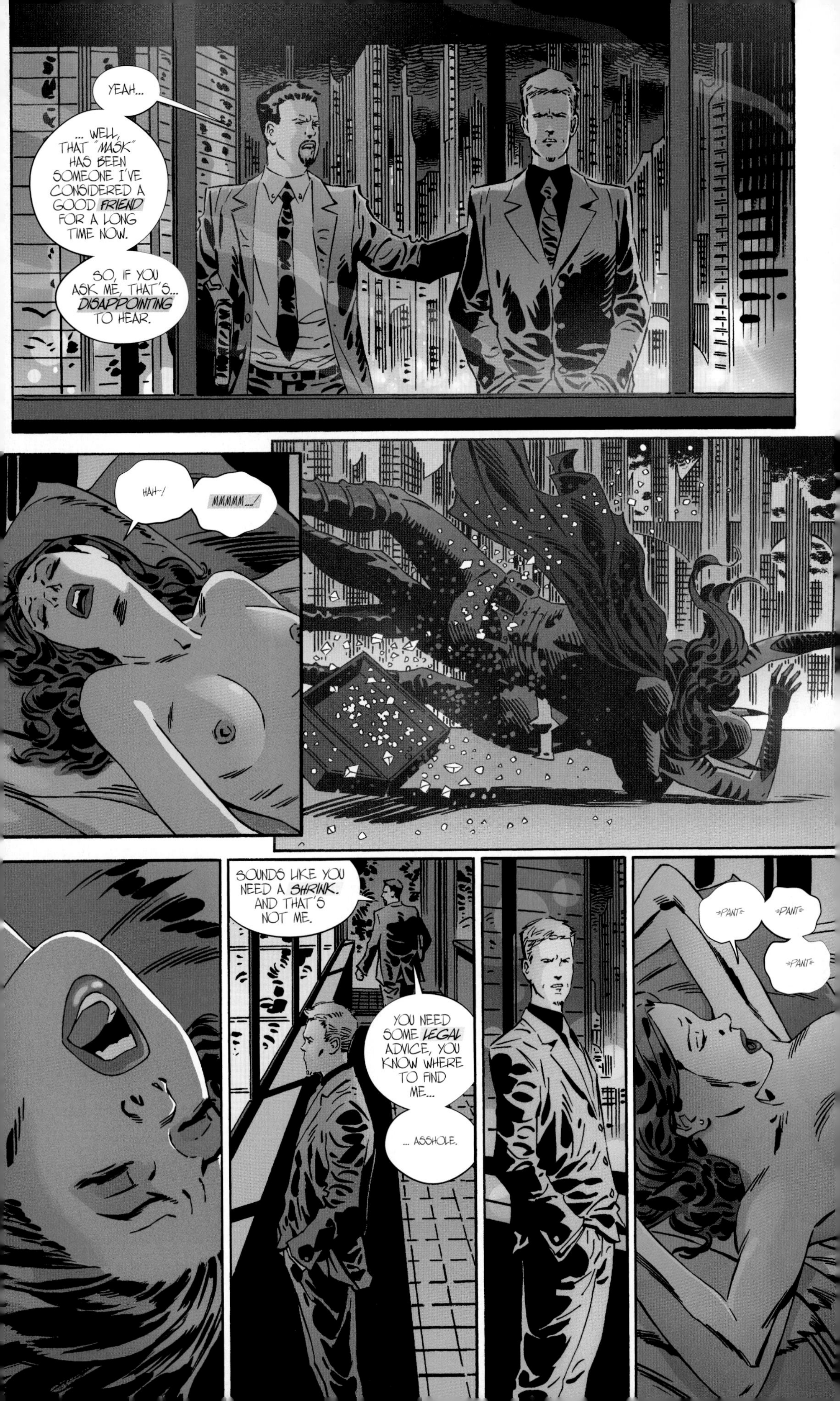

YEAH...
... WELL, THAT "MASK" HAS BEEN SOMEONE I'VE CONSIDERED A GOOD FRIEND FOR A LONG TIME NOW.
SO, IF YOU ASK ME, THAT'S... DISAPPOINTING TO HEAR.
HAH-!
MMMMM...!
SOUNDS LIKE YOU NEED A SHRINK. AND THAT'S NOT ME.
YOU NEED SOME LEGAL ADVICE, YOU KNOW WHERE TO FIND ME...
... ASSHOLE.
PANT
PANT
PANT

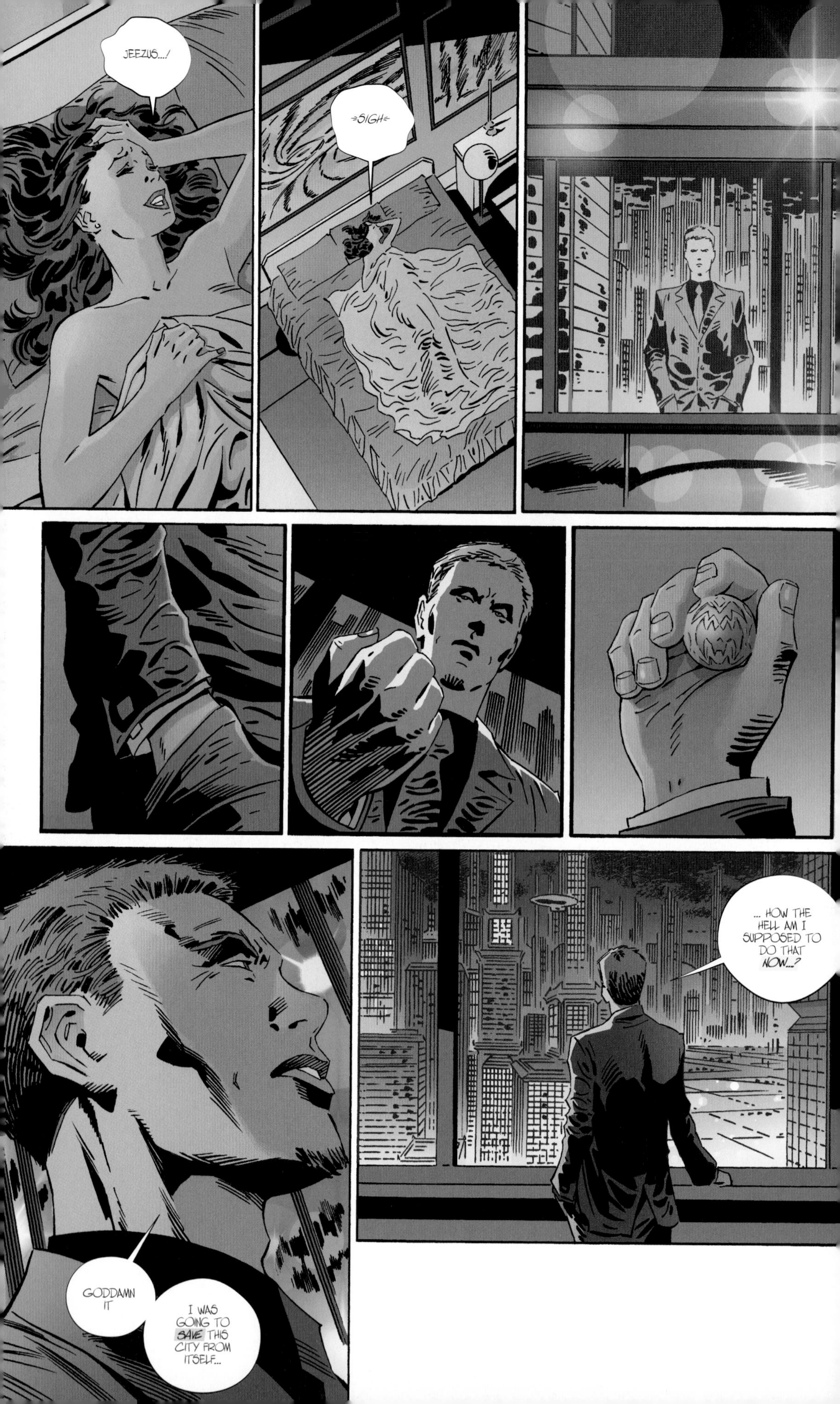
JEEZUS...!
=SIGH=
GODDAMN IT
I WAS GOING TO SAVE THIS CITY FROM ITSELF...
... HOW THE HELL AM I SUPPOSED TO DO THAT NOW...?

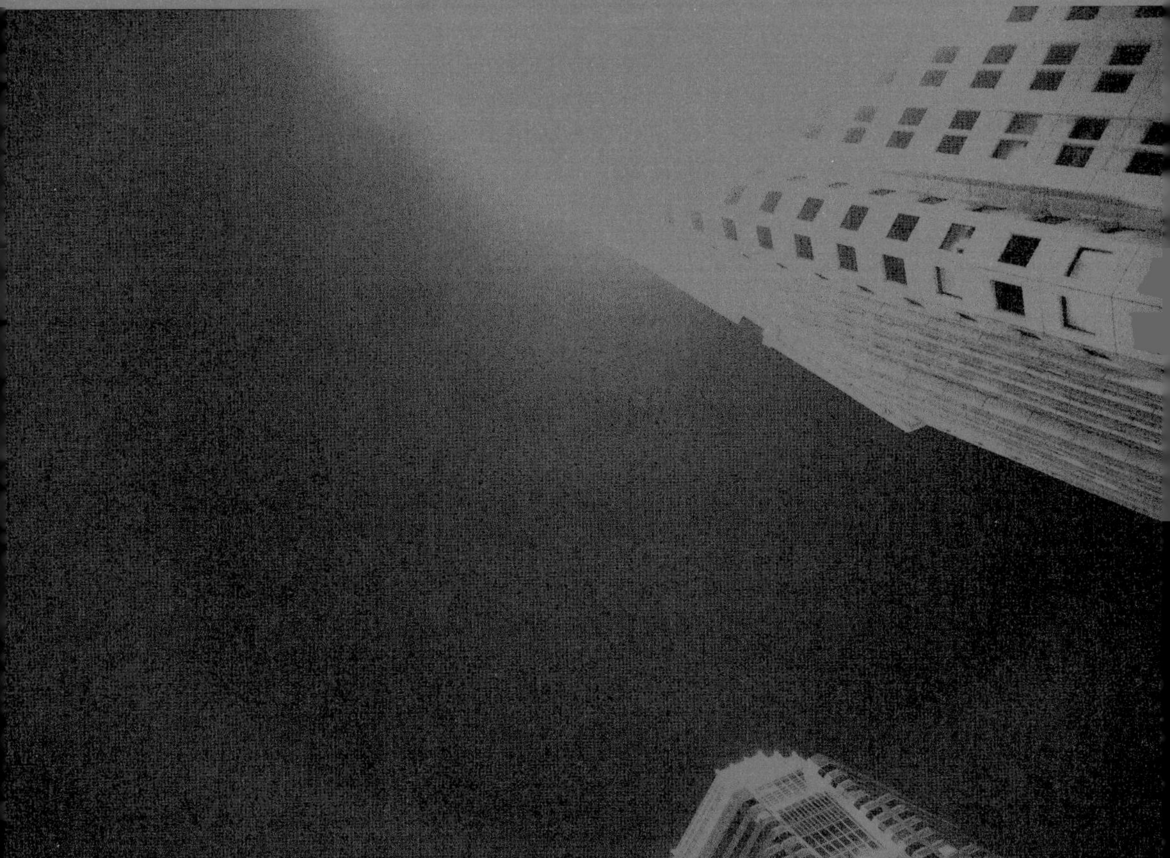

SEX

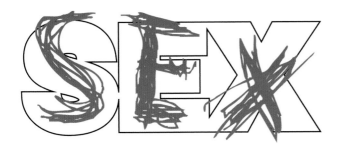

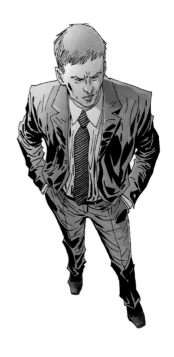

CHAPTER FOUR
FACE OF THE HUMAN RACE

JOE CASEY WRITER   PIOTR KOWALSKI ARTIST   BRAD SIMPSON COLORIST   RUS WOOTON LETTERER   SONIA HARRIS GRAPHIC DESIGNER

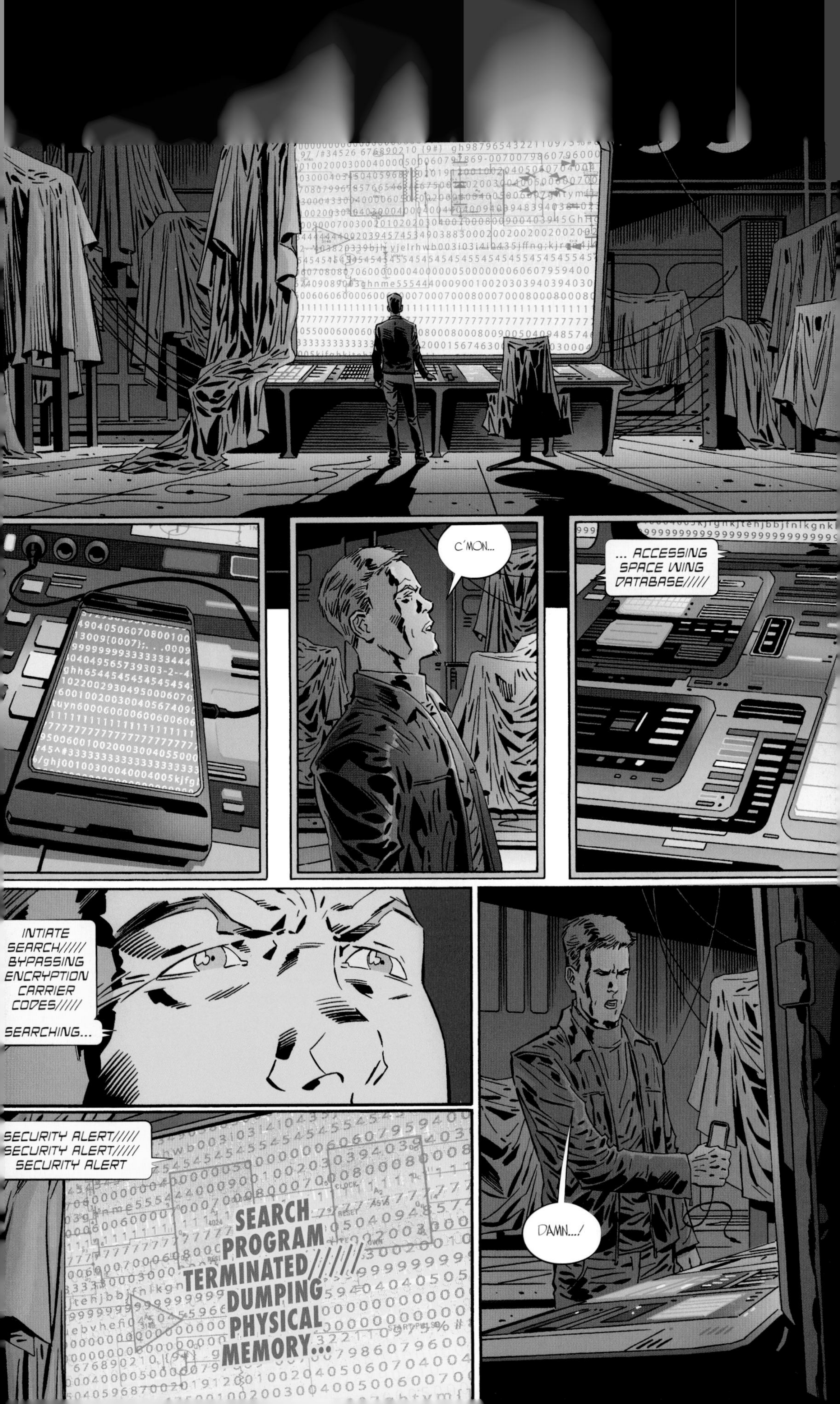
C'MON...
... ACCESSING SPACE WING DATABASE/////
INTIATE SEARCH///// BYPASSING ENCRYPTION CARRIER CODES/////
SEARCHING...
SECURITY ALERT///// SECURITY ALERT///// SECURITY ALERT
SEARCH PROGRAM TERMINATED///// DUMPING PHYSICAL MEMORY...
DAMN...!

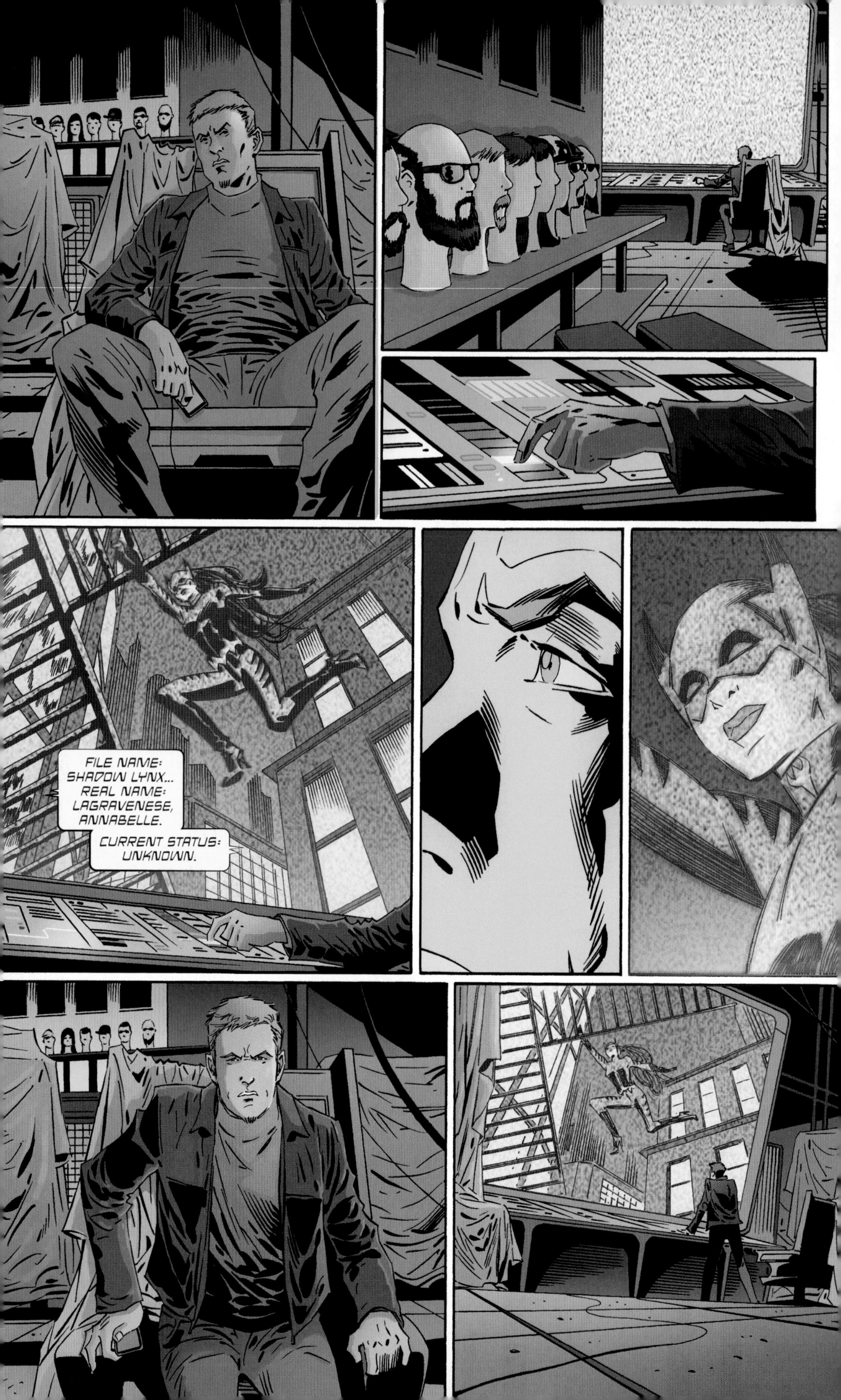
FILE NAME: SHADOW LYNX... REAL NAME: LAGRAVENESE, ANNABELLE.
CURRENT STATUS: UNKNOWN.

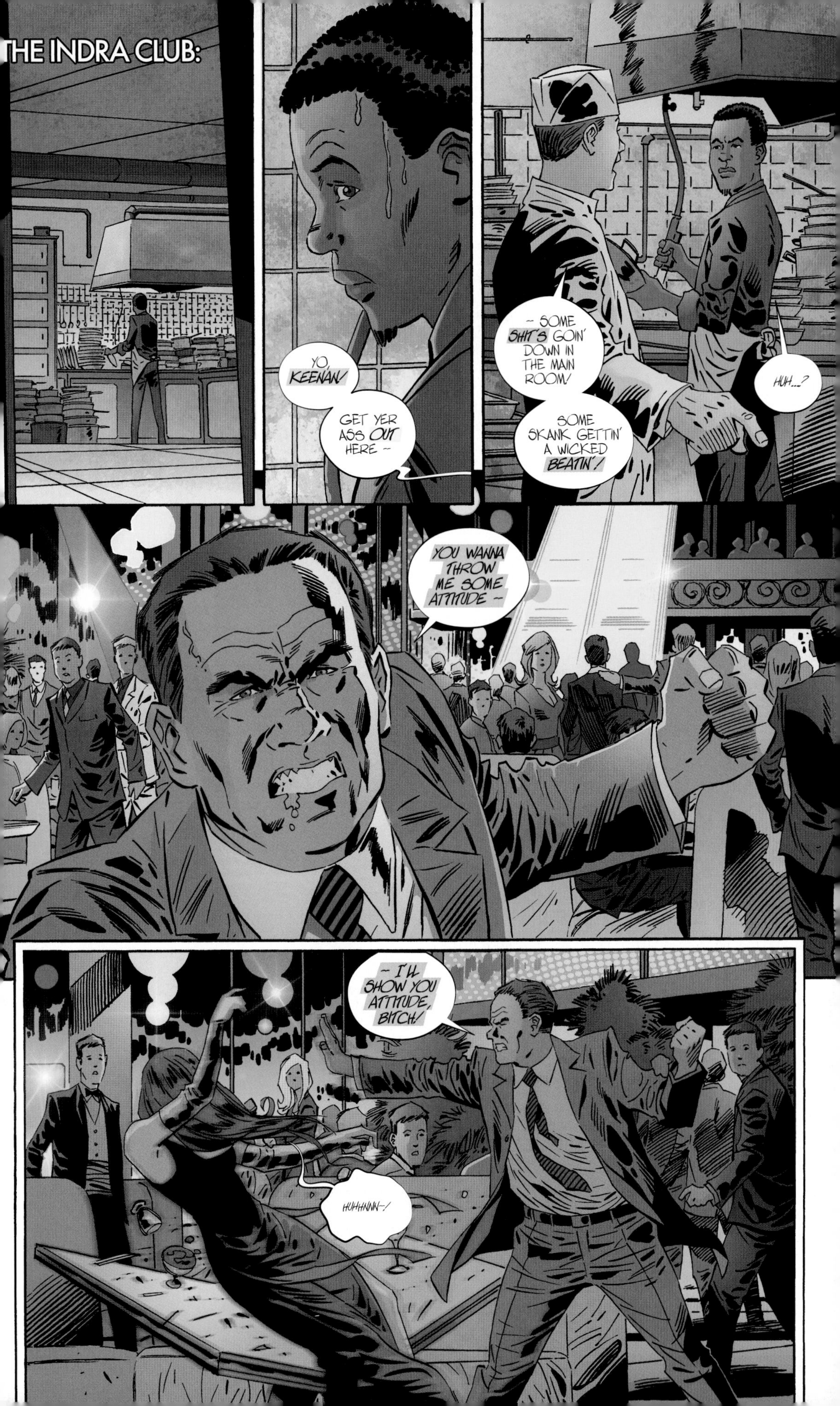
THE INDRA CLUB:
YO, KEENAN!
GET YER ASS OUT HERE --
-- SOME SHIT'S GOIN' DOWN IN THE MAIN ROOM!
SOME SKANK GETTIN' A WICKED BEATIN'!
HUH...?
YOU WANNA THROW ME SOME ATTITUDE --
-- I'LL SHOW YOU ATTITUDE, BITCH!
HUHHNNN--!

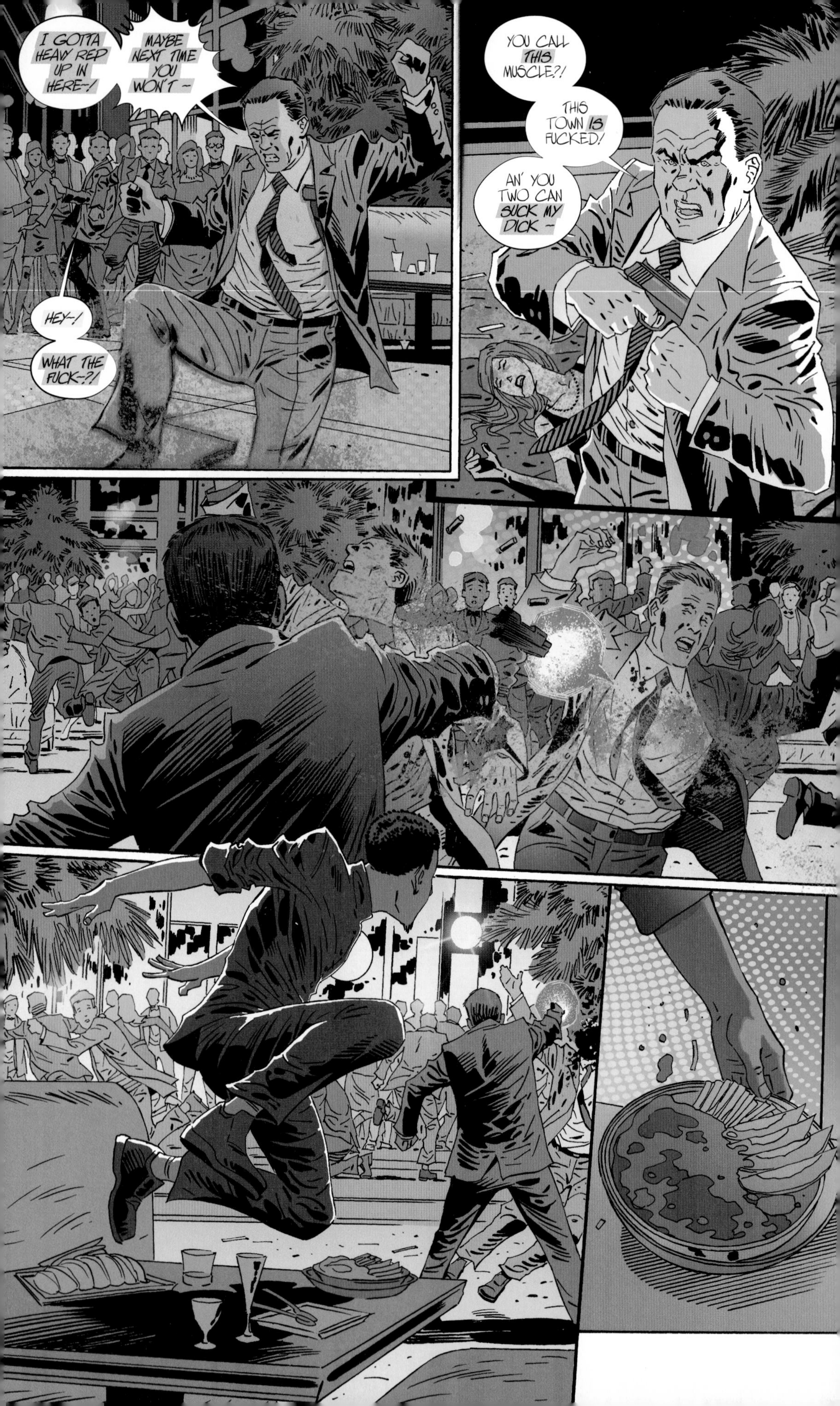
I GOTTA HEAVY REP UP IN HERE--!
MAYBE NEXT TIME YOU WON'T --
HEY--!
WHAT THE FUCK--?!
YOU CALL THIS MUSCLE?!
THIS TOWN IS FUCKED!
AN' YOU TWO CAN SUCK MY DICK --

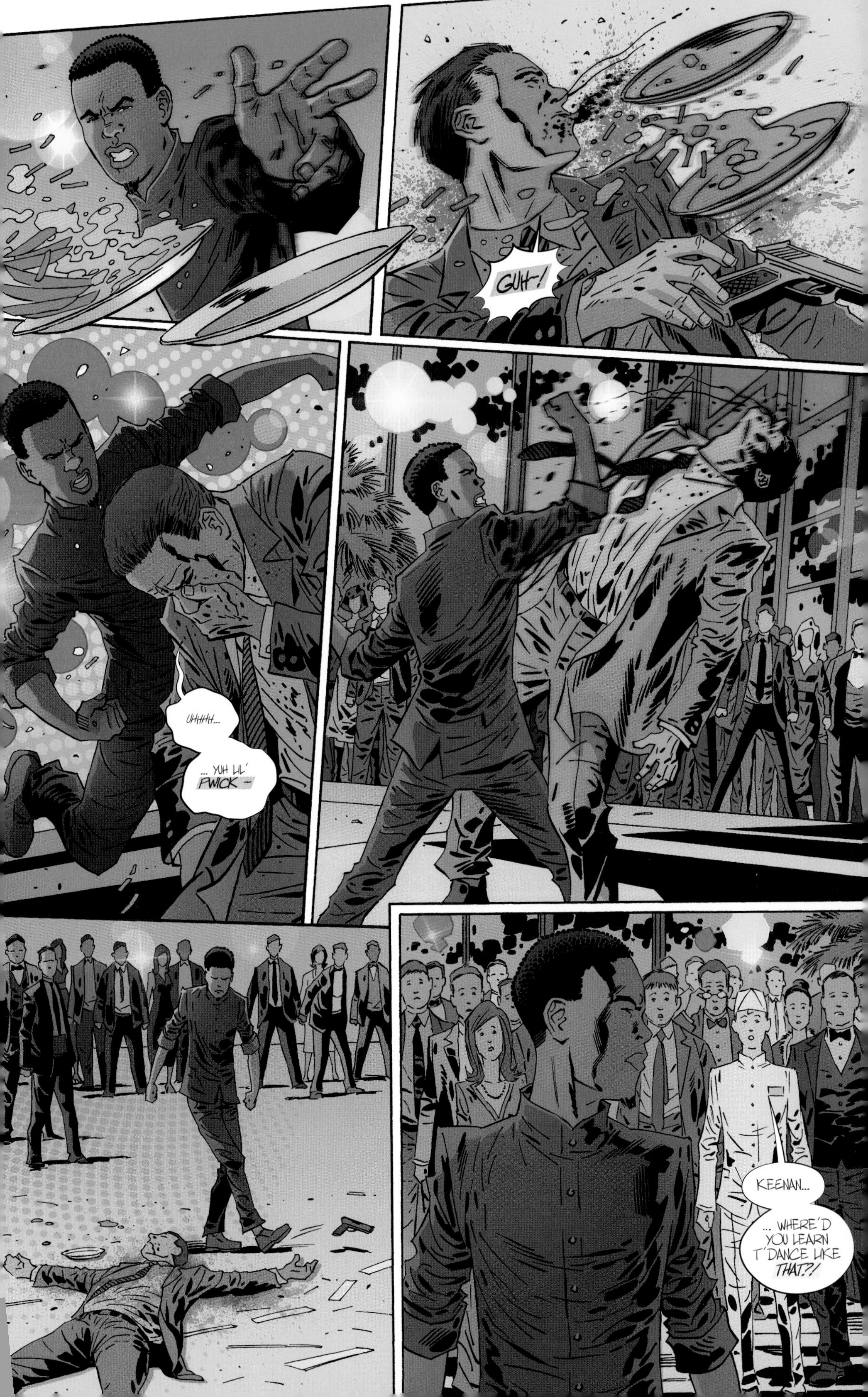
GUH-!
UHHHH...
... YUH LIL' PWICK -
KEENAN...
... WHERE'D YOU LEARN T'DANCE LIKE THAT?!

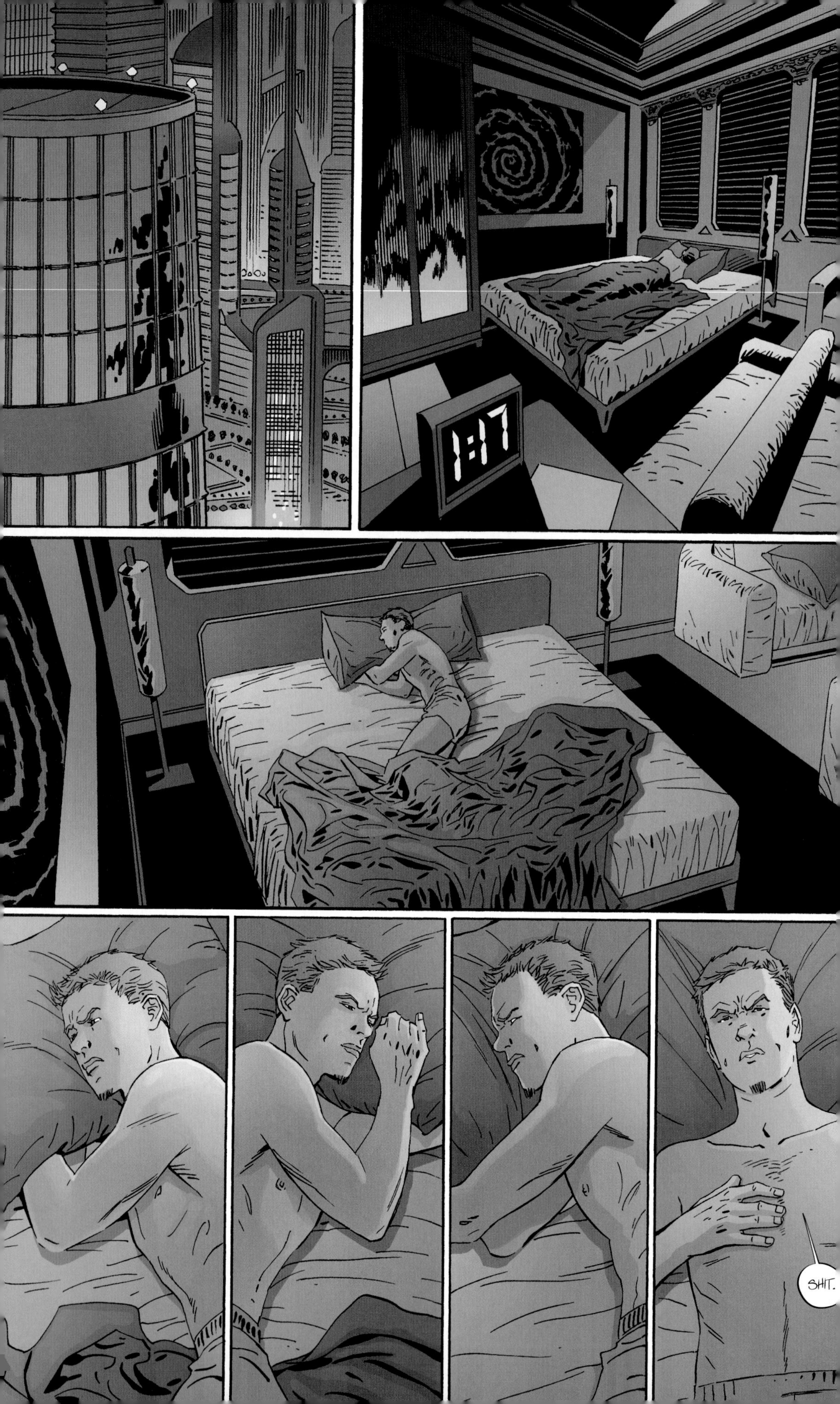
1:17
SHIT.

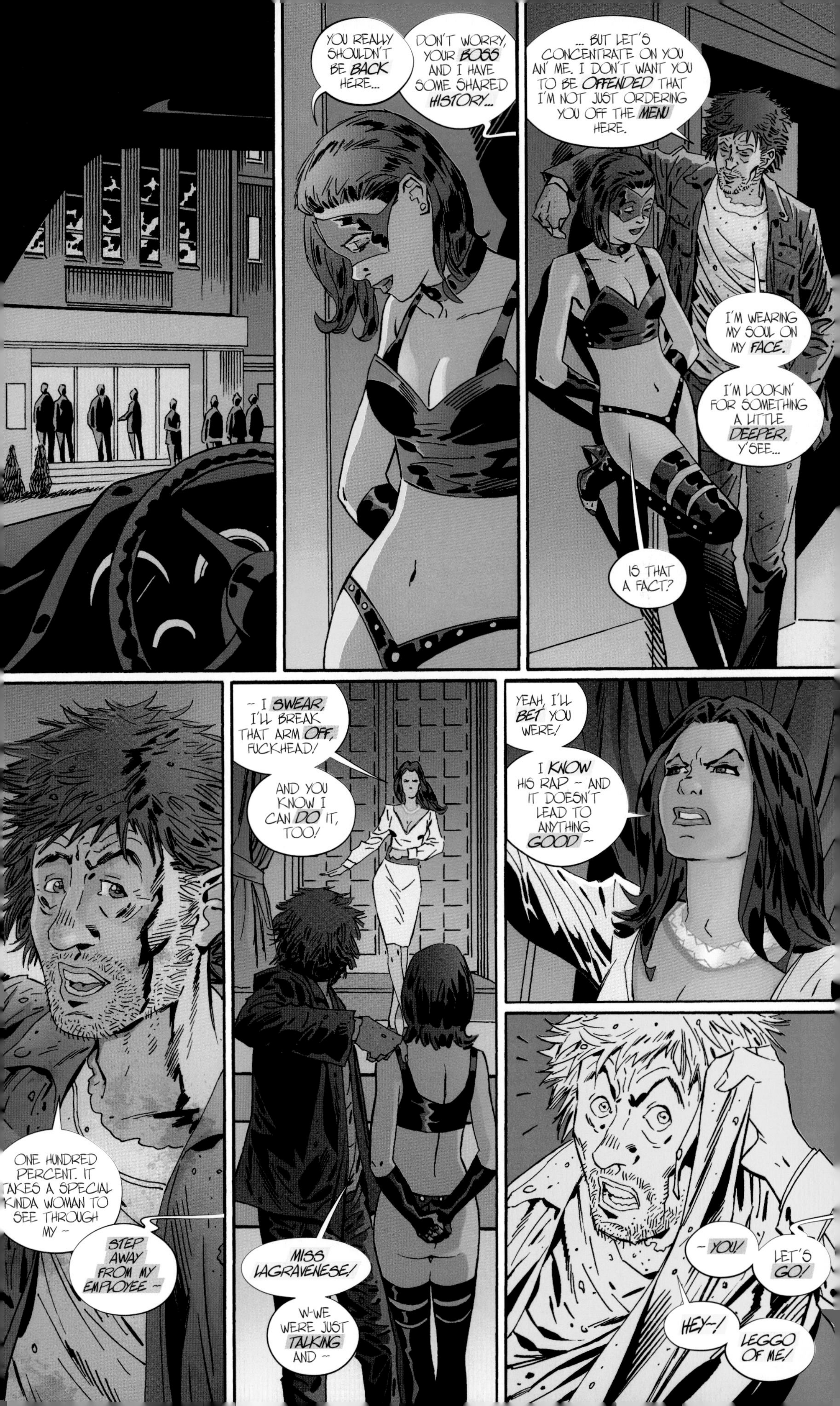
YOU REALLY SHOULDN'T BE BACK HERE...
DON'T WORRY, YOUR BOSS AND I HAVE SOME SHARED HISTORY...
... BUT LET'S CONCENTRATE ON YOU AN' ME. I DON'T WANT YOU TO BE OFFENDED THAT I'M NOT JUST ORDERING YOU OFF THE MENU HERE.
I'M WEARING MY SOUL ON MY FACE.
I'M LOOKIN' FOR SOMETHING A LITTLE DEEPER, Y'SEE...
IS THAT A FACT?
ONE HUNDRED PERCENT. IT TAKES A SPECIAL KINDA WOMAN TO SEE THROUGH MY --
STEP AWAY FROM MY EMPLOYEE --
-- I SWEAR, I'LL BREAK THAT ARM OFF, FUCKHEAD!
AND YOU KNOW I CAN DO IT, TOO!
MISS LAGRAVENESE!
W-WE WERE JUST TALKING AND --
YEAH, I'LL BET YOU WERE!
I KNOW HIS RAP -- AND IT DOESN'T LEAD TO ANYTHING GOOD --
-- YOU!
LET'S GO!
HEY--!
LEGGO OF ME!

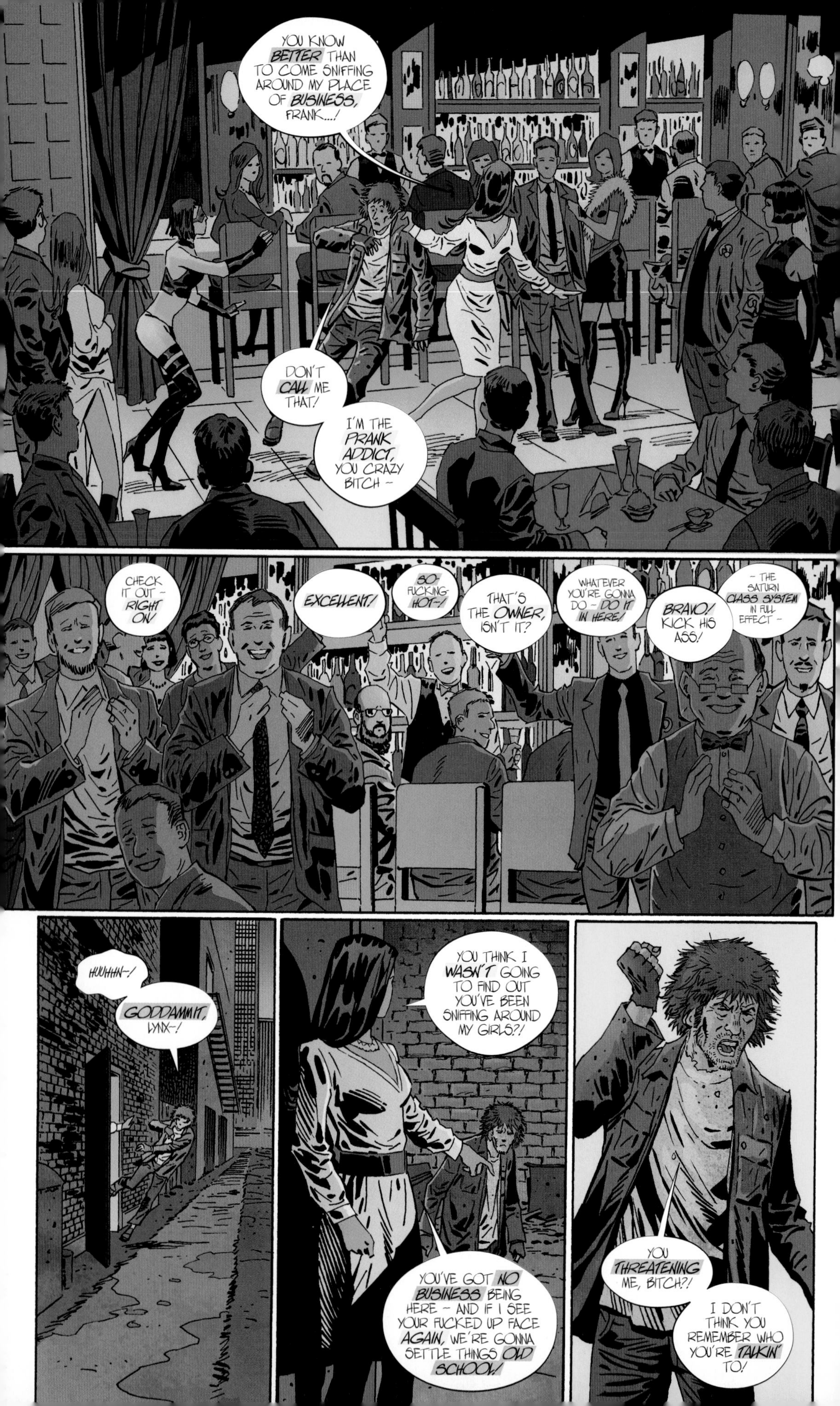
YOU KNOW BETTER THAN TO COME SNIFFING AROUND MY PLACE OF BUSINESS, FRANK...!
DON'T CALL ME THAT!
I'M THE PRANK ADDICT, YOU CRAZY BITCH –
CHECK IT OUT – RIGHT ON!
EXCELLENT!
SO-FUCKING-HOT–!
THAT'S THE OWNER, ISN'T IT?
WHATEVER YOU'RE GONNA DO – DO IT IN HERE!
BRAVO! KICK HIS ASS!
– THE SATURN CLASS SYSTEM IN FULL EFFECT –
HUUHHN–!
GODDAMMIT, LYNX–!
YOU THINK I WASN'T GOING TO FIND OUT YOU'VE BEEN SNIFFING AROUND MY GIRLS?!
YOU'VE GOT NO BUSINESS BEING HERE – AND IF I SEE YOUR FUCKED UP FACE AGAIN, WE'RE GONNA SETTLE THINGS OLD SCHOOL!
YOU THREATENING ME, BITCH?!
I DON'T THINK YOU REMEMBER WHO YOU'RE TALKIN' TO!

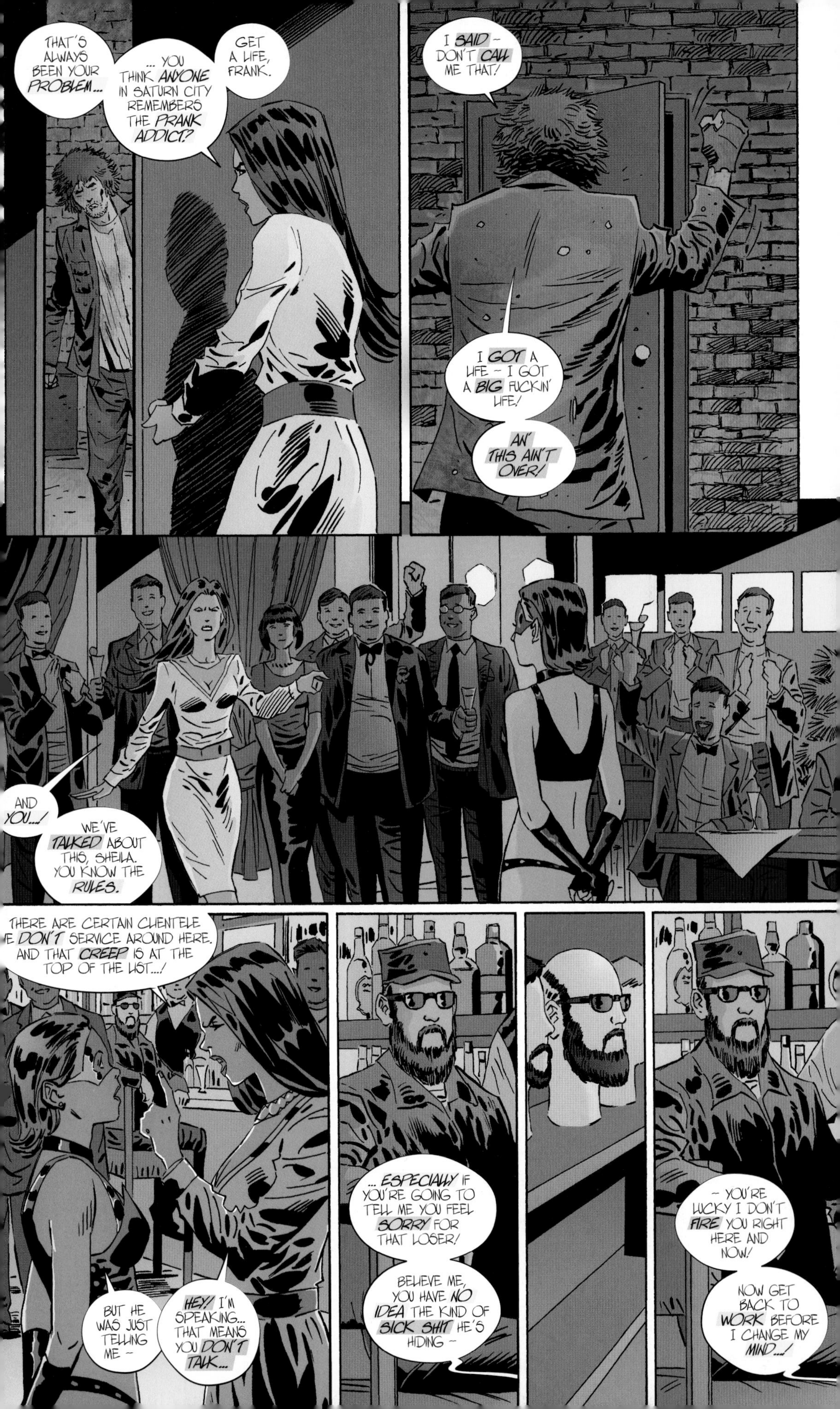
THAT'S ALWAYS BEEN YOUR PROBLEM...
... YOU THINK ANYONE IN SATURN CITY REMEMBERS THE PRANK ADDICT?
GET A LIFE, FRANK.
I SAID -- DON'T CALL ME THAT!
I GOT A LIFE -- I GOT A BIG FUCKIN' LIFE!
AN' THIS AIN'T OVER!
AND YOU...!
WE'VE TALKED ABOUT THIS, SHEILA. YOU KNOW THE RULES.
THERE ARE CERTAIN CLIENTELE WE DON'T SERVICE AROUND HERE. AND THAT CREEP IS AT THE TOP OF THE LIST...!
BUT HE WAS JUST TELLING ME --
HEY! I'M SPEAKING... THAT MEANS YOU DON'T TALK...
... ESPECIALLY IF YOU'RE GOING TO TELL ME YOU FEEL SORRY FOR THAT LOSER!
BELIEVE ME, YOU HAVE NO IDEA THE KIND OF SICK SHIT HE'S HIDING --
-- YOU'RE LUCKY I DON'T FIRE YOU RIGHT HERE AND NOW!
NOW GET BACK TO WORK BEFORE I CHANGE MY MIND...!

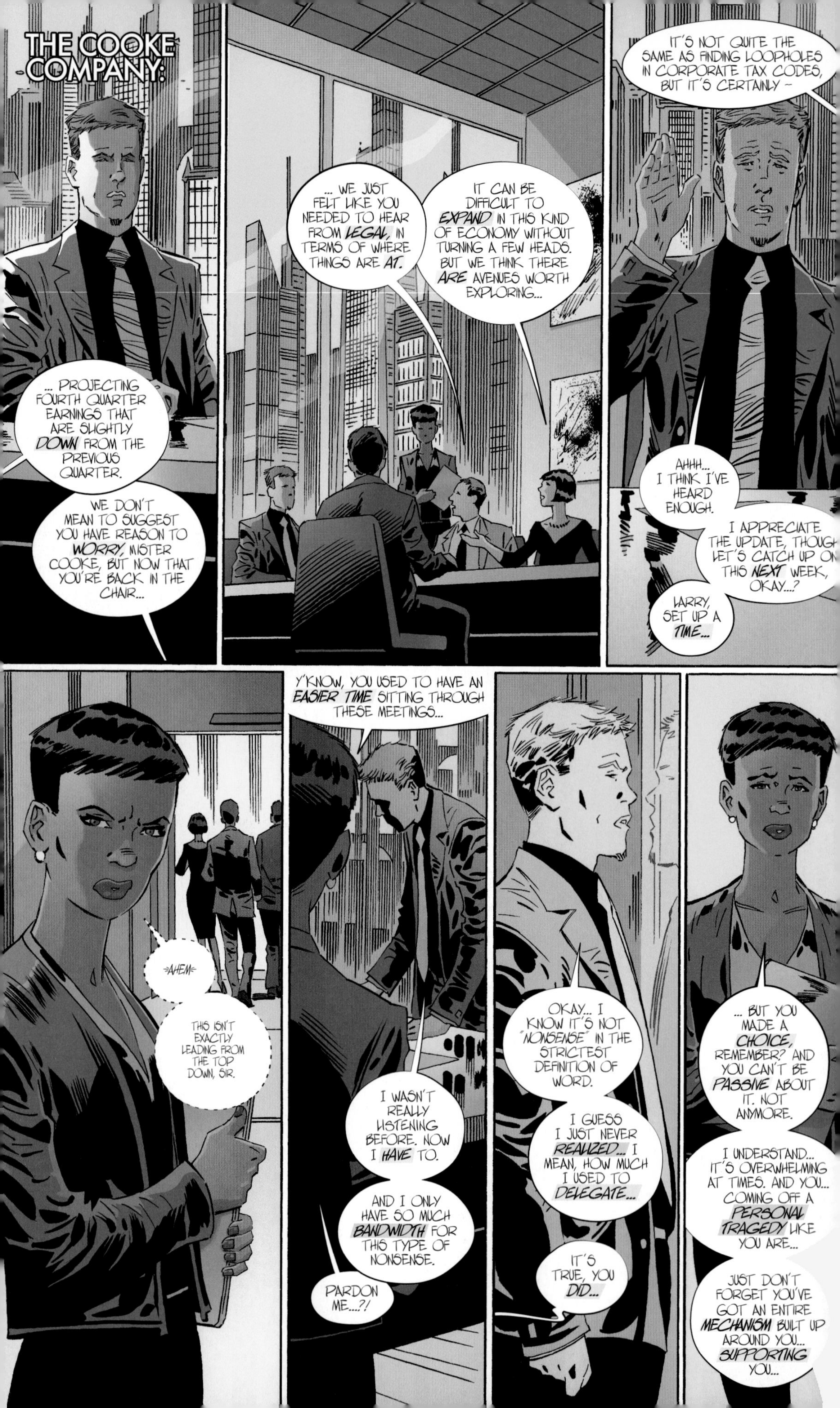

THE COOKE COMPANY:
... PROJECTING FOURTH QUARTER EARNINGS THAT ARE SLIGHTLY DOWN FROM THE PREVIOUS QUARTER.
WE DON'T MEAN TO SUGGEST YOU HAVE REASON TO WORRY, MISTER COOKE, BUT NOW THAT YOU'RE BACK IN THE CHAIR...
... WE JUST FELT LIKE YOU NEEDED TO HEAR FROM LEGAL, IN TERMS OF WHERE THINGS ARE AT.
IT CAN BE DIFFICULT TO EXPAND IN THIS KIND OF ECONOMY WITHOUT TURNING A FEW HEADS. BUT WE THINK THERE ARE AVENUES WORTH EXPLORING...
IT'S NOT QUITE THE SAME AS FINDING LOOPHOLES IN CORPORATE TAX CODES, BUT IT'S CERTAINLY --
AHHH... I THINK I'VE HEARD ENOUGH.
I APPRECIATE THE UPDATE, THOUGH LET'S CATCH UP ON THIS NEXT WEEK, OKAY...?
LARRY, SET UP A TIME...
AHEM
THIS ISN'T EXACTLY LEADING FROM THE TOP DOWN, SIR.
Y'KNOW, YOU USED TO HAVE AN EASIER TIME SITTING THROUGH THESE MEETINGS...
I WASN'T REALLY LISTENING BEFORE. NOW I HAVE TO.
AND I ONLY HAVE SO MUCH BANDWIDTH FOR THIS TYPE OF NONSENSE.
PARDON ME...?!
OKAY... I KNOW IT'S NOT "NONSENSE" IN THE STRICTEST DEFINITION OF WORD.
I GUESS I JUST NEVER REALIZED... I MEAN, HOW MUCH I USED TO DELEGATE...
IT'S TRUE, YOU DID...
... BUT YOU MADE A CHOICE, REMEMBER? AND YOU CAN'T BE PASSIVE ABOUT IT. NOT ANYMORE.
I UNDERSTAND... IT'S OVERWHELMING AT TIMES. AND YOU... COMING OFF A PERSONAL TRAGEDY LIKE YOU ARE...
JUST DON'T FORGET YOU'VE GOT AN ENTIRE MECHANISM BUILT UP AROUND YOU... SUPPORTING YOU...

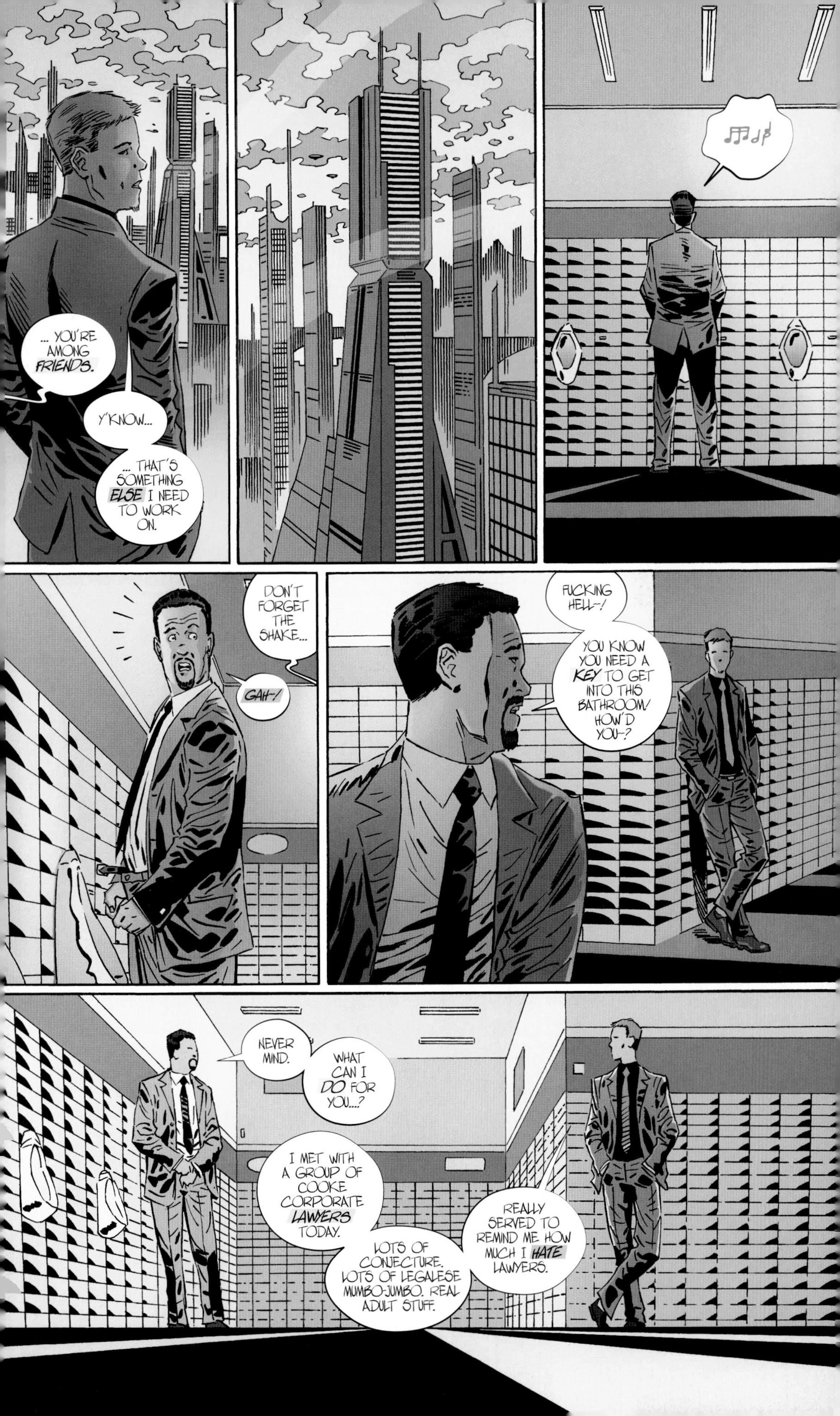
... YOU'RE AMONG FRIENDS.
Y'KNOW...
... THAT'S SOMETHING ELSE I NEED TO WORK ON.
DON'T FORGET THE SHAKE...
GAH--!
FUCKING HELL--!
YOU KNOW YOU NEED A KEY TO GET INTO THIS BATHROOM! HOW'D YOU--?
NEVER MIND.
WHAT CAN I DO FOR YOU...?
I MET WITH A GROUP OF COOKE CORPORATE LAWYERS TODAY.
LOTS OF CONJECTURE. LOTS OF LEGALESE MUMBO-JUMBO. REAL ADULT STUFF.
REALLY SERVED TO REMIND ME HOW MUCH I HATE LAWYERS.

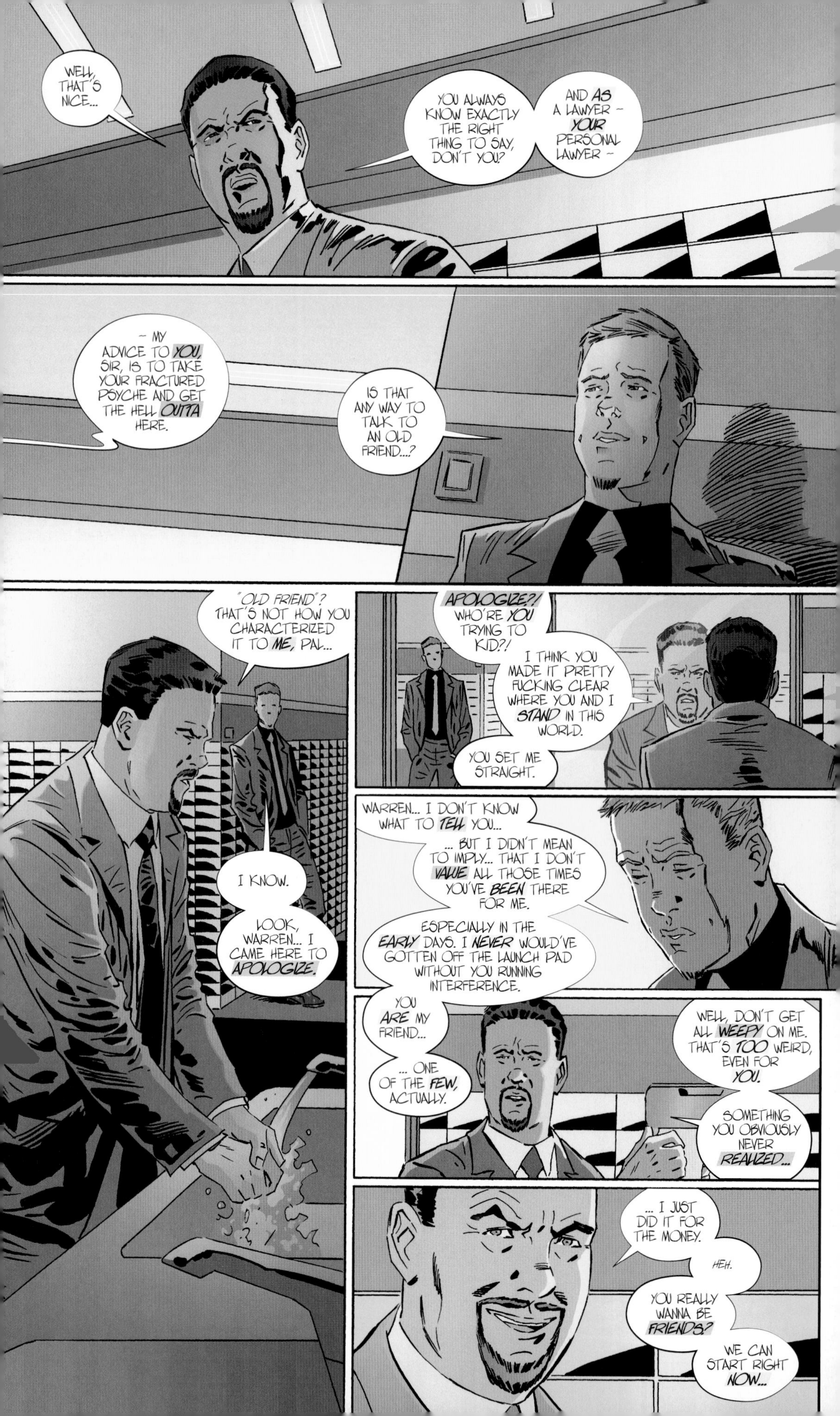
WELL, THAT'S NICE...
YOU ALWAYS KNOW EXACTLY THE RIGHT THING TO SAY, DON'T YOU?
AND AS A LAWYER -- YOUR PERSONAL LAWYER --
-- MY ADVICE TO YOU, SIR, IS TO TAKE YOUR FRACTURED PSYCHE AND GET THE HELL OUTTA HERE.
IS THAT ANY WAY TO TALK TO AN OLD FRIEND...?
"OLD FRIEND"? THAT'S NOT HOW YOU CHARACTERIZED IT TO ME, PAL...
APOLOGIZE?! WHO'RE YOU TRYING TO KID?!
I THINK YOU MADE IT PRETTY FUCKING CLEAR WHERE YOU AND I STAND IN THIS WORLD.
YOU SET ME STRAIGHT.
I KNOW.
LOOK, WARREN... I CAME HERE TO APOLOGIZE.
WARREN... I DON'T KNOW WHAT TO TELL YOU...
... BUT I DIDN'T MEAN TO IMPLY... THAT I DON'T VALUE ALL THOSE TIMES YOU'VE BEEN THERE FOR ME.
ESPECIALLY IN THE EARLY DAYS. I NEVER WOULD'VE GOTTEN OFF THE LAUNCH PAD WITHOUT YOU RUNNING INTERFERENCE.
YOU ARE MY FRIEND...
... ONE OF THE FEW, ACTUALLY.
WELL, DON'T GET ALL WEEPY ON ME. THAT'S TOO WEIRD, EVEN FOR YOU.
SOMETHING YOU OBVIOUSLY NEVER REALIZED...
... I JUST DID IT FOR THE MONEY.
HEH.
YOU REALLY WANNA BE FRIENDS?
WE CAN START RIGHT NOW...

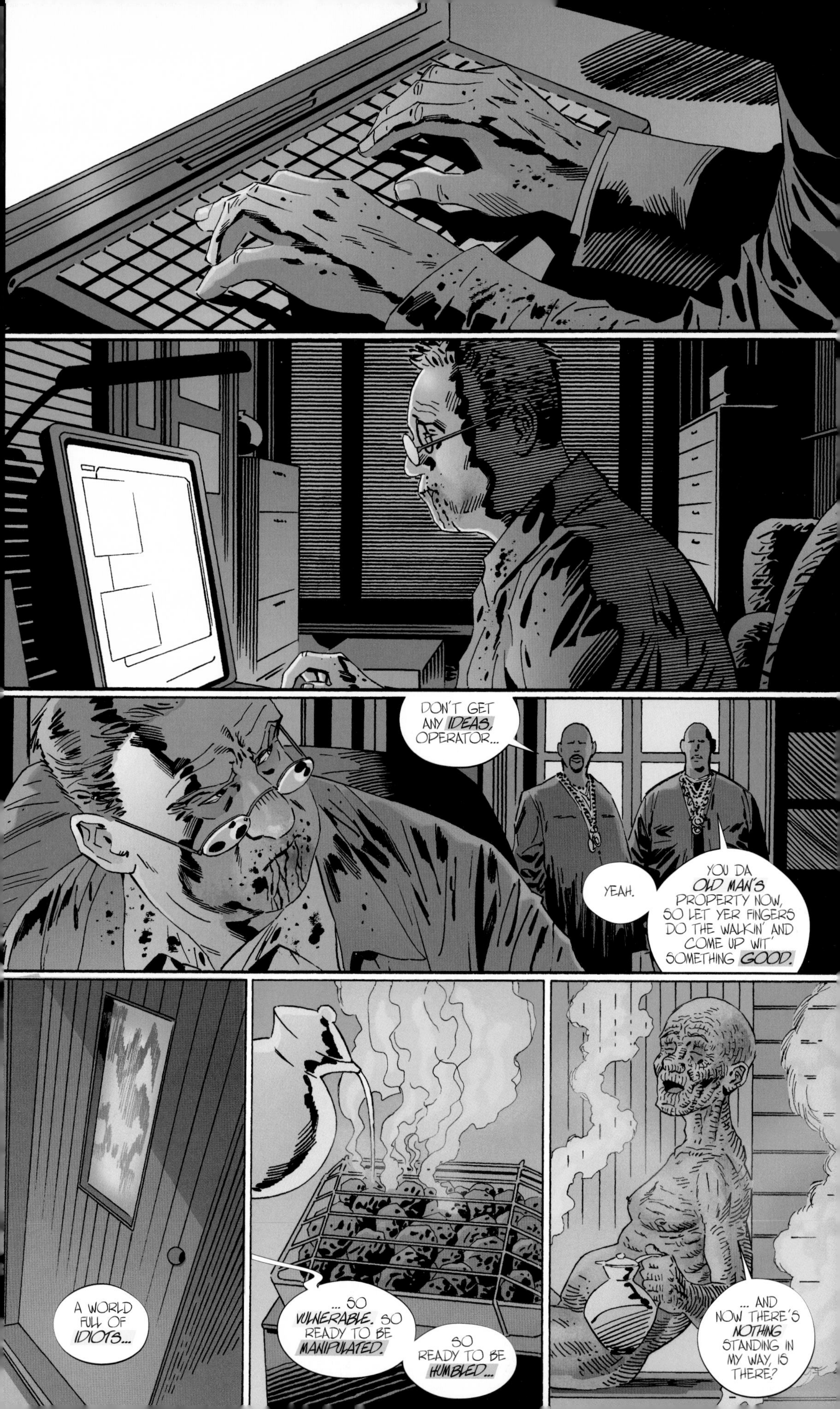
DON'T GET ANY IDEAS, OPERATOR...
YEAH.
YOU DA OLD MAN'S PROPERTY NOW, SO LET YER FINGERS DO THE WALKIN' AND COME UP WIT' SOMETHING GOOD.
A WORLD FULL OF IDIOTS...
... SO VULNERABLE. SO READY TO BE MANIPULATED.
SO READY TO BE HUMBLED...
... AND NOW THERE'S NOTHING STANDING IN MY WAY, IS THERE?

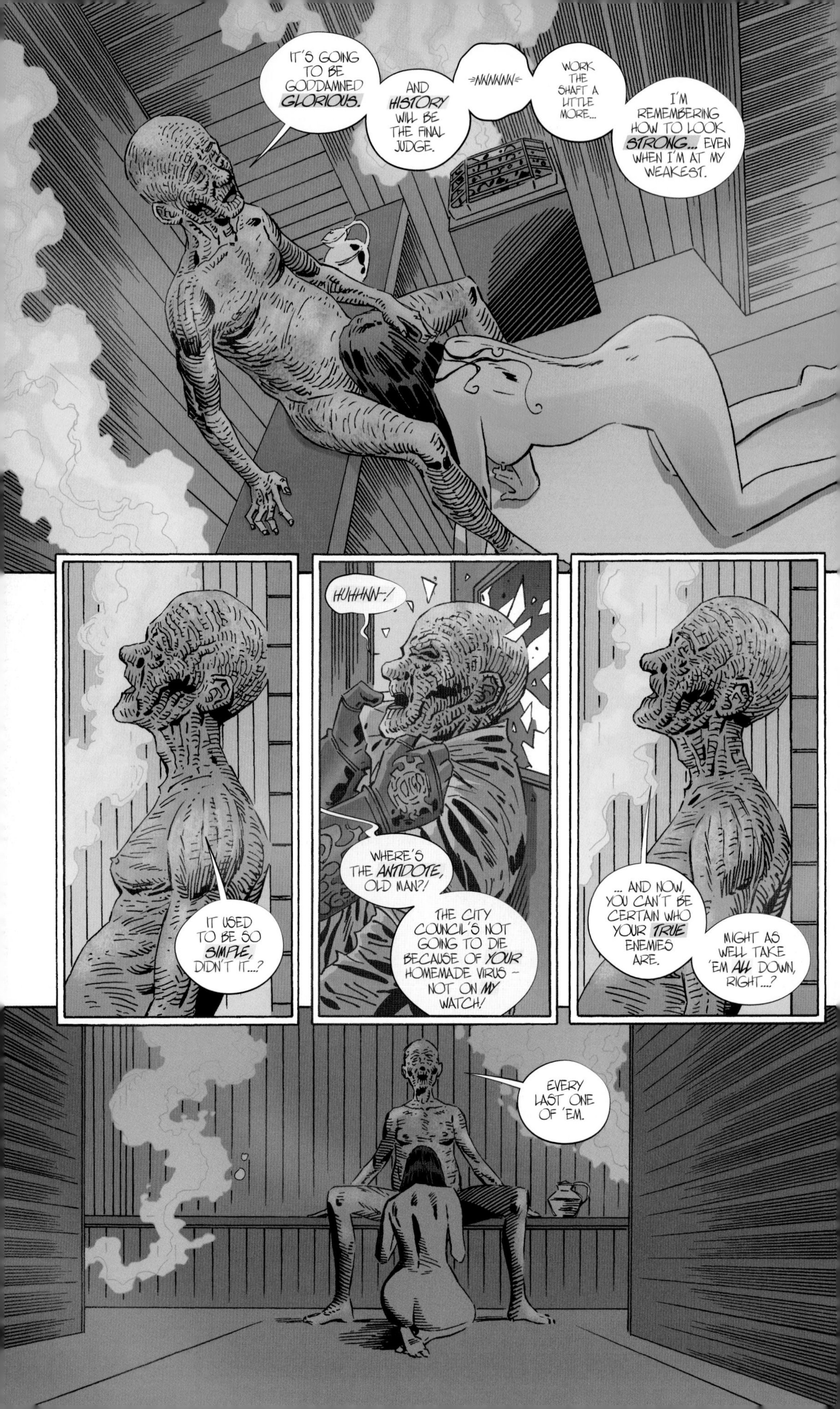
IT'S GOING TO BE GODDAMNED GLORIOUS.
AND HISTORY WILL BE THE FINAL JUDGE.
-NNNNNN-
WORK THE SHAFT A LITTLE MORE...
I'M REMEMBERING HOW TO LOOK STRONG... EVEN WHEN I'M AT MY WEAKEST.
IT USED TO BE SO SIMPLE, DIDN'T IT...?
HUHHNN-!
WHERE'S THE ANTIDOTE, OLD MAN?!
THE CITY COUNCIL'S NOT GOING TO DIE BECAUSE OF YOUR HOMEMADE VIRUS -- NOT ON MY WATCH!
... AND NOW, YOU CAN'T BE CERTAIN WHO YOUR TRUE ENEMIES ARE.
MIGHT AS WELL TAKE 'EM ALL DOWN, RIGHT...?
EVERY LAST ONE OF 'EM.

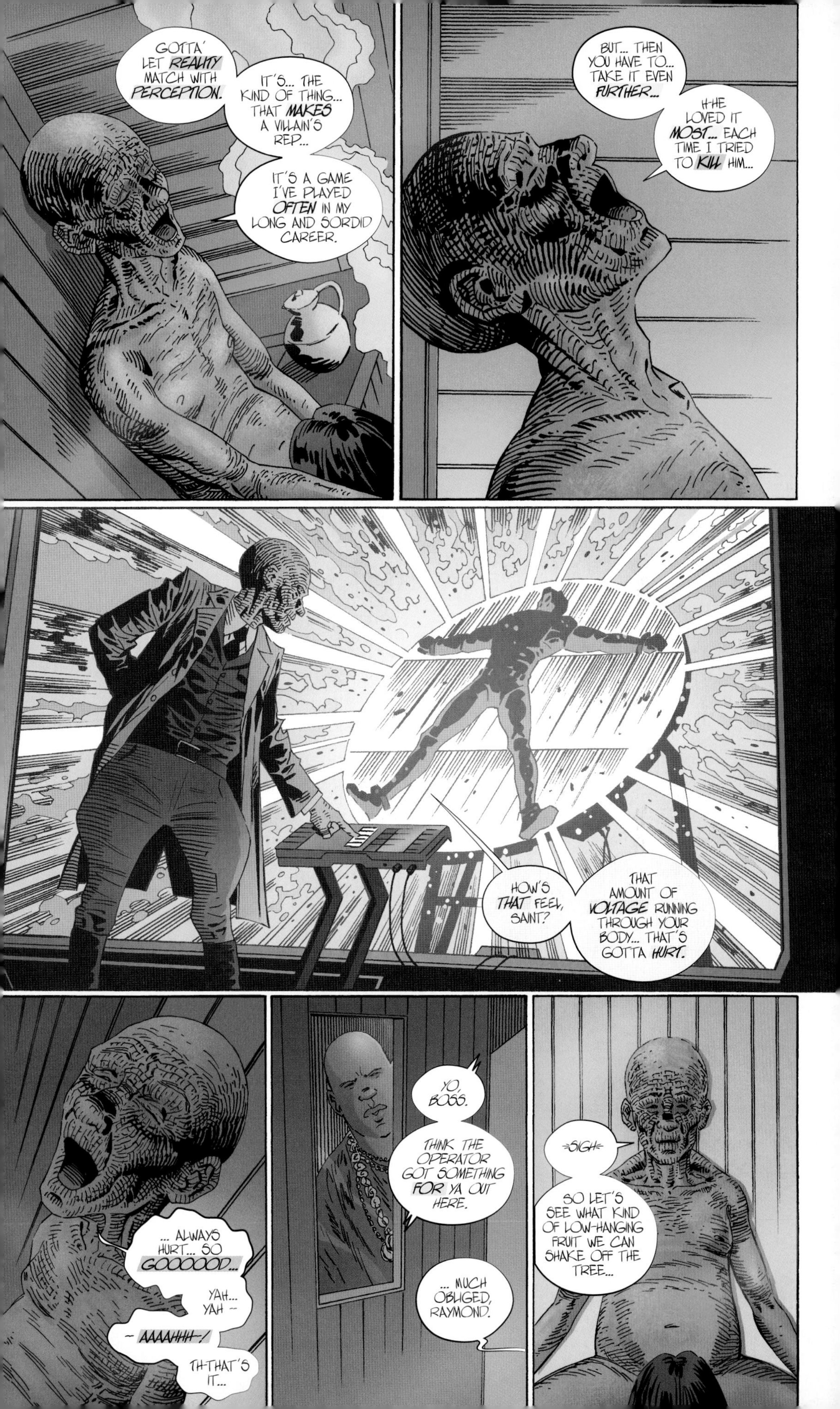
GOTTA' LET REALITY MATCH WITH PERCEPTION.
IT'S... THE KIND OF THING... THAT MAKES A VILLAIN'S REP...
IT'S A GAME I'VE PLAYED OFTEN IN MY LONG AND SORDID CAREER.
BUT... THEN YOU HAVE TO... TAKE IT EVEN FURTHER...
H-HE LOVED IT MOST... EACH TIME I TRIED TO KILL HIM...
HOW'S THAT FEEL, SAINT?
THAT AMOUNT OF VOLTAGE RUNNING THROUGH YOUR BODY... THAT'S GOTTA HURT.
... ALWAYS HURT... SO GOOOOOD...
YAH... YAH --
-- AAAAHHH--!
TH-THAT'S IT...
YO, BOSS.
THINK THE OPERATOR GOT SOMETHING FOR YA OUT HERE.
... MUCH OBLIGED, RAYMOND.
~SIGH~
SO LET'S SEE WHAT KIND OF LOW-HANGING FRUIT WE CAN SHAKE OFF THE TREE...

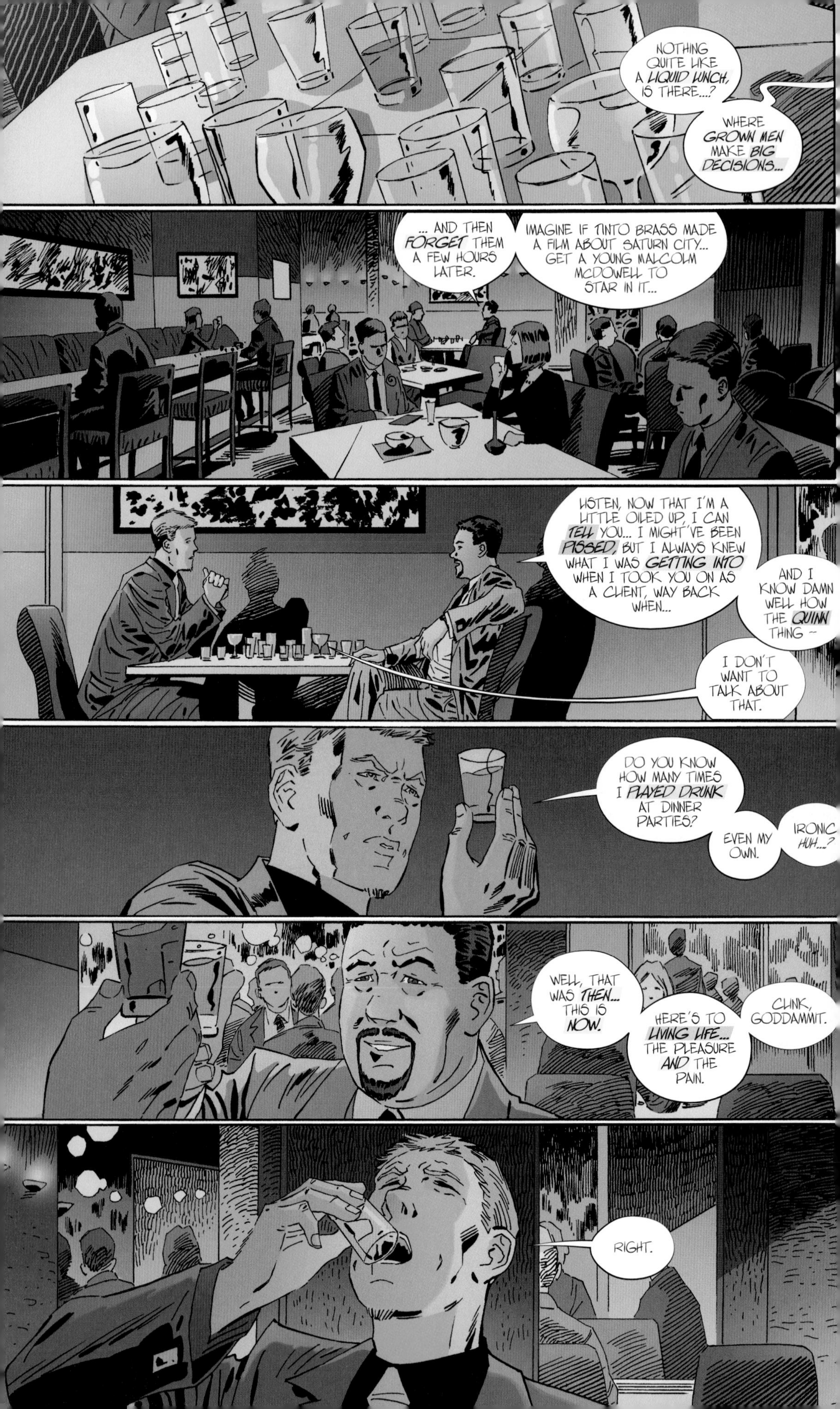
NOTHING QUITE LIKE A LIQUID LUNCH, IS THERE...?
WHERE GROWN MEN MAKE BIG DECISIONS...
... AND THEN FORGET THEM A FEW HOURS LATER.
IMAGINE IF TINTO BRASS MADE A FILM ABOUT SATURN CITY... GET A YOUNG MALCOLM MCDOWELL TO STAR IN IT...
LISTEN, NOW THAT I'M A LITTLE OILED UP, I CAN TELL YOU... I MIGHT'VE BEEN PISSED, BUT I ALWAYS KNEW WHAT I WAS GETTING INTO WHEN I TOOK YOU ON AS A CLIENT, WAY BACK WHEN...
AND I KNOW DAMN WELL HOW THE QUINN THING --
I DON'T WANT TO TALK ABOUT THAT.
DO YOU KNOW HOW MANY TIMES I PLAYED DRUNK AT DINNER PARTIES?
EVEN MY OWN.
IRONIC HUH...?
WELL, THAT WAS THEN... THIS IS NOW.
HERE'S TO LIVING LIFE... THE PLEASURE AND THE PAIN.
CLINK, GODDAMMIT.
RIGHT.

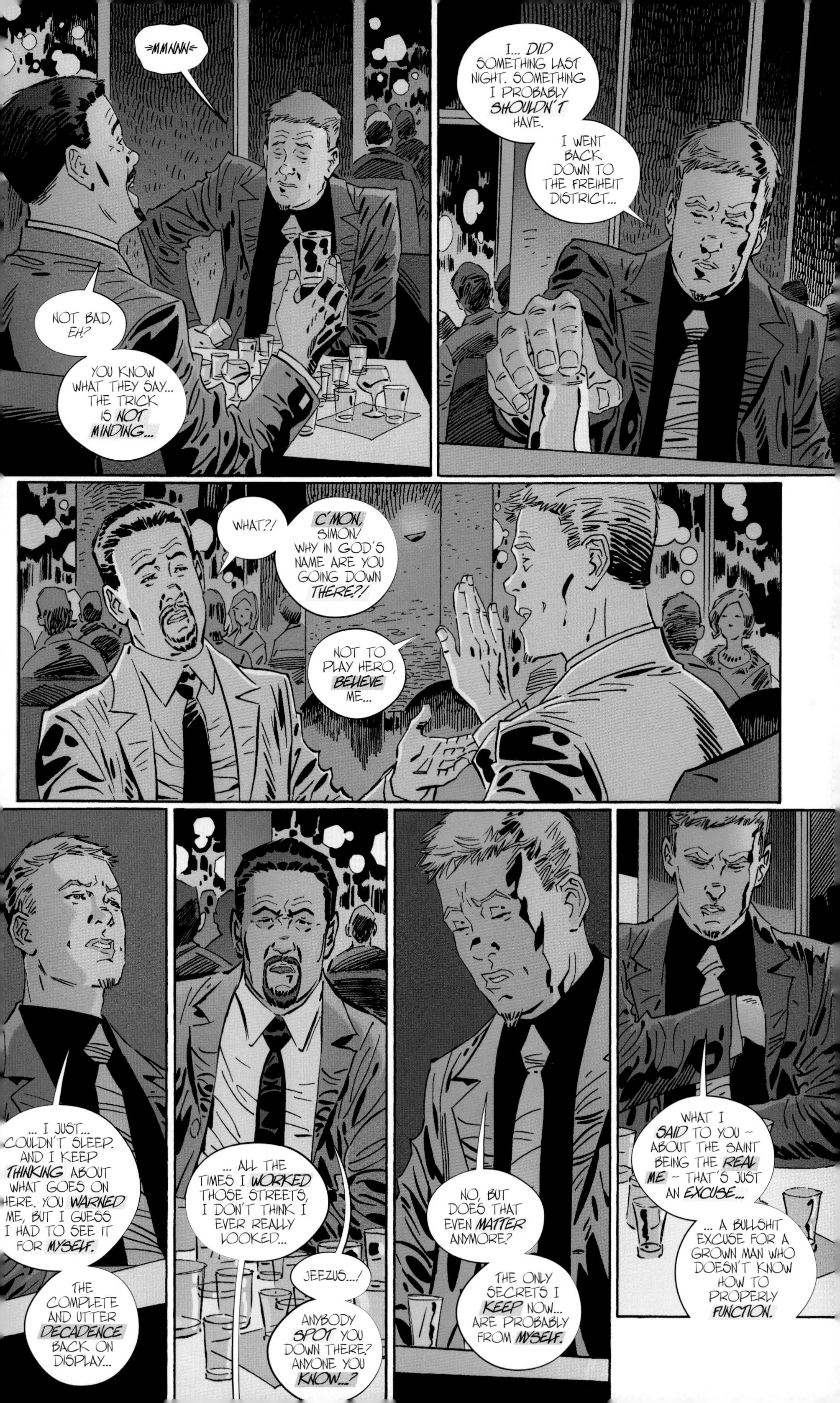

~MMNNN~
NOT BAD, EH?
YOU KNOW WHAT THEY SAY... THE TRICK IS NOT MINDING...
I... DID SOMETHING LAST NIGHT. SOMETHING I PROBABLY SHOULDN'T HAVE.
I WENT BACK DOWN TO THE FREIHEIT DISTRICT...
WHAT?!
C'MON, SIMON! WHY IN GOD'S NAME ARE YOU GOING DOWN THERE?!
NOT TO PLAY HERO, BELIEVE ME...
... I JUST... COULDN'T SLEEP. AND I KEEP THINKING ABOUT WHAT GOES ON HERE. YOU WARNED ME, BUT I GUESS I HAD TO SEE IT FOR MYSELF.
THE COMPLETE AND UTTER DECADENCE BACK ON DISPLAY...
... ALL THE TIMES I WORKED THOSE STREETS, I DON'T THINK I EVER REALLY LOOKED...
JEEZUS...!
ANYBODY SPOT YOU DOWN THERE? ANYONE YOU KNOW...?
NO, BUT DOES THAT EVEN MATTER ANYMORE?
THE ONLY SECRETS I KEEP NOW... ARE PROBABLY FROM MYSELF.
WHAT I SAID TO YOU -- ABOUT THE SAINT BEING THE REAL ME -- THAT'S JUST AN EXCUSE...
... A BULLSHIT EXCUSE FOR A GROWN MAN WHO DOESN'T KNOW HOW TO PROPERLY FUNCTION.

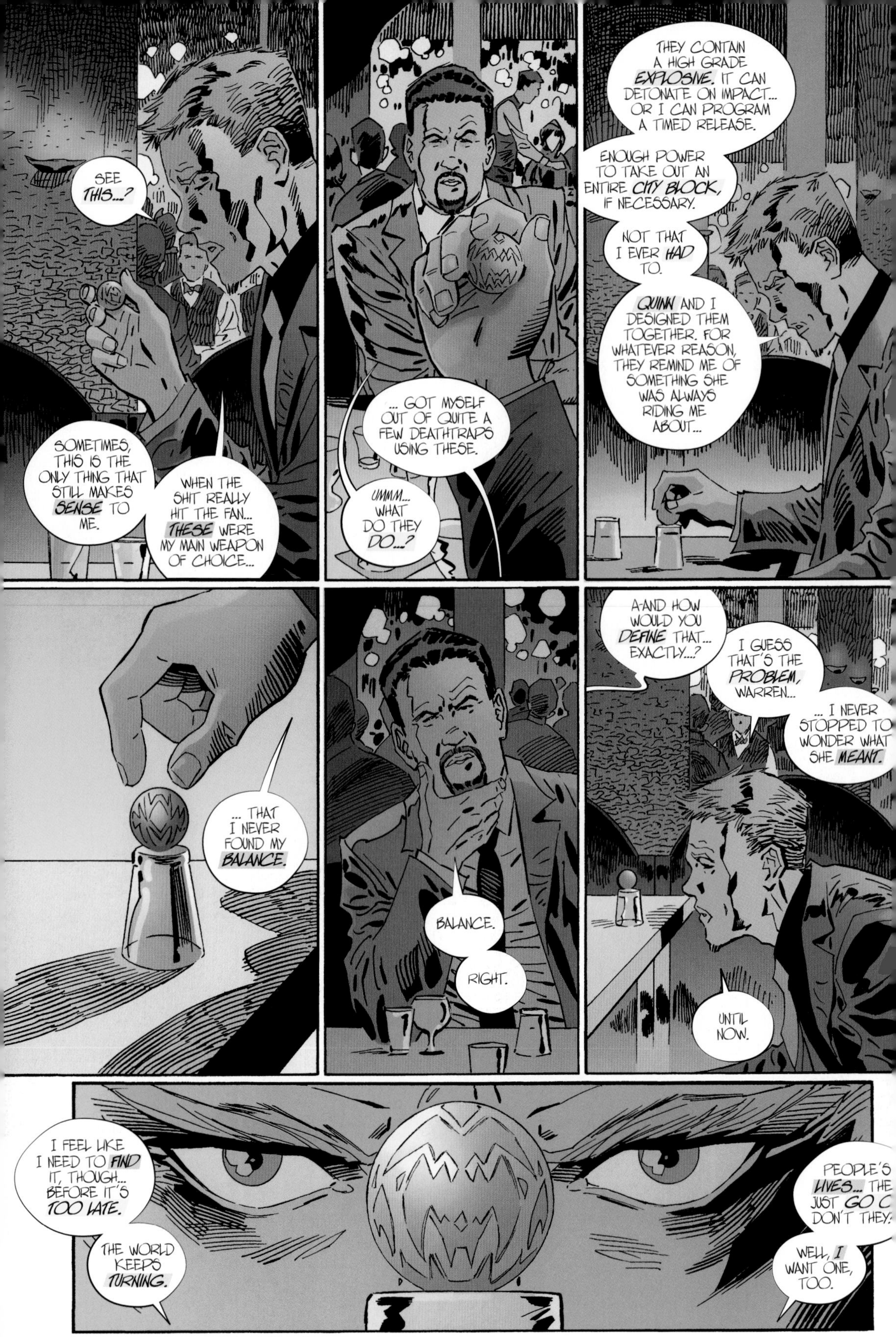

SEE THIS...?
SOMETIMES, THIS IS THE ONLY THING THAT STILL MAKES SENSE TO ME.
WHEN THE SHIT REALLY HIT THE FAN... THESE WERE MY MAIN WEAPON OF CHOICE...
... GOT MYSELF OUT OF QUITE A FEW DEATHTRAPS USING THESE.
UMMM... WHAT DO THEY DO...?
THEY CONTAIN A HIGH GRADE EXPLOSIVE. IT CAN DETONATE ON IMPACT... OR I CAN PROGRAM A TIMED RELEASE.
ENOUGH POWER TO TAKE OUT AN ENTIRE CITY BLOCK, IF NECESSARY.
NOT THAT I EVER HAD TO.
QUINN AND I DESIGNED THEM TOGETHER. FOR WHATEVER REASON, THEY REMIND ME OF SOMETHING SHE WAS ALWAYS RIDING ME ABOUT...
... THAT I NEVER FOUND MY BALANCE.
BALANCE.
RIGHT.
A-AND HOW WOULD YOU DEFINE THAT... EXACTLY...?
I GUESS THAT'S THE PROBLEM, WARREN...
... I NEVER STOPPED TO WONDER WHAT SHE MEANT.
UNTIL NOW.
I FEEL LIKE I NEED TO FIND IT, THOUGH... BEFORE IT'S TOO LATE.
THE WORLD KEEPS TURNING.
PEOPLE'S LIVES... THE JUST GO C DON'T THEY
WELL, I WANT ONE, TOO.

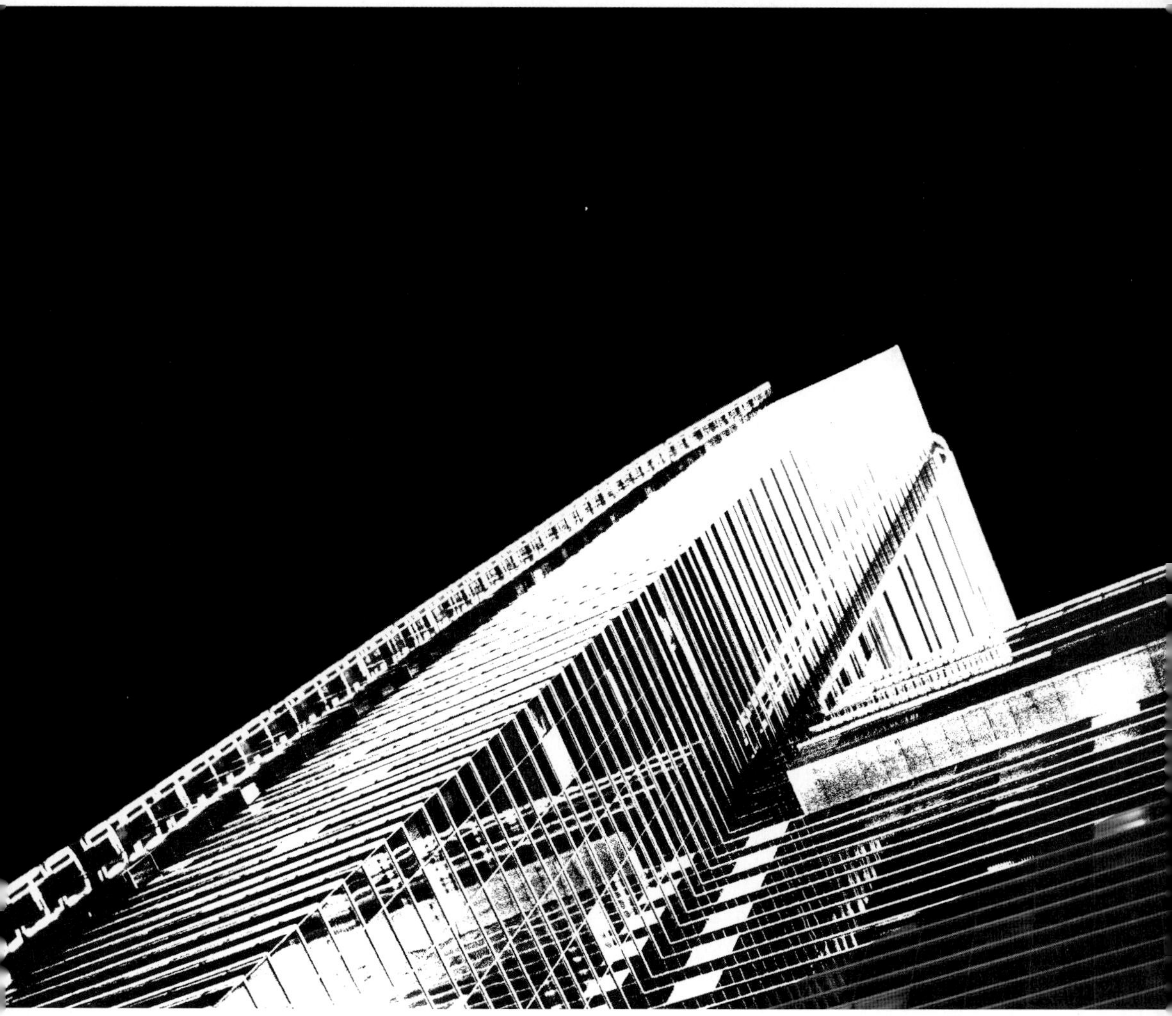

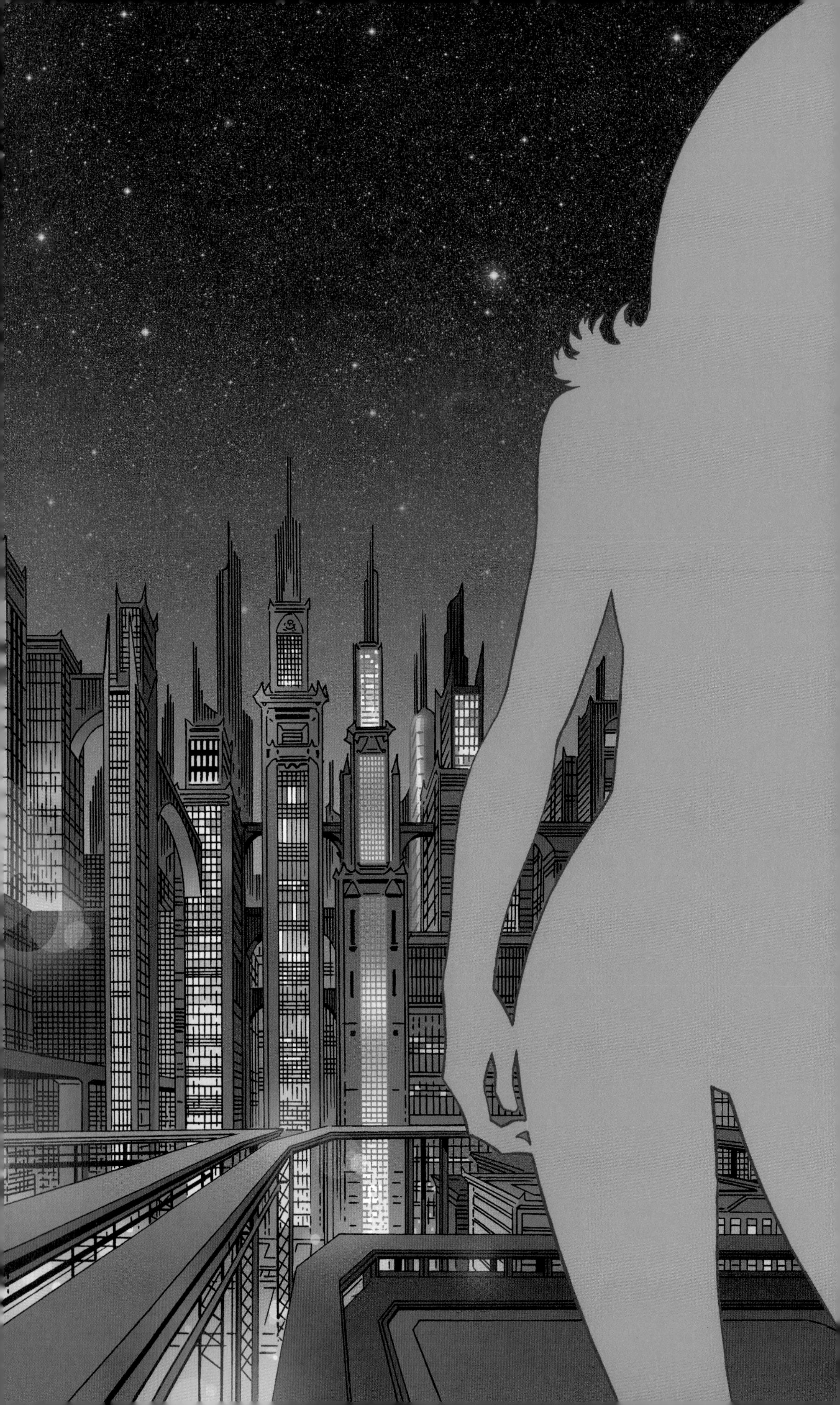

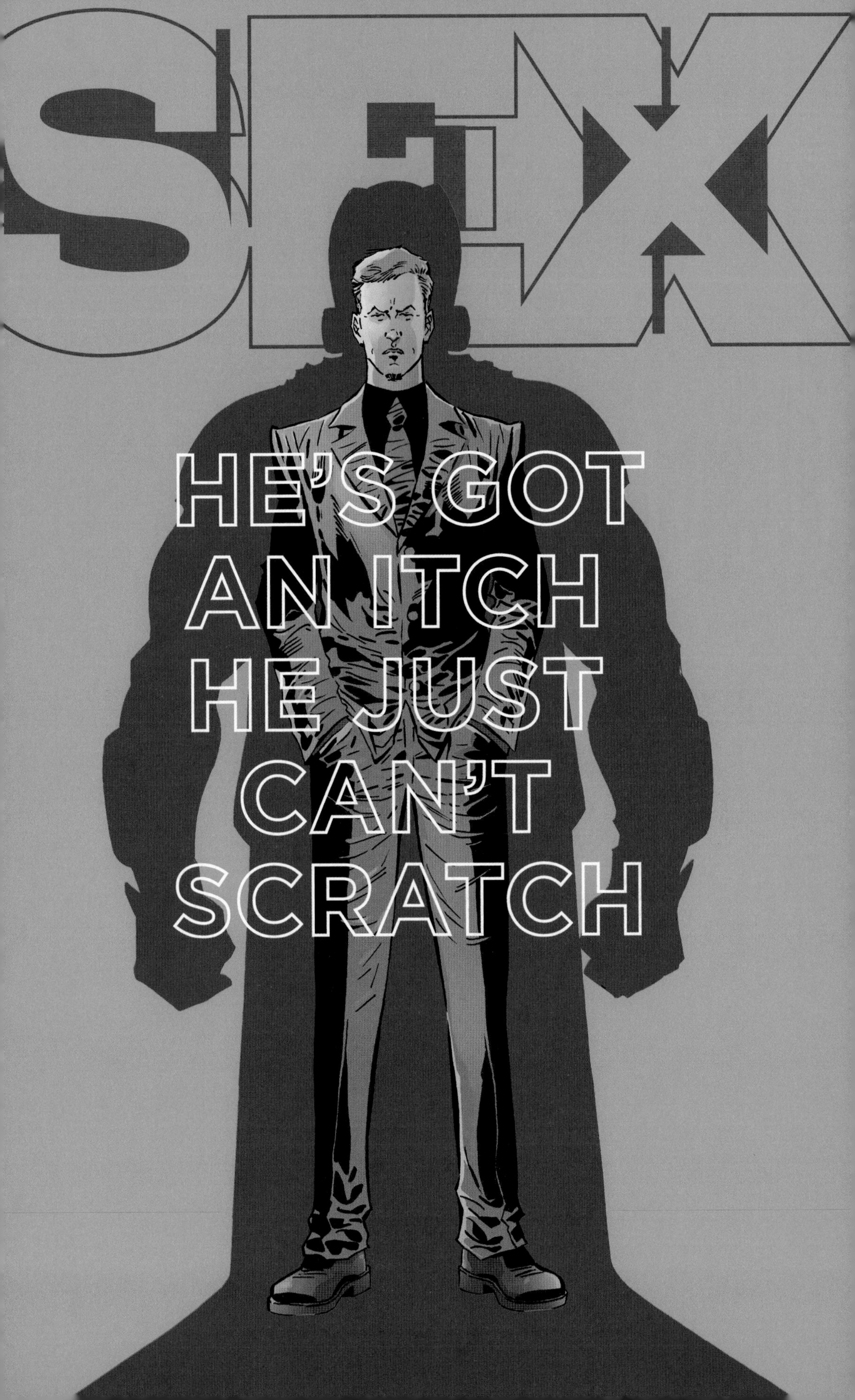
SEX
HE'S GOT AN ITCH HE JUST CAN'T SCRATCH

CHAPTER FIVE
QUIVERS N' SHAKES

JOE CASEY WRITER   **PIOTR KOWALSKI** ARTIST   **BRAD SIMPSON** COLORIST   **RUS WOOTON** LETTERER   **SONIA HARRIS** GRAPHIC DESIGNER

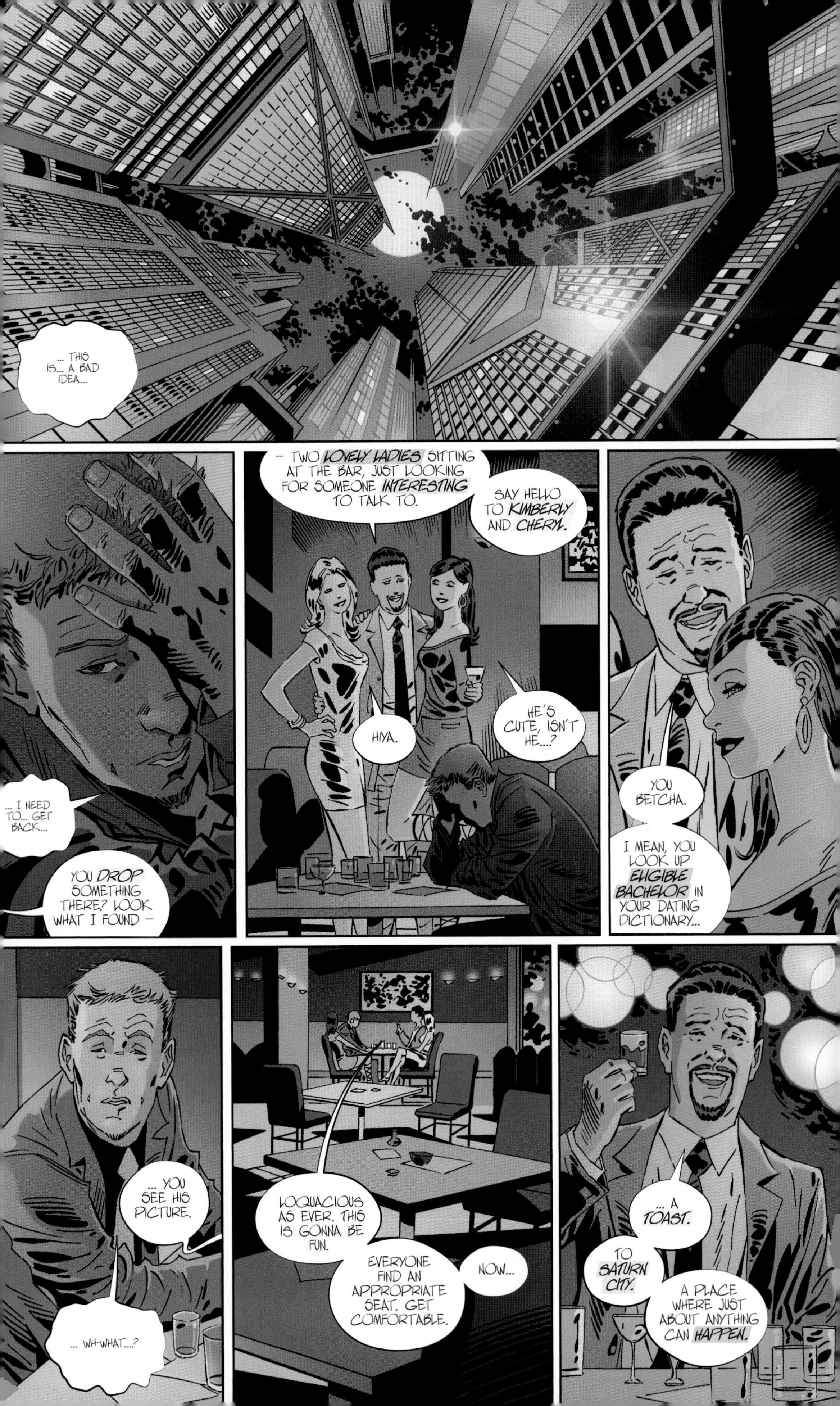
... THIS IS... A BAD IDEA...
... I NEED TO... GET BACK...
YOU DROP SOMETHING THERE? LOOK WHAT I FOUND --
-- TWO LOVELY LADIES SITTING AT THE BAR, JUST LOOKING FOR SOMEONE INTERESTING TO TALK TO.
SAY HELLO TO KIMBERLY AND CHERYL.
HIYA.
HE'S CUTE, ISN'T HE...?
YOU BETCHA.
I MEAN, YOU LOOK UP ELIGIBLE BACHELOR IN YOUR DATING DICTIONARY...
... YOU SEE HIS PICTURE.
... WH-WHAT...?
LOQUACIOUS AS EVER. THIS IS GONNA BE FUN.
EVERYONE FIND AN APPROPRIATE SEAT. GET COMFORTABLE.
NOW...
... A TOAST.
TO SATURN CITY.
A PLACE WHERE JUST ABOUT ANYTHING CAN HAPPEN.

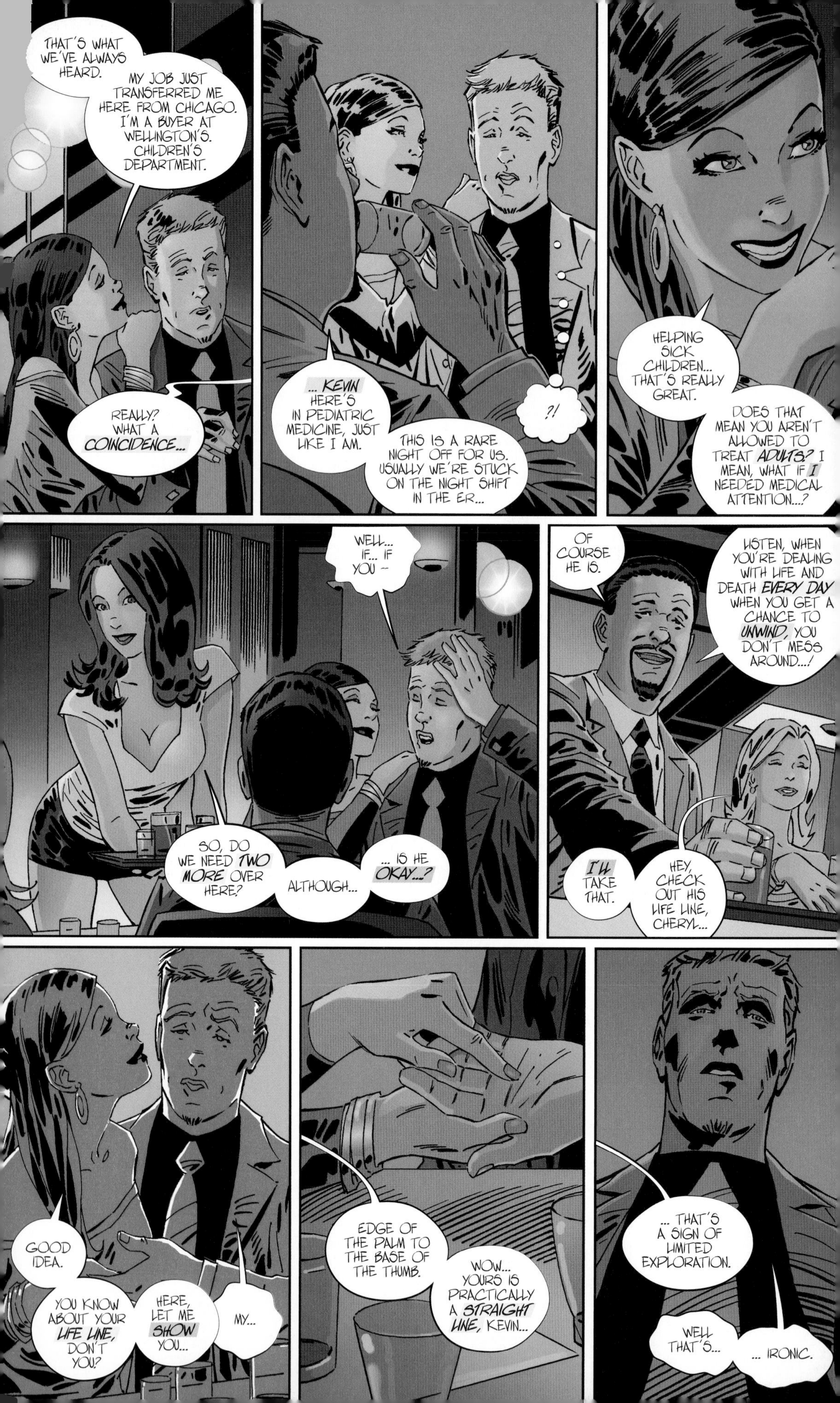

THAT'S WHAT WE'VE ALWAYS HEARD.
MY JOB JUST TRANSFERRED ME HERE FROM CHICAGO. I'M A BUYER AT WELLINGTON'S. CHILDREN'S DEPARTMENT.
REALLY? WHAT A COINCIDENCE...
... KEVIN HERE'S IN PEDIATRIC MEDICINE, JUST LIKE I AM.
THIS IS A RARE NIGHT OFF FOR US. USUALLY WE'RE STUCK ON THE NIGHT SHIFT IN THE ER...
?!
HELPING SICK CHILDREN... THAT'S REALLY GREAT.
DOES THAT MEAN YOU AREN'T ALLOWED TO TREAT ADULTS? I MEAN, WHAT IF I NEEDED MEDICAL ATTENTION...?
WELL... IF... IF YOU --
SO, DO WE NEED TWO MORE OVER HERE?
ALTHOUGH...
... IS HE OKAY...?
OF COURSE HE IS.
LISTEN, WHEN YOU'RE DEALING WITH LIFE AND DEATH EVERY DAY WHEN YOU GET A CHANCE TO UNWIND, YOU DON'T MESS AROUND...!
I'LL TAKE THAT.
HEY, CHECK OUT HIS LIFE LINE, CHERYL...
GOOD IDEA.
YOU KNOW ABOUT YOUR LIFE LINE, DON'T YOU?
HERE, LET ME SHOW YOU...
MY...
EDGE OF THE PALM TO THE BASE OF THE THUMB.
WOW... YOURS IS PRACTICALLY A STRAIGHT LINE, KEVIN...
... THAT'S A SIGN OF LIMITED EXPLORATION.
WELL THAT'S...
... IRONIC.

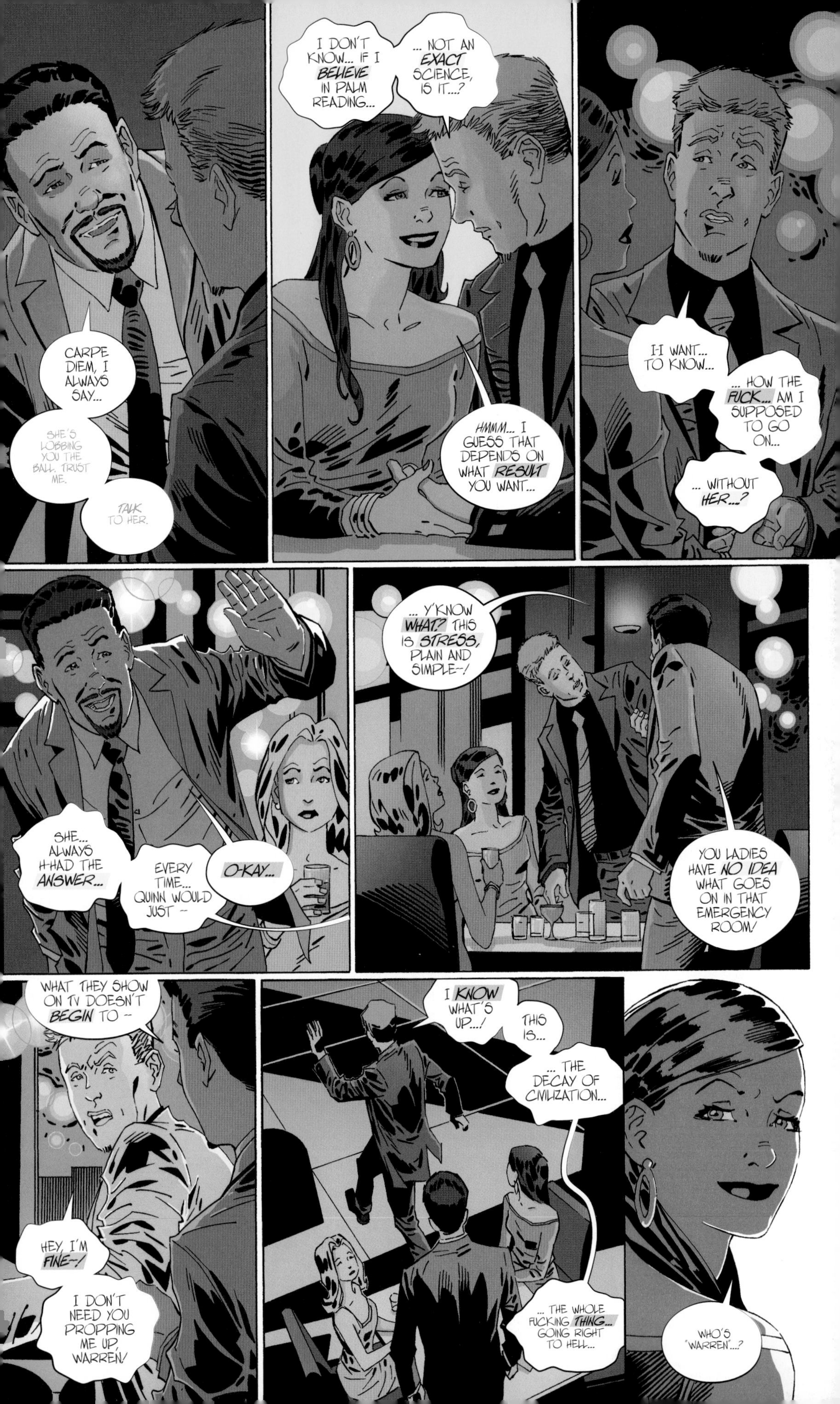
CARPE DIEM, I ALWAYS SAY...
SHE'S LOBBING YOU THE BALL. TRUST ME.
TALK TO HER.
I DON'T KNOW... IF I BELIEVE IN PALM READING...
... NOT AN EXACT SCIENCE, IS IT...?
HMMM... I GUESS THAT DEPENDS ON WHAT RESULT YOU WANT...
I-I WANT... TO KNOW...
... HOW THE FUCK... AM I SUPPOSED TO GO ON...
... WITHOUT HER...?
SHE... ALWAYS H-HAD THE ANSWER...
EVERY TIME... QUINN WOULD JUST --
O-KAY...
... Y'KNOW WHAT? THIS IS STRESS, PLAIN AND SIMPLE--!
YOU LADIES HAVE NO IDEA WHAT GOES ON IN THAT EMERGENCY ROOM!
WHAT THEY SHOW ON TV DOESN'T BEGIN TO --
HEY, I'M FINE--!
I DON'T NEED YOU PROPPING ME UP, WARREN!
I KNOW WHAT'S UP...!
THIS IS...
... THE DECAY OF CIVILIZATION...
... THE WHOLE FUCKING THING... GOING RIGHT TO HELL...
WHO'S "WARREN"...?

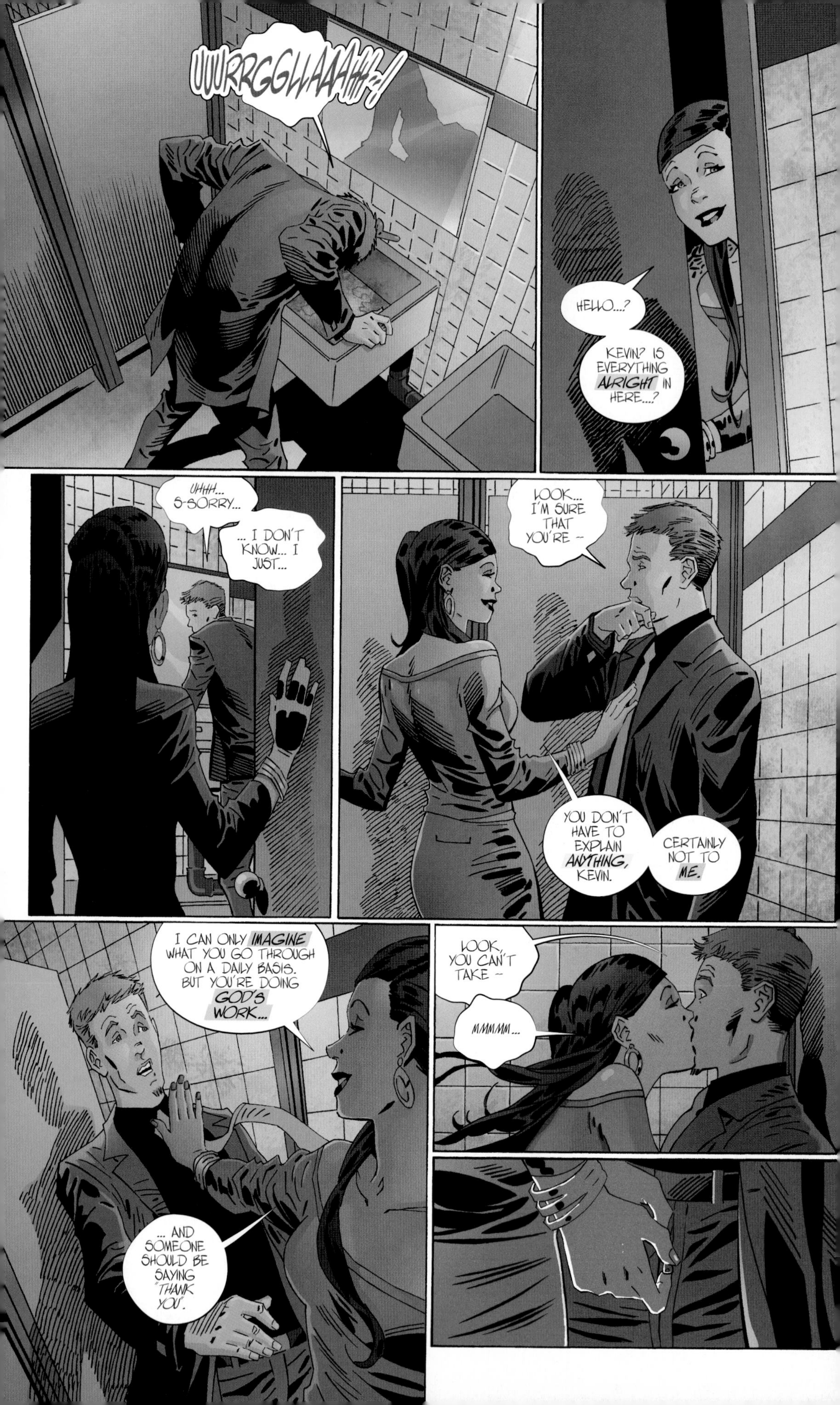
UUURRGGLLAAAHH-!
HELLO...?
KEVIN? IS EVERYTHING ALRIGHT IN HERE...?
UHHH... S-SORRY...
... I DON'T KNOW... I JUST...
LOOK... I'M SURE THAT YOU'RE --
YOU DON'T HAVE TO EXPLAIN ANYTHING, KEVIN.
CERTAINLY NOT TO ME.
I CAN ONLY IMAGINE WHAT YOU GO THROUGH ON A DAILY BASIS. BUT YOU'RE DOING GOD'S WORK...
... AND SOMEONE SHOULD BE SAYING "THANK YOU".
LOOK, YOU CAN'T TAKE --
MMMMM...

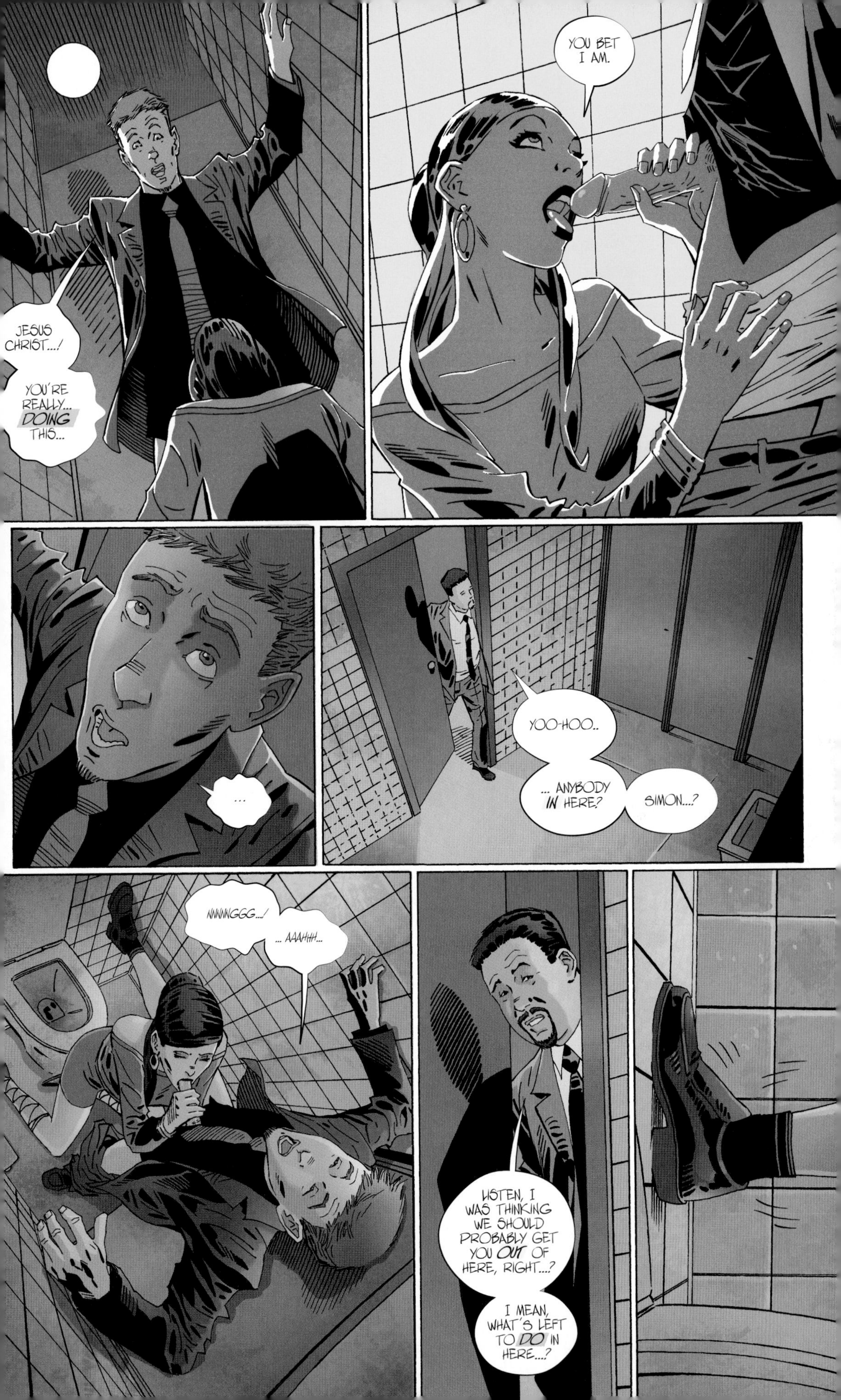
JESUS CHRIST...!
YOU'RE REALLY... DOING THIS...
YOU BET I AM.
...
YOO-HOO..
... ANYBODY IN HERE?
SIMON...?
NNNNNGGG...!
... AAAHHH...
LISTEN, I WAS THINKING WE SHOULD PROBABLY GET YOU OUT OF HERE, RIGHT...?
I MEAN, WHAT'S LEFT TO DO IN HERE...?

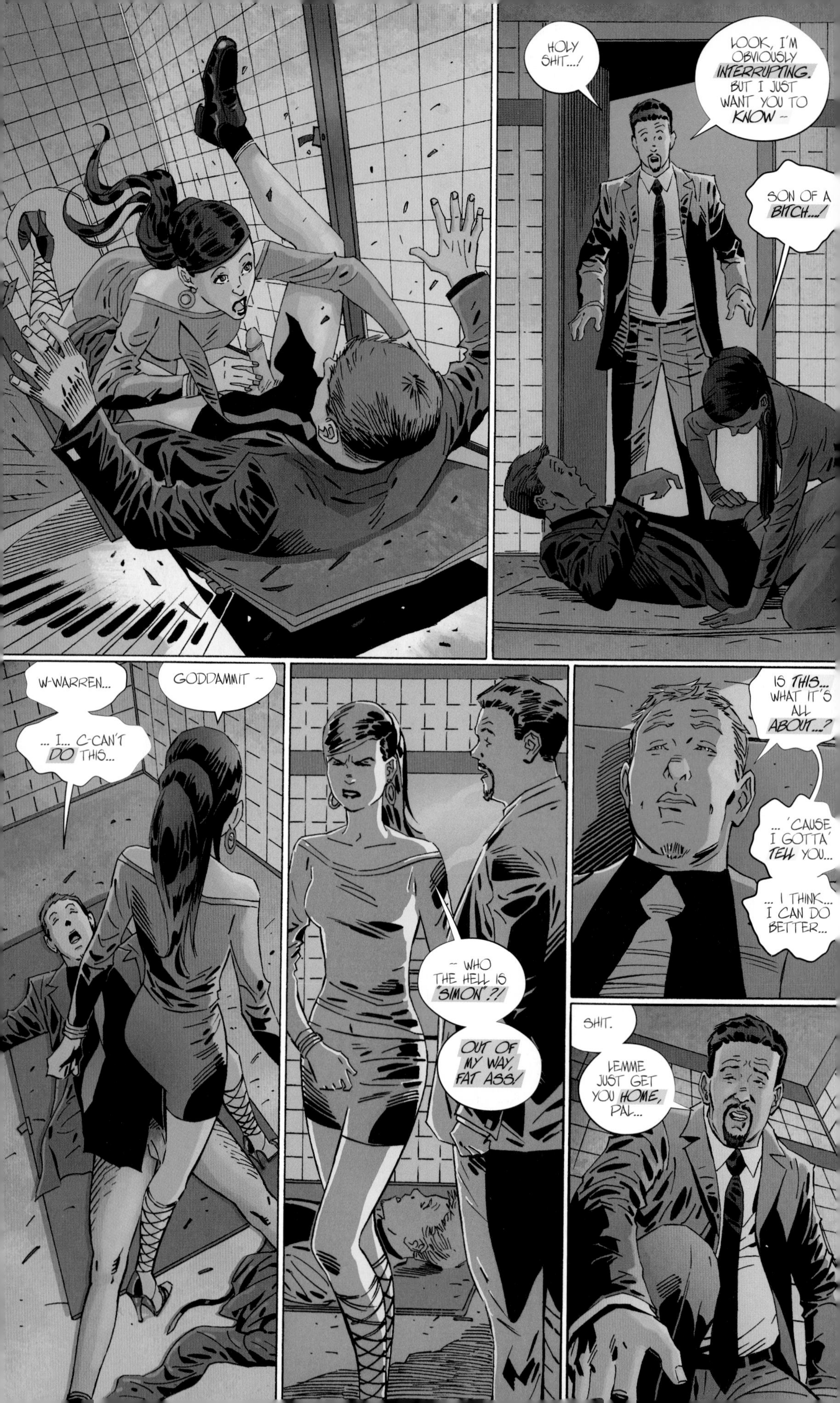
HOLY SHIT...!
LOOK, I'M OBVIOUSLY INTERRUPTING. BUT I JUST WANT YOU TO KNOW --
SON OF A BITCH...!
W-WARREN...
GODDAMMIT --
... I... C-CAN'T DO THIS...
-- WHO THE HELL IS "SIMON"?!
OUT OF MY WAY, FAT ASS!
IS THIS... WHAT IT'S ALL ABOUT...?
... 'CAUSE I GOTTA' TELL YOU...
... I THINK... I CAN DO BETTER...
SHIT.
LEMME JUST GET YOU HOME, PAL...

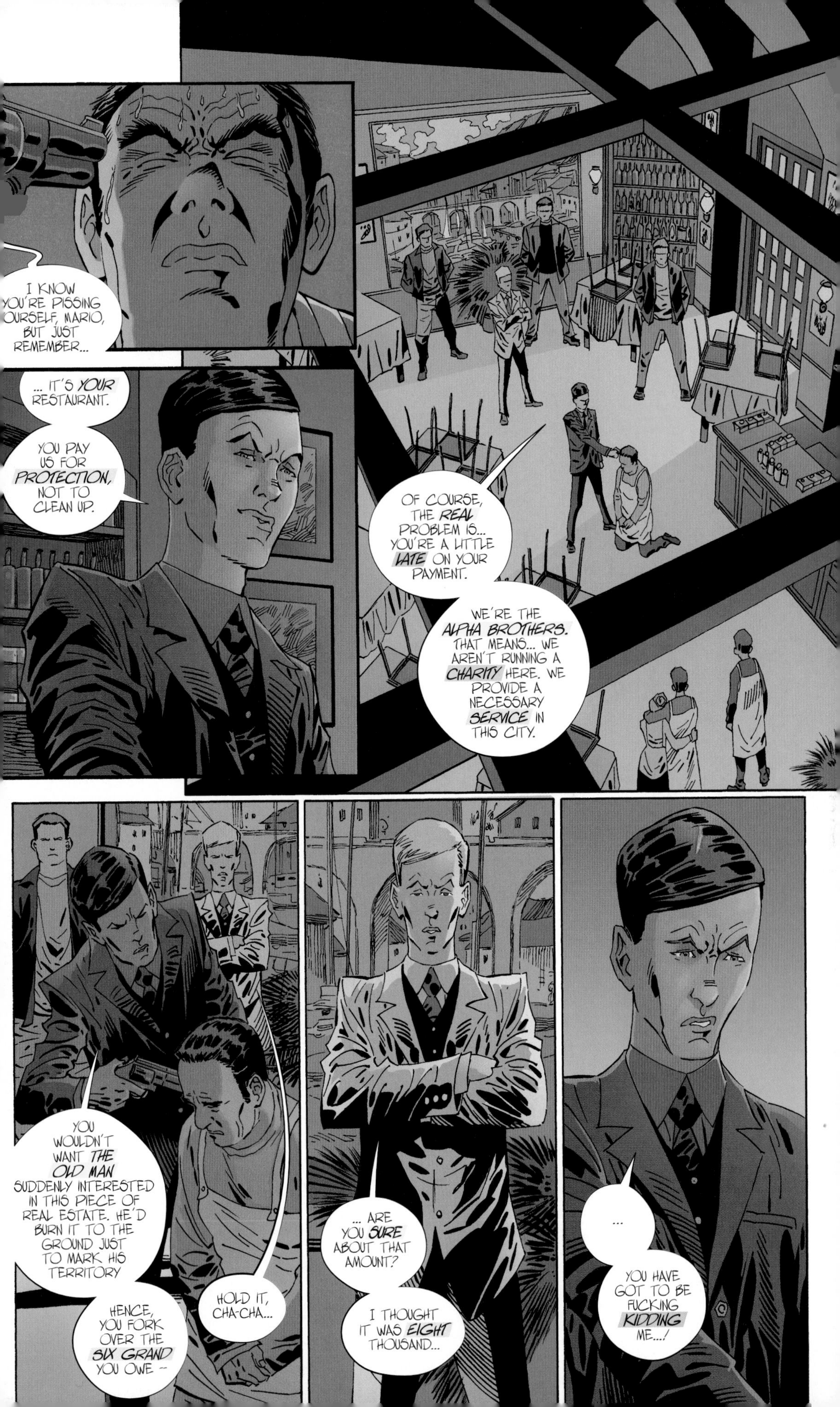

I KNOW YOU'RE PISSING OURSELF, MARIO, BUT JUST REMEMBER...
... IT'S YOUR RESTAURANT.
YOU PAY US FOR PROTECTION, NOT TO CLEAN UP.
OF COURSE, THE REAL PROBLEM IS... YOU'RE A LITTLE LATE ON YOUR PAYMENT.
WE'RE THE ALPHA BROTHERS. THAT MEANS... WE AREN'T RUNNING A CHARITY HERE. WE PROVIDE A NECESSARY SERVICE IN THIS CITY.
YOU WOULDN'T WANT THE OLD MAN SUDDENLY INTERESTED IN THIS PIECE OF REAL ESTATE. HE'D BURN IT TO THE GROUND JUST TO MARK HIS TERRITORY
HENCE, YOU FORK OVER THE SIX GRAND YOU OWE --
HOLD IT, CHA-CHA...
... ARE YOU SURE ABOUT THAT AMOUNT?
I THOUGHT IT WAS EIGHT THOUSAND...
...
YOU HAVE GOT TO BE FUCKING KIDDING ME...!

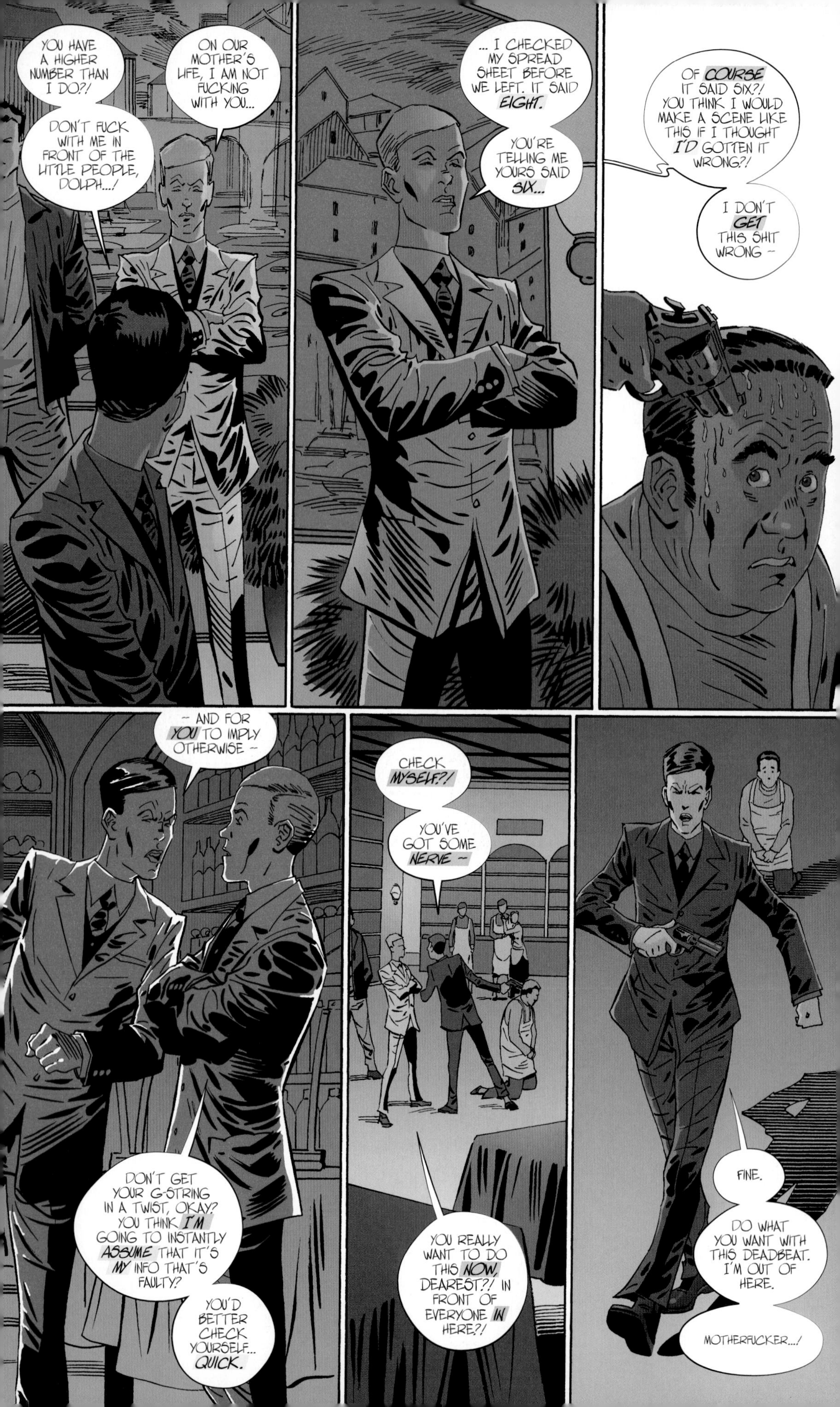
YOU HAVE A HIGHER NUMBER THAN I DO?!
DON'T FUCK WITH ME IN FRONT OF THE LITTLE PEOPLE, DOLPH...!
ON OUR MOTHER'S LIFE, I AM NOT FUCKING WITH YOU...
... I CHECKED MY SPREAD SHEET BEFORE WE LEFT. IT SAID EIGHT.
YOU'RE TELLING ME YOURS SAID SIX...
OF COURSE IT SAID SIX?! YOU THINK I WOULD MAKE A SCENE LIKE THIS IF I THOUGHT I'D GOTTEN IT WRONG?!
I DON'T GET THIS SHIT WRONG --
-- AND FOR YOU TO IMPLY OTHERWISE --
DON'T GET YOUR G-STRING IN A TWIST, OKAY? YOU THINK I'M GOING TO INSTANTLY ASSUME THAT IT'S MY INFO THAT'S FAULTY?
YOU'D BETTER CHECK YOURSELF... QUICK.
CHECK MYSELF?!
YOU'VE GOT SOME NERVE --
YOU REALLY WANT TO DO THIS NOW, DEAREST?! IN FRONT OF EVERYONE IN HERE?!
FINE.
DO WHAT YOU WANT WITH THIS DEADBEAT. I'M OUT OF HERE.
MOTHERFUCKER...!

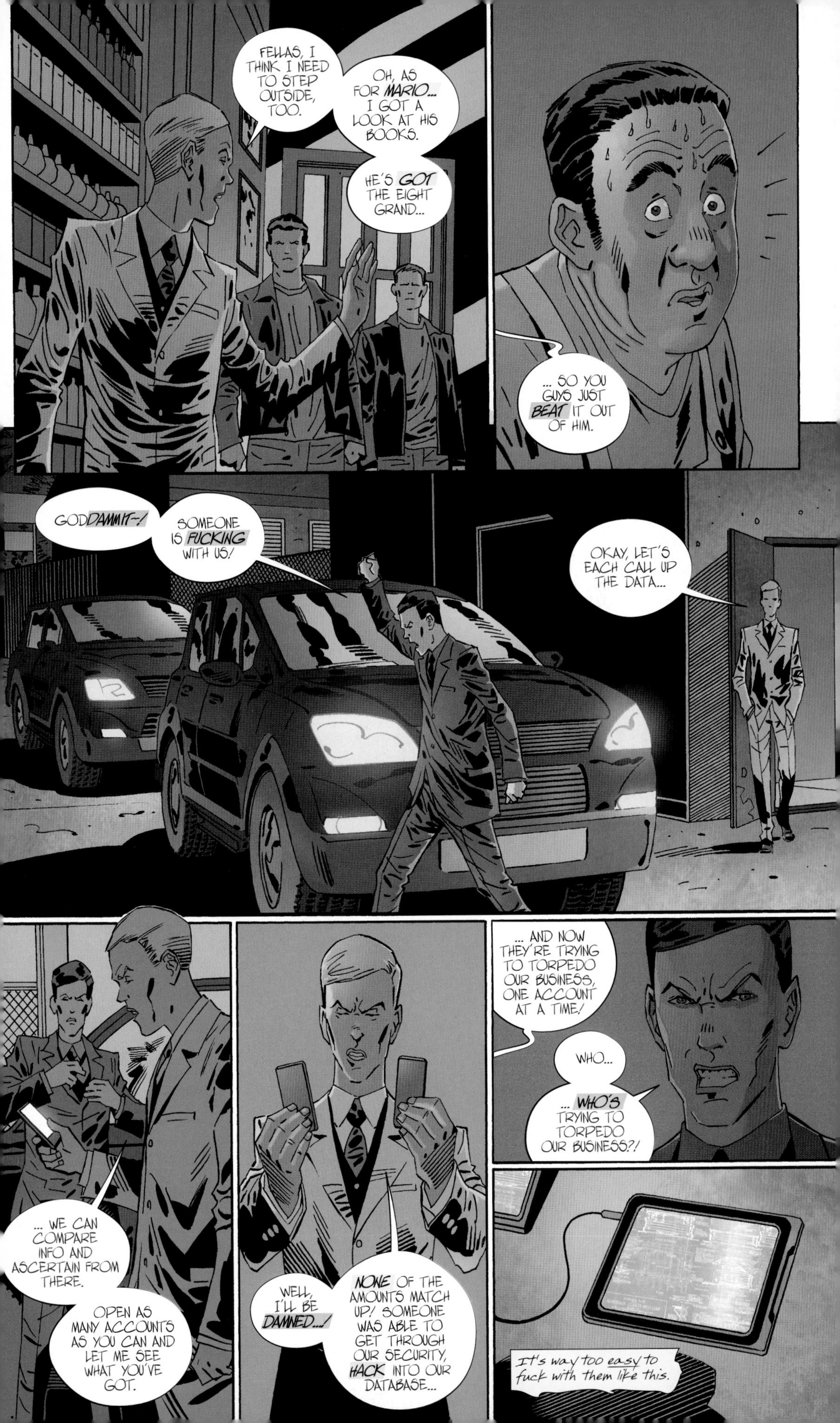
FELLAS, I THINK I NEED TO STEP OUTSIDE, TOO.
OH, AS FOR MARIO... I GOT A LOOK AT HIS BOOKS.
HE'S GOT THE EIGHT GRAND...
... SO YOU GUYS JUST BEAT IT OUT OF HIM.
GODDAMMIT--!
SOMEONE IS FUCKING WITH US!
OKAY, LET'S EACH CALL UP THE DATA...
... WE CAN COMPARE INFO AND ASCERTAIN FROM THERE.
OPEN AS MANY ACCOUNTS AS YOU CAN AND LET ME SEE WHAT YOU'VE GOT.
WELL, I'LL BE DAMNED...!
NONE OF THE AMOUNTS MATCH UP! SOMEONE WAS ABLE TO GET THROUGH OUR SECURITY, HACK INTO OUR DATABASE...
... AND NOW THEY'RE TRYING TO TORPEDO OUR BUSINESS, ONE ACCOUNT AT A TIME!
WHO...
... WHO'S TRYING TO TORPEDO OUR BUSINESS?!
It's way too easy to fuck with them like this.

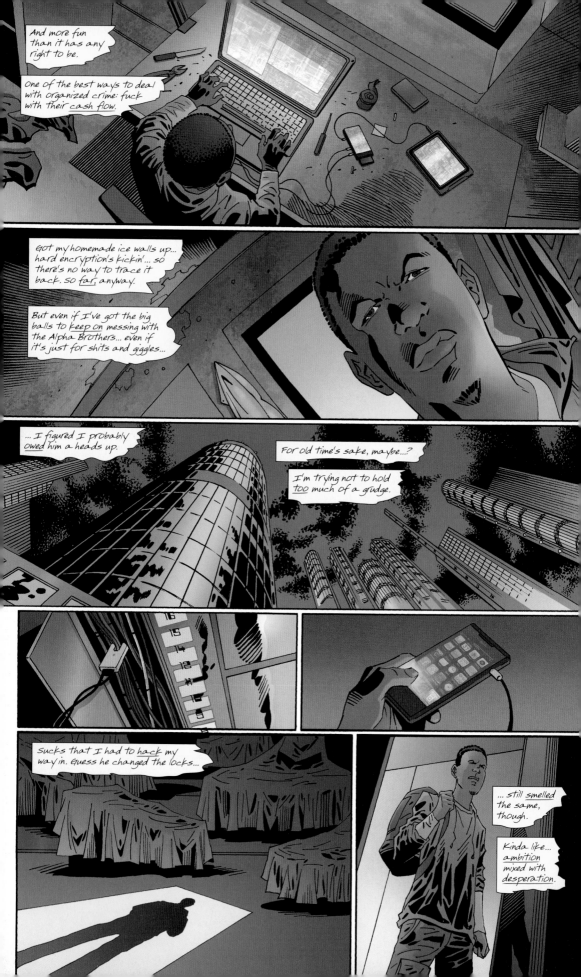

And more fun than it has any right to be.

One of the best ways to deal with organized crime: fuck with their cash flow.

Got my homemade ice walls up... hard encryption's kickin'... so there's no way to trace it back. So far, anyway.

But even if I've got the big balls to keep on messing with the Alpha Brothers... even if it's just for shits and giggles...

...I figured I probably owed him a heads up.

For old time's sake, maybe...?

I'm trying not to hold too much of a grudge.

Sucks that I had to hack my way in. Guess he changed the locks...

...still smelled the same, though.

Kinda like... ambition mixed with desperation.

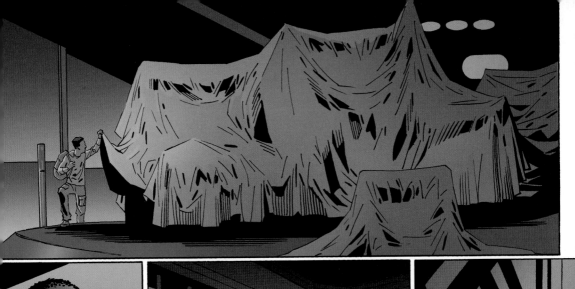

Okay, I knew he wouldn't be hanging around on the Thirteenth floor...

...but I was stalling.

JEEZUS CHRIST... YOU'RE HEAVIER THAN YOU LOOK...

... LET'S JUST... G-GET UP TO YOUR GODDAMN BED...

=HUHHN=

COME ON... HELP ME OUT HERE...

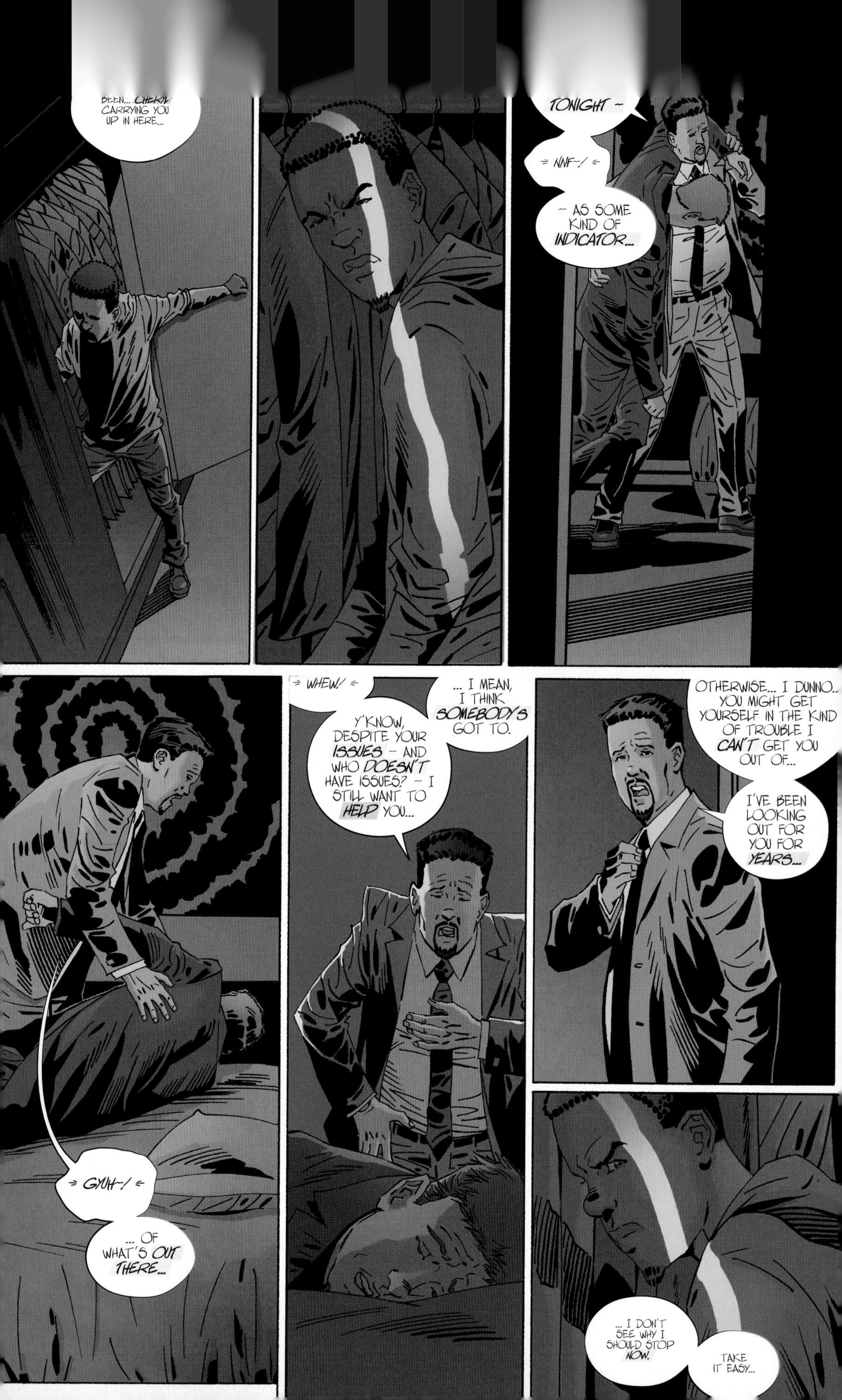

BEEN... CHERYL CARRYING YOU UP IN HERE...
TONIGHT --
NNF--!
-- AS SOME KIND OF INDICATOR...
GYUH--!
... OF WHAT'S OUT THERE...
WHEW!
Y'KNOW, DESPITE YOUR ISSUES -- AND WHO DOESN'T HAVE ISSUES? -- I STILL WANT TO HELP YOU...
... I MEAN, I THINK SOMEBODY'S GOT TO.
OTHERWISE... I DUNNO... YOU MIGHT GET YOURSELF IN THE KIND OF TROUBLE I CAN'T GET YOU OUT OF...
I'VE BEEN LOOKING OUT FOR YOU FOR YEARS...
... I DON'T SEE WHY I SHOULD STOP NOW.
TAKE IT EASY...

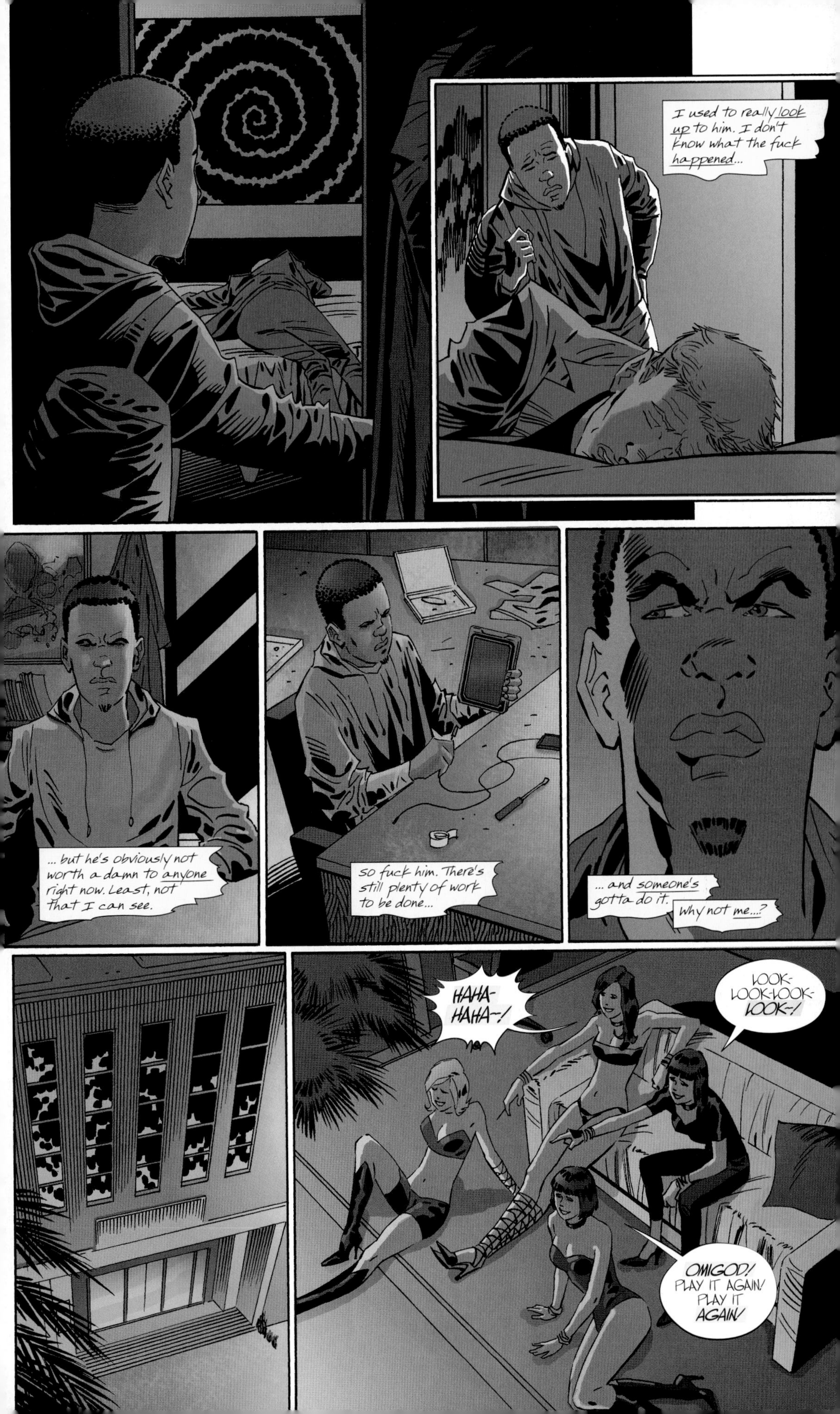
I used to really look up to him. I don't know what the fuck happened...
... but he's obviously not worth a damn to anyone right now. Least, not that I can see.
so fuck him. There's still plenty of work to be done...
... and someone's gotta do it.
Why not me...?
HAHA-HAHA--!
LOOK-LOOK-LOOK-LOOK--!
OMIGOD! PLAY IT AGAIN! PLAY IT AGAIN!

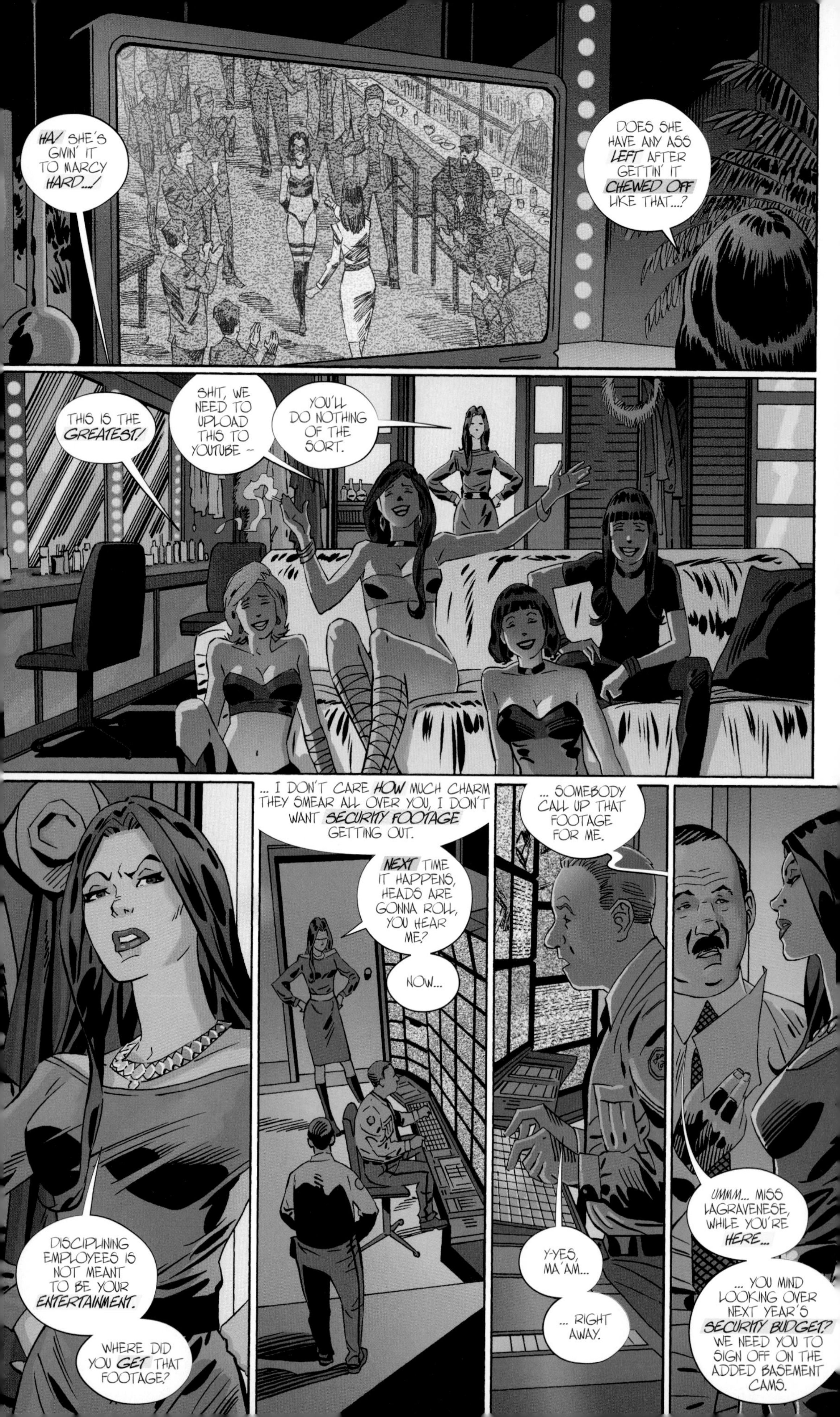
HA! SHE'S GIVIN' IT TO MARCY HARD...!
DOES SHE HAVE ANY ASS LEFT AFTER GETTIN' IT CHEWED OFF LIKE THAT...?
THIS IS THE GREATEST!
SHIT, WE NEED TO UPLOAD THIS TO YOUTUBE --
YOU'LL DO NOTHING OF THE SORT.
DISCIPLINING EMPLOYEES IS NOT MEANT TO BE YOUR ENTERTAINMENT.
WHERE DID YOU GET THAT FOOTAGE?
... I DON'T CARE HOW MUCH CHARM THEY SMEAR ALL OVER YOU, I DON'T WANT SECURITY FOOTAGE GETTING OUT.
NEXT TIME IT HAPPENS, HEADS ARE GONNA ROLL, YOU HEAR ME?
NOW...
... SOMEBODY CALL UP THAT FOOTAGE FOR ME.
Y-YES, MA'AM...
... RIGHT AWAY.
UMMM... MISS LAGRAVENESE, WHILE YOU'RE HERE...
... YOU MIND LOOKING OVER NEXT YEAR'S SECURITY BUDGET? WE NEED YOU TO SIGN OFF ON THE ADDED BASEMENT CAMS.

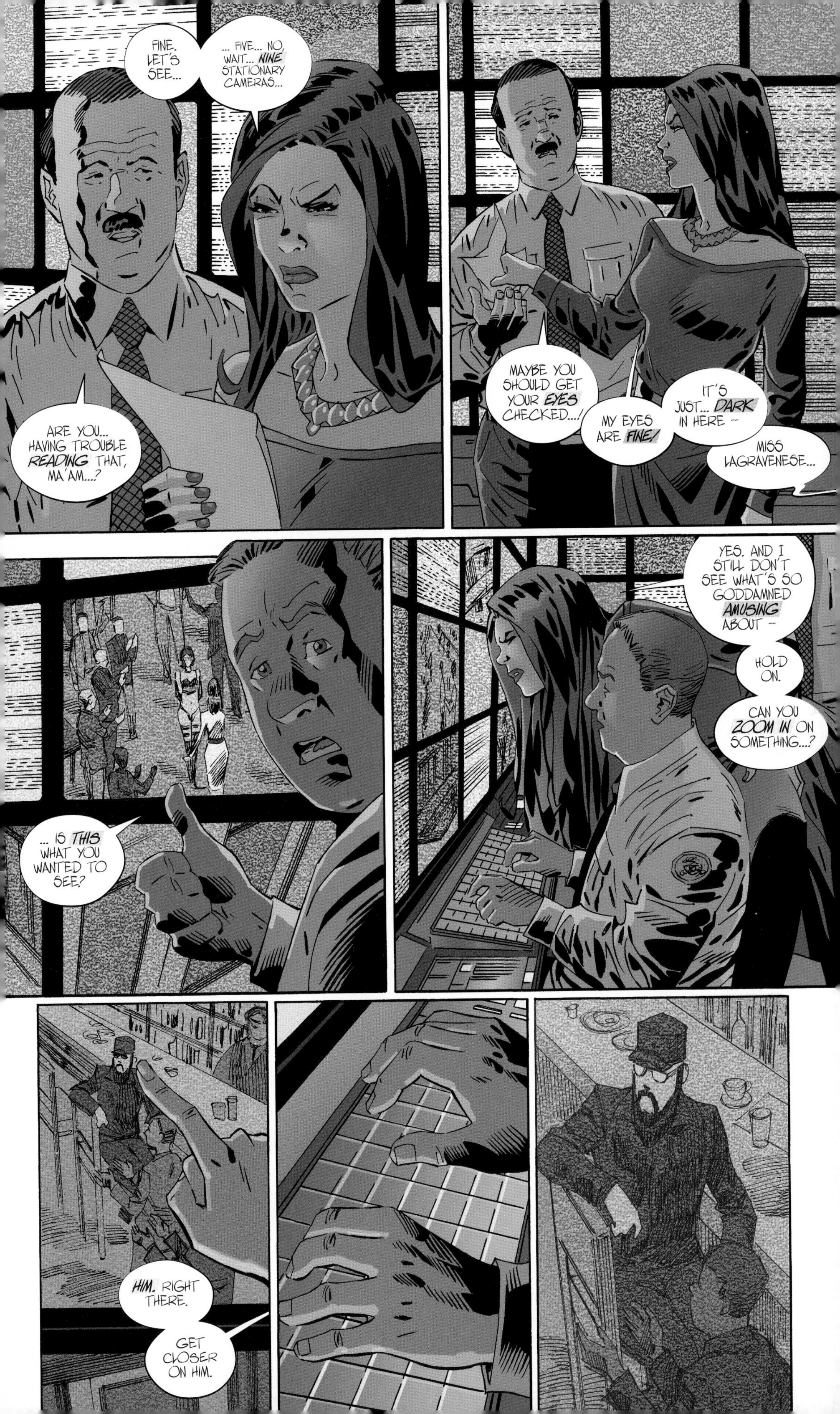
FINE. LET'S SEE...
... FIVE... NO, WAIT... NINE STATIONARY CAMERAS...
ARE YOU... HAVING TROUBLE READING THAT, MA'AM...?
MAYBE YOU SHOULD GET YOUR EYES CHECKED...!
MY EYES ARE FINE!
IT'S JUST... DARK IN HERE --
MISS LAGRAVENESE...
... IS THIS WHAT YOU WANTED TO SEE?
YES. AND I STILL DON'T SEE WHAT'S SO GODDAMNED AMUSING ABOUT --
HOLD ON.
CAN YOU ZOOM IN ON SOMETHING...?
HIM. RIGHT THERE.
GET CLOSER ON HIM.

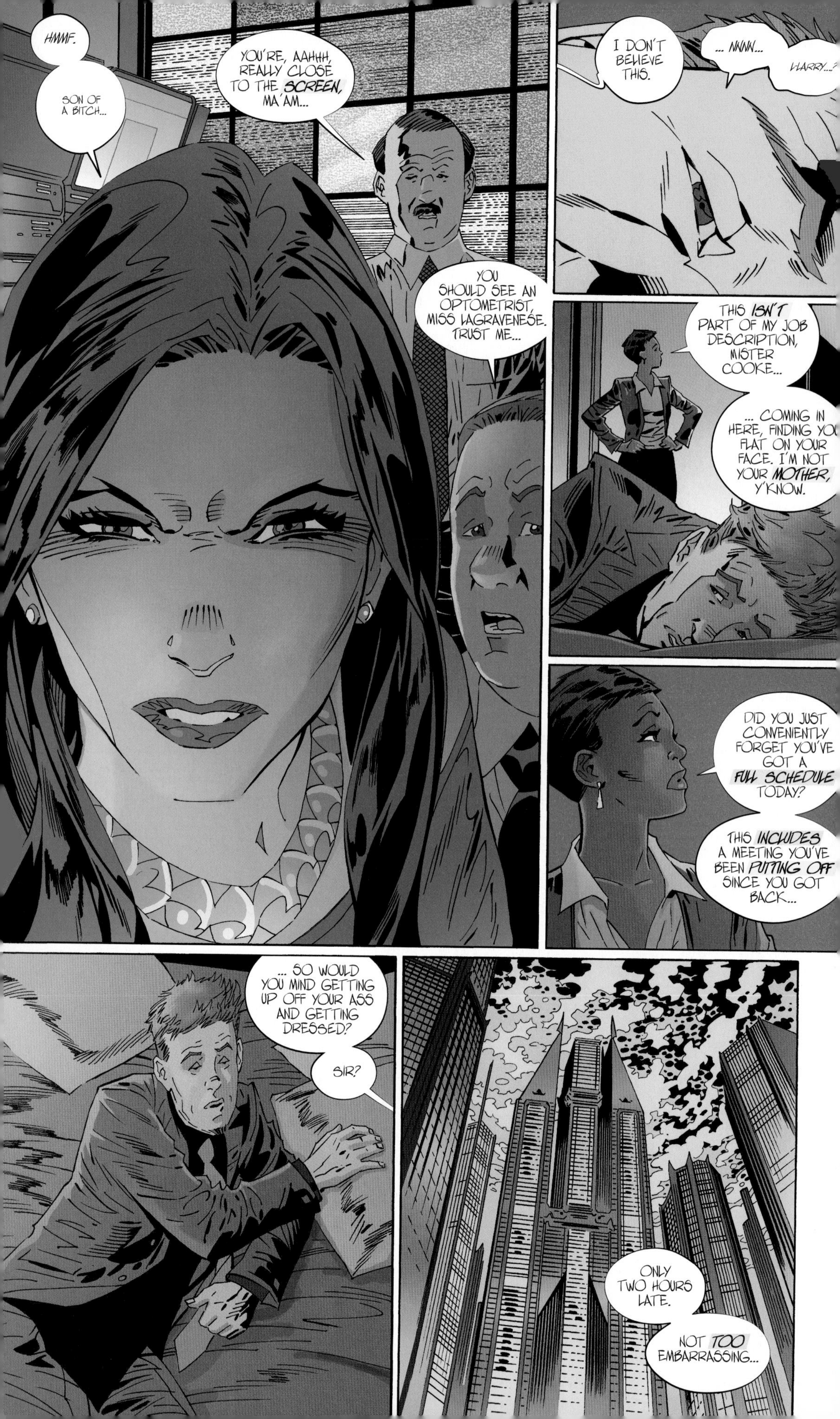
HMMF.
SON OF A BITCH...
YOU'RE, AAHHH, REALLY CLOSE TO THE SCREEN, MA'AM...
YOU SHOULD SEE AN OPTOMETRIST, MISS LAGRAVENESE. TRUST ME...
I DON'T BELIEVE THIS.
... NNNN...
HARRY...?
THIS ISN'T PART OF MY JOB DESCRIPTION, MISTER COOKE...
... COMING IN HERE, FINDING YOU FLAT ON YOUR FACE. I'M NOT YOUR MOTHER, Y'KNOW.
DID YOU JUST CONVENIENTLY FORGET YOU'VE GOT A FULL SCHEDULE TODAY?
THIS INCLUDES A MEETING YOU'VE BEEN PUTTING OFF SINCE YOU GOT BACK...
... SO WOULD YOU MIND GETTING UP OFF YOUR ASS AND GETTING DRESSED?
SIR?
ONLY TWO HOURS LATE.
NOT TOO EMBARRASSING...

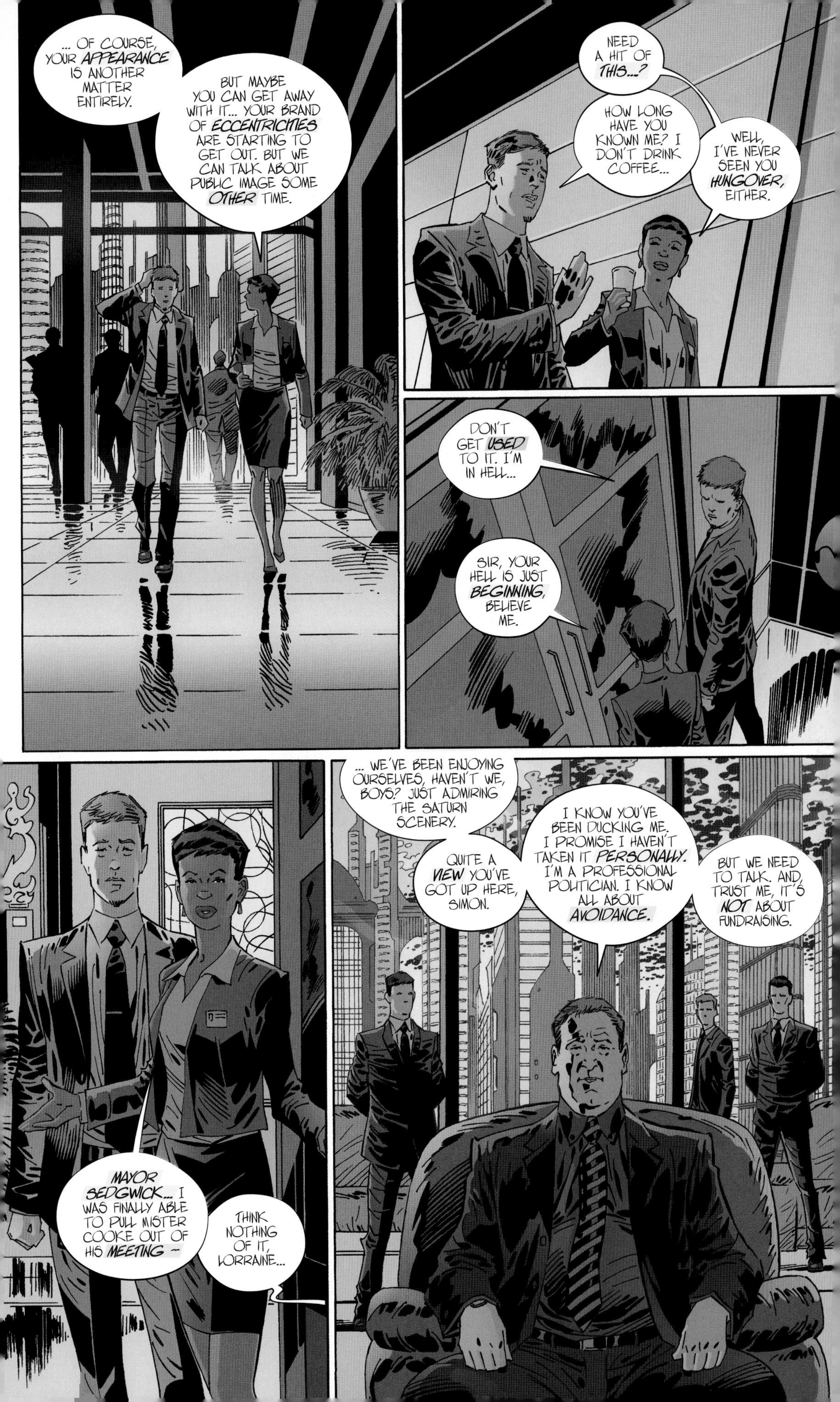
... OF COURSE, YOUR APPEARANCE IS ANOTHER MATTER ENTIRELY.
BUT MAYBE YOU CAN GET AWAY WITH IT... YOUR BRAND OF ECCENTRICITIES ARE STARTING TO GET OUT. BUT WE CAN TALK ABOUT PUBLIC IMAGE SOME OTHER TIME.
NEED A HIT OF THIS...?
HOW LONG HAVE YOU KNOWN ME? I DON'T DRINK COFFEE...
WELL, I'VE NEVER SEEN YOU HUNGOVER, EITHER.
DON'T GET USED TO IT. I'M IN HELL...
SIR, YOUR HELL IS JUST BEGINNING, BELIEVE ME.
MAYOR SEDGWICK... I WAS FINALLY ABLE TO PULL MISTER COOKE OUT OF HIS MEETING --
THINK NOTHING OF IT, LORRAINE...
... WE'VE BEEN ENJOYING OURSELVES, HAVEN'T WE, BOYS? JUST ADMIRING THE SATURN SCENERY.
QUITE A VIEW YOU'VE GOT UP HERE, SIMON.
I KNOW YOU'VE BEEN DUCKING ME. I PROMISE I HAVEN'T TAKEN IT PERSONALLY. I'M A PROFESSIONAL POLITICIAN. I KNOW ALL ABOUT AVOIDANCE.
BUT WE NEED TO TALK. AND, TRUST ME, IT'S NOT ABOUT FUNDRAISING.

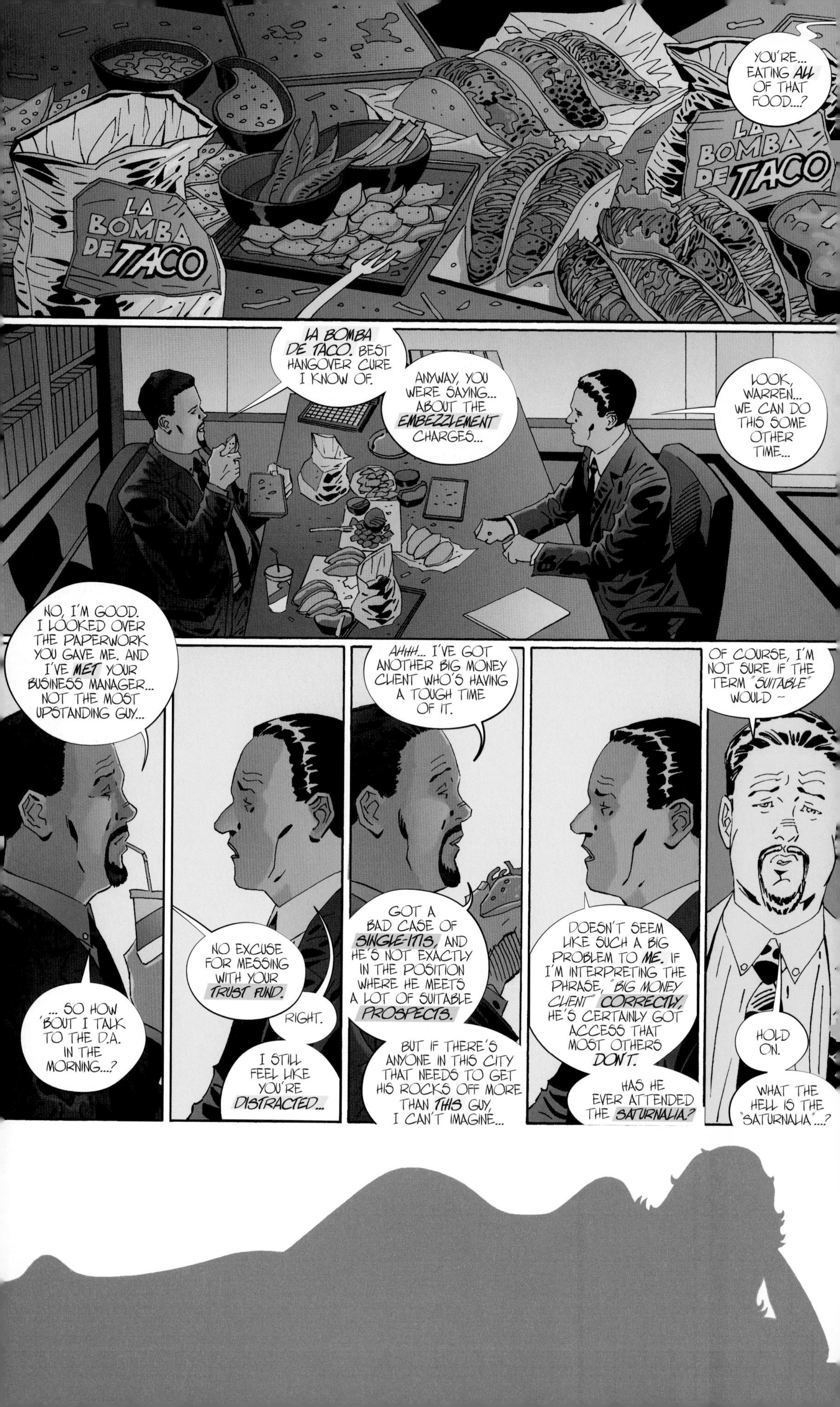
YOU'RE... EATING ALL OF THAT FOOD...?
LA BOMBA DE TACO
LA BOMBA DE TACO
LA BOMBA DE TACO. BEST HANGOVER CURE I KNOW OF.
ANYWAY, YOU WERE SAYING... ABOUT THE EMBEZZLEMENT CHARGES...
LOOK, WARREN... WE CAN DO THIS SOME OTHER TIME...
NO, I'M GOOD. I LOOKED OVER THE PAPERWORK YOU GAVE ME. AND I'VE MET YOUR BUSINESS MANAGER... NOT THE MOST UPSTANDING GUY...
... SO HOW 'BOUT I TALK TO THE D.A. IN THE MORNING...?
NO EXCUSE FOR MESSING WITH YOUR TRUST FUND.
RIGHT.
I STILL FEEL LIKE YOU'RE DISTRACTED...
AHHH... I'VE GOT ANOTHER BIG MONEY CLIENT WHO'S HAVING A TOUGH TIME OF IT.
GOT A BAD CASE OF SINGLE-ITIS, AND HE'S NOT EXACTLY IN THE POSITION WHERE HE MEETS A LOT OF SUITABLE PROSPECTS.
BUT IF THERE'S ANYONE IN THIS CITY THAT NEEDS TO GET HIS ROCKS OFF MORE THAN THIS GUY, I CAN'T IMAGINE...
DOESN'T SEEM LIKE SUCH A BIG PROBLEM TO ME. IF I'M INTERPRETING THE PHRASE, "BIG MONEY CLIENT" CORRECTLY, HE'S CERTAINLY GOT ACCESS THAT MOST OTHERS DON'T.
HAS HE EVER ATTENDED THE SATURNALIA?
OF COURSE, I'M NOT SURE IF THE TERM "SUITABLE" WOULD --
HOLD ON.
WHAT THE HELL IS THE "SATURNALIA"...?

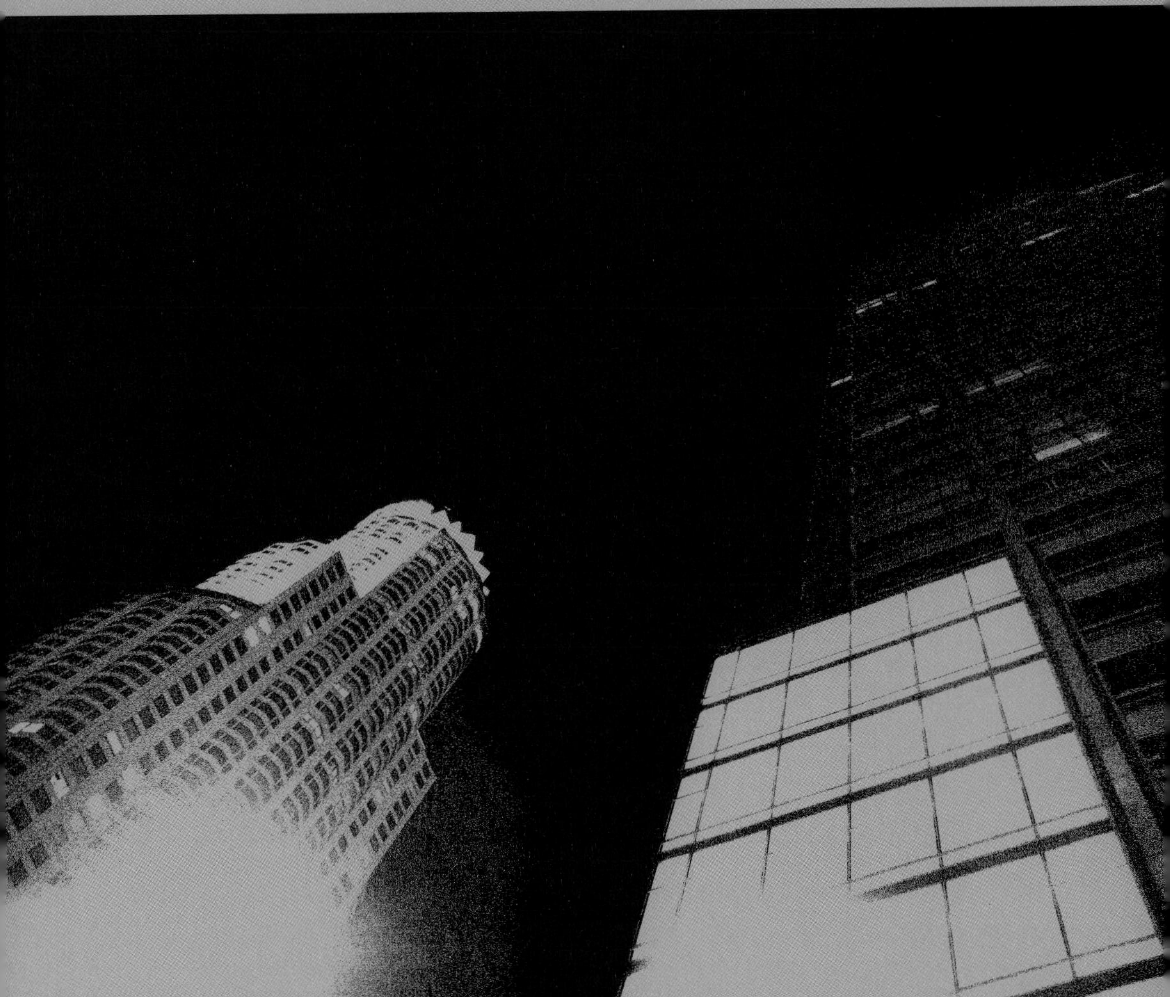

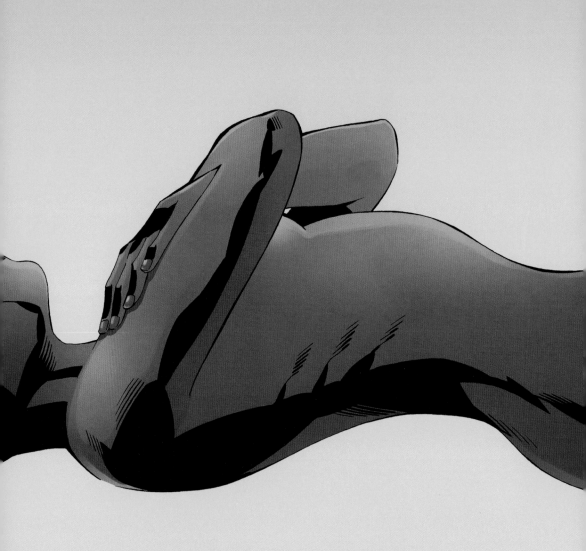

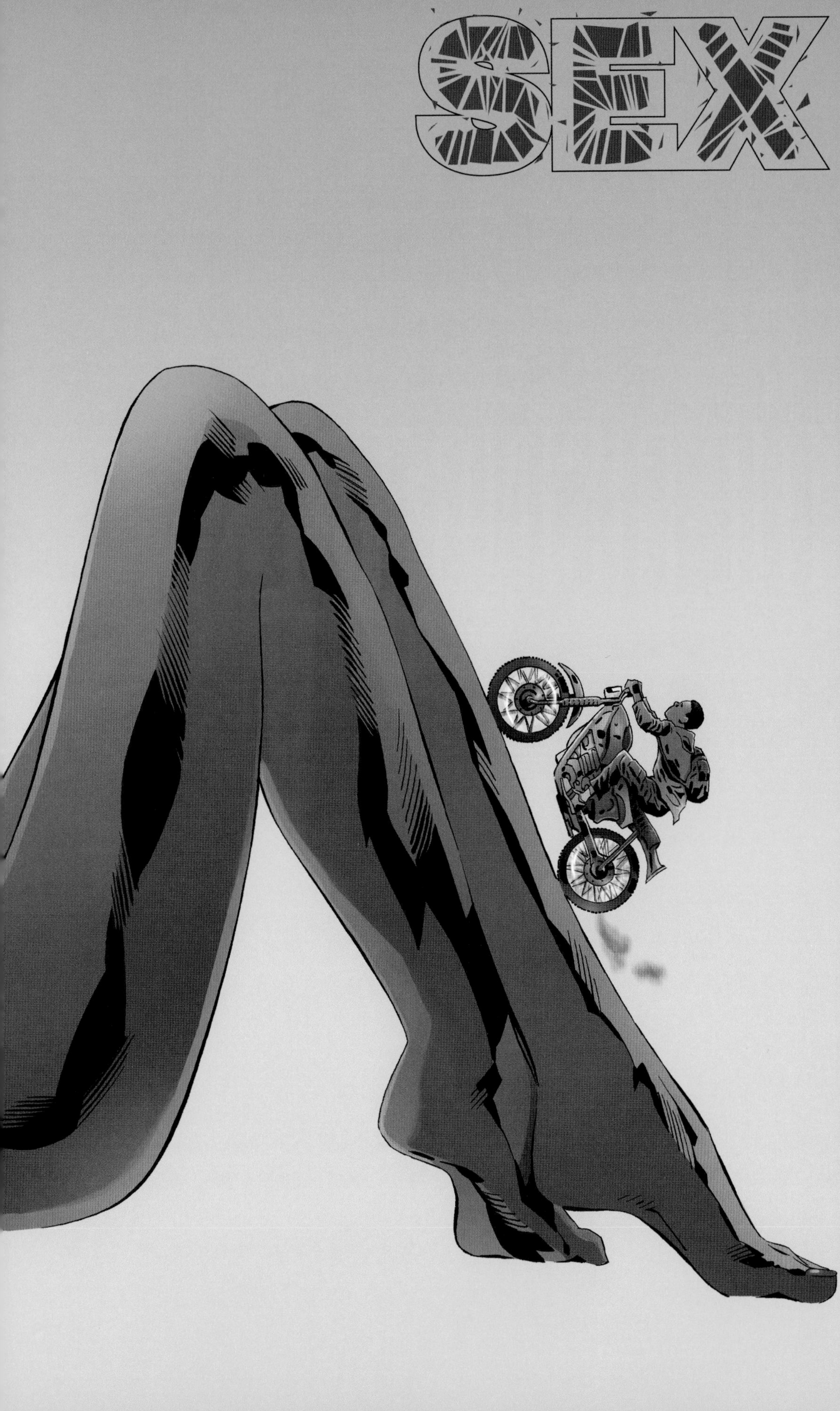
SEX

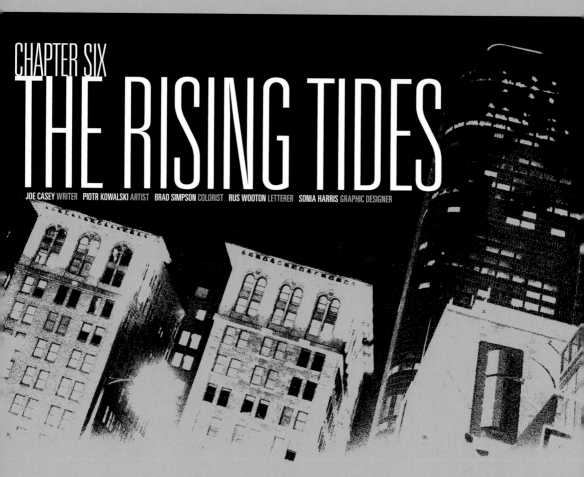

CHAPTER SIX
THE RISING TIDES

JOE CASEY WRITER PIOTR KOWALSKI ARTIST BRAD SIMPSON COLORIST RUS WOOTON LETTERER SONIA HARRIS GRAPHIC DESIGNER

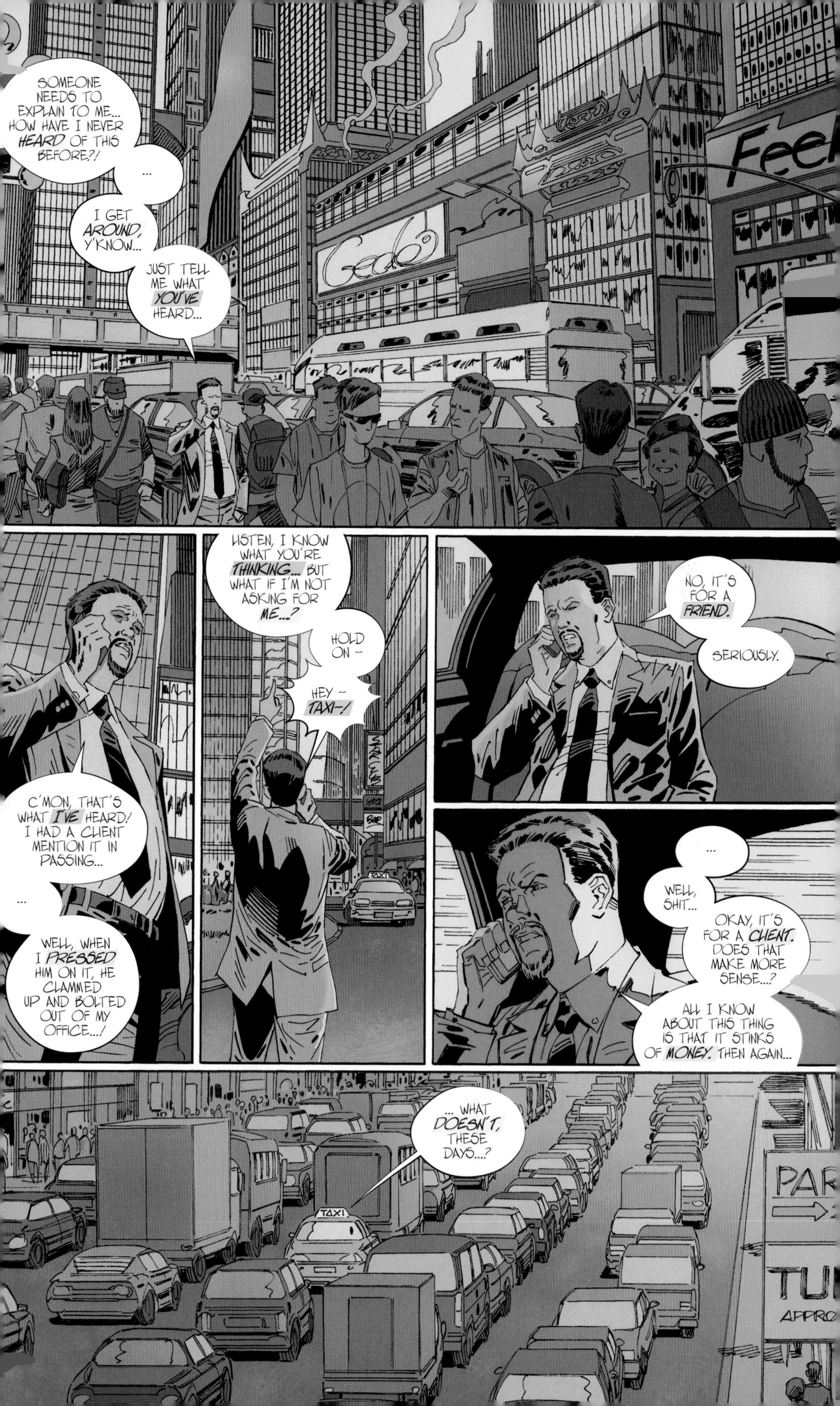

SOMEONE NEEDS TO EXPLAIN TO ME... HOW HAVE I NEVER HEARD OF THIS BEFORE?!
...
I GET AROUND, Y'KNOW...
JUST TELL ME WHAT YOU'VE HEARD...
C'MON, THAT'S WHAT I'VE HEARD! I HAD A CLIENT MENTION IT IN PASSING...
...
WELL, WHEN I PRESSED HIM ON IT, HE CLAMMED UP AND BOLTED OUT OF MY OFFICE...!
LISTEN, I KNOW WHAT YOU'RE THINKING... BUT WHAT IF I'M NOT ASKING FOR ME...?
HOLD ON --
HEY -- TAXI~!
TAXI
NO, IT'S FOR A FRIEND.
SERIOUSLY.
...
WELL, SHIT...
OKAY, IT'S FOR A CLIENT. DOES THAT MAKE MORE SENSE...?
ALL I KNOW ABOUT THIS THING IS THAT IT STINKS OF MONEY. THEN AGAIN...
... WHAT DOESN'T, THESE DAYS...?
TAXI

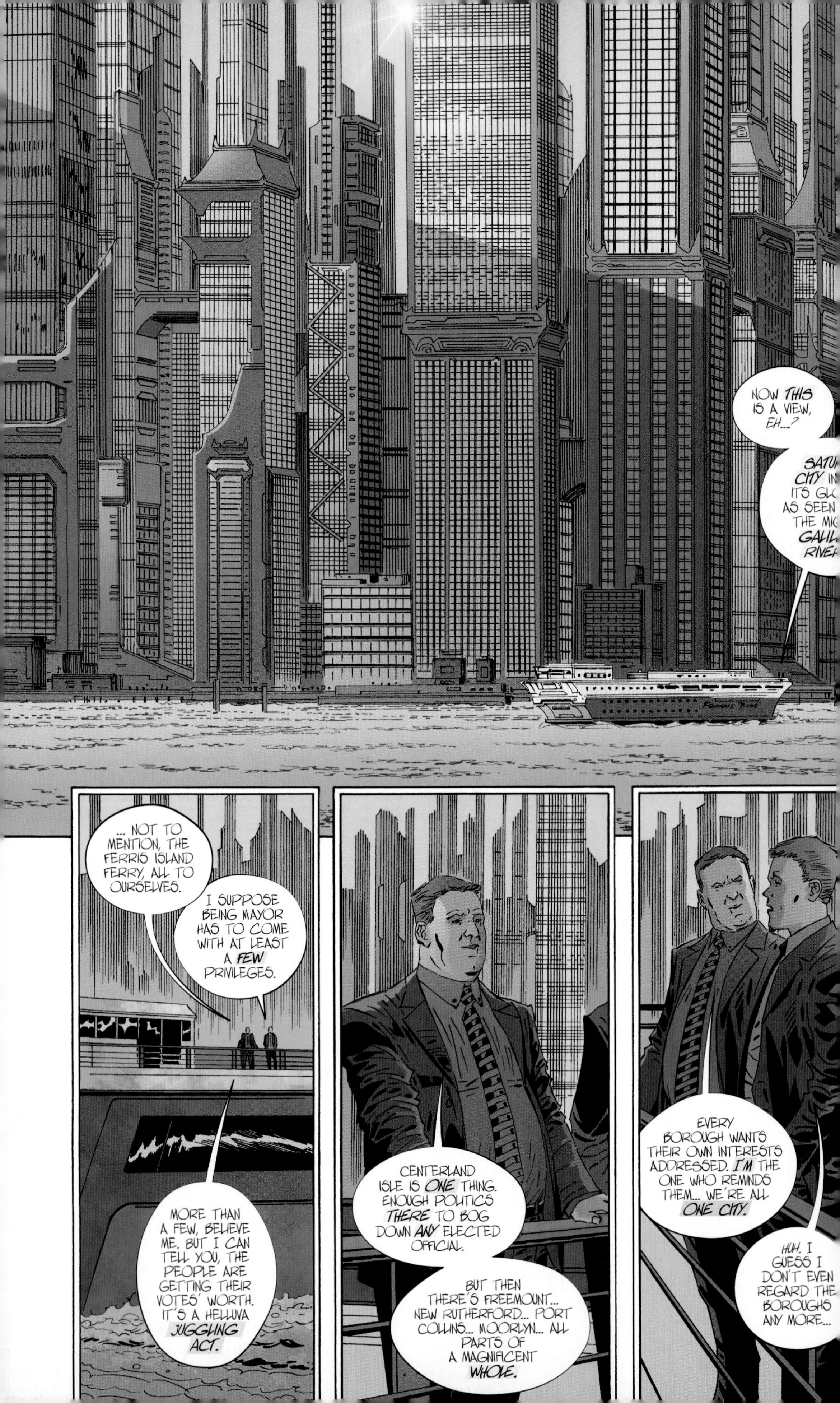
NOW THIS IS A VIEW, EH...?
SATU
CITY IN
ITS GLO
AS SEEN
THE MIG
GALIL
RIVER
... NOT TO MENTION, THE FERRIS ISLAND FERRY, ALL TO OURSELVES.
I SUPPOSE BEING MAYOR HAS TO COME WITH AT LEAST A FEW PRIVILEGES.
MORE THAN A FEW, BELIEVE ME. BUT I CAN TELL YOU, THE PEOPLE ARE GETTING THEIR VOTES' WORTH. IT'S A HELLUVA JUGGLING ACT.
CENTERLAND ISLE IS ONE THING. ENOUGH POLITICS THERE TO BOG DOWN ANY ELECTED OFFICIAL.
BUT THEN THERE'S FREEMOUNT... NEW RUTHERFORD... PORT COLLINS... MOORLYN... ALL PARTS OF A MAGNIFICENT WHOLE.
EVERY BOROUGH WANTS THEIR OWN INTERESTS ADDRESSED. I'M THE ONE WHO REMINDS THEM... WE'RE ALL ONE CITY.
HUH. I GUESS I DON'T EVEN REGARD THE BOROUGHS ANY MORE...

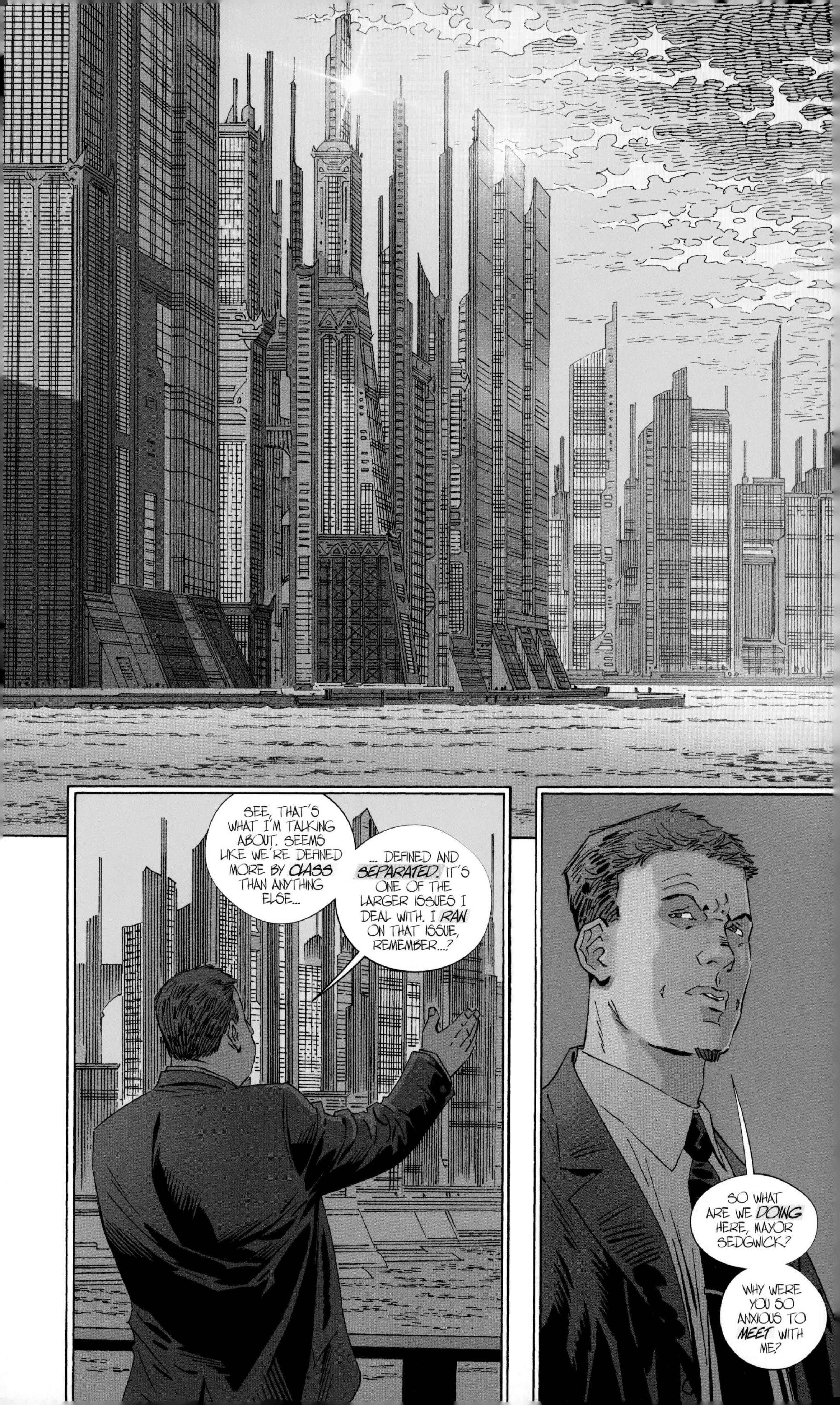
SEE, THAT'S WHAT I'M TALKING ABOUT. SEEMS LIKE WE'RE DEFINED MORE BY CLASS THAN ANYTHING ELSE...
... DEFINED AND SEPARATED. IT'S ONE OF THE LARGER ISSUES I DEAL WITH. I RAN ON THAT ISSUE, REMEMBER...?
SO WHAT ARE WE DOING HERE, MAYOR SEDGWICK?
WHY WERE YOU SO ANXIOUS TO MEET WITH ME?

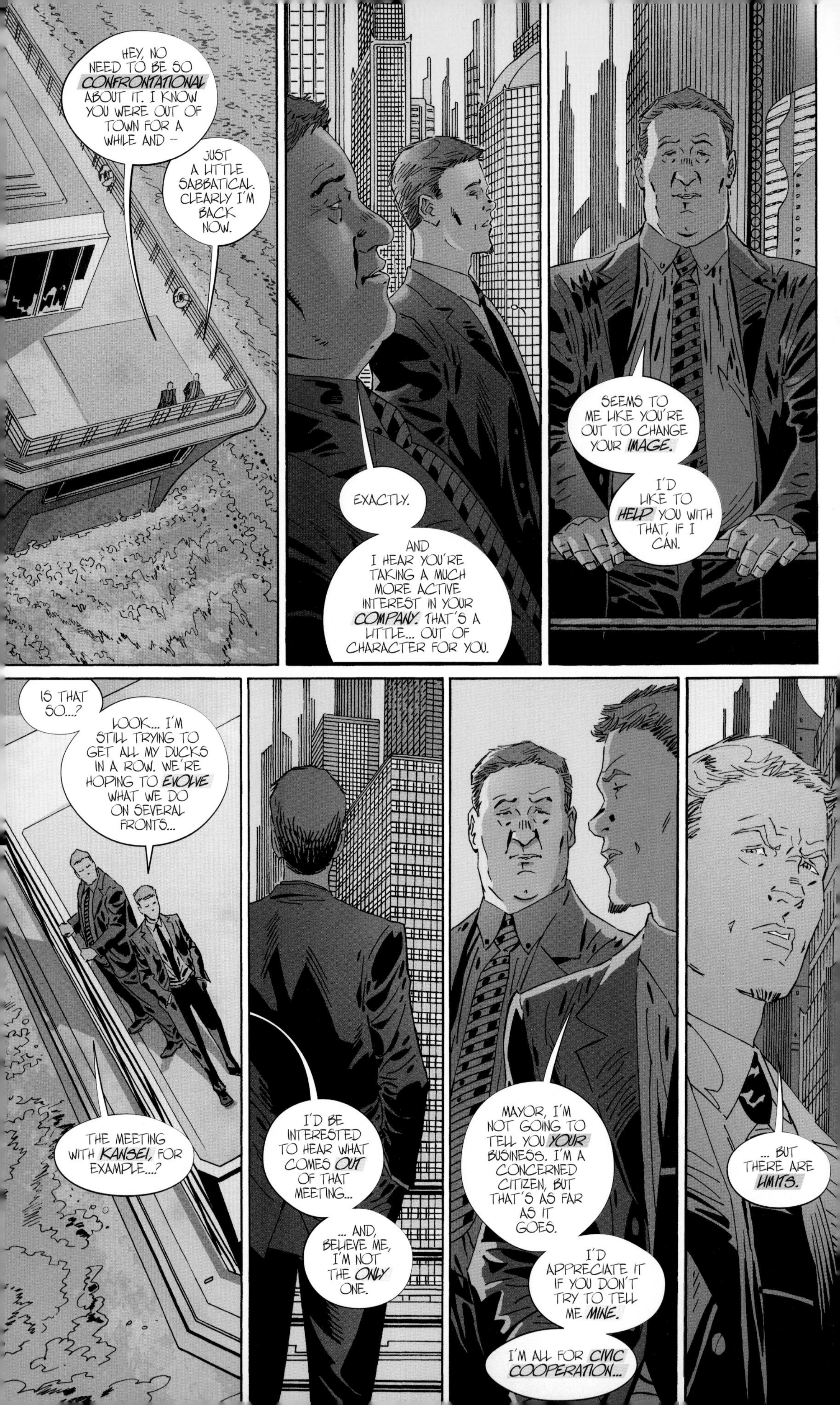
HEY, NO NEED TO BE SO CONFRONTATIONAL ABOUT IT. I KNOW YOU WERE OUT OF TOWN FOR A WHILE AND --
JUST A LITTLE SABBATICAL. CLEARLY I'M BACK NOW.
EXACTLY.
AND I HEAR YOU'RE TAKING A MUCH MORE ACTIVE INTEREST IN YOUR COMPANY. THAT'S A LITTLE... OUT OF CHARACTER FOR YOU.
SEEMS TO ME LIKE YOU'RE OUT TO CHANGE YOUR IMAGE.
I'D LIKE TO HELP YOU WITH THAT, IF I CAN.
IS THAT SO...?
LOOK... I'M STILL TRYING TO GET ALL MY DUCKS IN A ROW. WE'RE HOPING TO EVOLVE WHAT WE DO ON SEVERAL FRONTS...
THE MEETING WITH KANSEI, FOR EXAMPLE...?
I'D BE INTERESTED TO HEAR WHAT COMES OUT OF THAT MEETING...
... AND, BELIEVE ME, I'M NOT THE ONLY ONE.
MAYOR, I'M NOT GOING TO TELL YOU YOUR BUSINESS. I'M A CONCERNED CITIZEN, BUT THAT'S AS FAR AS IT GOES.
I'D APPRECIATE IT IF YOU DON'T TRY TO TELL ME MINE.
I'M ALL FOR CIVIC COOPERATION...
... BUT THERE ARE LIMITS.

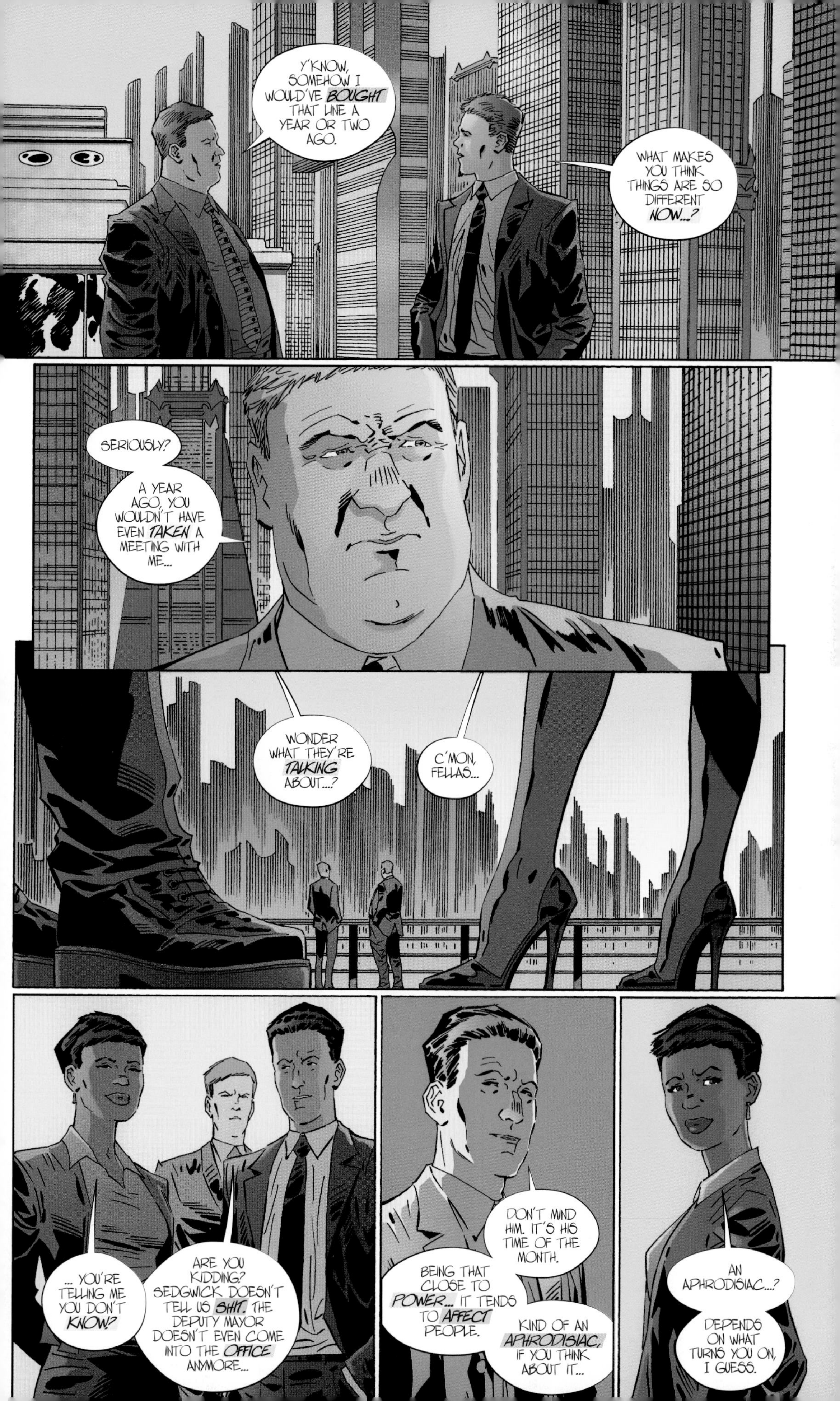
Y'KNOW, SOMEHOW I WOULD'VE BOUGHT THAT LINE A YEAR OR TWO AGO.
WHAT MAKES YOU THINK THINGS ARE SO DIFFERENT NOW...?
SERIOUSLY?
A YEAR AGO, YOU WOULDN'T HAVE EVEN TAKEN A MEETING WITH ME...
WONDER WHAT THEY'RE TALKING ABOUT...?
C'MON, FELLAS...
... YOU'RE TELLING ME YOU DON'T KNOW?
ARE YOU KIDDING? SEDGWICK DOESN'T TELL US SHIT. THE DEPUTY MAYOR DOESN'T EVEN COME INTO THE OFFICE ANYMORE...
DON'T MIND HIM. IT'S HIS TIME OF THE MONTH.
BEING THAT CLOSE TO POWER... IT TENDS TO AFFECT PEOPLE.
KIND OF AN APHRODISIAC, IF YOU THINK ABOUT IT...
AN APHRODISIAC...?
DEPENDS ON WHAT TURNS YOU ON, I GUESS.

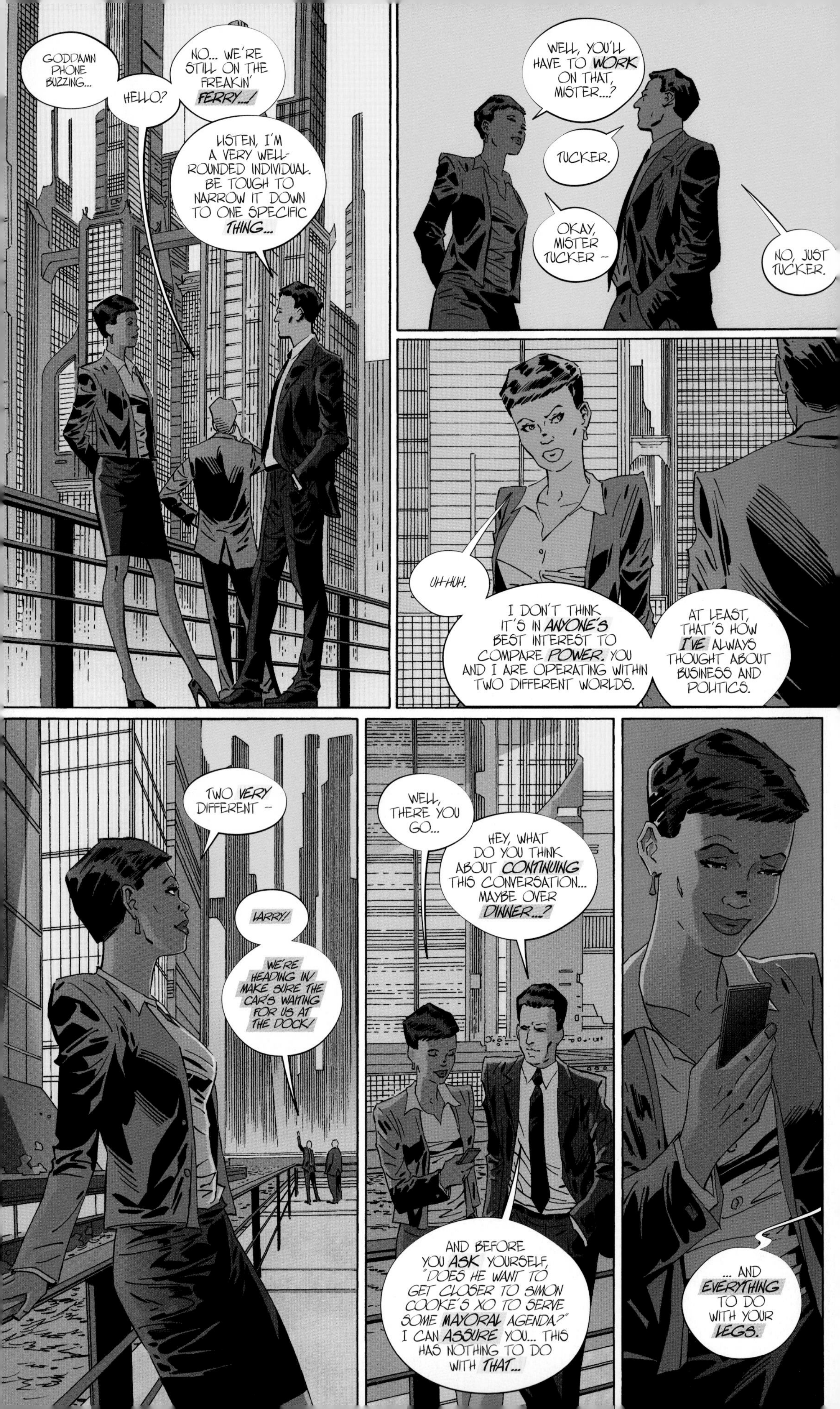
GODDAMN PHONE BUZZING...
HELLO?
NO... WE'RE STILL ON THE FREAKIN' FERRY...!
LISTEN, I'M A VERY WELL-ROUNDED INDIVIDUAL. BE TOUGH TO NARROW IT DOWN TO ONE SPECIFIC THING...
WELL, YOU'LL HAVE TO WORK ON THAT, MISTER...?
TUCKER.
OKAY, MISTER TUCKER --
NO, JUST TUCKER.
UH-HUH.
I DON'T THINK IT'S IN ANYONE'S BEST INTEREST TO COMPARE POWER. YOU AND I ARE OPERATING WITHIN TWO DIFFERENT WORLDS.
AT LEAST, THAT'S HOW I'VE ALWAYS THOUGHT ABOUT BUSINESS AND POLITICS.
TWO VERY DIFFERENT --
LARRY!
WE'RE HEADING IN! MAKE SURE THE CAR'S WAITING FOR US AT THE DOCK!
WELL, THERE YOU GO...
HEY, WHAT DO YOU THINK ABOUT CONTINUING THIS CONVERSATION... MAYBE OVER DINNER...?
AND BEFORE YOU ASK YOURSELF, "DOES HE WANT TO GET CLOSER TO SIMON COOKE'S XO TO SERVE SOME MAYORAL AGENDA?" I CAN ASSURE YOU... THIS HAS NOTHING TO DO WITH THAT...
... AND EVERYTHING TO DO WITH YOUR LEGS.

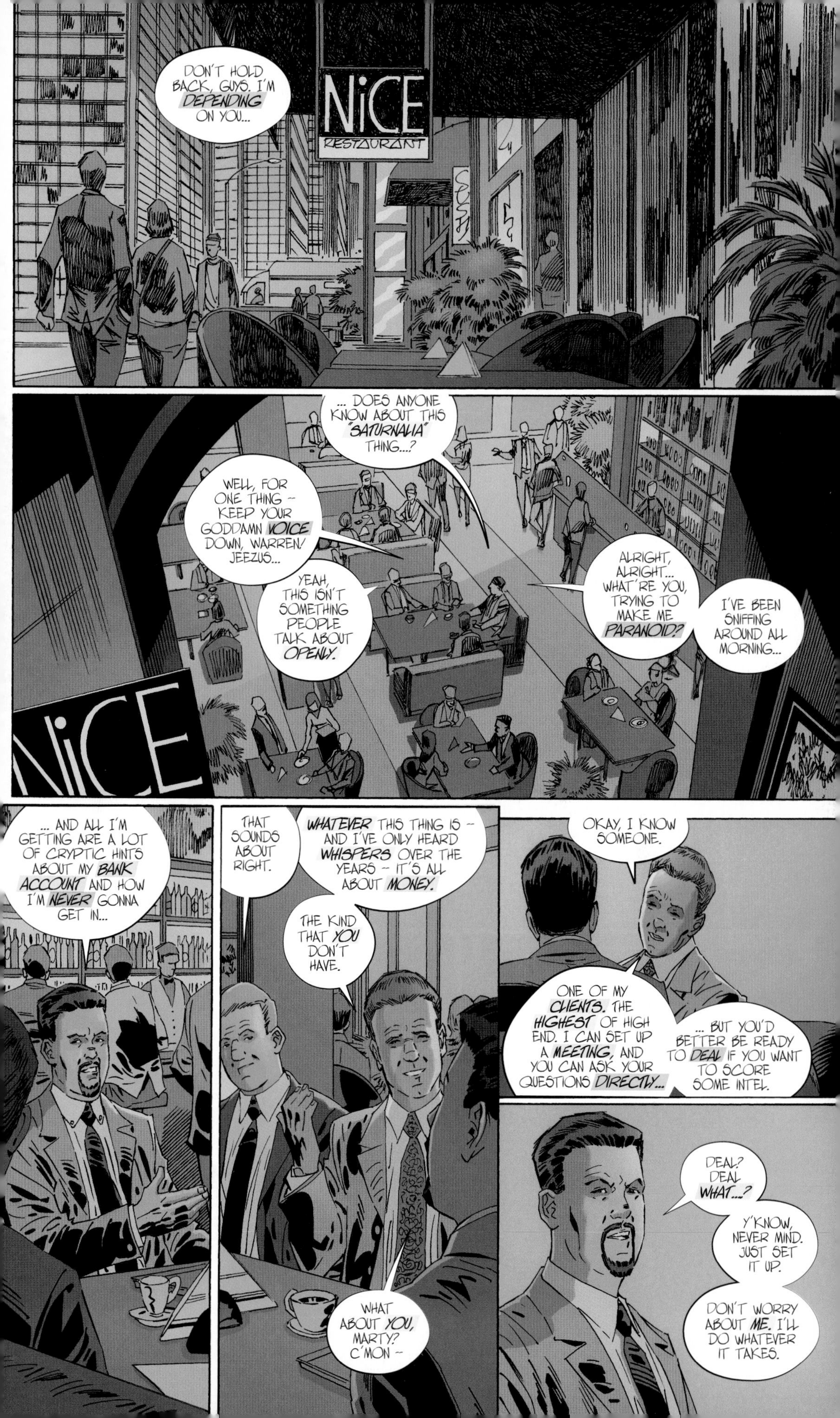

NiCE RESTAURANT
SUSHI
DON'T HOLD BACK, GUYS. I'M DEPENDING ON YOU...
... DOES ANYONE KNOW ABOUT THIS "SATURNALIA" THING...?
WELL, FOR ONE THING -- KEEP YOUR GODDAMN VOICE DOWN, WARREN! JEEZUS...
YEAH, THIS ISN'T SOMETHING PEOPLE TALK ABOUT OPENLY.
ALRIGHT, ALRIGHT... WHAT'RE YOU, TRYING TO MAKE ME PARANOID?
I'VE BEEN SNIFFING AROUND ALL MORNING...
NiCE
... AND ALL I'M GETTING ARE A LOT OF CRYPTIC HINTS ABOUT MY BANK ACCOUNT AND HOW I'M NEVER GONNA GET IN...
THAT SOUNDS ABOUT RIGHT.
WHATEVER THIS THING IS -- AND I'VE ONLY HEARD WHISPERS OVER THE YEARS -- IT'S ALL ABOUT MONEY.
THE KIND THAT YOU DON'T HAVE.
WHAT ABOUT YOU, MARTY? C'MON --
OKAY, I KNOW SOMEONE.
ONE OF MY CLIENTS. THE HIGHEST OF HIGH END. I CAN SET UP A MEETING, AND YOU CAN ASK YOUR QUESTIONS DIRECTLY...
... BUT YOU'D BETTER BE READY TO DEAL IF YOU WANT TO SCORE SOME INTEL.
DEAL? DEAL WHAT...?
Y'KNOW, NEVER MIND. JUST SET IT UP.
DON'T WORRY ABOUT ME. I'LL DO WHATEVER IT TAKES.

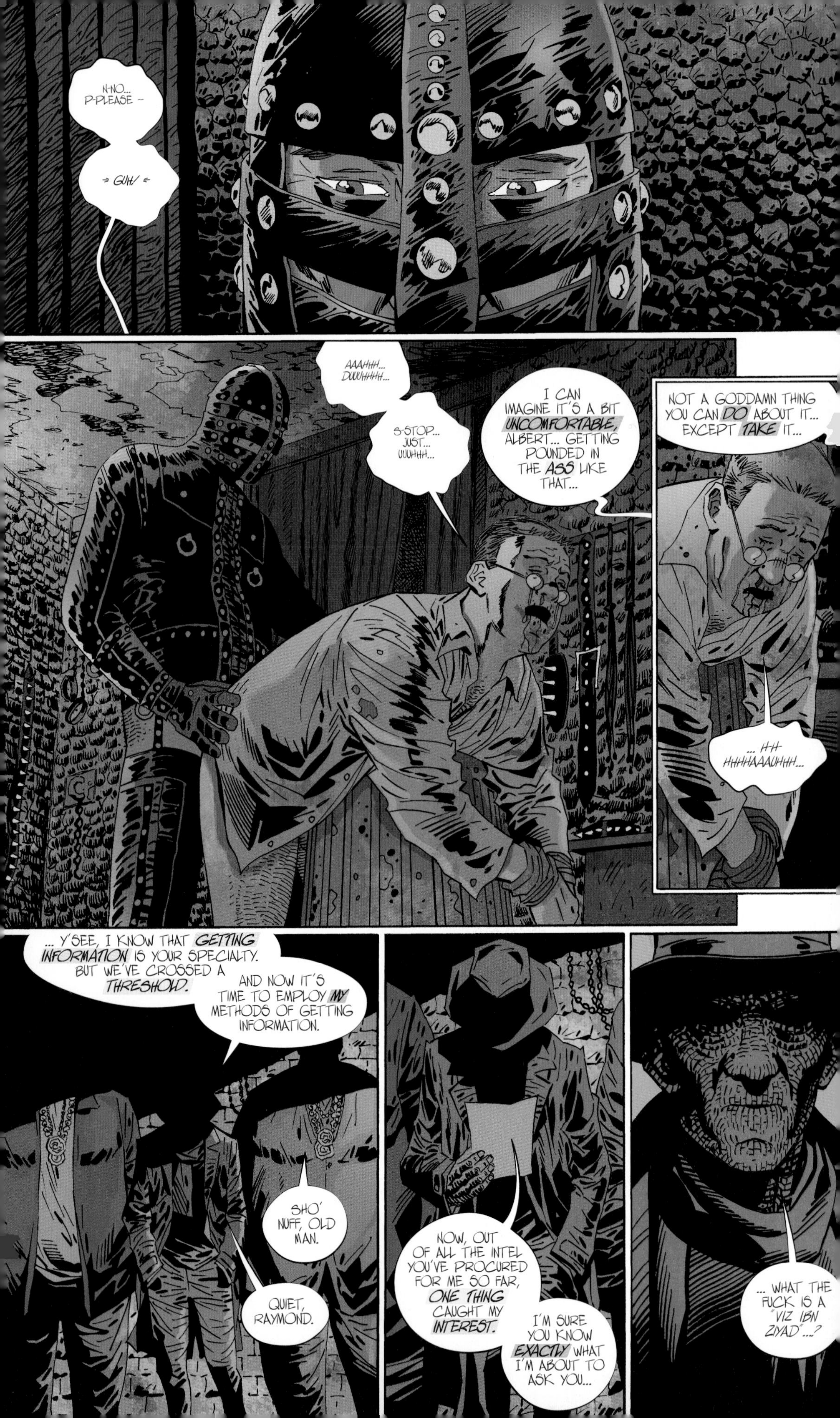
N-NO... P-PLEASE --
GUH!
AAAHHH... DUUUHHHH...
S-STOP... JUST... UUUHHH...
I CAN IMAGINE IT'S A BIT UNCOMFORTABLE, ALBERT... GETTING POUNDED IN THE ASS LIKE THAT...
NOT A GODDAMN THING YOU CAN DO ABOUT IT... EXCEPT TAKE IT...
... H-H HHHHAAAUHHH...
... Y'SEE, I KNOW THAT GETTING INFORMATION IS YOUR SPECIALTY. BUT WE'VE CROSSED A THRESHOLD.
AND NOW IT'S TIME TO EMPLOY MY METHODS OF GETTING INFORMATION.
SHO' NUFF, OLD MAN.
QUIET, RAYMOND.
NOW, OUT OF ALL THE INTEL YOU'VE PROCURED FOR ME SO FAR, ONE THING CAUGHT MY INTEREST.
I'M SURE YOU KNOW EXACTLY WHAT I'M ABOUT TO ASK YOU...
... WHAT THE FUCK IS A "VIZ IBN ZIYAD"...?

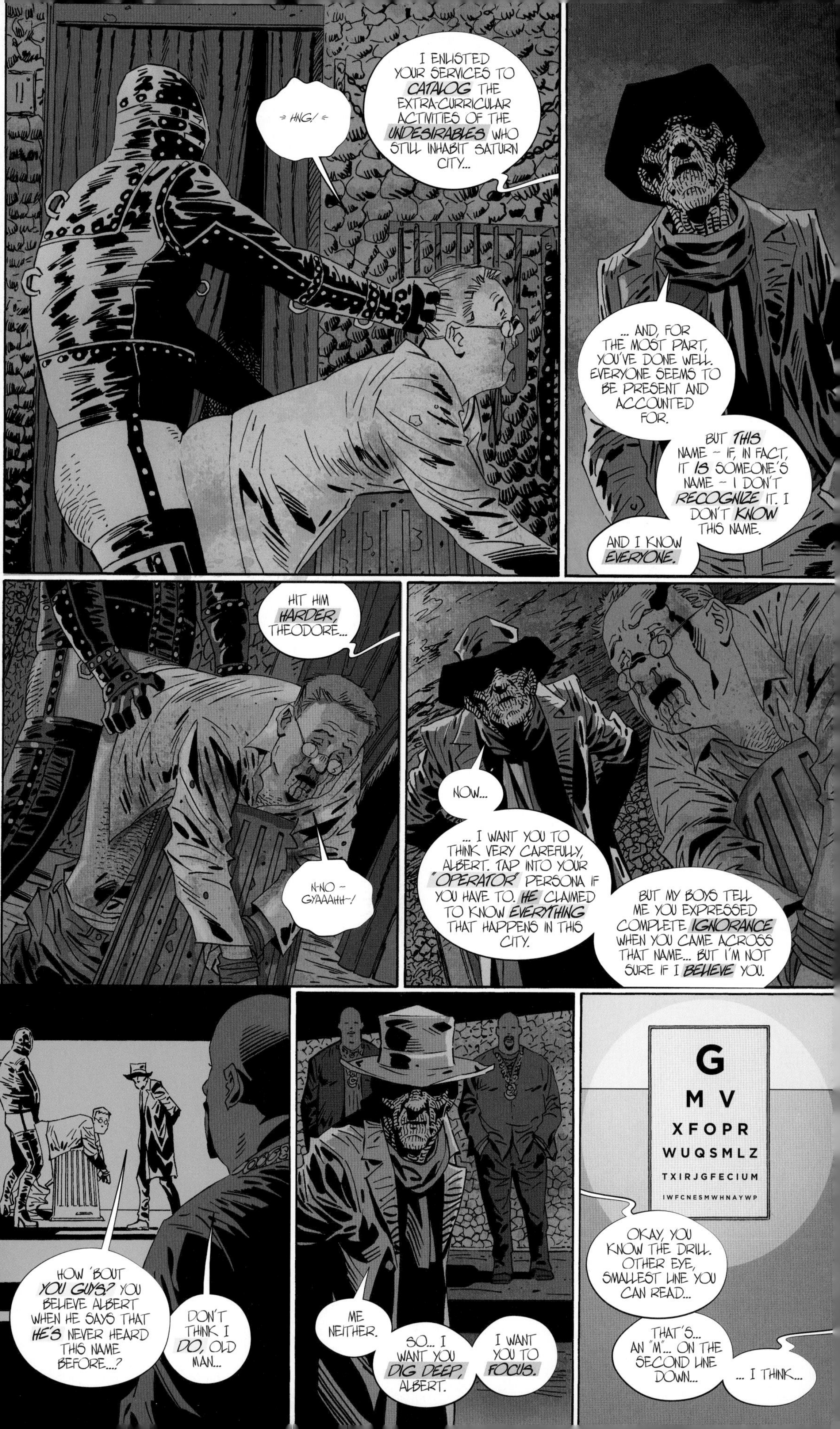
HNG!
I ENLISTED YOUR SERVICES TO CATALOG THE EXTRA-CURRICULAR ACTIVITIES OF THE UNDESIRABLES WHO STILL INHABIT SATURN CITY...
... AND, FOR THE MOST PART, YOU'VE DONE WELL. EVERYONE SEEMS TO BE PRESENT AND ACCOUNTED FOR.
BUT THIS NAME -- IF, IN FACT, IT IS SOMEONE'S NAME -- I DON'T RECOGNIZE IT. I DON'T KNOW THIS NAME.
AND I KNOW EVERYONE.
HIT HIM HARDER, THEODORE...
N-NO -- GYAAAHH--!
NOW...
... I WANT YOU TO THINK VERY CAREFULLY, ALBERT. TAP INTO YOUR "OPERATOR" PERSONA IF YOU HAVE TO. HE CLAIMED TO KNOW EVERYTHING THAT HAPPENS IN THIS CITY.
BUT MY BOYS TELL ME YOU EXPRESSED COMPLETE IGNORANCE WHEN YOU CAME ACROSS THAT NAME... BUT I'M NOT SURE IF I BELIEVE YOU.
HOW 'BOUT YOU GUYS? YOU BELIEVE ALBERT WHEN HE SAYS THAT HE'S NEVER HEARD THIS NAME BEFORE...?
DON'T THINK I DO, OLD MAN...
ME NEITHER.
SO... I WANT YOU DIG DEEP, ALBERT.
I WANT YOU TO FOCUS.
G
M V
X F O P R
W U Q S M L Z
T X I R J G F E C I U M
I W F C N E S M W H N A Y W P
OKAY, YOU KNOW THE DRILL. OTHER EYE, SMALLEST LINE YOU CAN READ...
THAT'S... AN "M"... ON THE SECOND LINE DOWN...
... I THINK...

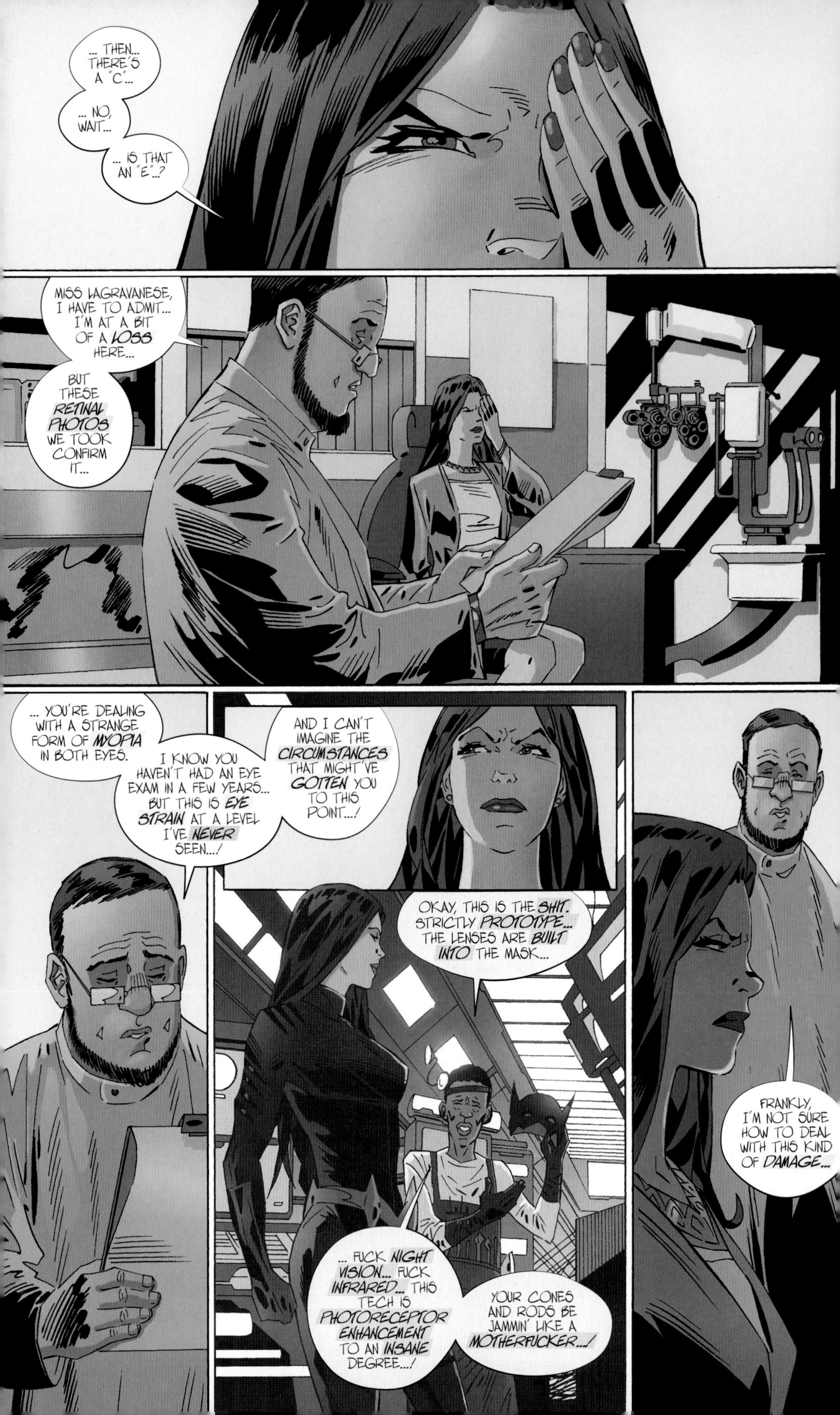

... THEN... THERE'S A "C"...
... NO, WAIT...
... IS THAT AN "E"...?
MISS LAGRAVANESE, I HAVE TO ADMIT... I'M AT A BIT OF A LOSS HERE...
BUT THESE RETINAL PHOTOS WE TOOK CONFIRM IT...
... YOU'RE DEALING WITH A STRANGE FORM OF MYOPIA IN BOTH EYES.
I KNOW YOU HAVEN'T HAD AN EYE EXAM IN A FEW YEARS... BUT THIS IS EYE STRAIN AT A LEVEL I'VE NEVER SEEN...!
AND I CAN'T IMAGINE THE CIRCUMSTANCES THAT MIGHT'VE GOTTEN YOU TO THIS POINT...!
OKAY, THIS IS THE SHIT. STRICTLY PROTOTYPE... THE LENSES ARE BUILT INTO THE MASK...
... FUCK NIGHT VISION... FUCK INFRARED... THIS TECH IS PHOTORECEPTOR ENHANCEMENT TO AN INSANE DEGREE...!
YOUR CONES AND RODS BE JAMMIN' LIKE A MOTHERFUCKER...!
FRANKLY, I'M NOT SURE HOW TO DEAL WITH THIS KIND OF DAMAGE...

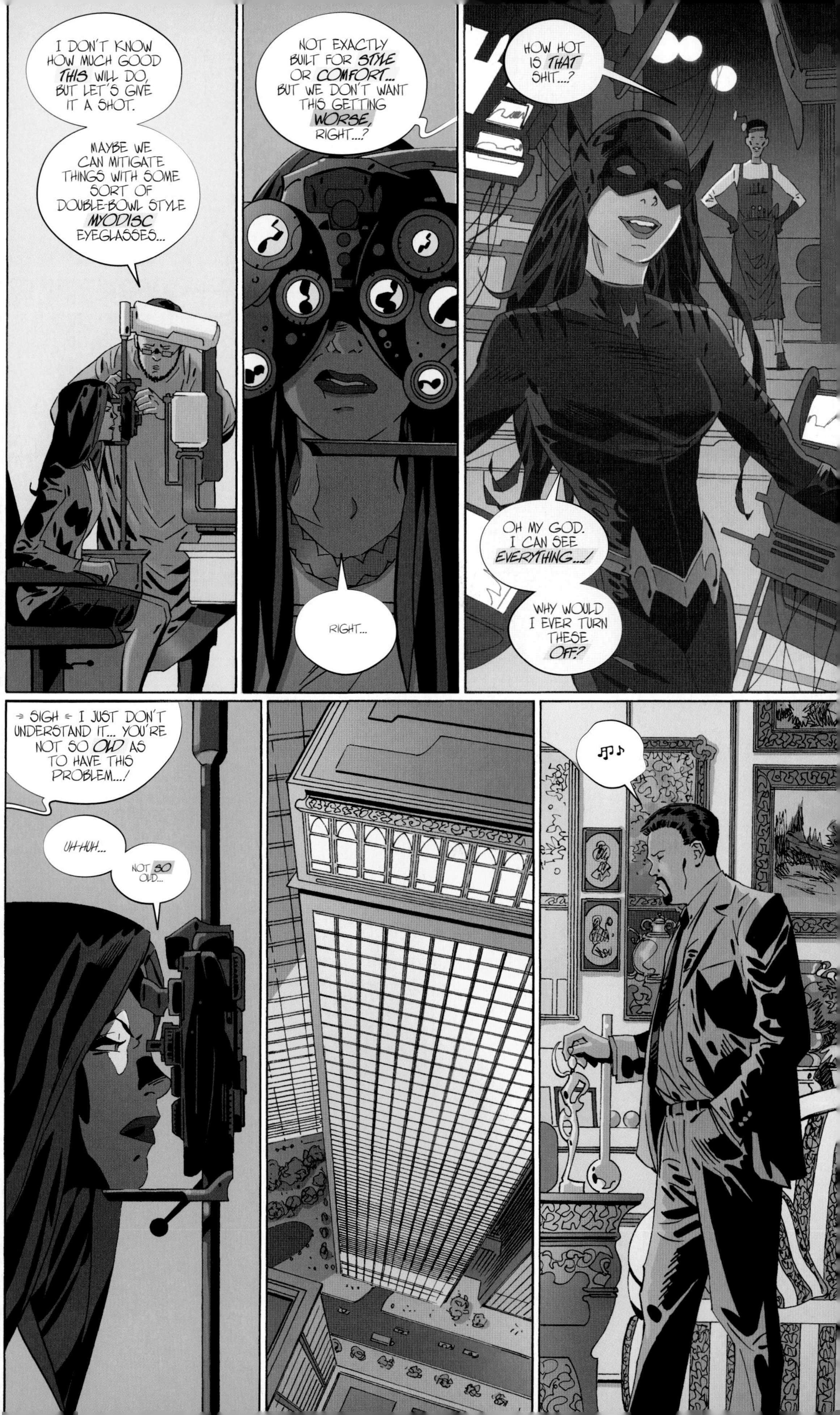
I DON'T KNOW HOW MUCH GOOD THIS WILL DO, BUT LET'S GIVE IT A SHOT.
MAYBE WE CAN MITIGATE THINGS WITH SOME SORT OF DOUBLE-BOWL STYLE MYODISC EYEGLASSES...
NOT EXACTLY BUILT FOR STYLE OR COMFORT... BUT WE DON'T WANT THIS GETTING WORSE, RIGHT...?
RIGHT...
HOW HOT IS THAT SHIT...?
OH MY GOD. I CAN SEE EVERYTHING...!
WHY WOULD I EVER TURN THESE OFF?
⇒ SIGH ⇐ I JUST DON'T UNDERSTAND IT... YOU'RE NOT SO OLD AS TO HAVE THIS PROBLEM...!
UH-HUH...
NOT SO OLD...
♫♪

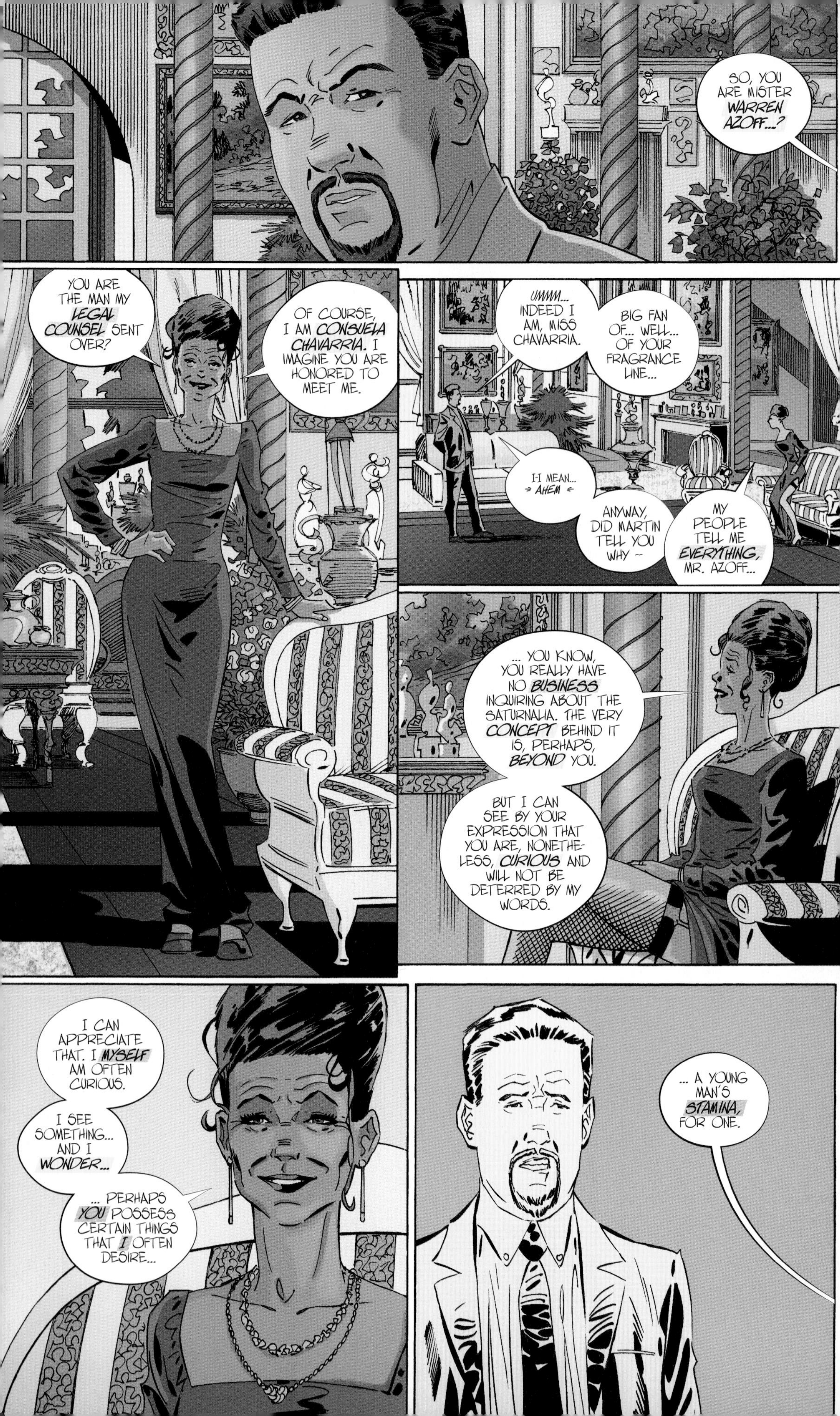
SO, YOU ARE MISTER WARREN AZOFF...?
YOU ARE THE MAN MY LEGAL COUNSEL SENT OVER?
OF COURSE, I AM CONSUELA CHAVARRIA. I IMAGINE YOU ARE HONORED TO MEET ME.
UMMM... INDEED I AM, MISS CHAVARRIA.
BIG FAN OF... WELL... OF YOUR FRAGRANCE LINE...
I-I MEAN... AHEM
ANYWAY, DID MARTIN TELL YOU WHY --
MY PEOPLE TELL ME EVERYTHING, MR. AZOFF...
... YOU KNOW, YOU REALLY HAVE NO BUSINESS INQUIRING ABOUT THE SATURNALIA. THE VERY CONCEPT BEHIND IT IS, PERHAPS, BEYOND YOU.
BUT I CAN SEE BY YOUR EXPRESSION THAT YOU ARE, NONETHE-LESS, CURIOUS AND WILL NOT BE DETERRED BY MY WORDS.
I CAN APPRECIATE THAT. I MYSELF AM OFTEN CURIOUS.
I SEE SOMETHING... AND I WONDER...
... PERHAPS YOU POSSESS CERTAIN THINGS THAT I OFTEN DESIRE...
... A YOUNG MAN'S STAMINA, FOR ONE.

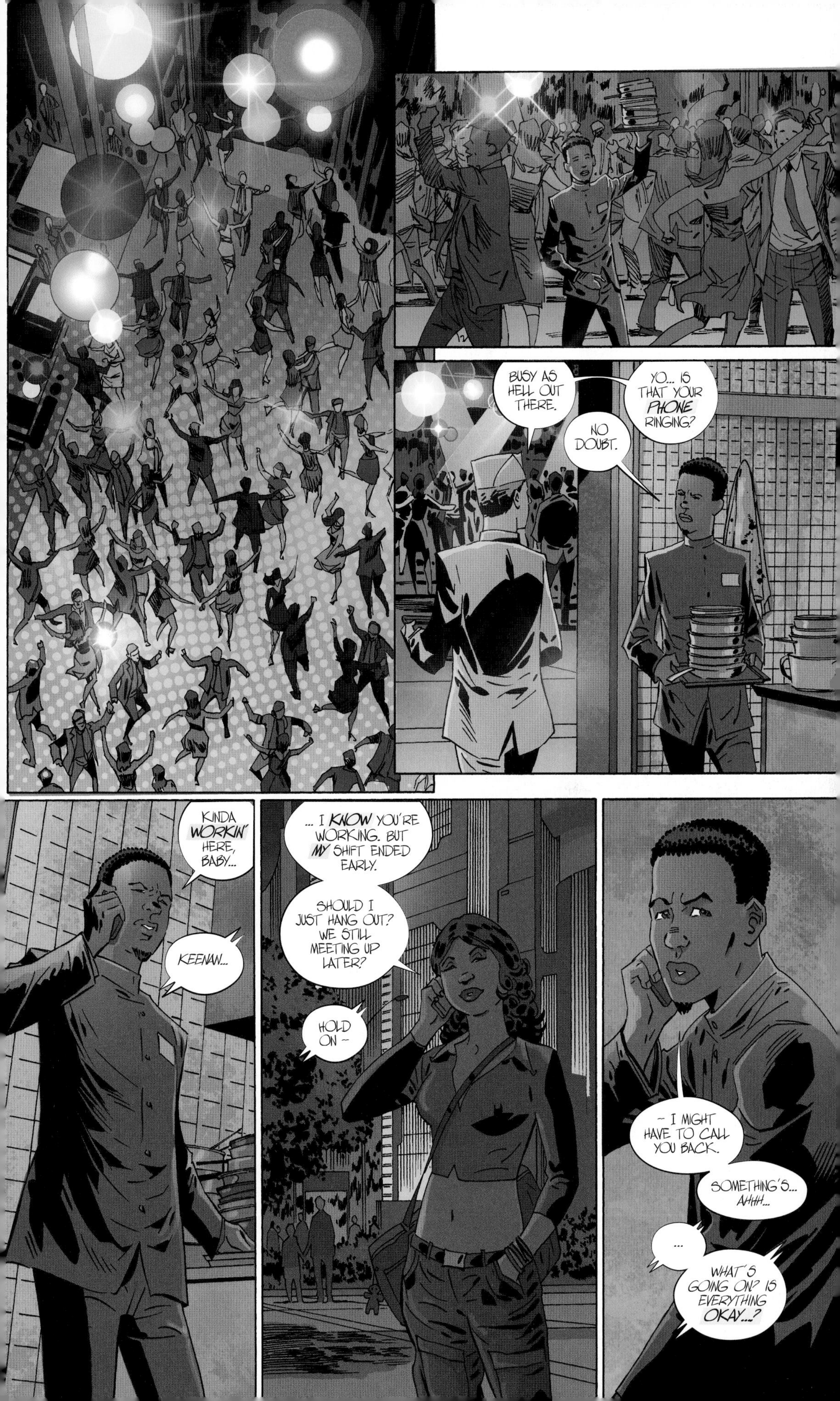
BUSY AS HELL OUT THERE.
YO... IS THAT YOUR PHONE RINGING?
NO DOUBT.
KINDA WORKIN' HERE, BABY...
KEENAN...
... I KNOW YOU'RE WORKING. BUT MY SHIFT ENDED EARLY.
SHOULD I JUST HANG OUT? WE STILL MEETING UP LATER?
HOLD ON --
-- I MIGHT HAVE TO CALL YOU BACK.
SOMETHING'S... AHHH...
...
WHAT'S GOING ON? IS EVERYTHING OKAY...?

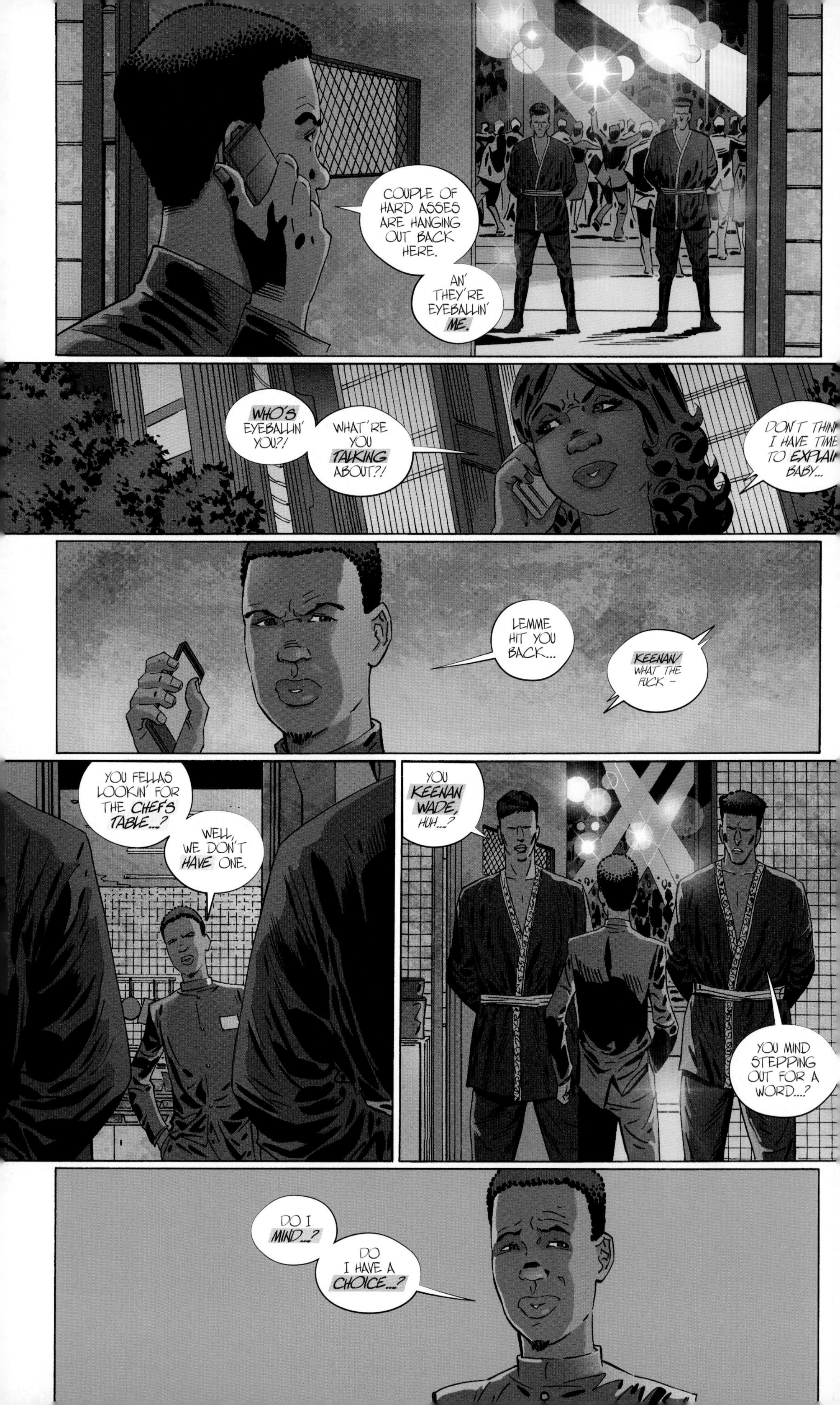
COUPLE OF HARD ASSES ARE HANGING OUT BACK HERE.
AN' THEY'RE EYEBALLIN' ME.
WHO'S EYEBALLIN' YOU?!
WHAT'RE YOU TALKING ABOUT?!
DON'T THINK I HAVE TIME TO EXPLAIN BABY...
LEMME HIT YOU BACK...
KEENAN! WHAT THE FUCK --
YOU FELLAS LOOKIN' FOR THE CHEF'S TABLE...?
WELL, WE DON'T HAVE ONE.
YOU KEENAN WADE, HUH...?
YOU MIND STEPPING OUT FOR A WORD...?
DO I MIND...?
DO I HAVE A CHOICE...?

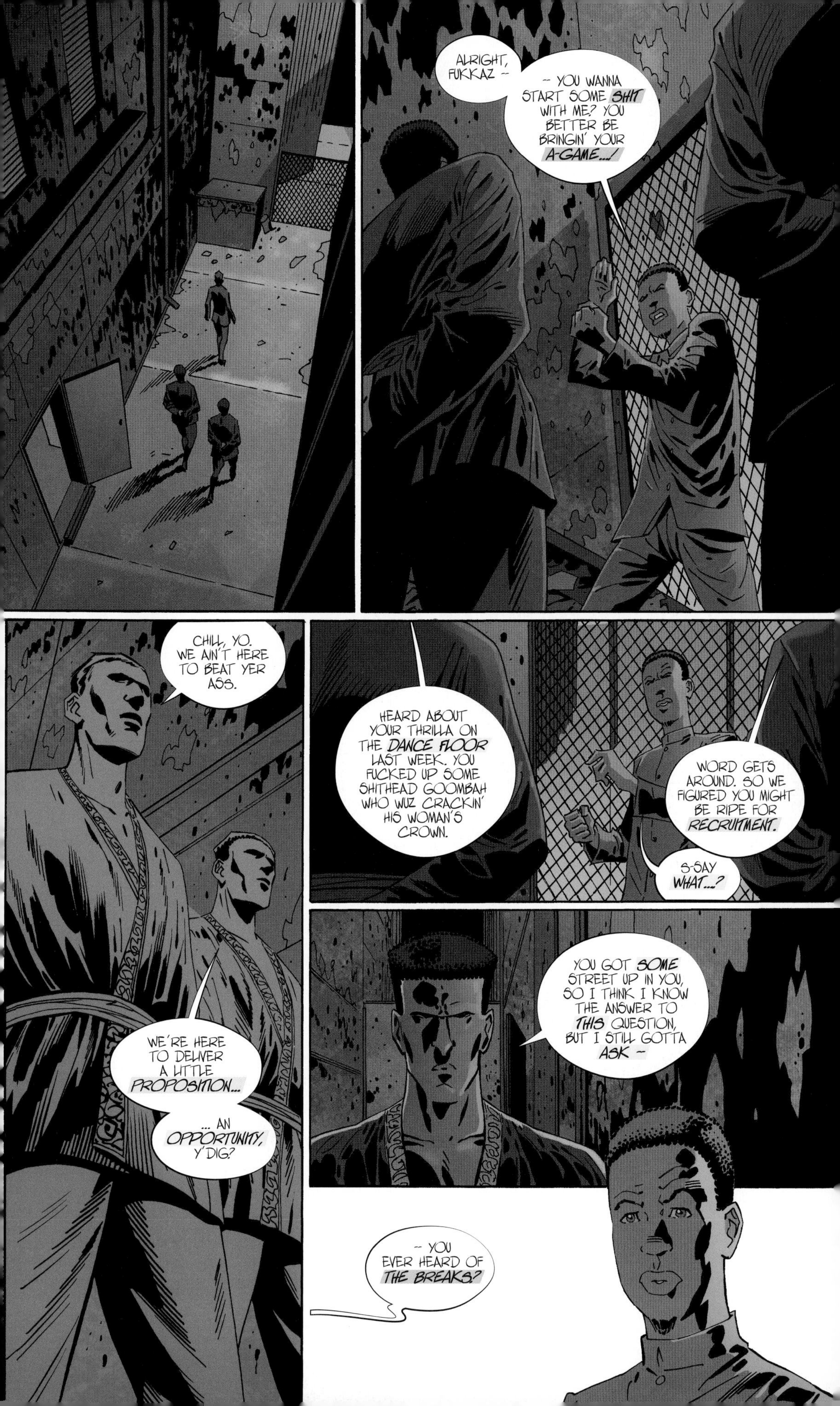
ALRIGHT, FUKKAZ --
-- YOU WANNA START SOME SHIT WITH ME? YOU BETTER BE BRINGIN' YOUR A-GAME...!
CHILL, YO. WE AIN'T HERE TO BEAT YER ASS.
WE'RE HERE TO DELIVER A LITTLE PROPOSITION...
... AN OPPORTUNITY, Y'DIG?
HEARD ABOUT YOUR THRILLA ON THE DANCE FLOOR LAST WEEK. YOU FUCKED UP SOME SHITHEAD GOOMBAH WHO WUZ CRACKIN' HIS WOMAN'S CROWN.
WORD GETS AROUND. SO WE FIGURED YOU MIGHT BE RIPE FOR RECRUITMENT.
S-SAY WHAT...?
YOU GOT SOME STREET UP IN YOU, SO I THINK I KNOW THE ANSWER TO THIS QUESTION, BUT I STILL GOTTA ASK --
-- YOU EVER HEARD OF THE BREAKS?

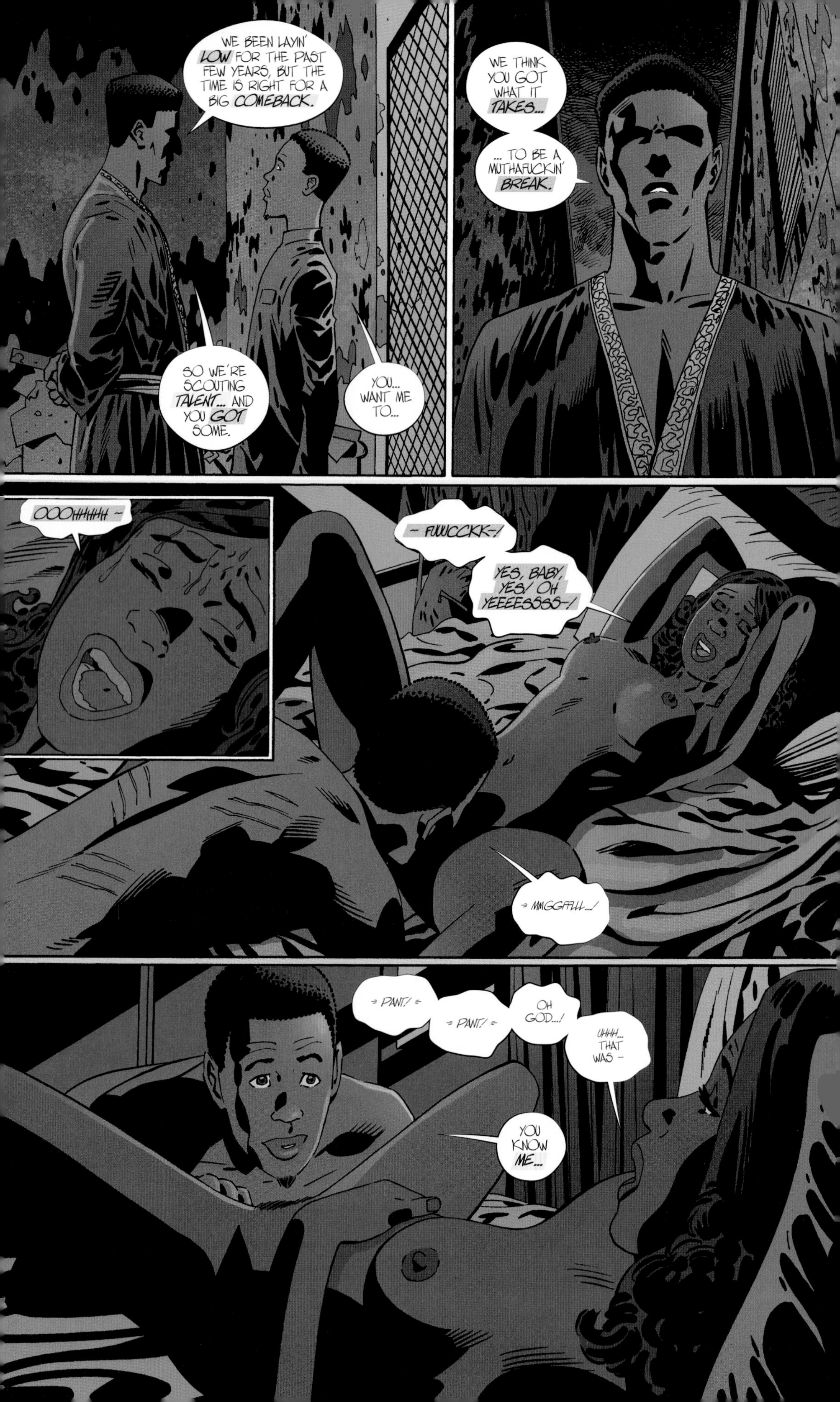
WE BEEN LAYIN' LOW FOR THE PAST FEW YEARS, BUT THE TIME IS RIGHT FOR A BIG COMEBACK.
SO WE'RE SCOUTING TALENT... AND YOU GOT SOME.
YOU... WANT ME TO...
WE THINK YOU GOT WHAT IT TAKES...
... TO BE A MUTHAFUCKIN' BREAK.
OOOHHHHH ~
~ FUUUCCKK~!
YES, BABY, YES! OH YEEEESSSS~!
MMGGFFLLL...!
PANT!
PANT!
OH GOD...!
UHHH... THAT WAS ~
YOU KNOW ME...

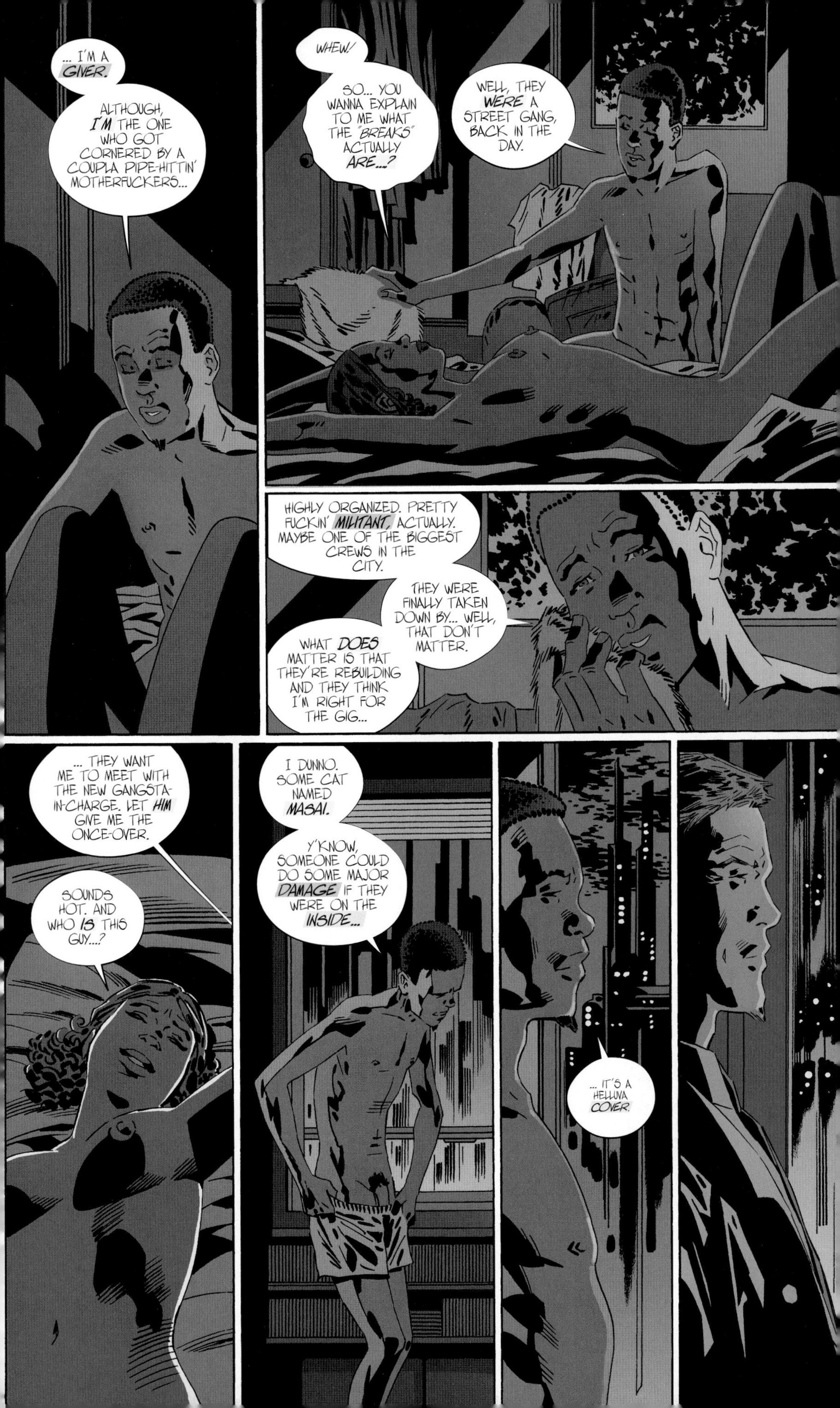
... I'M A GIVER.
ALTHOUGH, I'M THE ONE WHO GOT CORNERED BY A COUPLA PIPE-HITTIN' MOTHERFUCKERS...
WHEW!
SO... YOU WANNA EXPLAIN TO ME WHAT THE "BREAKS" ACTUALLY ARE...?
WELL, THEY WERE A STREET GANG, BACK IN THE DAY.
HIGHLY ORGANIZED. PRETTY FUCKIN' MILITANT, ACTUALLY. MAYBE ONE OF THE BIGGEST CREWS IN THE CITY.
THEY WERE FINALLY TAKEN DOWN BY... WELL, THAT DON'T MATTER.
WHAT DOES MATTER IS THAT THEY'RE REBUILDING AND THEY THINK I'M RIGHT FOR THE GIG...
... THEY WANT ME TO MEET WITH THE NEW GANGSTA-IN-CHARGE. LET HIM GIVE ME THE ONCE-OVER.
SOUNDS HOT. AND WHO IS THIS GUY...?
I DUNNO. SOME CAT NAMED MASAI.
Y'KNOW, SOMEONE COULD DO SOME MAJOR DAMAGE IF THEY WERE ON THE INSIDE...
... IT'S A HELLUVA COVER.

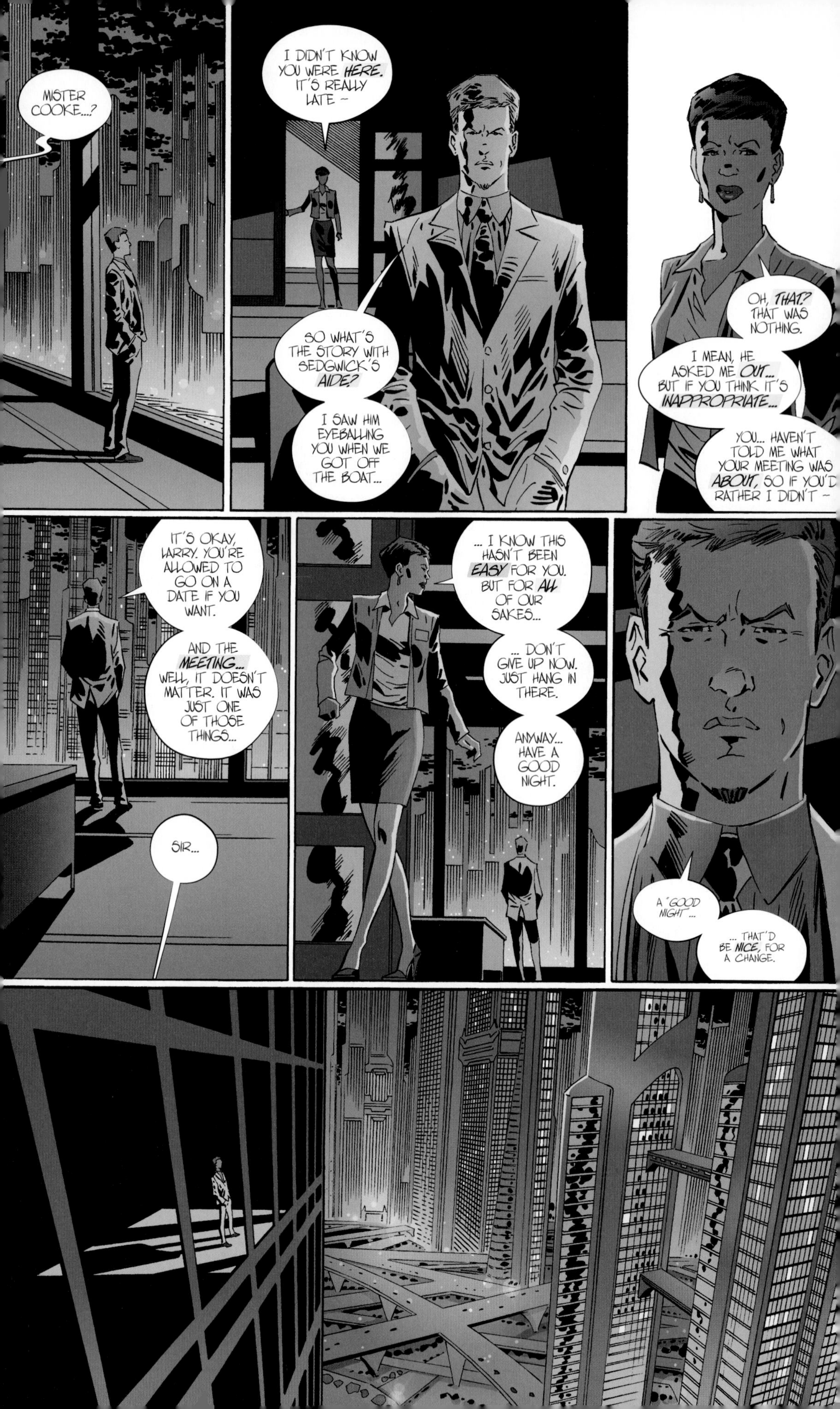
MISTER COOKE...?
I DIDN'T KNOW YOU WERE HERE. IT'S REALLY LATE --
SO WHAT'S THE STORY WITH SEDGWICK'S AIDE?
I SAW HIM EYEBALLING YOU WHEN WE GOT OFF THE BOAT...
OH, THAT? THAT WAS NOTHING.
I MEAN, HE ASKED ME OUT... BUT IF YOU THINK IT'S INAPPROPRIATE...
YOU... HAVEN'T TOLD ME WHAT YOUR MEETING WAS ABOUT, SO IF YOU'D RATHER I DIDN'T --
IT'S OKAY, LARRY. YOU'RE ALLOWED TO GO ON A DATE IF YOU WANT.
AND THE MEETING... WELL, IT DOESN'T MATTER. IT WAS JUST ONE OF THOSE THINGS...
SIR...
... I KNOW THIS HASN'T BEEN EASY FOR YOU. BUT FOR ALL OF OUR SAKES...
... DON'T GIVE UP NOW. JUST HANG IN THERE.
ANYWAY... HAVE A GOOD NIGHT.
A "GOOD NIGHT"...
... THAT'D BE NICE, FOR A CHANGE.

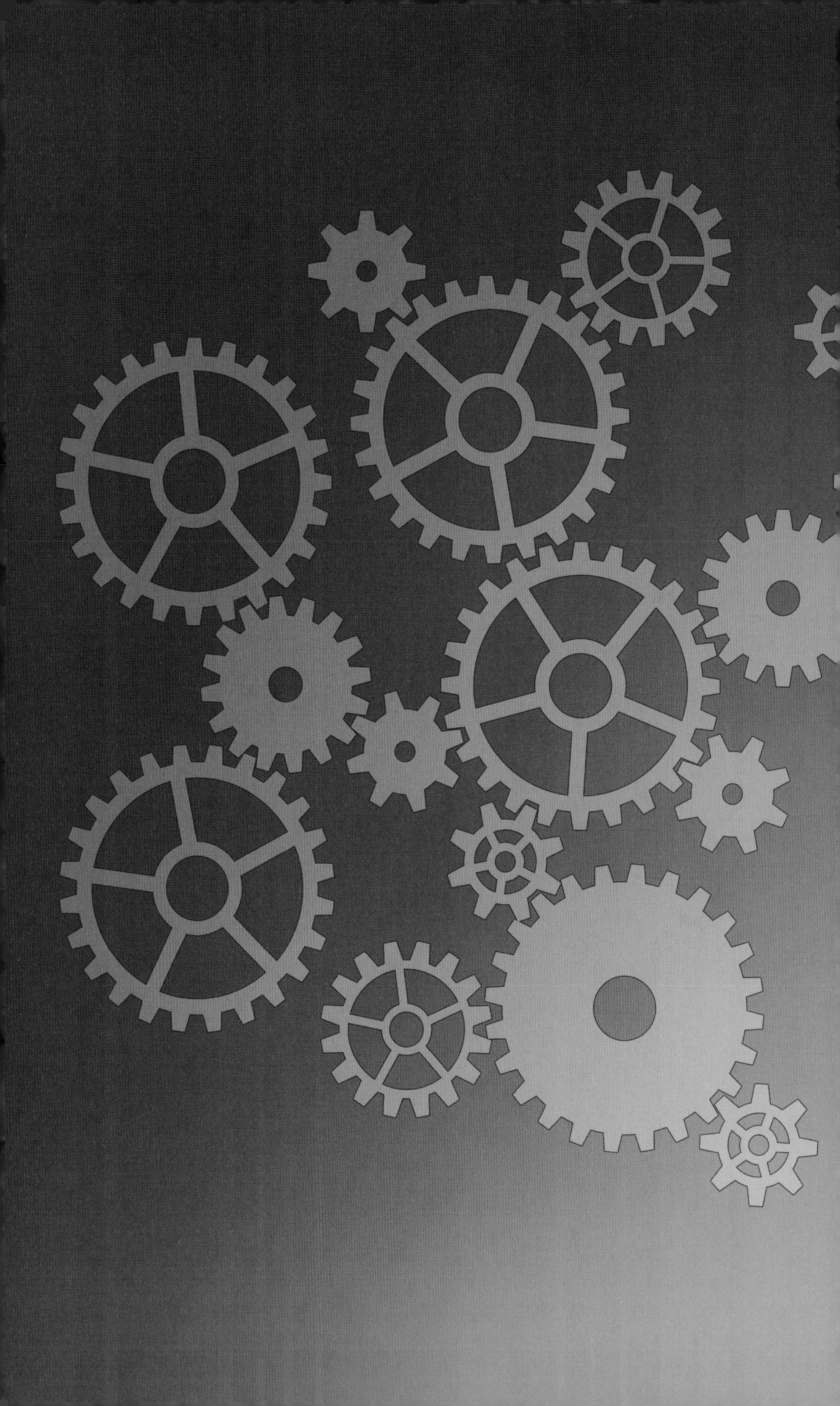

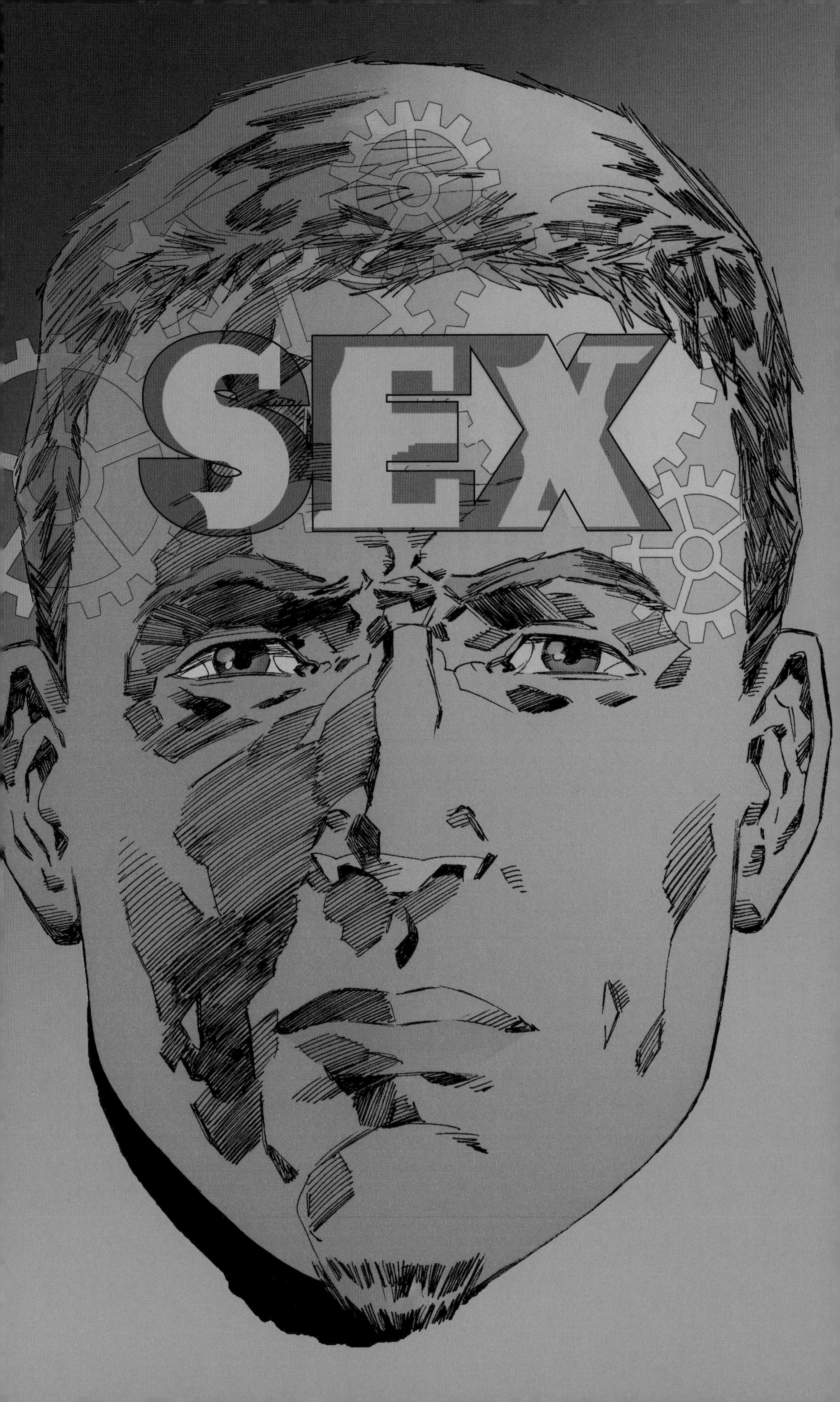
SEX

CHAPTER SEVEN

EVERLASTING GOBSTOPPER

JOE CASEY WRITER PIOTR KOWALSKI ARTIST BRAD SIMPSON COLORIST RUS WOOTON LETTERER SONIA HARRIS GRAPHIC DESIGNER

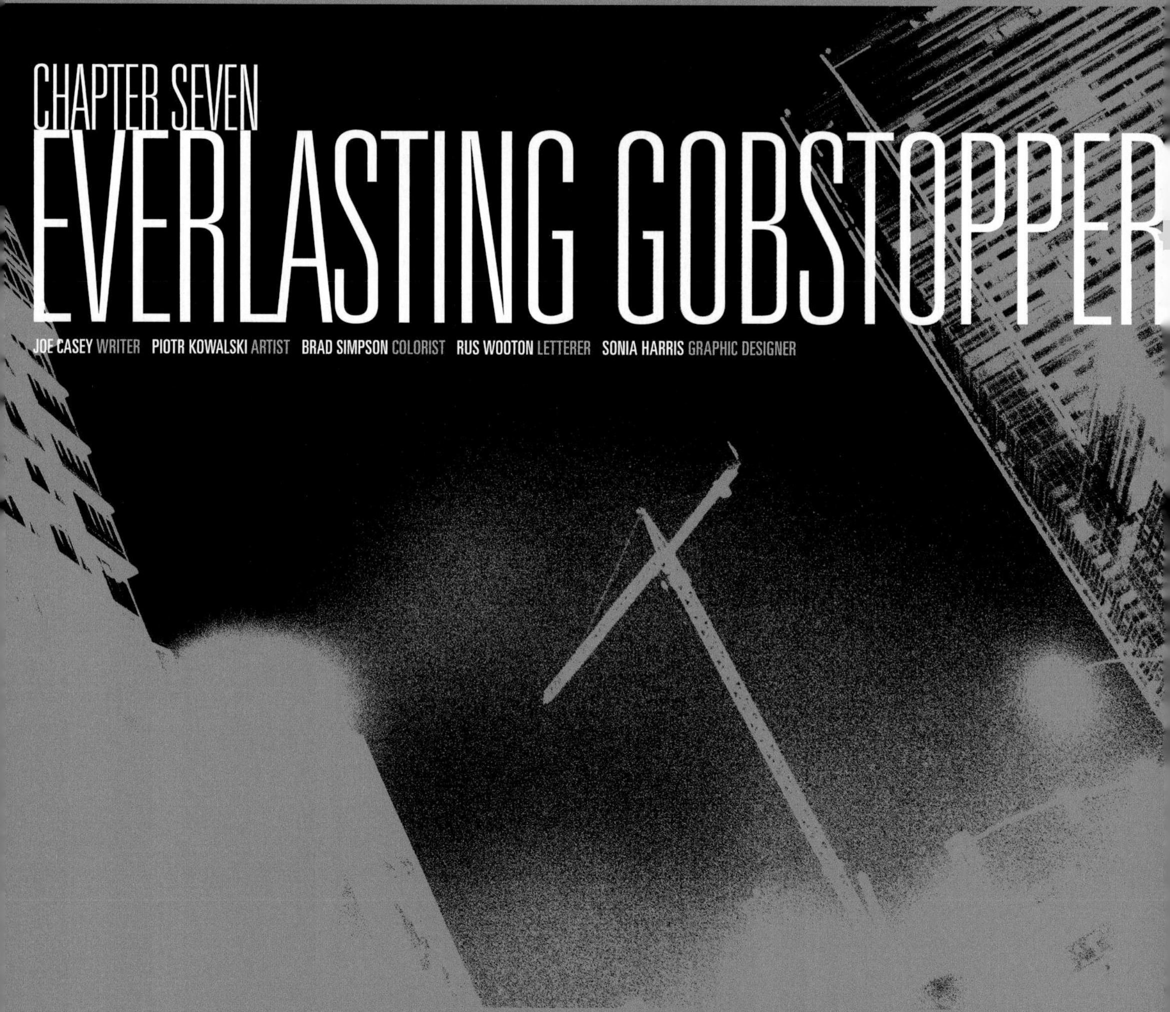

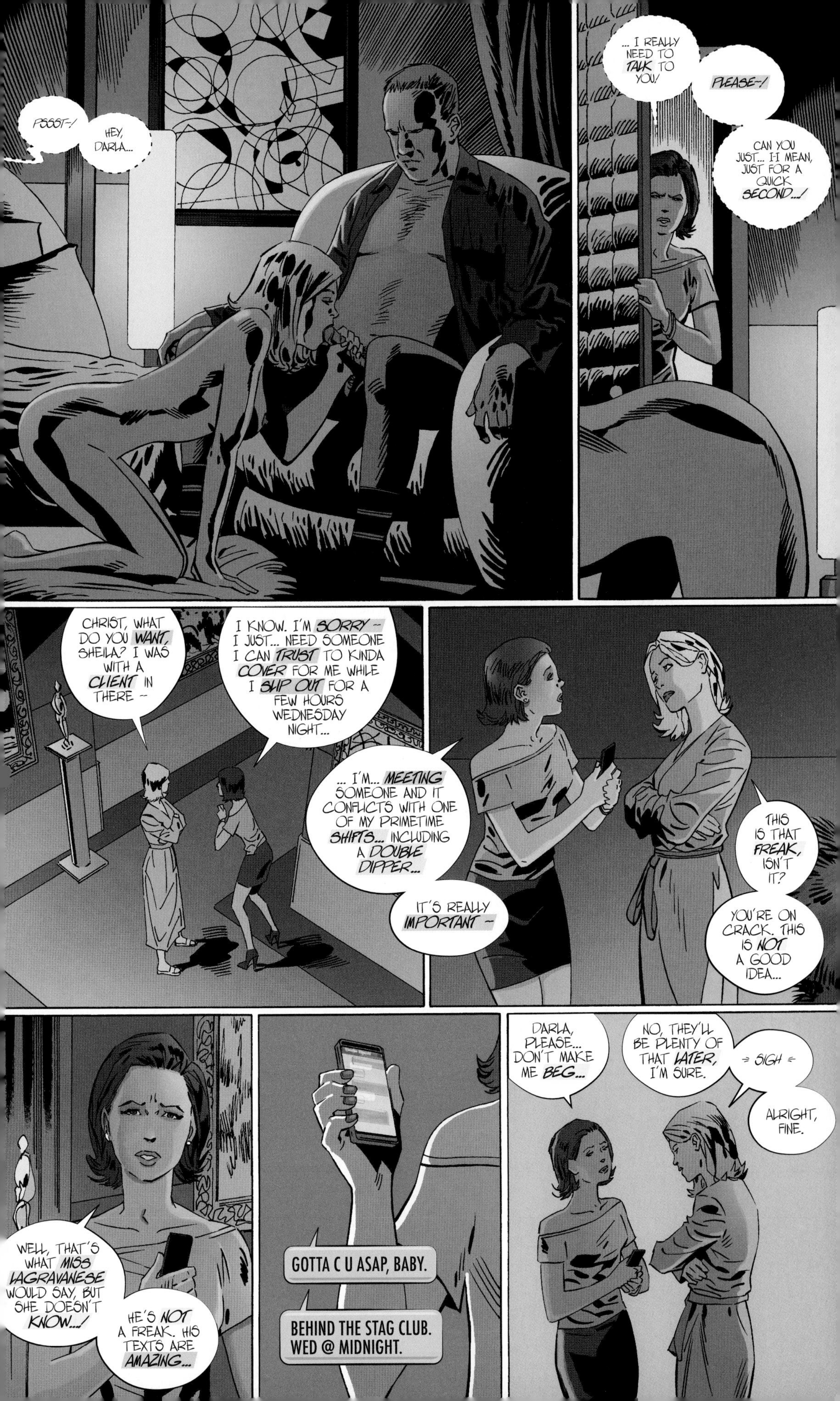
PSSST-!
HEY, DARLA...
... I REALLY NEED TO TALK TO YOU!
PLEASE-!
CAN YOU JUST... I-I MEAN, JUST FOR A QUICK SECOND...!
CHRIST, WHAT DO YOU WANT, SHEILA? I WAS WITH A CLIENT IN THERE --
I KNOW. I'M SORRY -- I JUST... NEED SOMEONE I CAN TRUST TO KINDA COVER FOR ME WHILE I SLIP OUT FOR A FEW HOURS WEDNESDAY NIGHT...
... I'M... MEETING SOMEONE AND IT CONFLICTS WITH ONE OF MY PRIMETIME SHIFTS... INCLUDING A DOUBLE DIPPER...
IT'S REALLY IMPORTANT --
THIS IS THAT FREAK, ISN'T IT?
YOU'RE ON CRACK. THIS IS NOT A GOOD IDEA...
WELL, THAT'S WHAT MISS LAGRAVANESE WOULD SAY, BUT SHE DOESN'T KNOW...!
HE'S NOT A FREAK. HIS TEXTS ARE AMAZING...
GOTTA C U ASAP, BABY.
BEHIND THE STAG CLUB. WED @ MIDNIGHT.
DARLA, PLEASE... DON'T MAKE ME BEG...
NO, THEY'LL BE PLENTY OF THAT LATER, I'M SURE.
SIGH
ALRIGHT, FINE.

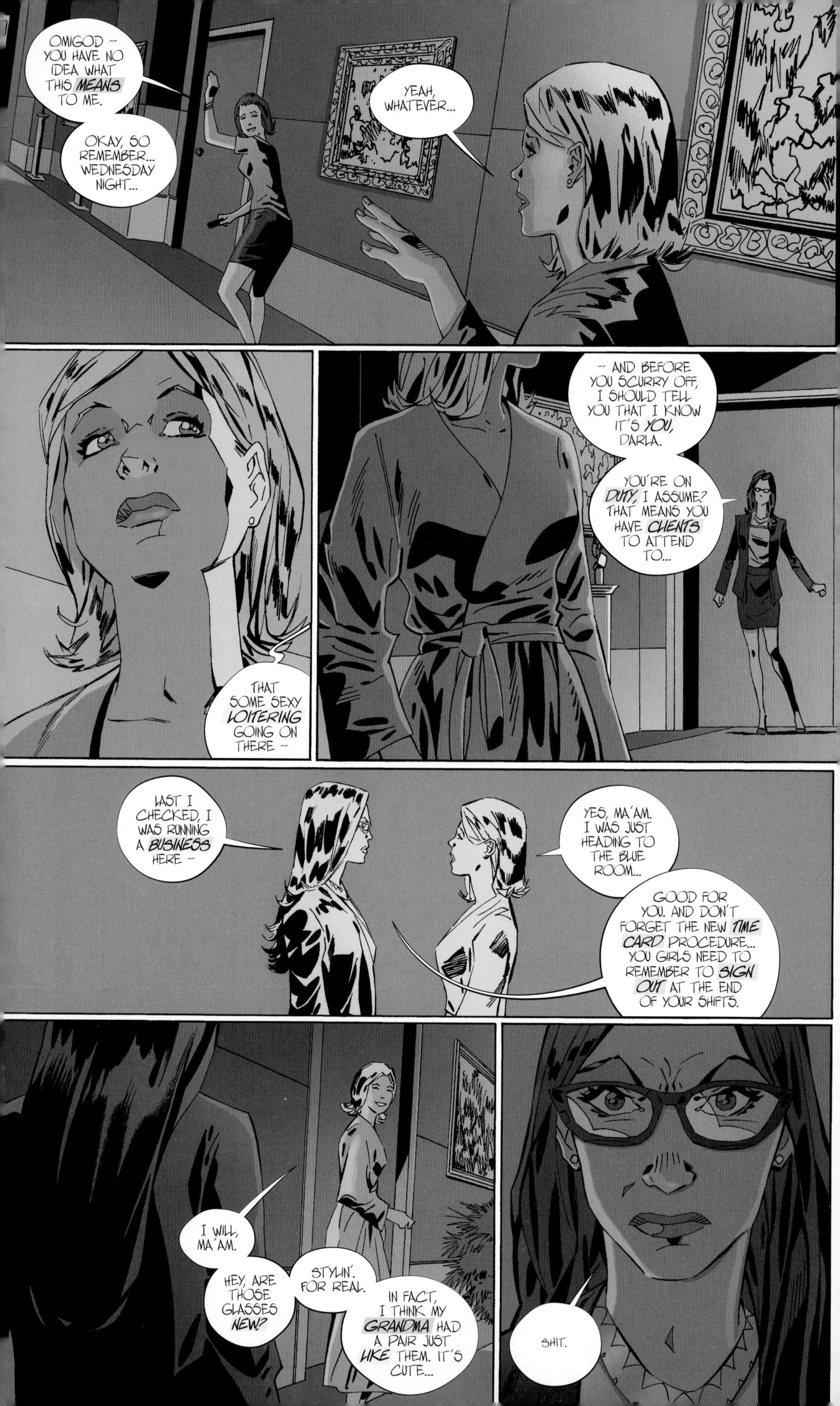
OMIGOD -- YOU HAVE NO IDEA WHAT THIS MEANS TO ME.
OKAY, SO REMEMBER... WEDNESDAY NIGHT...
YEAH, WHATEVER...
THAT SOME SEXY LOITERING GOING ON THERE --
-- AND BEFORE YOU SCURRY OFF, I SHOULD TELL YOU THAT I KNOW IT'S YOU, DARLA.
YOU'RE ON DUTY, I ASSUME? THAT MEANS YOU HAVE CLIENTS TO ATTEND TO...
LAST I CHECKED, I WAS RUNNING A BUSINESS HERE --
YES, MA'AM. I WAS JUST HEADING TO THE BLUE ROOM...
GOOD FOR YOU. AND DON'T FORGET THE NEW TIME CARD PROCEDURE... YOU GIRLS NEED TO REMEMBER TO SIGN OUT AT THE END OF YOUR SHIFTS.
I WILL, MA'AM.
HEY, ARE THOSE GLASSES NEW?
STYLIN'. FOR REAL.
IN FACT, I THINK MY GRANDMA HAD A PAIR JUST LIKE THEM. IT'S CUTE...
SHIT.

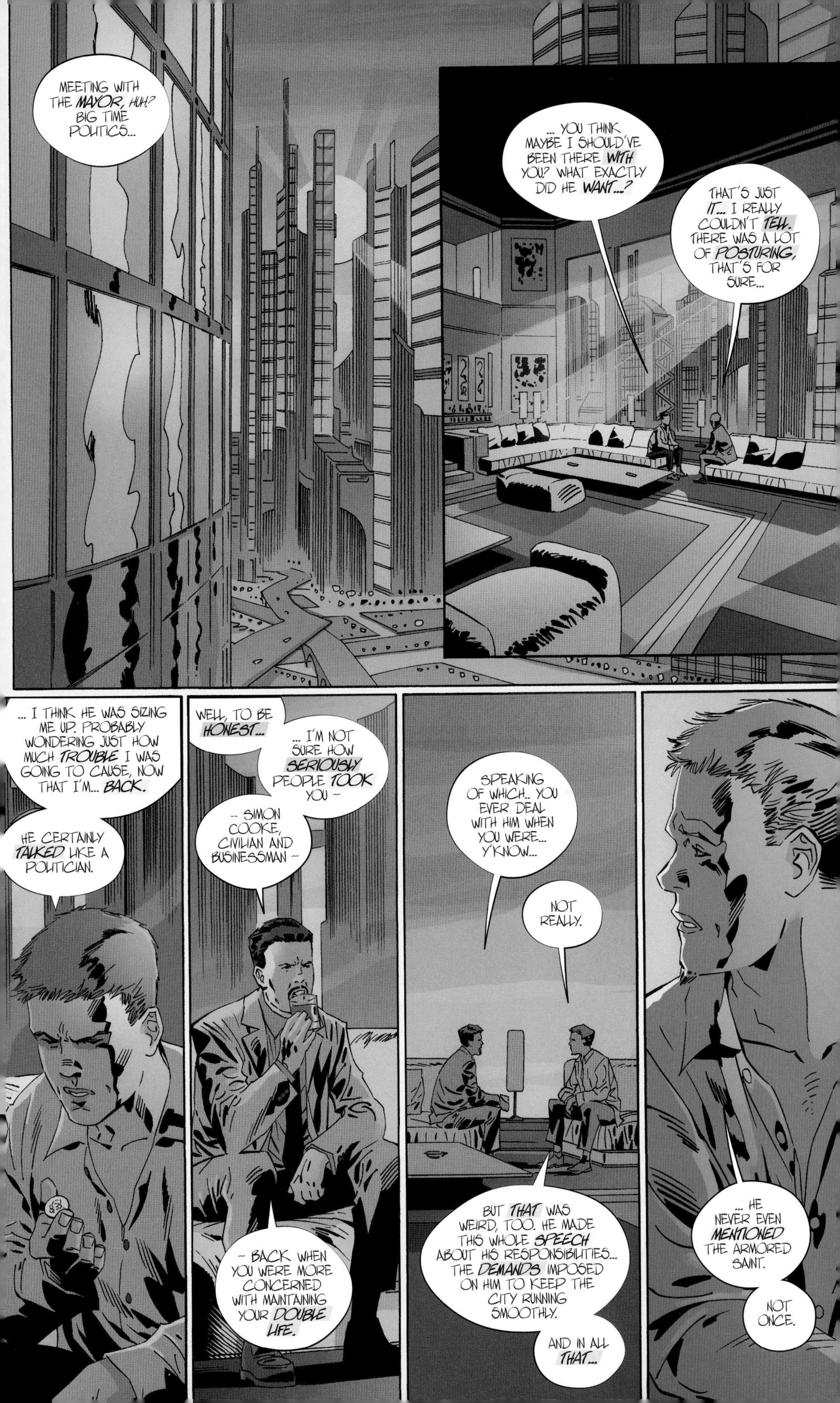
MEETING WITH THE MAYOR, HUH? BIG TIME POLITICS...
... YOU THINK MAYBE I SHOULD'VE BEEN THERE WITH YOU? WHAT EXACTLY DID HE WANT...?
THAT'S JUST IT... I REALLY COULDN'T TELL. THERE WAS A LOT OF POSTURING, THAT'S FOR SURE...
... I THINK HE WAS SIZING ME UP. PROBABLY WONDERING JUST HOW MUCH TROUBLE I WAS GOING TO CAUSE, NOW THAT I'M... BACK.
HE CERTAINLY TALKED LIKE A POLITICIAN.
WELL, TO BE HONEST...
... I'M NOT SURE HOW SERIOUSLY PEOPLE TOOK YOU --
-- SIMON COOKE, CIVILIAN AND BUSINESSMAN --
-- BACK WHEN YOU WERE MORE CONCERNED WITH MAINTAINING YOUR DOUBLE LIFE.
SPEAKING OF WHICH.. YOU EVER DEAL WITH HIM WHEN YOU WERE... Y'KNOW...
NOT REALLY.
BUT THAT WAS WEIRD, TOO. HE MADE THIS WHOLE SPEECH ABOUT HIS RESPONSIBILITIES... THE DEMANDS IMPOSED ON HIM TO KEEP THE CITY RUNNING SMOOTHLY.
AND IN ALL THAT...
... HE NEVER EVEN MENTIONED THE ARMORED SAINT.
NOT ONCE.

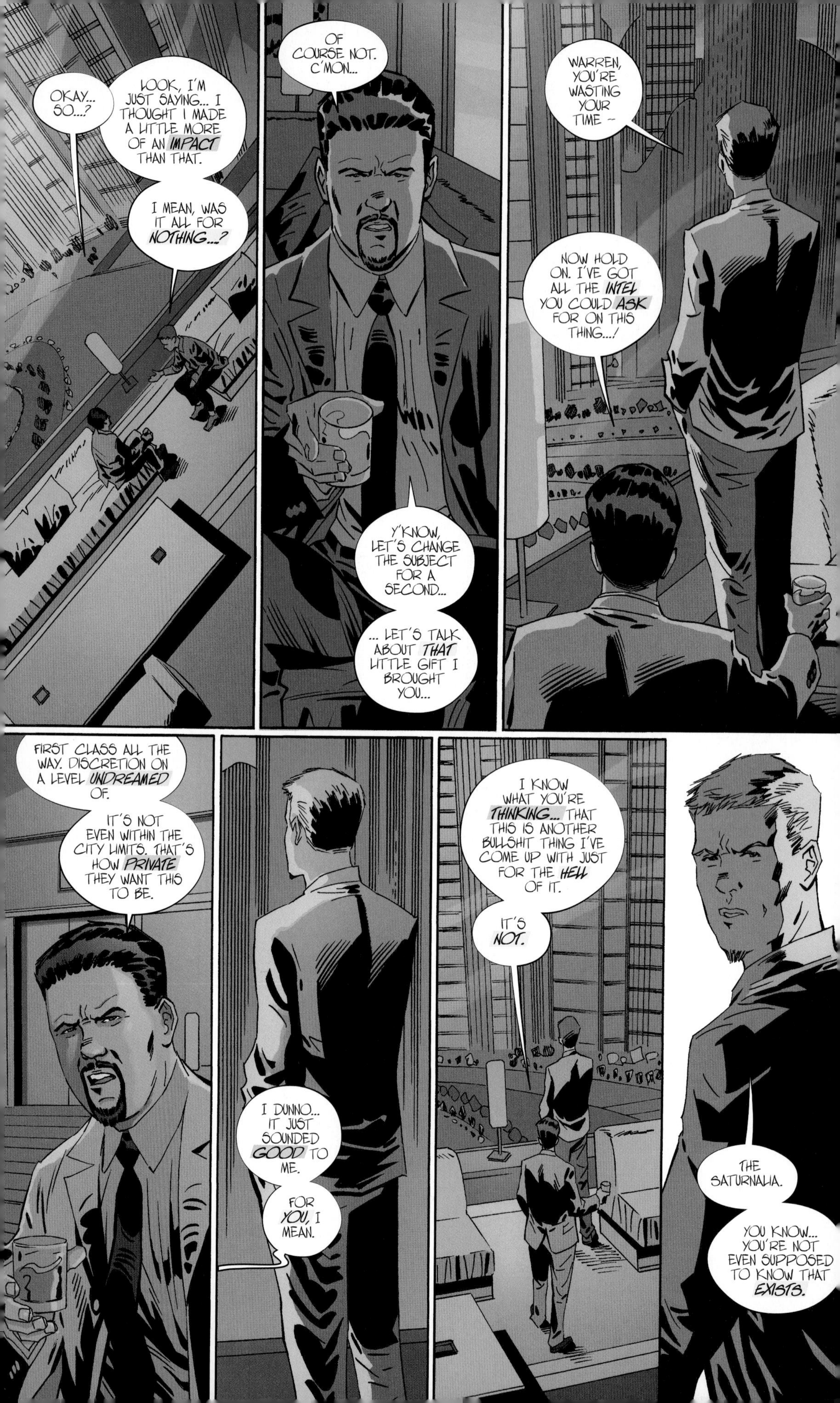
OKAY... SO...?
LOOK, I'M JUST SAYING... I THOUGHT I MADE A LITTLE MORE OF AN IMPACT THAN THAT.
I MEAN, WAS IT ALL FOR NOTHING...?
OF COURSE NOT. C'MON...
Y'KNOW, LET'S CHANGE THE SUBJECT FOR A SECOND...
... LET'S TALK ABOUT THAT LITTLE GIFT I BROUGHT YOU...
WARREN, YOU'RE WASTING YOUR TIME --
NOW HOLD ON. I'VE GOT ALL THE INTEL YOU COULD ASK FOR ON THIS THING...!
FIRST CLASS ALL THE WAY. DISCRETION ON A LEVEL UNDREAMED OF.
IT'S NOT EVEN WITHIN THE CITY LIMITS. THAT'S HOW PRIVATE THEY WANT THIS TO BE.
I DUNNO... IT JUST SOUNDED GOOD TO ME.
FOR YOU, I MEAN.
I KNOW WHAT YOU'RE THINKING... THAT THIS IS ANOTHER BULLSHIT THING I'VE COME UP WITH JUST FOR THE HELL OF IT.
IT'S NOT.
THE SATURNALIA.
YOU KNOW... YOU'RE NOT EVEN SUPPOSED TO KNOW THAT EXISTS.

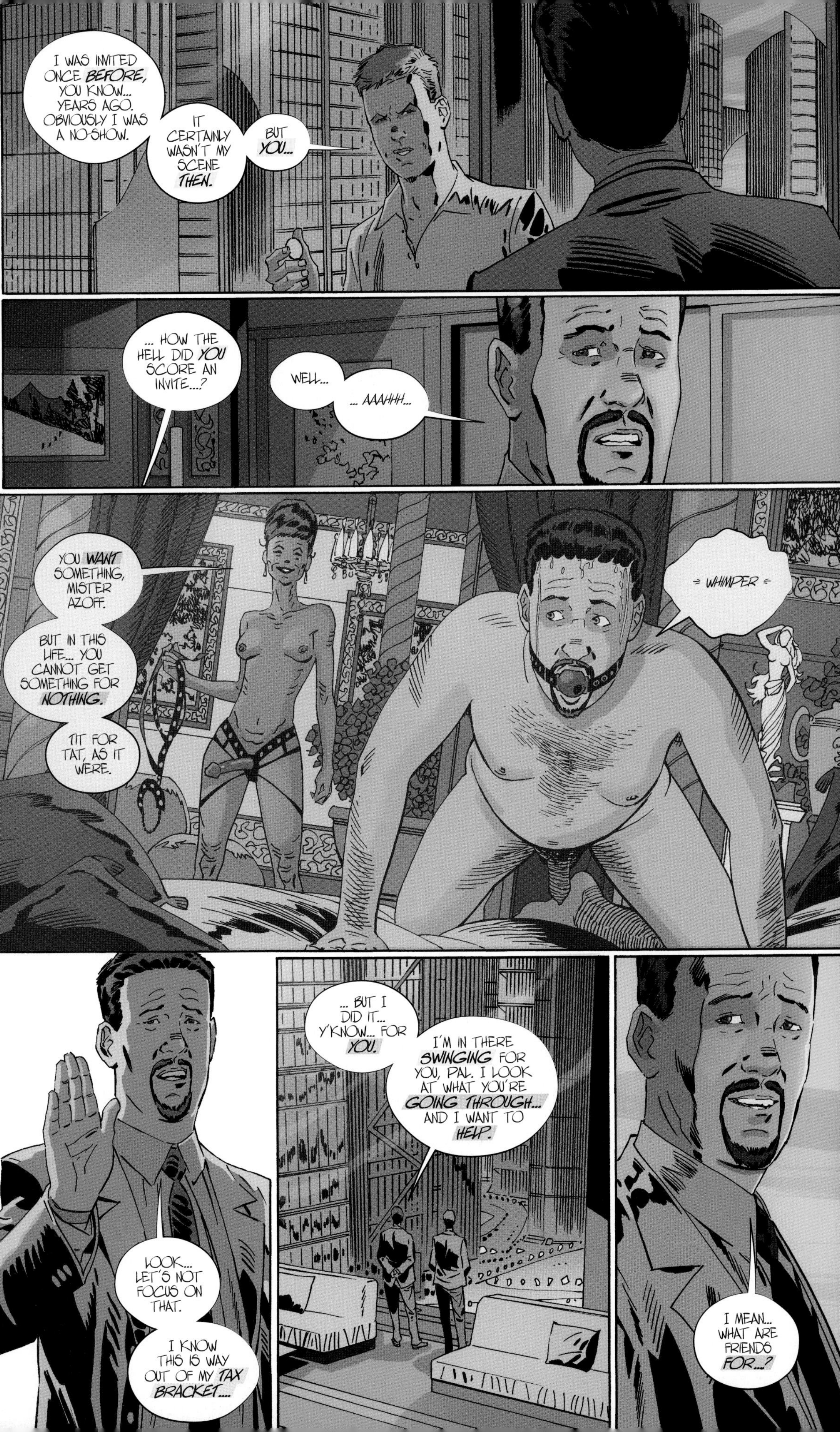

I WAS INVITED ONCE BEFORE, YOU KNOW... YEARS AGO. OBVIOUSLY I WAS A NO-SHOW.
IT CERTAINLY WASN'T MY SCENE THEN.
BUT YOU...
... HOW THE HELL DID YOU SCORE AN INVITE...?
WELL...
... AAAHHH...
YOU WANT SOMETHING, MISTER AZOFF.
BUT IN THIS LIFE... YOU CANNOT GET SOMETHING FOR NOTHING.
TIT FOR TAT, AS IT WERE.
= WHIMPER =
LOOK... LET'S NOT FOCUS ON THAT.
I KNOW THIS IS WAY OUT OF MY TAX BRACKET....
... BUT I DID IT... Y'KNOW... FOR YOU.
I'M IN THERE SWINGING FOR YOU, PAL. I LOOK AT WHAT YOU'RE GOING THROUGH... AND I WANT TO HELP.
I MEAN... WHAT ARE FRIENDS FOR...?

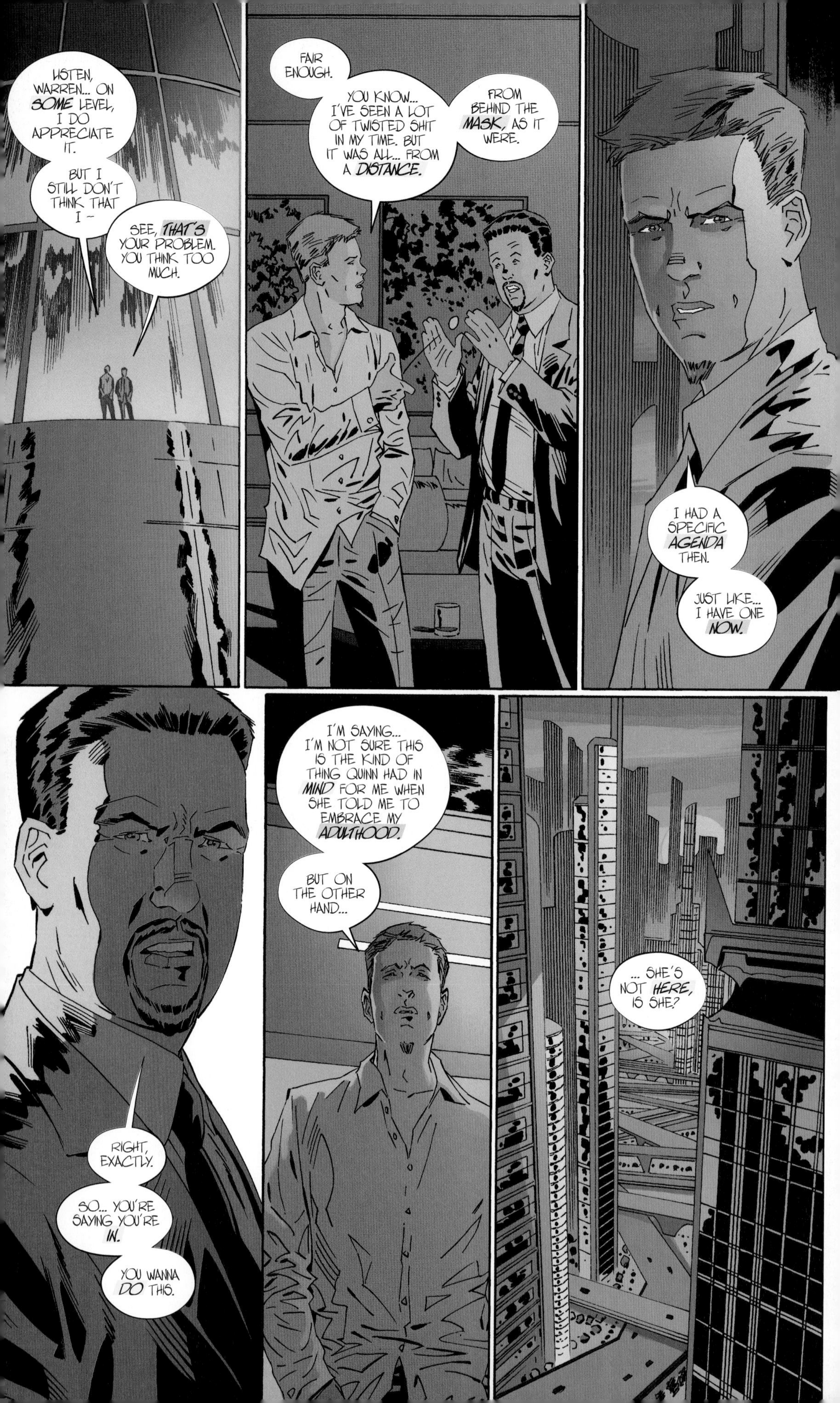
LISTEN, WARREN... ON SOME LEVEL, I DO APPRECIATE IT.
BUT I STILL DON'T THINK THAT I --
SEE, THAT'S YOUR PROBLEM. YOU THINK TOO MUCH.
FAIR ENOUGH.
YOU KNOW... I'VE SEEN A LOT OF TWISTED SHIT IN MY TIME. BUT IT WAS ALL... FROM A DISTANCE.
FROM BEHIND THE MASK, AS IT WERE.
I HAD A SPECIFIC AGENDA THEN.
JUST LIKE... I HAVE ONE NOW.
RIGHT, EXACTLY.
SO... YOU'RE SAYING YOU'RE IN.
YOU WANNA DO THIS.
I'M SAYING... I'M NOT SURE THIS IS THE KIND OF THING QUINN HAD IN MIND FOR ME WHEN SHE TOLD ME TO EMBRACE MY ADULTHOOD.
BUT ON THE OTHER HAND...
... SHE'S NOT HERE, IS SHE?

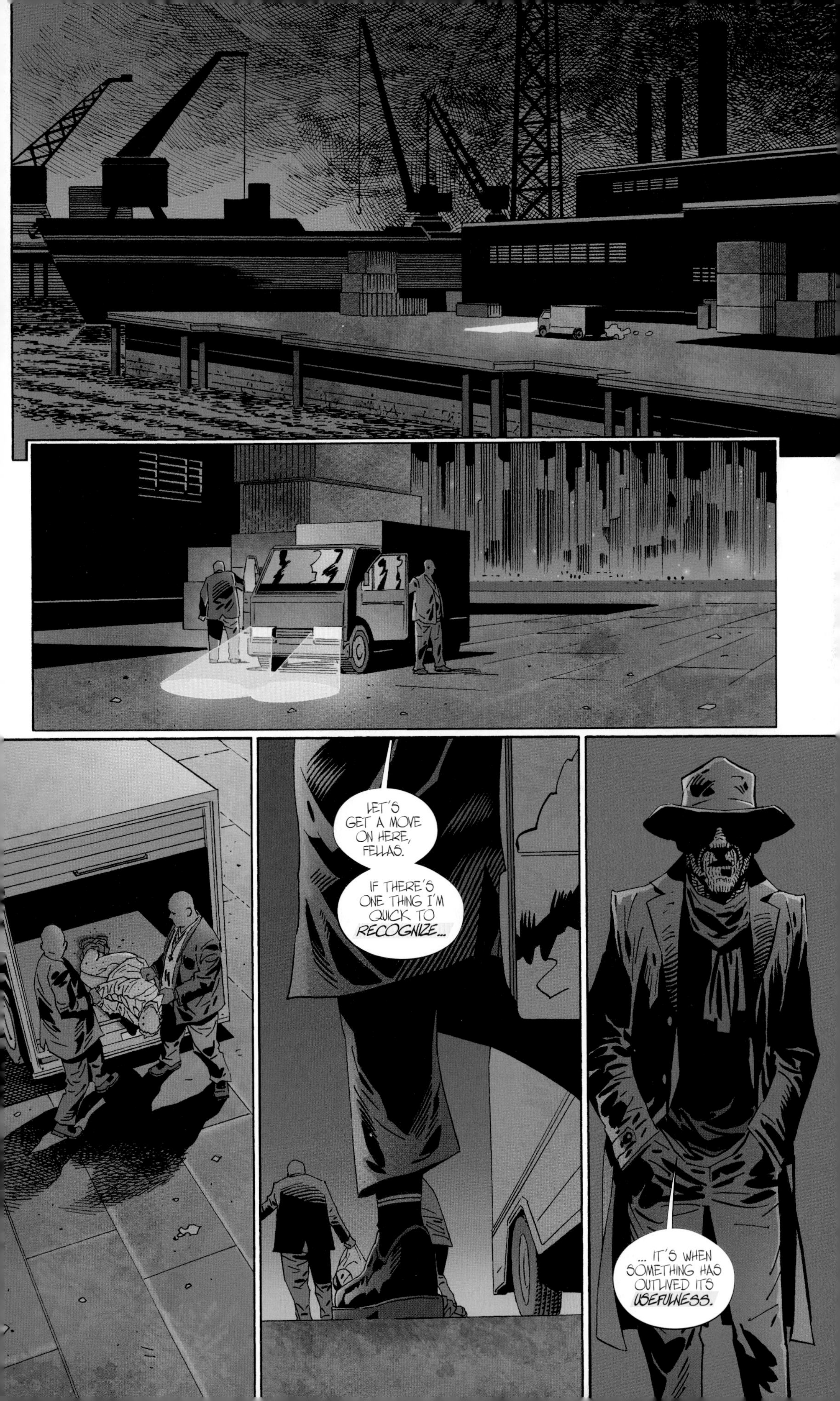

LET'S GET A MOVE ON HERE, FELLAS.
IF THERE'S ONE THING I'M QUICK TO RECOGNIZE...
... IT'S WHEN SOMETHING HAS OUTLIVED ITS USEFULNESS.

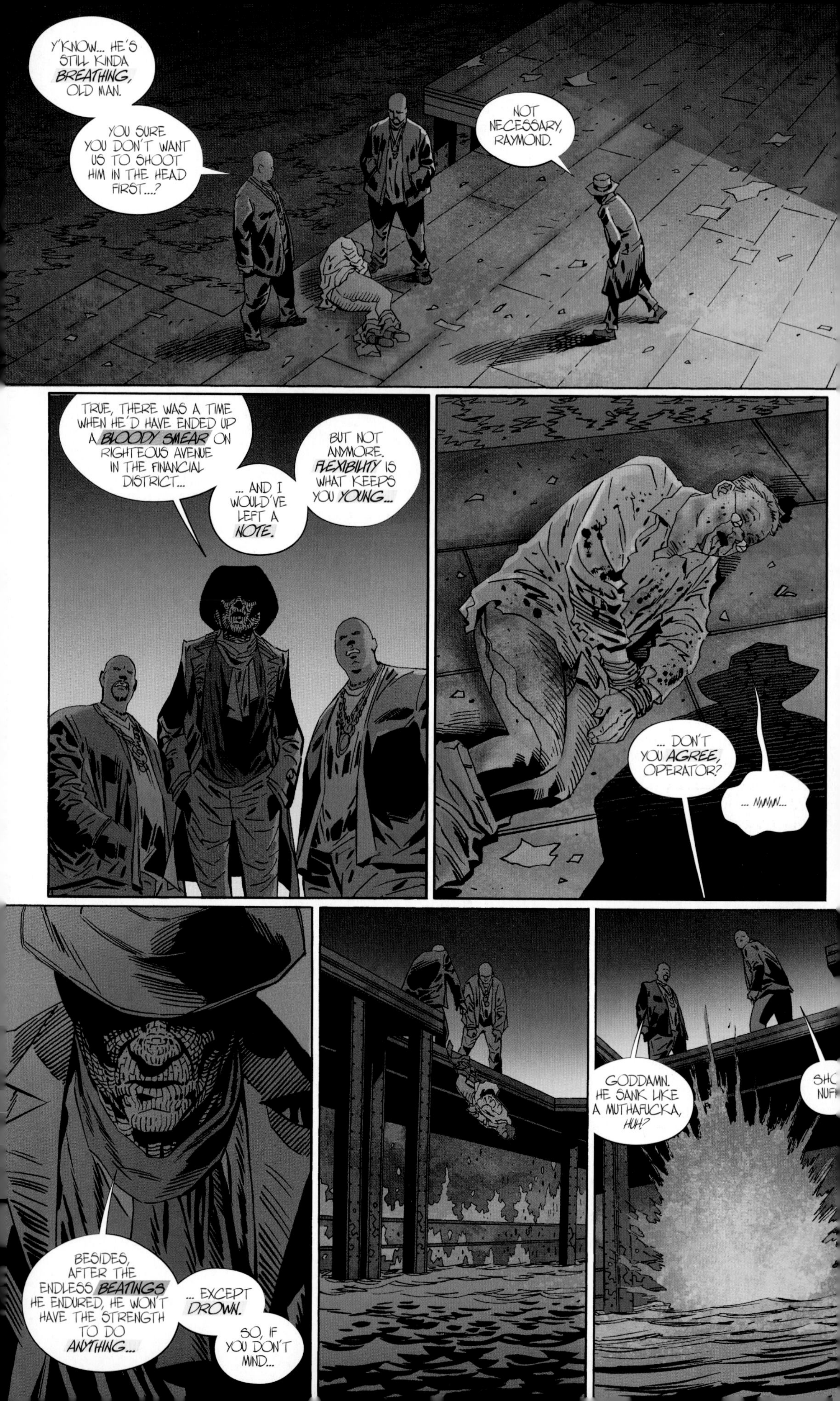

Y'KNOW... HE'S STILL KINDA BREATHING, OLD MAN.
YOU SURE YOU DON'T WANT US TO SHOOT HIM IN THE HEAD FIRST...?
NOT NECESSARY, RAYMOND.
TRUE, THERE WAS A TIME WHEN HE'D HAVE ENDED UP A BLOODY SMEAR ON RIGHTEOUS AVENUE IN THE FINANCIAL DISTRICT...
... AND I WOULD'VE LEFT A NOTE.
BUT NOT ANYMORE. FLEXIBILITY IS WHAT KEEPS YOU YOUNG...
... DON'T YOU AGREE, OPERATOR?
... NNNNN...
BESIDES, AFTER THE ENDLESS BEATINGS HE ENDURED, HE WON'T HAVE THE STRENGTH TO DO ANYTHING...
... EXCEPT DROWN.
SO, IF YOU DON'T MIND...
GODDAMN. HE SANK LIKE A MUTHAFUCKA, HUH?

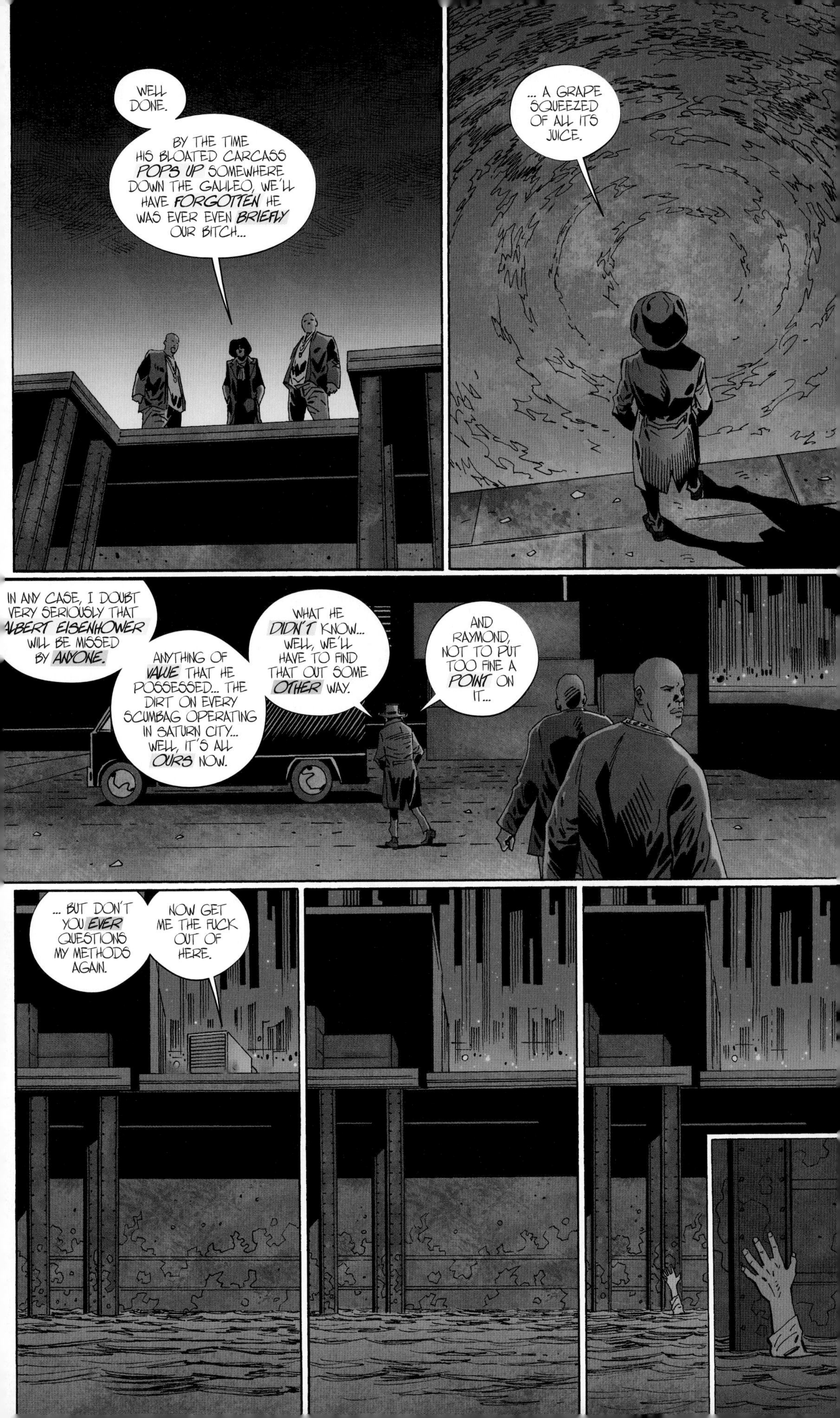
WELL DONE.
BY THE TIME HIS BLOATED CARCASS POPS UP SOMEWHERE DOWN THE GALILEO, WE'LL HAVE FORGOTTEN HE WAS EVER EVEN BRIEFLY OUR BITCH...
... A GRAPE SQUEEZED OF ALL ITS JUICE.
IN ANY CASE, I DOUBT VERY SERIOUSLY THAT ALBERT EISENHOWER WILL BE MISSED BY ANYONE.
ANYTHING OF VALUE THAT HE POSSESSED... THE DIRT ON EVERY SCUMBAG OPERATING IN SATURN CITY... WELL, IT'S ALL OURS NOW.
WHAT HE DIDN'T KNOW... WELL, WE'LL HAVE TO FIND THAT OUT SOME OTHER WAY.
AND RAYMOND, NOT TO PUT TOO FINE A POINT ON IT...
... BUT DON'T YOU EVER QUESTIONS MY METHODS AGAIN.
NOW GET ME THE FUCK OUT OF HERE.

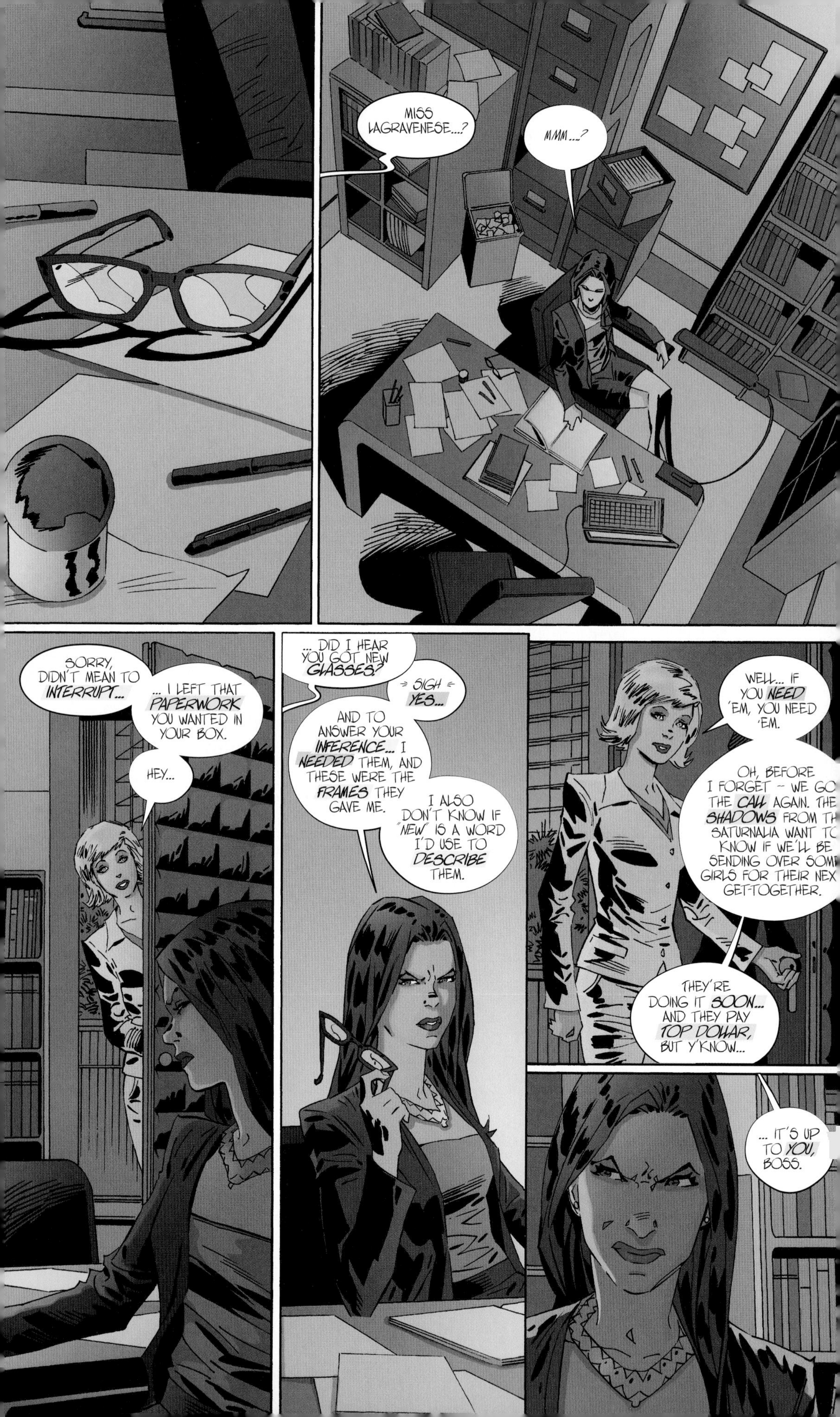
MISS LAGRAVENESE...?
MMM...?
SORRY, DIDN'T MEAN TO INTERRUPT...
... I LEFT THAT PAPERWORK YOU WANTED IN YOUR BOX.
HEY...
... DID I HEAR YOU GOT NEW GLASSES?
SIGH YES...
AND TO ANSWER YOUR INFERENCE... I NEEDED THEM, AND THESE WERE THE FRAMES THEY GAVE ME.
I ALSO DON'T KNOW IF "NEW" IS A WORD I'D USE TO DESCRIBE THEM.
WELL... IF YOU NEED 'EM, YOU NEED 'EM.
OH, BEFORE I FORGET -- WE GO THE CALL AGAIN. THE SHADOWS FROM TH SATURNALIA WANT TO KNOW IF WE'LL BE SENDING OVER SOM GIRLS FOR THEIR NEX GET-TOGETHER.
THEY'RE DOING IT SOON... AND THEY PAY TOP DOLLAR, BUT Y'KNOW...
... IT'S UP TO YOU, BOSS.

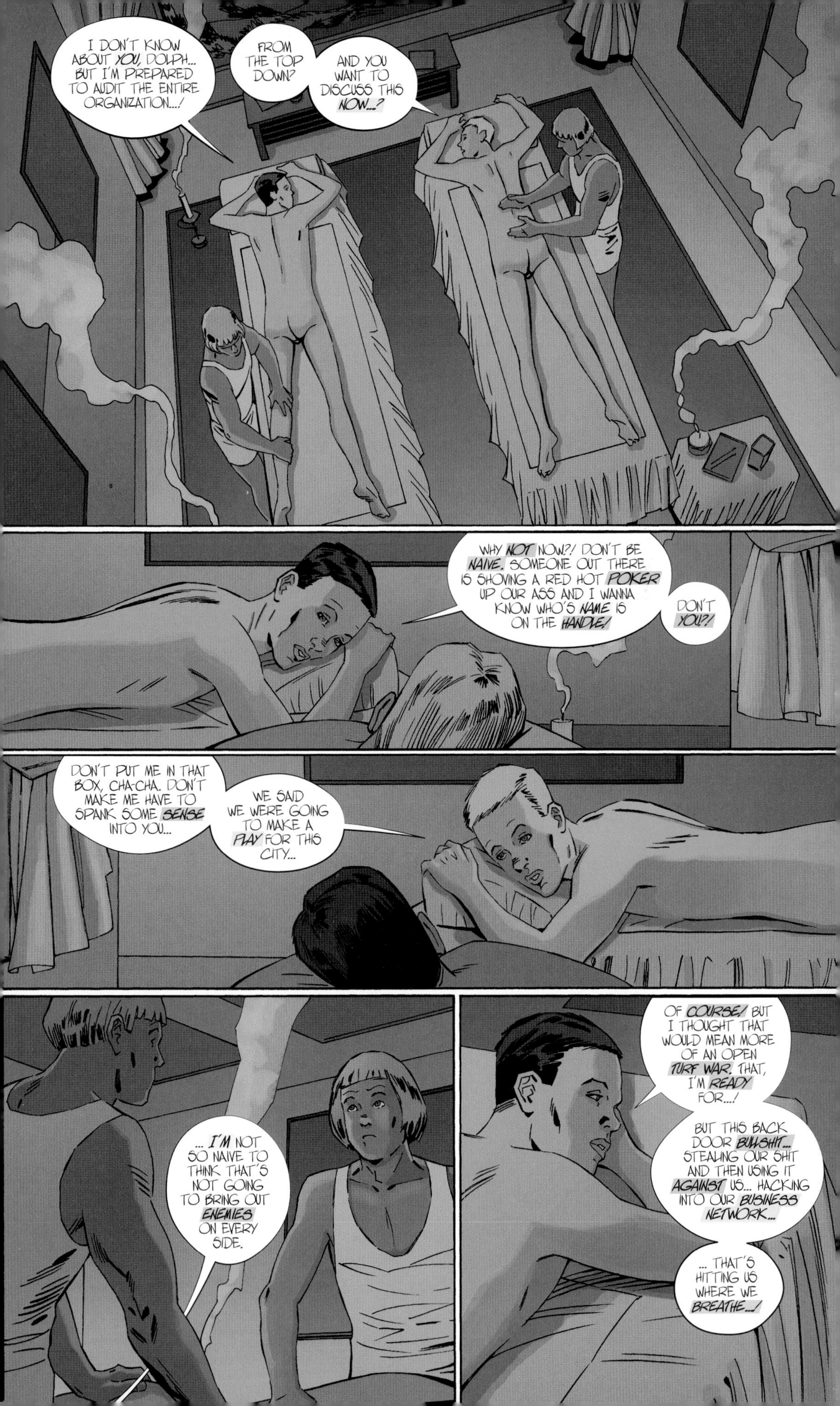

I DON'T KNOW ABOUT YOU, DOLPH... BUT I'M PREPARED TO AUDIT THE ENTIRE ORGANIZATION...!
FROM THE TOP DOWN?
AND YOU WANT TO DISCUSS THIS NOW...?
WHY NOT NOW?! DON'T BE NAIVE. SOMEONE OUT THERE IS SHOVING A RED HOT POKER UP OUR ASS AND I WANNA KNOW WHO'S NAME IS ON THE HANDLE!
DON'T YOU?!
DON'T PUT ME IN THAT BOX, CHA-CHA. DON'T MAKE ME HAVE TO SPANK SOME SENSE INTO YOU...
WE SAID WE WERE GOING TO MAKE A PLAY FOR THIS CITY...
... I'M NOT SO NAIVE TO THINK THAT'S NOT GOING TO BRING OUT ENEMIES ON EVERY SIDE.
OF COURSE! BUT I THOUGHT THAT WOULD MEAN MORE OF AN OPEN TURF WAR. THAT, I'M READY FOR...!
BUT THIS BACK DOOR BULLSHIT... STEALING OUR SHIT AND THEN USING IT AGAINST US... HACKING INTO OUR BUSINESS NETWORK...
... THAT'S HITTING US WHERE WE BREATHE...!

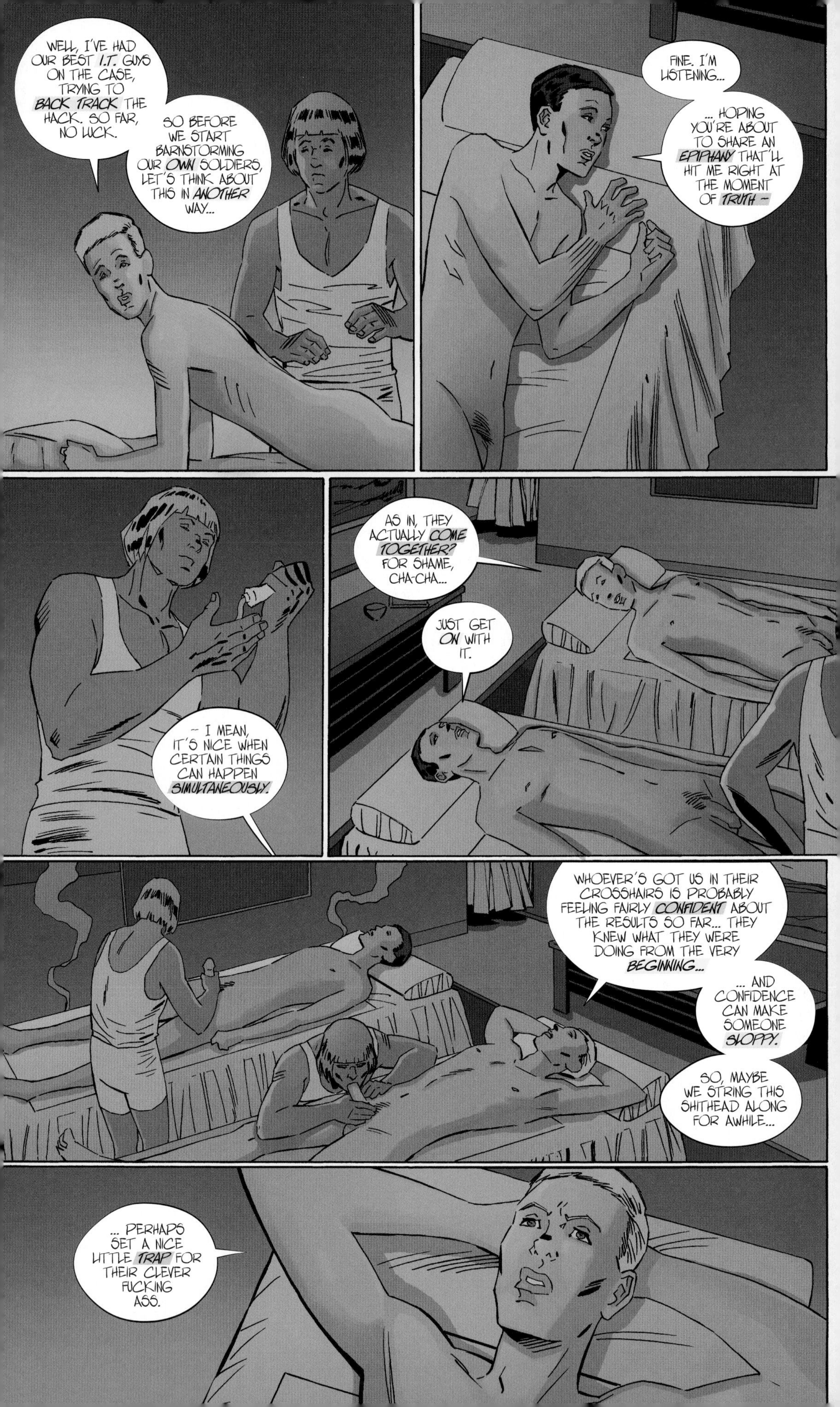
WELL, I'VE HAD OUR BEST I.T. GUYS ON THE CASE, TRYING TO BACK TRACK THE HACK. SO FAR, NO LUCK.
SO BEFORE WE START BARNSTORMING OUR OWN SOLDIERS, LET'S THINK ABOUT THIS IN ANOTHER WAY...
FINE. I'M LISTENING...
... HOPING YOU'RE ABOUT TO SHARE AN EPIPHANY THAT'LL HIT ME RIGHT AT THE MOMENT OF TRUTH --
-- I MEAN, IT'S NICE WHEN CERTAIN THINGS CAN HAPPEN SIMULTANEOUSLY.
AS IN, THEY ACTUALLY COME TOGETHER? FOR SHAME, CHA-CHA...
JUST GET ON WITH IT.
WHOEVER'S GOT US IN THEIR CROSSHAIRS IS PROBABLY FEELING FAIRLY CONFIDENT ABOUT THE RESULTS SO FAR... THEY KNEW WHAT THEY WERE DOING FROM THE VERY BEGINNING...
... AND CONFIDENCE CAN MAKE SOMEONE SLOPPY.
SO, MAYBE WE STRING THIS SHITHEAD ALONG FOR AWHILE...
... PERHAPS SET A NICE LITTLE TRAP FOR THEIR CLEVER FUCKING ASS.

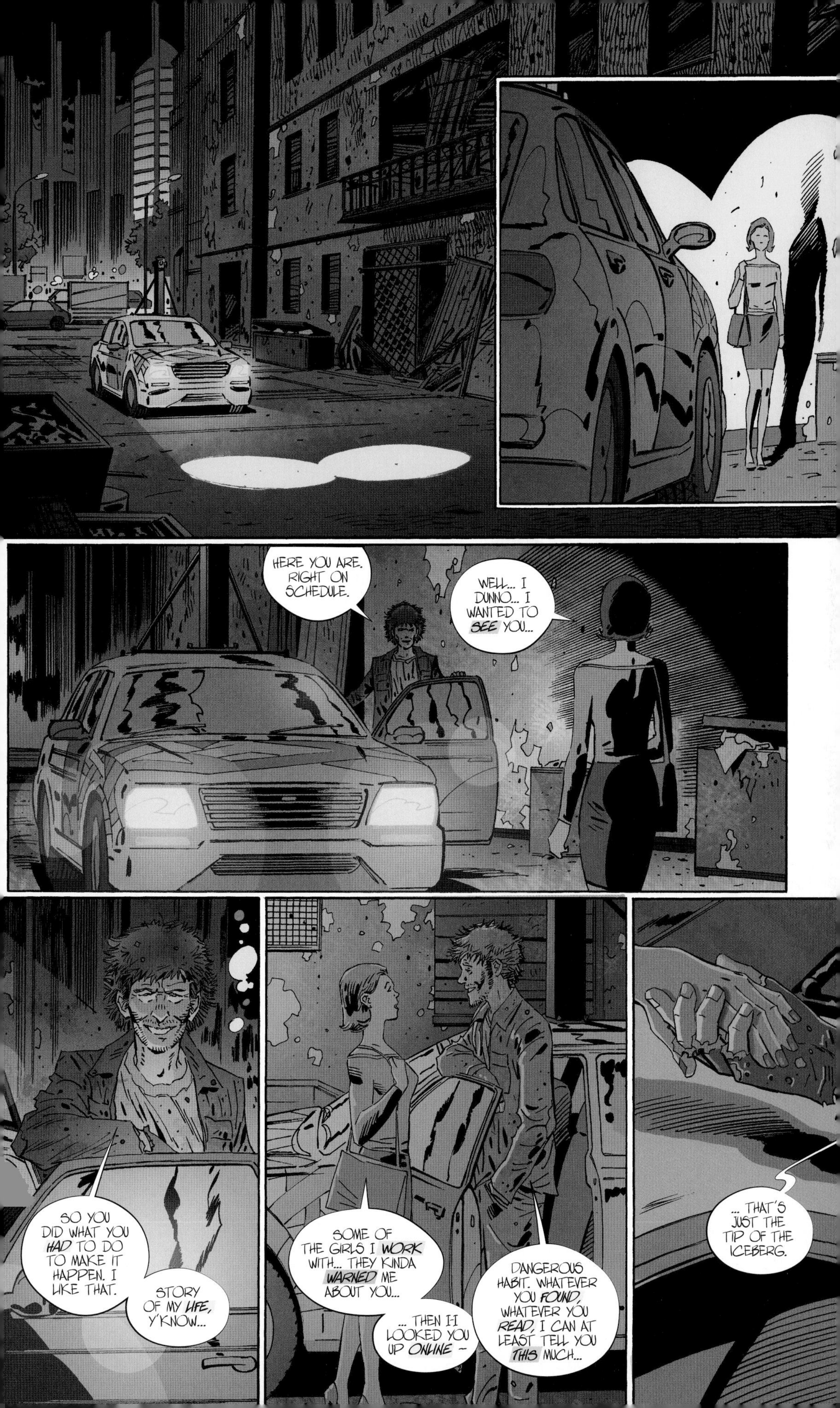
HERE YOU ARE. RIGHT ON SCHEDULE.
WELL... I DUNNO... I WANTED TO SEE YOU...
SO YOU DID WHAT YOU HAD TO DO TO MAKE IT HAPPEN. I LIKE THAT.
STORY OF MY LIFE, Y'KNOW...
SOME OF THE GIRLS I WORK WITH... THEY KINDA WARNED ME ABOUT YOU...
... THEN I-I LOOKED YOU UP ONLINE --
DANGEROUS HABIT. WHATEVER YOU FOUND, WHATEVER YOU READ, I CAN AT LEAST TELL YOU THIS MUCH...
... THAT'S JUST THE TIP OF THE ICEBERG.

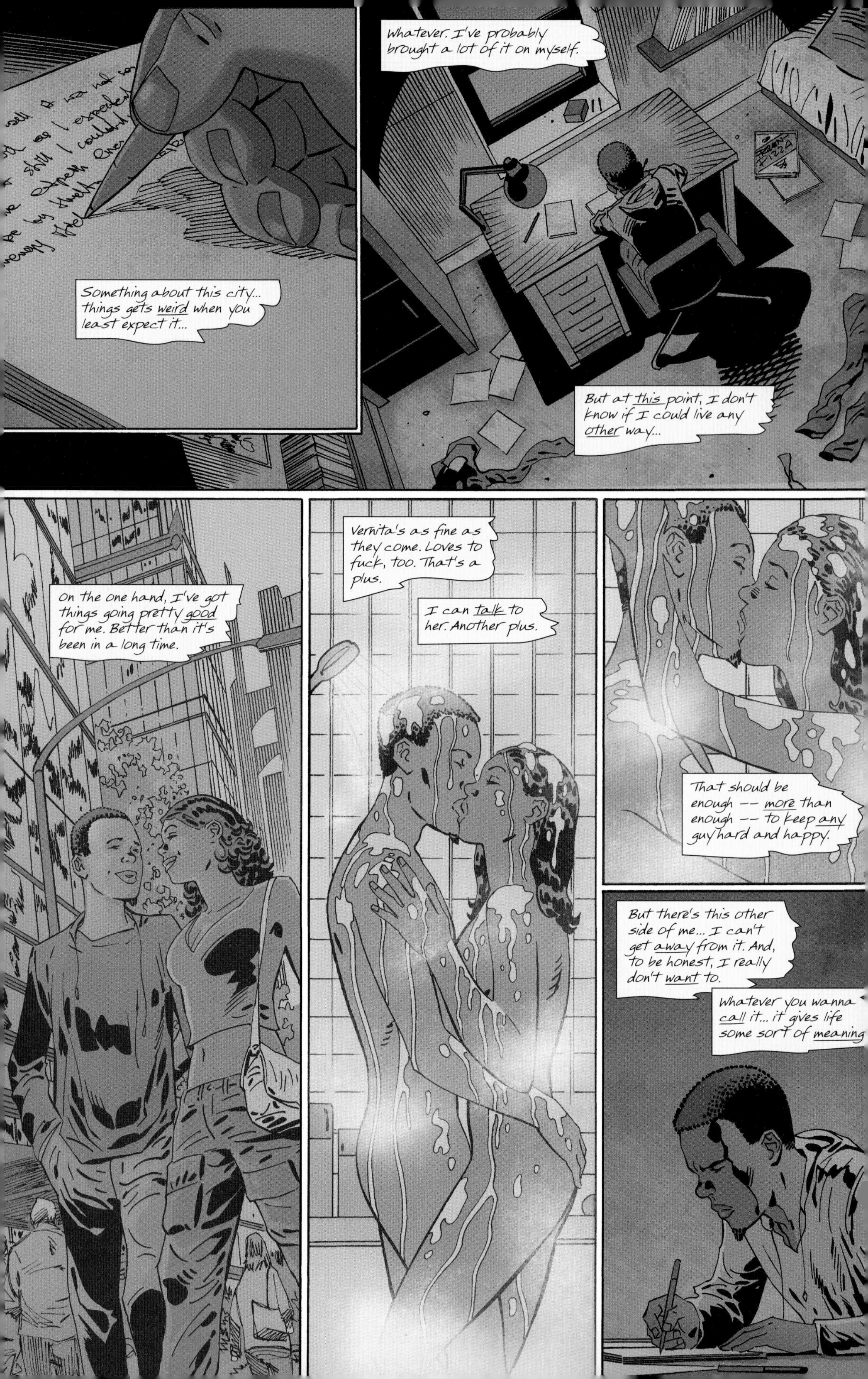
Something about this city... things gets weird when you least expect it...
Whatever. I've probably brought a lot of it on myself.
But at this point, I don't know if I could live any other way...
On the one hand, I've got things going pretty good for me. Better than it's been in a long time.
Vernita's as fine as they come. Loves to fuck, too. That's a plus.
I can talk to her. Another plus.
That should be enough -- more than enough -- to keep any guy hard and happy.
But there's this other side of me... I can't get away from it. And, to be honest, I really don't want to.
Whatever you wanna call it... it gives life some sort of meaning

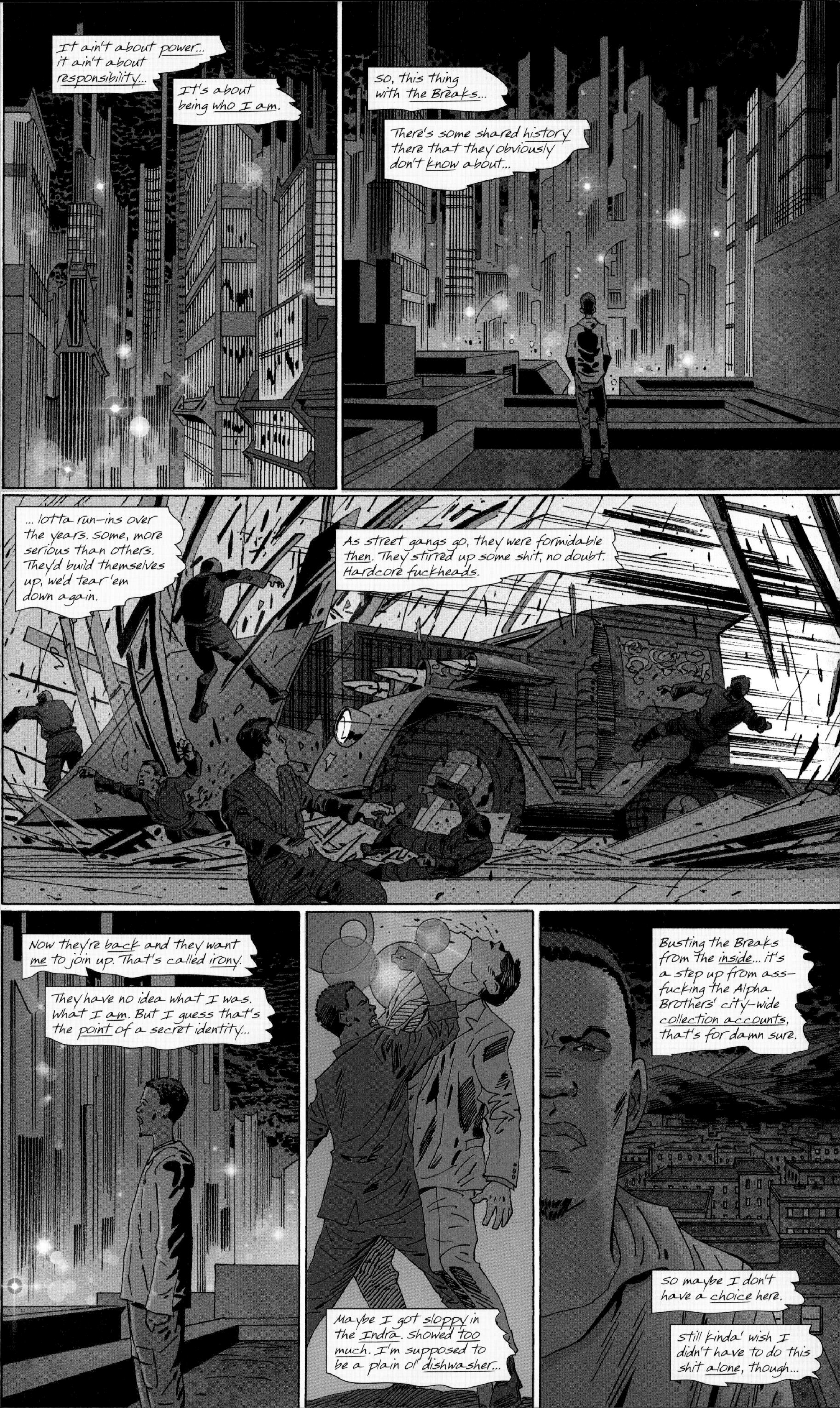
It ain't about power... it ain't about responsibility...
It's about being who I am.
So, this thing with the Breaks...
There's some shared history there that they obviously don't know about...
... lotta run-ins over the years. Some, more serious than others. They'd build themselves up, we'd tear 'em down again.
As street gangs go, they were formidable then. They stirred up some shit, no doubt. Hardcore fuckheads.
Now they're back and they want me to join up. That's called irony.
They have no idea what I was. What I am. But I guess that's the point of a secret identity...
Maybe I got sloppy in the Indra. Showed too much. I'm supposed to be a plain ol' dishwasher...
Busting the Breaks from the inside... it's a step up from ass-fucking the Alpha Brothers' city-wide collection accounts, that's for damn sure.
So maybe I don't have a choice here.
Still kinda' wish I didn't have to do this shit alone, though...

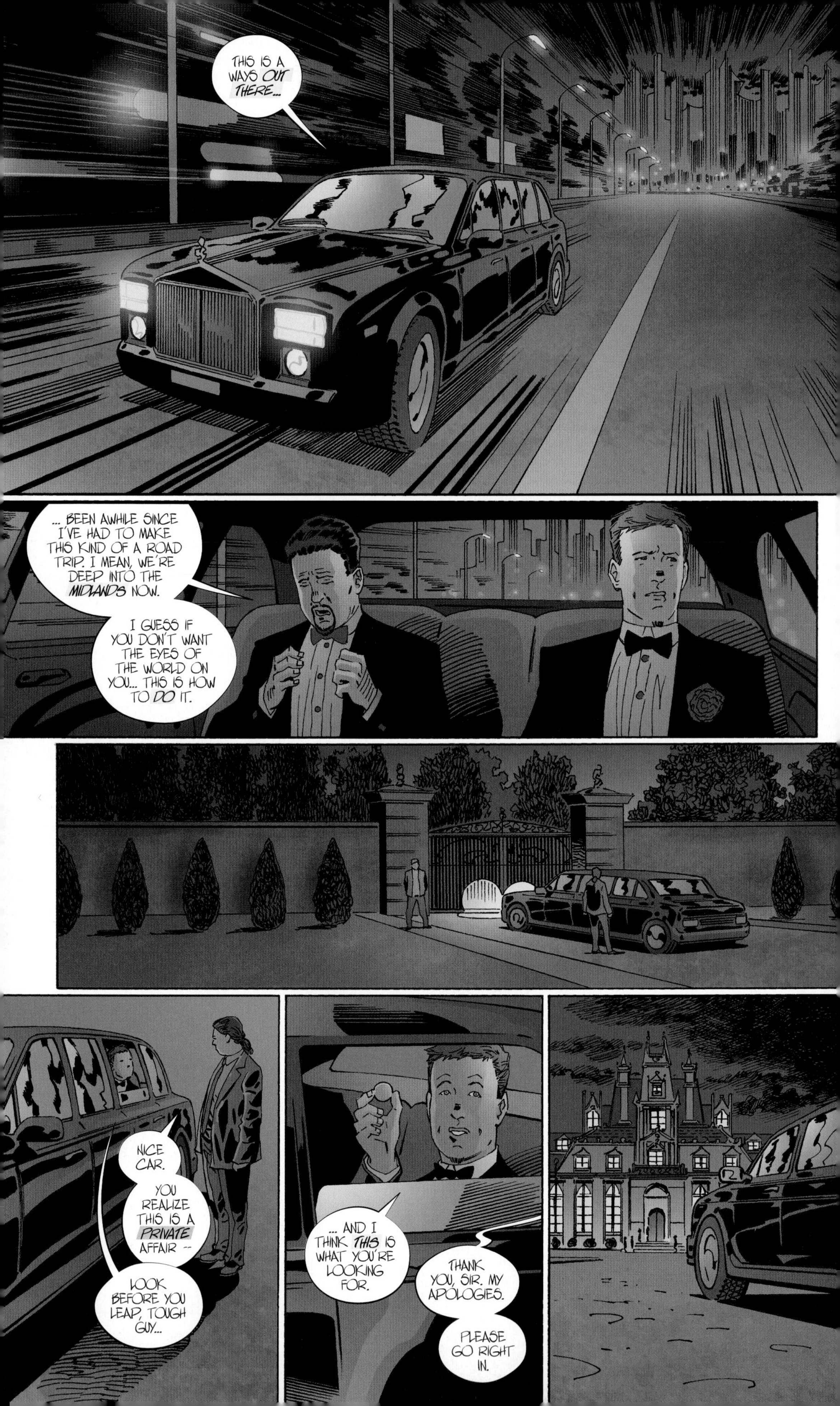
THIS IS A WAYS OUT THERE...
... BEEN AWHILE SINCE I'VE HAD TO MAKE THIS KIND OF A ROAD TRIP. I MEAN, WE'RE DEEP INTO THE MIDLANDS NOW.
I GUESS IF YOU DON'T WANT THE EYES OF THE WORLD ON YOU... THIS IS HOW TO DO IT.
NICE CAR.
YOU REALIZE THIS IS A PRIVATE AFFAIR --
LOOK BEFORE YOU LEAP, TOUGH GUY...
... AND I THINK THIS IS WHAT YOU'RE LOOKING FOR.
THANK YOU, SIR. MY APOLOGIES.
PLEASE GO RIGHT IN.

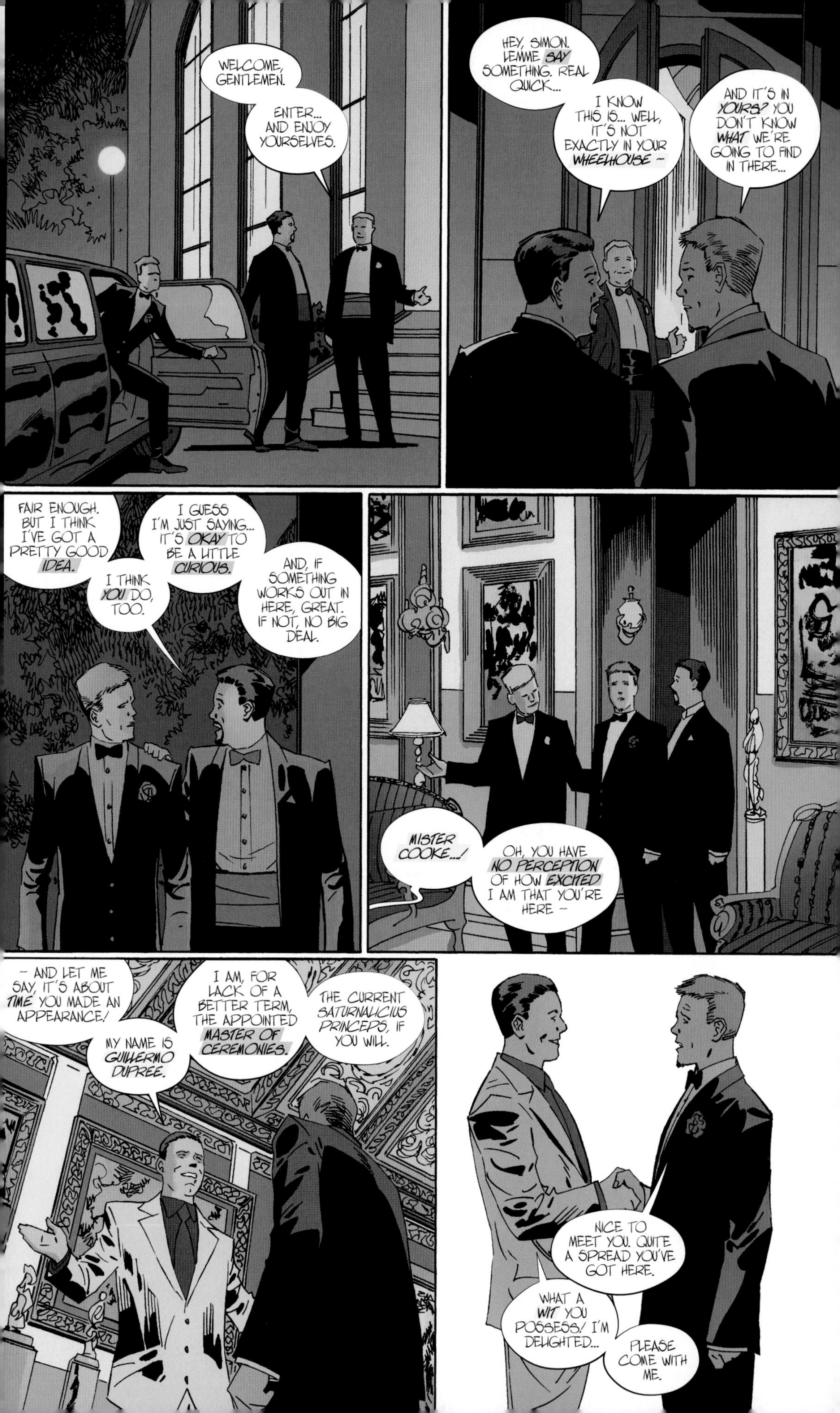
WELCOME, GENTLEMEN.
ENTER... AND ENJOY YOURSELVES.
HEY, SIMON. LEMME SAY SOMETHING. REAL QUICK...
I KNOW THIS IS... WELL, IT'S NOT EXACTLY IN YOUR WHEELHOUSE --
AND IT'S IN YOURS? YOU DON'T KNOW WHAT WE'RE GOING TO FIND IN THERE...
FAIR ENOUGH. BUT I THINK I'VE GOT A PRETTY GOOD IDEA.
I THINK YOU DO, TOO.
I GUESS I'M JUST SAYING... IT'S OKAY TO BE A LITTLE CURIOUS.
AND, IF SOMETHING WORKS OUT IN HERE, GREAT. IF NOT, NO BIG DEAL.
MISTER COOKE...!
OH, YOU HAVE NO PERCEPTION OF HOW EXCITED I AM THAT YOU'RE HERE --
-- AND LET ME SAY, IT'S ABOUT TIME YOU MADE AN APPEARANCE!
MY NAME IS GUILLERMO DUPREE.
I AM, FOR LACK OF A BETTER TERM, THE APPOINTED MASTER OF CEREMONIES.
THE CURRENT SATURNALICIUS PRINCEPS, IF YOU WILL.
NICE TO MEET YOU. QUITE A SPREAD YOU'VE GOT HERE.
WHAT A WIT YOU POSSESS! I'M DELIGHTED...
PLEASE COME WITH ME.

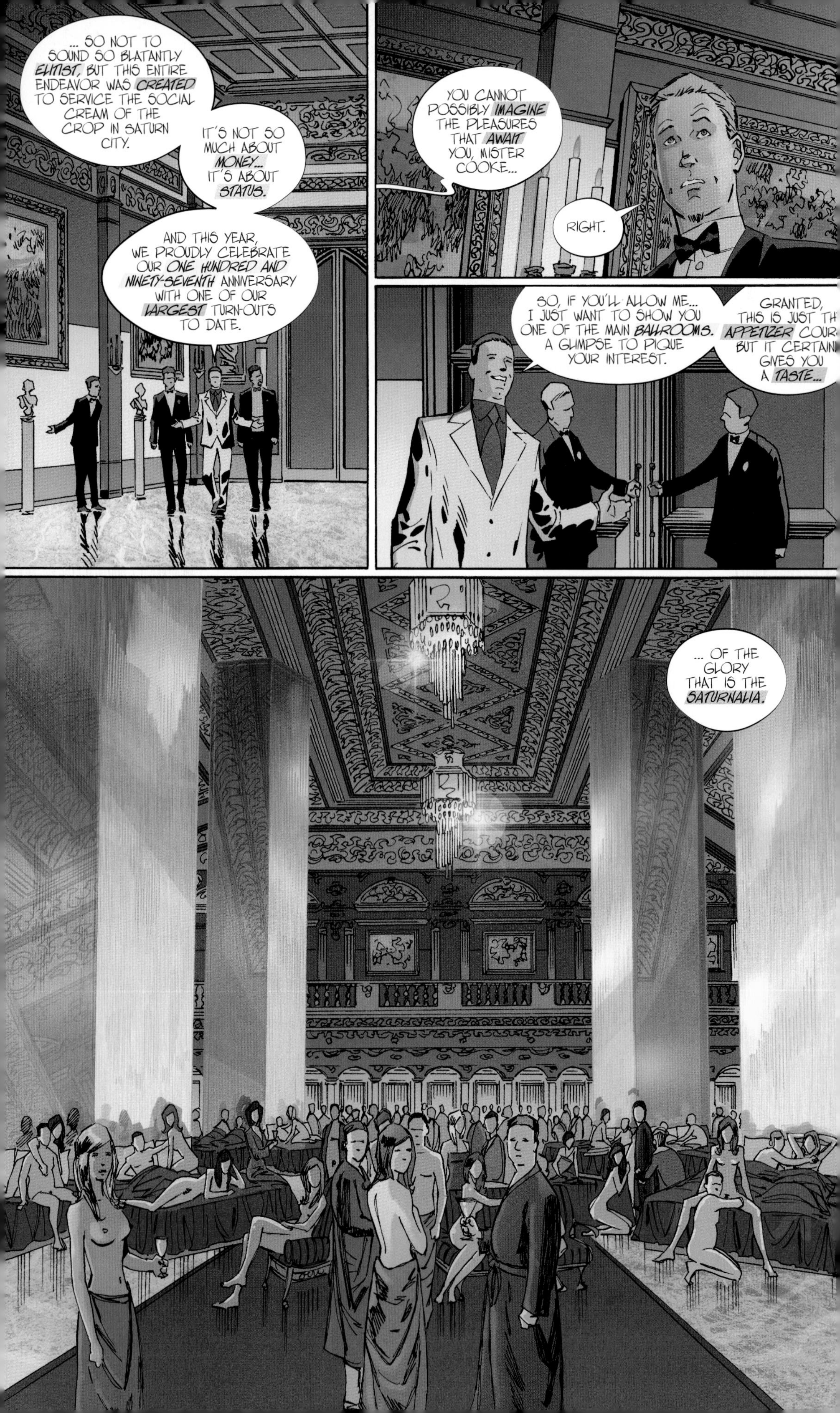
... SO NOT TO SOUND SO BLATANTLY ELITIST, BUT THIS ENTIRE ENDEAVOR WAS CREATED TO SERVICE THE SOCIAL CREAM OF THE CROP IN SATURN CITY.
IT'S NOT SO MUCH ABOUT MONEY... IT'S ABOUT STATUS.
AND THIS YEAR, WE PROUDLY CELEBRATE OUR ONE HUNDRED AND NINETY-SEVENTH ANNIVERSARY WITH ONE OF OUR LARGEST TURN-OUTS TO DATE.
YOU CANNOT POSSIBLY IMAGINE THE PLEASURES THAT AWAIT YOU, MISTER COOKE...
RIGHT.
SO, IF YOU'LL ALLOW ME... I JUST WANT TO SHOW YOU ONE OF THE MAIN BALLROOMS. A GLIMPSE TO PIQUE YOUR INTEREST.
GRANTED, THIS IS JUST TH APPETIZER COUR BUT IT CERTAIN GIVES YOU A TASTE...
... OF THE GLORY THAT IS THE SATURNALIA.

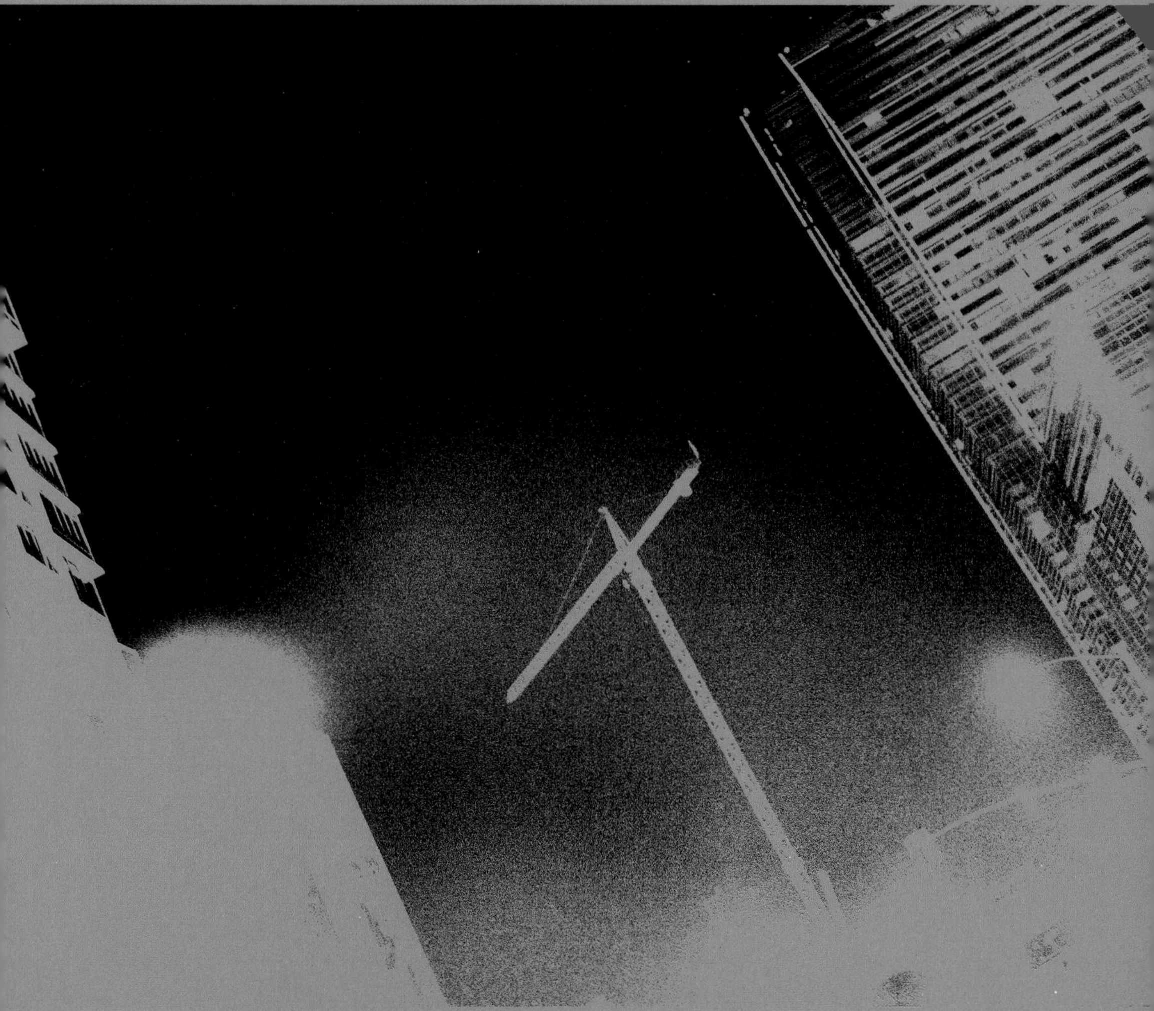

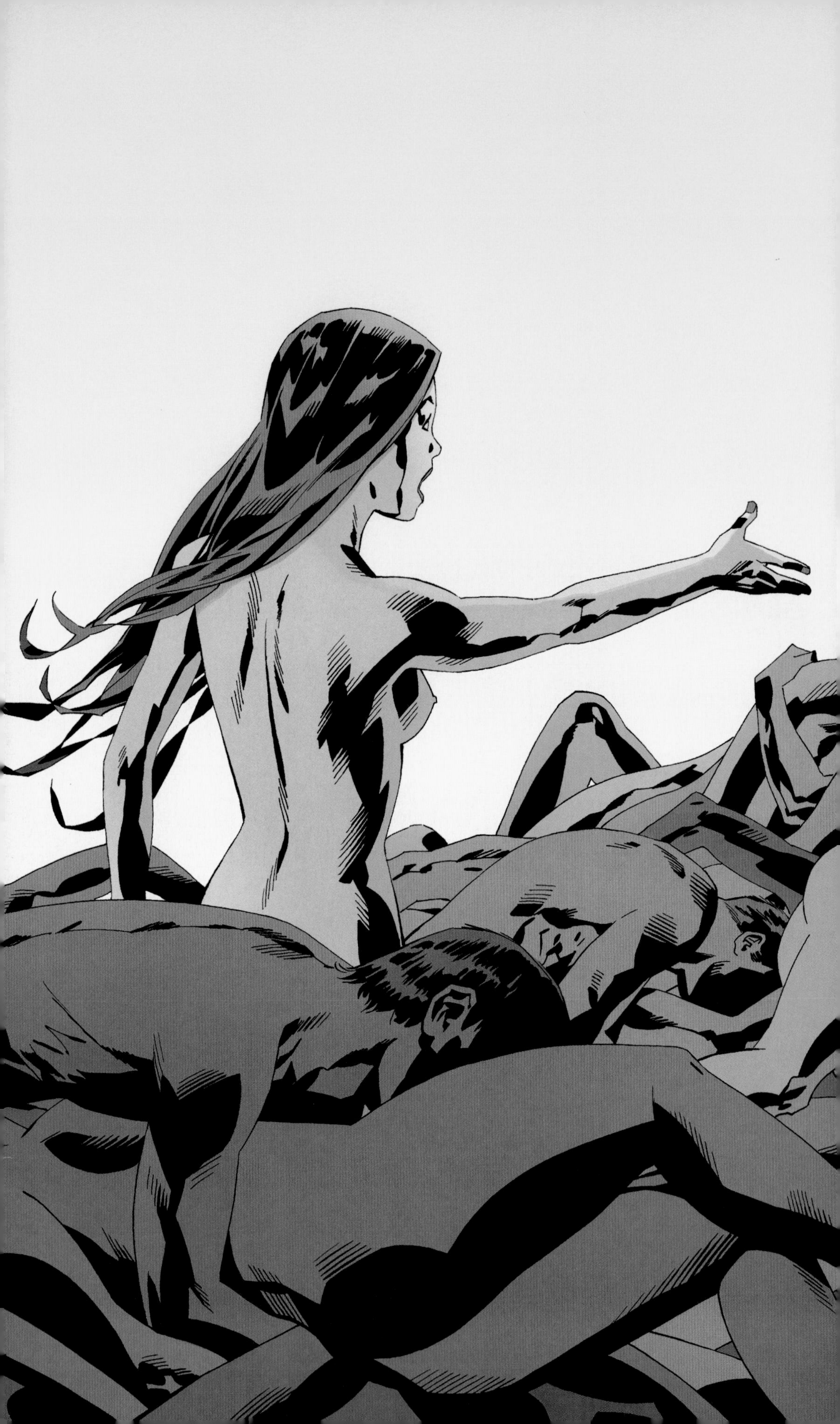

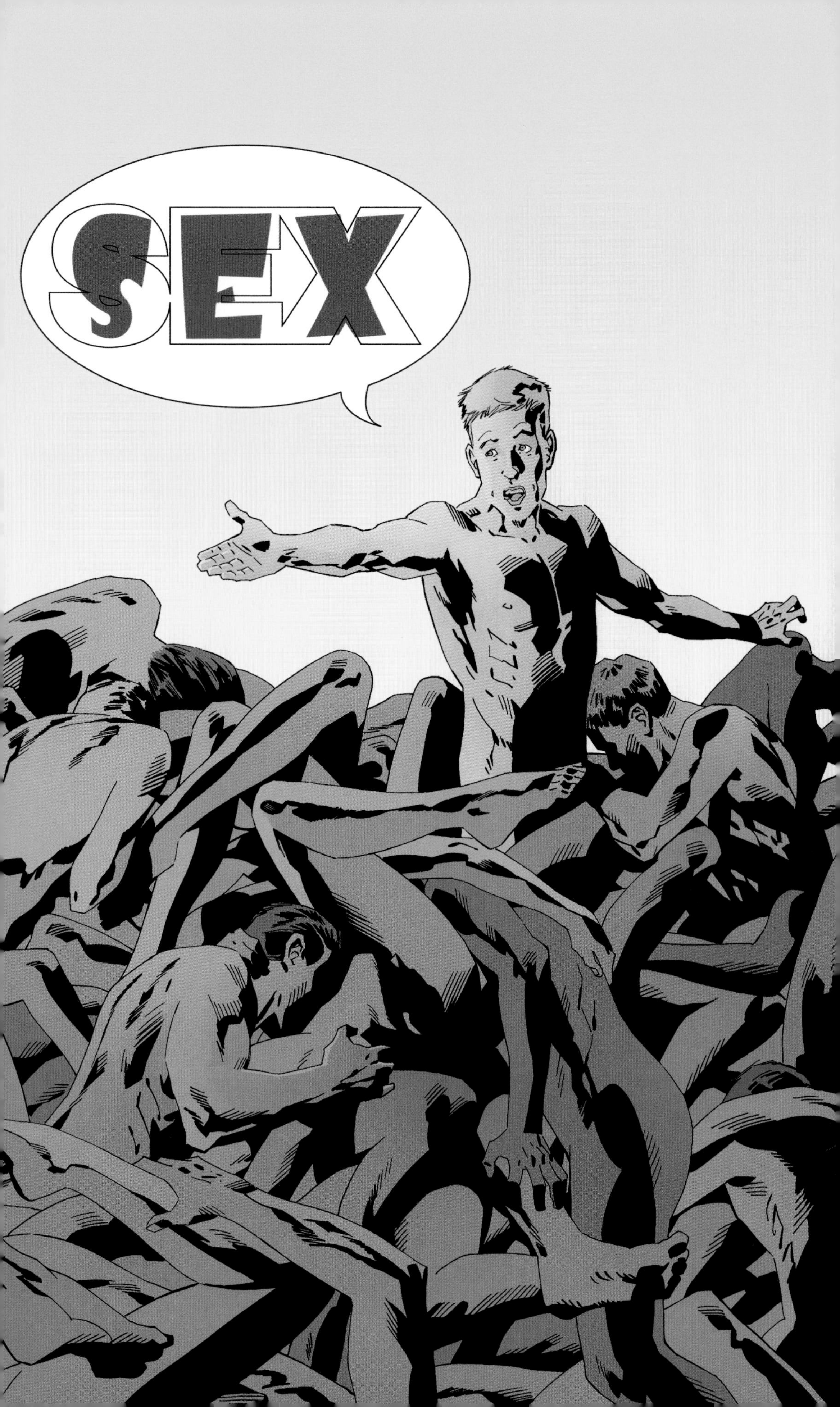
SEX

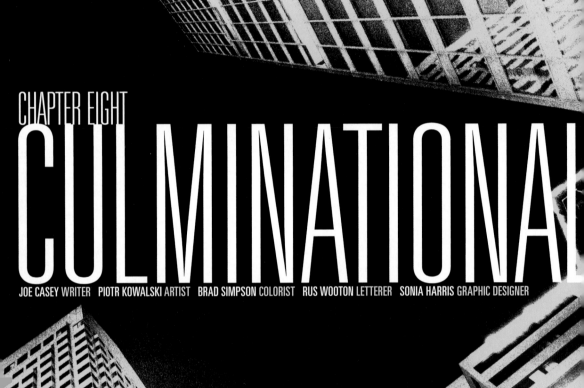

CHAPTER EIGHT
CULMINATIONAL

JOE CASEY WRITER   PIOTR KOWALSKI ARTIST   BRAD SIMPSON COLORIST   RUS WOOTON LETTERER   SONIA HARRIS GRAPHIC DESIGNER

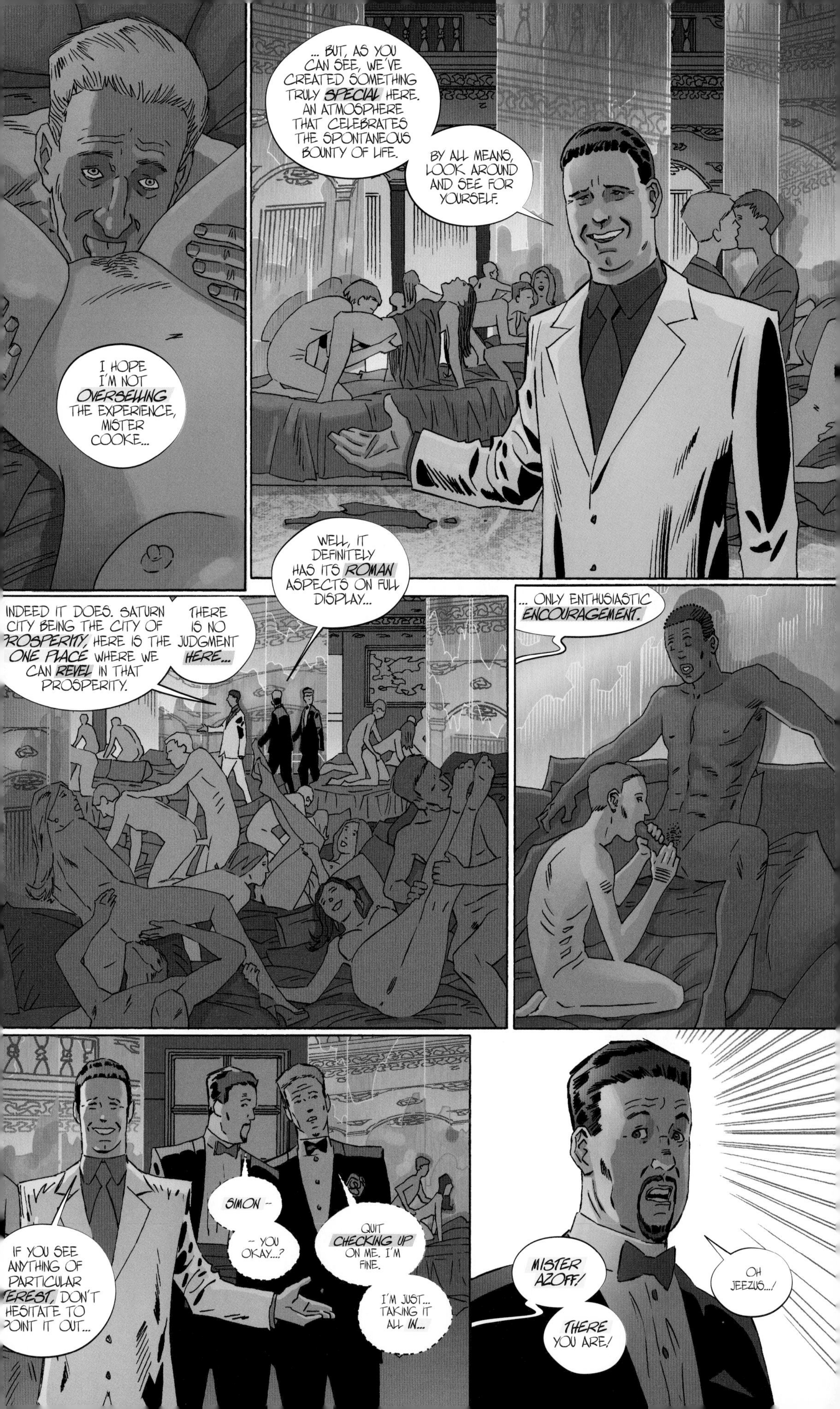
I HOPE I'M NOT OVERSELLING THE EXPERIENCE, MISTER COOKE...
... BUT, AS YOU CAN SEE, WE'VE CREATED SOMETHING TRULY SPECIAL HERE. AN ATMOSPHERE THAT CELEBRATES THE SPONTANEOUS BOUNTY OF LIFE.
BY ALL MEANS, LOOK AROUND AND SEE FOR YOURSELF.
WELL, IT DEFINITELY HAS ITS ROMAN ASPECTS ON FULL DISPLAY...
INDEED IT DOES. SATURN CITY BEING THE CITY OF PROSPERITY, HERE IS THE ONE PLACE WHERE WE CAN REVEL IN THAT PROSPERITY.
THERE IS NO JUDGMENT HERE...
... ONLY ENTHUSIASTIC ENCOURAGEMENT.
IF YOU SEE ANYTHING OF PARTICULAR EREST, DON'T HESITATE TO OINT IT OUT...
SIMON --
-- YOU OKAY...?
QUIT CHECKING UP ON ME. I'M FINE.
I'M JUST... TAKING IT ALL IN...
MISTER AZOFF!
THERE YOU ARE!
OH JEEZUS...!

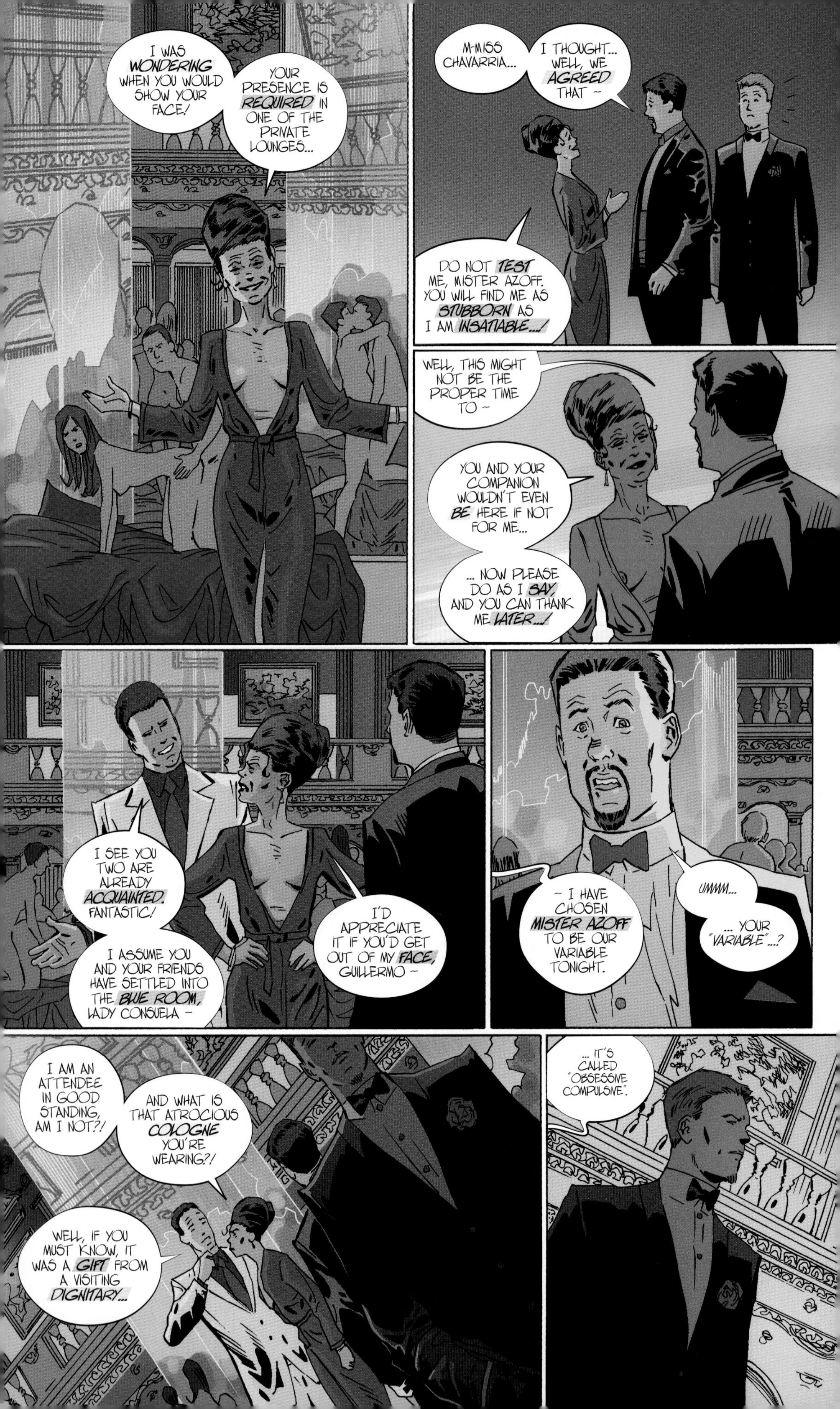

I WAS WONDERING WHEN YOU WOULD SHOW YOUR FACE!
YOUR PRESENCE IS REQUIRED IN ONE OF THE PRIVATE LOUNGES...
M-MISS CHAVARRIA...
I THOUGHT... WELL, WE AGREED THAT --
DO NOT TEST ME, MISTER AZOFF. YOU WILL FIND ME AS STUBBORN AS I AM INSATIABLE...!
WELL, THIS MIGHT NOT BE THE PROPER TIME TO --
YOU AND YOUR COMPANION WOULDN'T EVEN BE HERE IF NOT FOR ME...
... NOW PLEASE DO AS I SAY, AND YOU CAN THANK ME LATER...!
I SEE YOU TWO ARE ALREADY ACQUAINTED. FANTASTIC!
I ASSUME YOU AND YOUR FRIENDS HAVE SETTLED INTO THE BLUE ROOM, LADY CONSUELA --
I'D APPRECIATE IT IF YOU'D GET OUT OF MY FACE, GUILLERMO --
-- I HAVE CHOSEN MISTER AZOFF TO BE OUR VARIABLE TONIGHT.
UMMM...
... YOUR "VARIABLE"...?
I AM AN ATTENDEE IN GOOD STANDING, AM I NOT?!
AND WHAT IS THAT ATROCIOUS COLOGNE YOU'RE WEARING?!
WELL, IF YOU MUST KNOW, IT WAS A GIFT FROM A VISITING DIGNITARY...
... IT'S CALLED "OBSESSIVE COMPULSIVE".

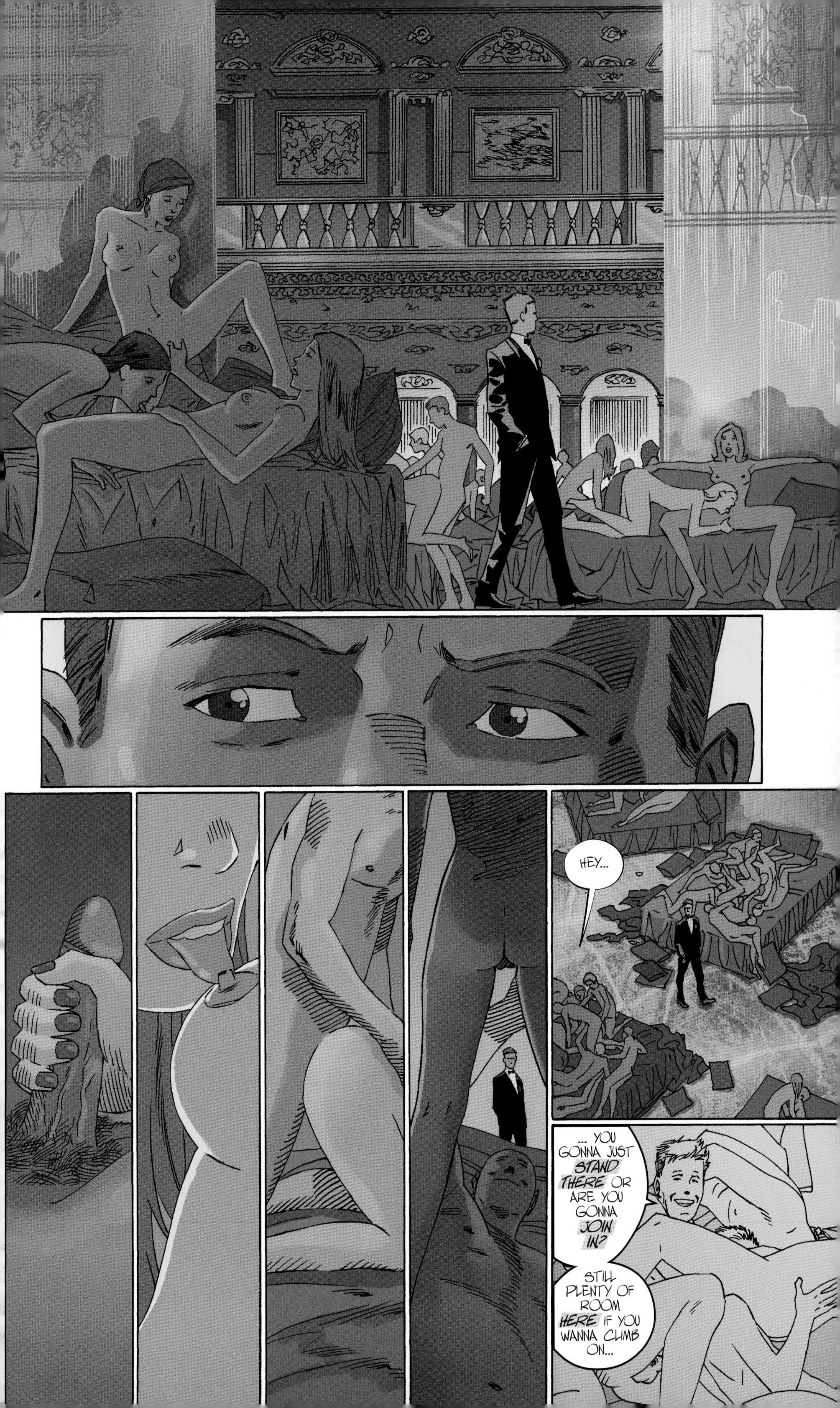
HEY...
... YOU GONNA JUST STAND THERE OR ARE YOU GONNA JOIN IN?
STILL PLENTY OF ROOM HERE IF YOU WANNA CLIMB ON...

I THOUGHT WE'D SETTLED UP IN YOUR *PENTHOUSE*, MISS CHAVARRIA --

OH, ON THE *CONTRARY...*

... MORE LIKE YOU OPENED A STANDING *ACCOUNT* WITH ME.

AFTER SEEING YOUR *SUBMISSIVE* SIDE, I KNEW YOU'D BE *PERFECT* TO PARTAKE IN THE ACTIVITIES *WE* INDULGE IN WHILE ATTENDING THE *SATURNALIA...*

WAIT A MINUTE...

... WHO'S *"WE"?*

HELLO, *DEARS!*

I HAVE RETURNED AND I'VE MADE GOOD ON MY *PROMISE...*

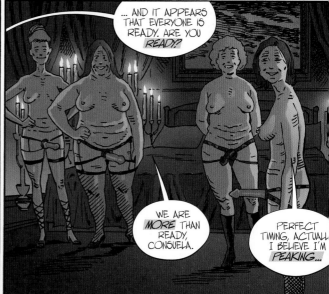

... AND IT APPEARS THAT EVERYONE IS READY. ARE YOU *READY?*

WE ARE *MORE* THAN READY, CONSUELA.

PERFECT TIMING, ACTUALL I BELIEVE I'M *PEAKING...*

THAT'S *WONDERFUL*, GRETA. AS YOU ALL CAN SEE, TONIGHT'S *VARIABLE* HAS ARRIVED.

AND I CAN TELL YOU FROM *PERSONAL EXPERIENCE...*

... HE WILL PERFORM AS *EXPECTED.*

I...

... DON'T KNOW... HO\ I FEEL ABOU THIS...

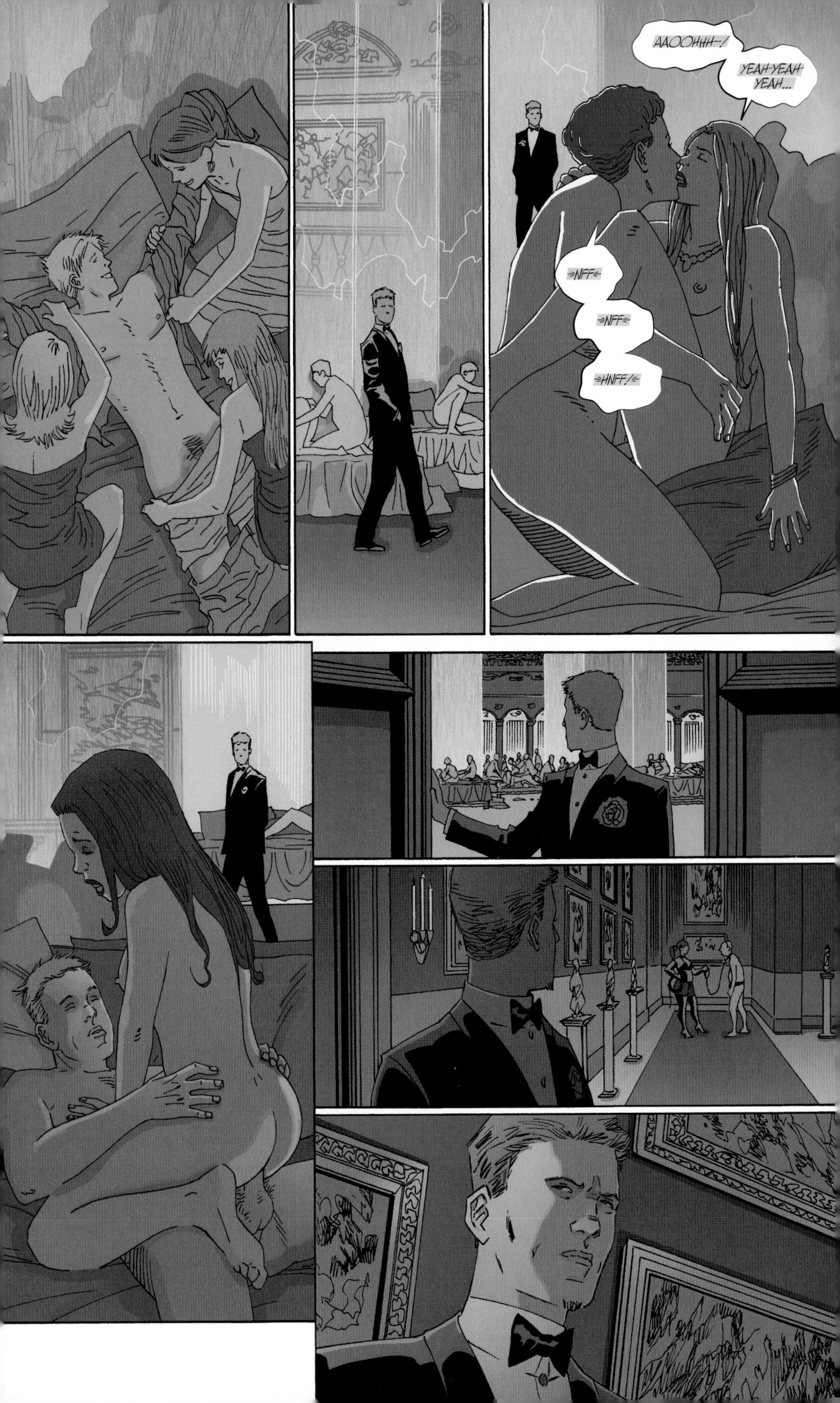

AAOOHHH--!
YEAH-YEAH-YEAH...
=NFF=
=NFF=
=HNFF/=

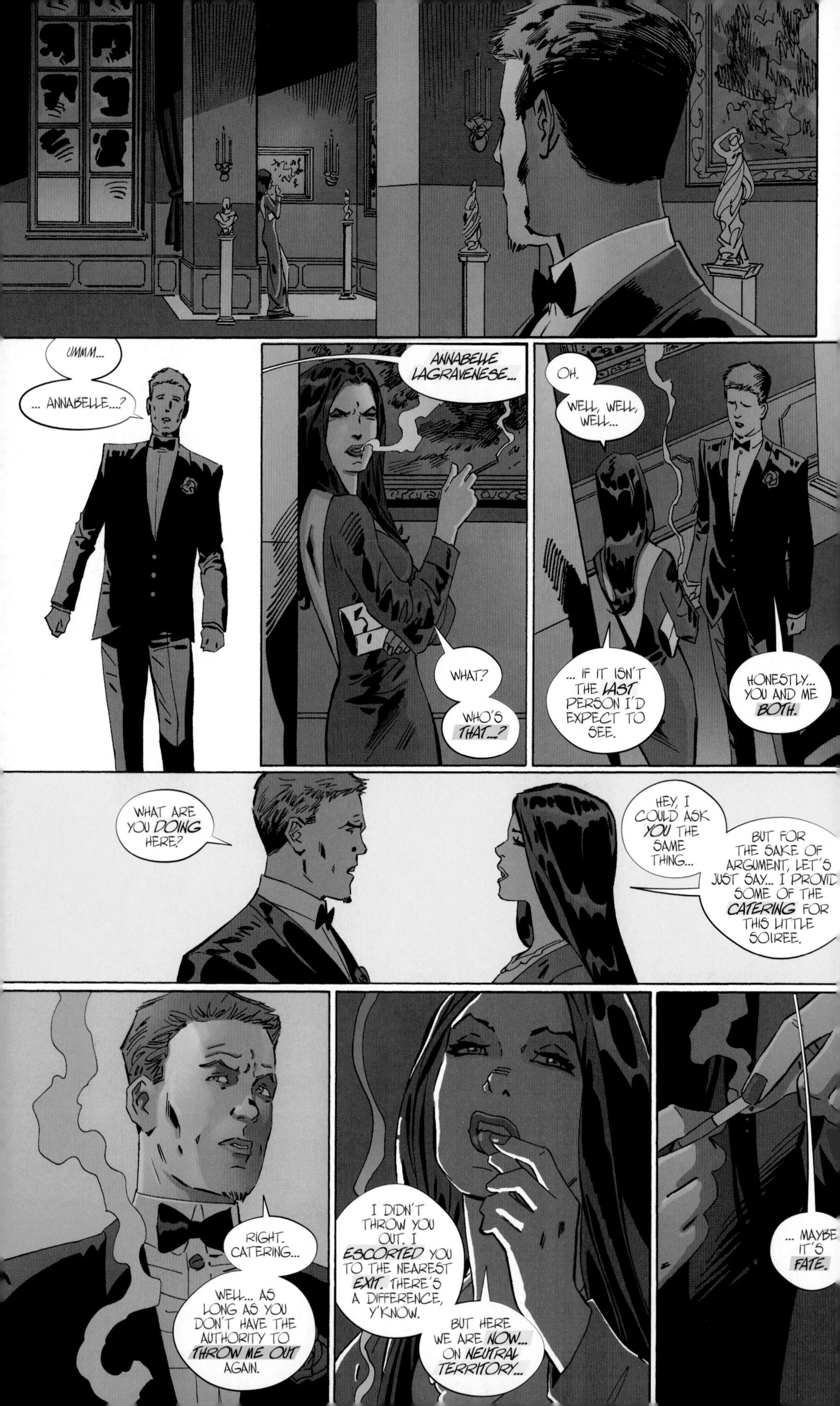
UMMM...
... ANNABELLE...?
ANNABELLE LAGRAVENESE...
WHAT?
WHO'S THAT...?
OH.
WELL, WELL, WELL...
... IF IT ISN'T THE LAST PERSON I'D EXPECT TO SEE.
HONESTLY... YOU AND ME BOTH.
WHAT ARE YOU DOING HERE?
HEY, I COULD ASK YOU THE SAME THING...
BUT FOR THE SAKE OF ARGUMENT, LET'S JUST SAY... I PROVID SOME OF THE CATERING FOR THIS LITTLE SOIREE.
RIGHT. CATERING...
WELL... AS LONG AS YOU DON'T HAVE THE AUTHORITY TO THROW ME OUT AGAIN.
I DIDN'T THROW YOU OUT. I ESCORTED YOU TO THE NEAREST EXIT. THERE'S A DIFFERENCE, Y'KNOW.
BUT HERE WE ARE NOW... ON NEUTRAL TERRITORY...
... MAYBE IT'S FATE.

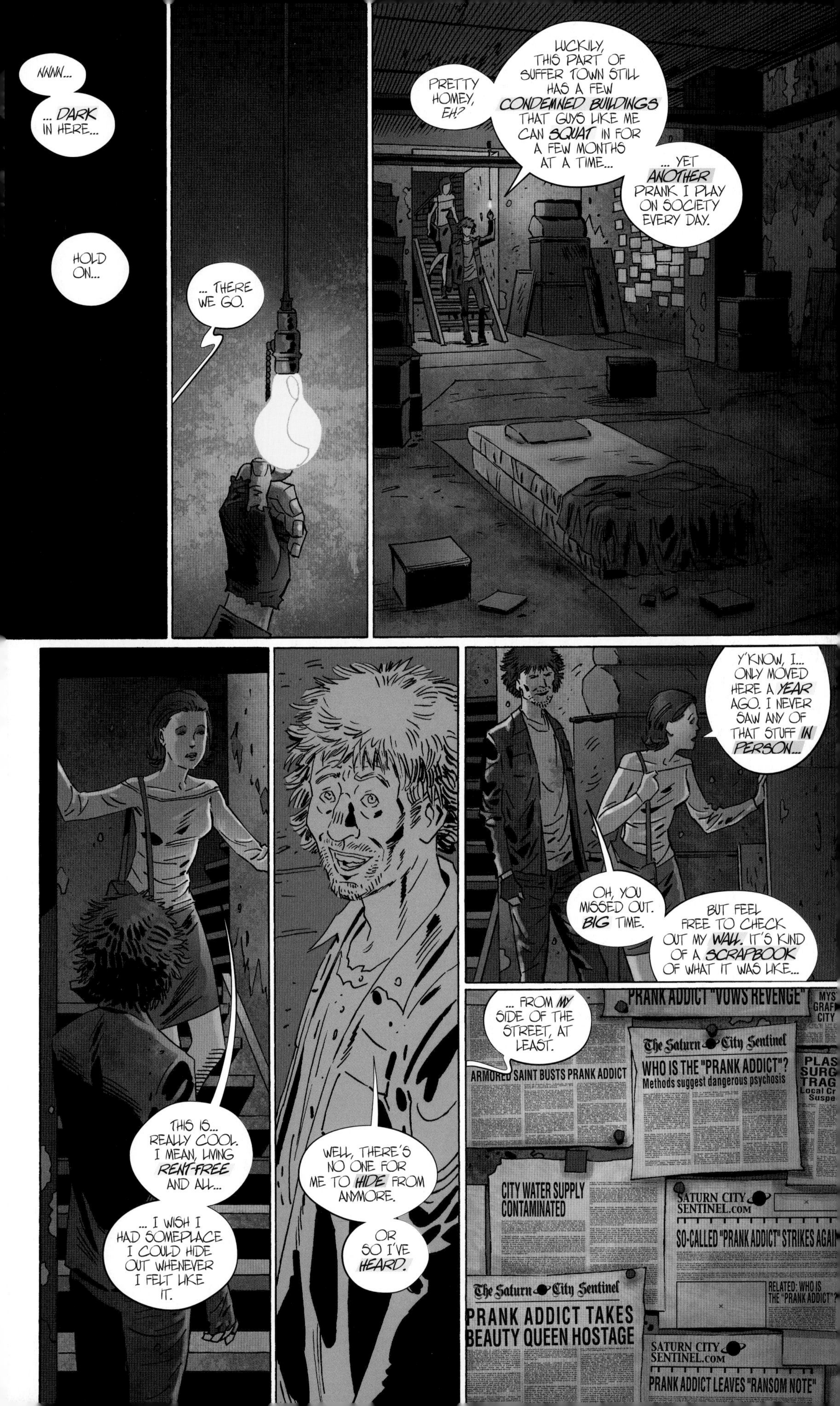
NNNN...
... DARK IN HERE...
HOLD ON...
... THERE WE GO.
PRETTY HOMEY, EH?
LUCKILY, THIS PART OF SUFFER TOWN STILL HAS A FEW CONDEMNED BUILDINGS THAT GUYS LIKE ME CAN SQUAT IN FOR A FEW MONTHS AT A TIME...
... YET ANOTHER PRANK I PLAY ON SOCIETY EVERY DAY.
THIS IS... REALLY COOL. I MEAN, LIVING RENT-FREE AND ALL...
... I WISH I HAD SOMEPLACE I COULD HIDE OUT WHENEVER I FELT LIKE IT.
WELL, THERE'S NO ONE FOR ME TO HIDE FROM ANYMORE.
OR SO I'VE HEARD.
Y'KNOW, I... ONLY MOVED HERE A YEAR AGO. I NEVER SAW ANY OF THAT STUFF IN PERSON...
OH, YOU MISSED OUT. BIG TIME.
BUT FEEL FREE TO CHECK OUT MY WALL. IT'S KIND OF A SCRAPBOOK OF WHAT IT WAS LIKE...
... FROM MY SIDE OF THE STREET, AT LEAST.
PRANK ADDICT "VOWS REVENGE"
ARMORED SAINT BUSTS PRANK ADDICT
The Saturn City Sentinel
WHO IS THE "PRANK ADDICT"?
Methods suggest dangerous psychosis
CITY WATER SUPPLY CONTAMINATED
SATURN CITY SENTINEL.COM
SO-CALLED "PRANK ADDICT" STRIKES AGAI
The Saturn City Sentinel
PRANK ADDICT TAKES BEAUTY QUEEN HOSTAGE
RELATED: WHO IS THE "PRANK ADDICT"?
SATURN CITY SENTINEL.COM
PRANK ADDICT LEAVES "RANSOM NOTE"

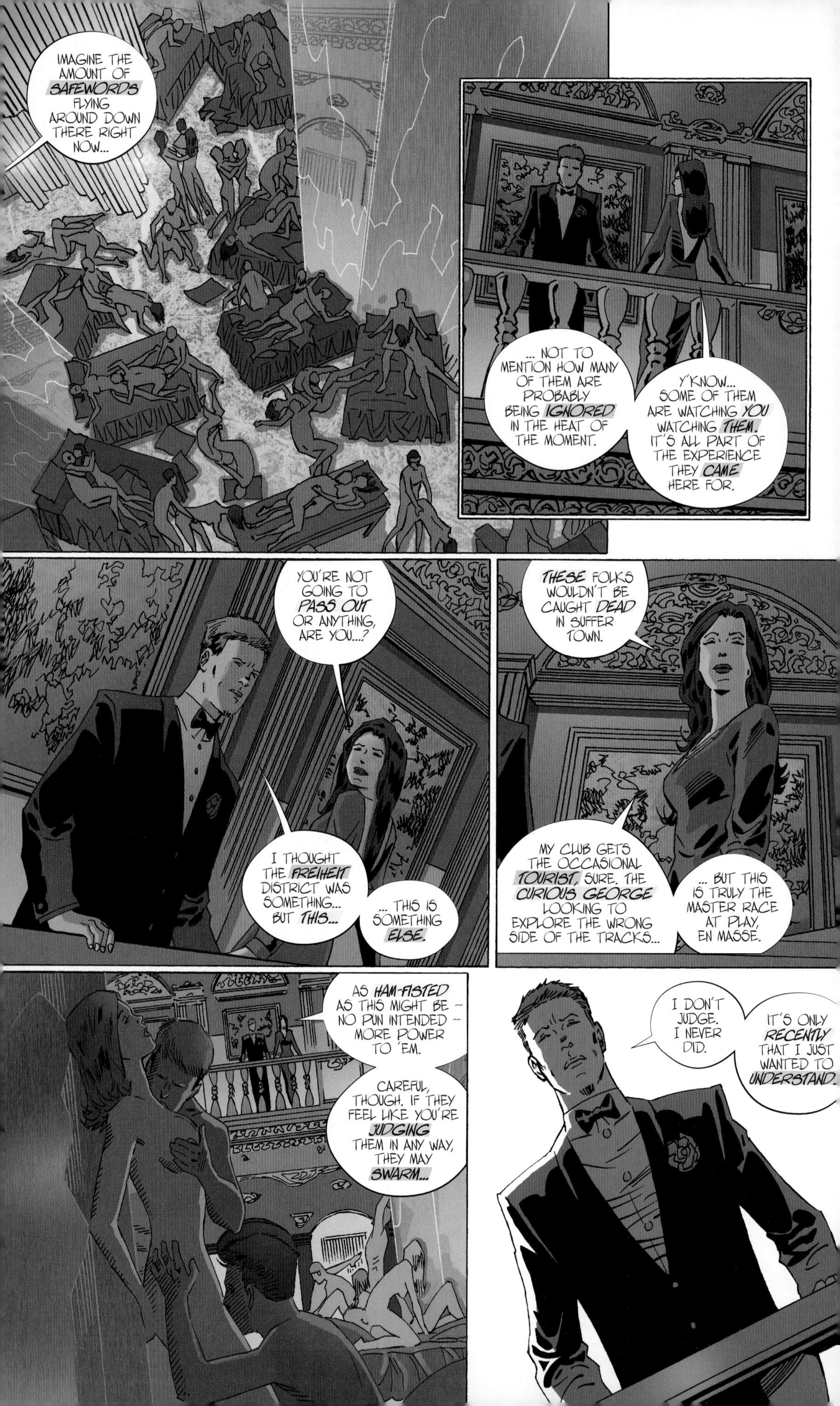
IMAGINE THE AMOUNT OF SAFEWORDS FLYING AROUND DOWN THERE RIGHT NOW...
... NOT TO MENTION HOW MANY OF THEM ARE PROBABLY BEING IGNORED IN THE HEAT OF THE MOMENT.
Y'KNOW... SOME OF THEM ARE WATCHING YOU WATCHING THEM. IT'S ALL PART OF THE EXPERIENCE THEY CAME HERE FOR.
YOU'RE NOT GOING TO PASS OUT OR ANYTHING, ARE YOU...?
I THOUGHT THE FREIHEIT DISTRICT WAS SOMETHING... BUT THIS...
... THIS IS SOMETHING ELSE.
THESE FOLKS WOULDN'T BE CAUGHT DEAD IN SUFFER TOWN.
MY CLUB GETS THE OCCASIONAL TOURIST, SURE. THE CURIOUS GEORGE LOOKING TO EXPLORE THE WRONG SIDE OF THE TRACKS...
... BUT THIS IS TRULY THE MASTER RACE AT PLAY, EN MASSE.
AS HAM-FISTED AS THIS MIGHT BE -- NO PUN INTENDED -- MORE POWER TO 'EM.
CAREFUL, THOUGH. IF THEY FEEL LIKE YOU'RE JUDGING THEM IN ANY WAY, THEY MAY SWARM...
I DON'T JUDGE. I NEVER DID.
IT'S ONLY RECENTLY THAT I JUST WANTED TO UNDERSTAND.

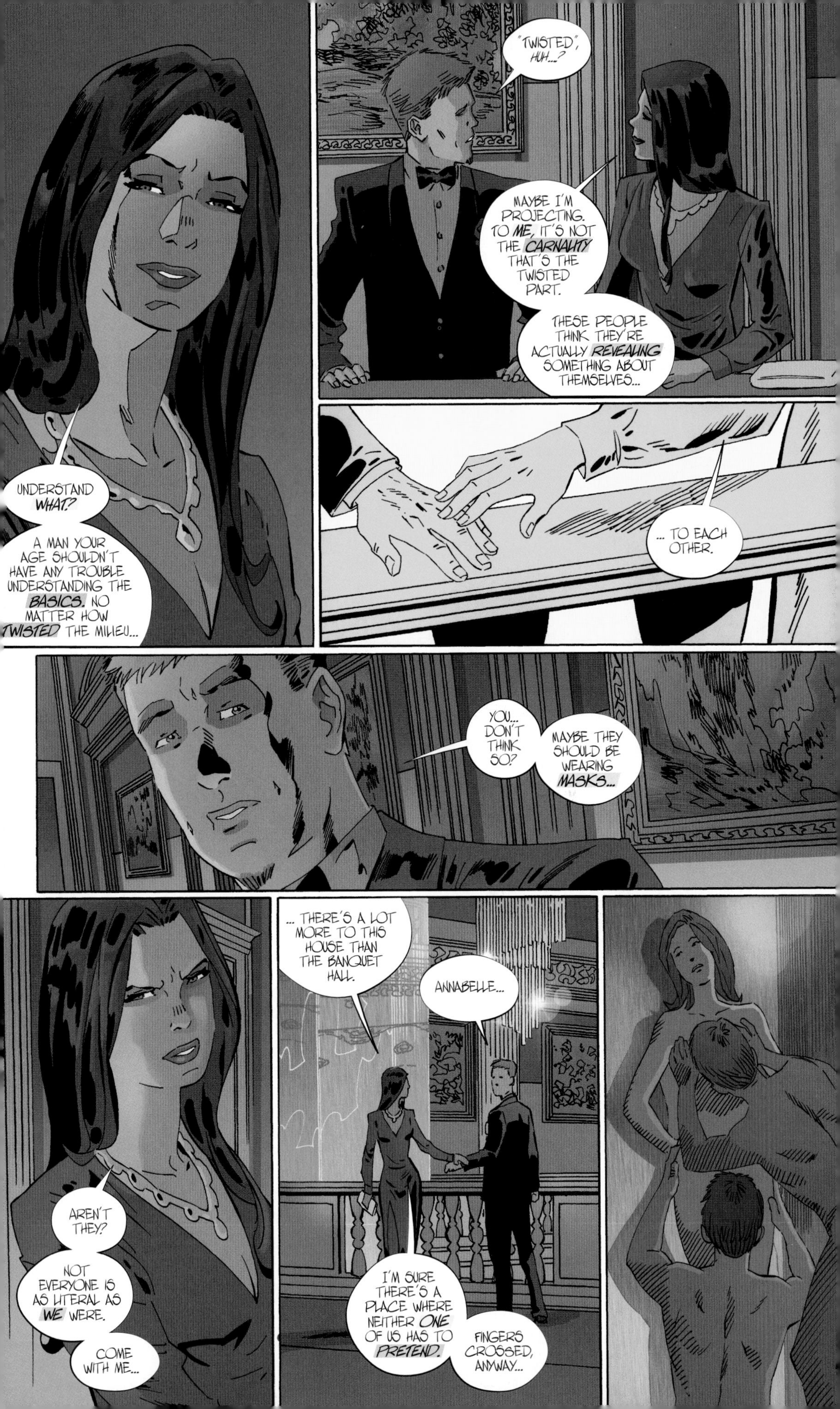
"TWISTED", HUH...?
MAYBE I'M PROJECTING. TO ME, IT'S NOT THE CARNALITY THAT'S THE TWISTED PART.
THESE PEOPLE THINK THEY'RE ACTUALLY REVEALING SOMETHING ABOUT THEMSELVES...
UNDERSTAND WHAT?
A MAN YOUR AGE SHOULDN'T HAVE ANY TROUBLE UNDERSTANDING THE BASICS. NO MATTER HOW TWISTED THE MILIEU...
... TO EACH OTHER.
YOU... DON'T THINK SO?
MAYBE THEY SHOULD BE WEARING MASKS...
AREN'T THEY?
NOT EVERYONE IS AS LITERAL AS WE WERE.
COME WITH ME...
... THERE'S A LOT MORE TO THIS HOUSE THAN THE BANQUET HALL.
ANNABELLE...
I'M SURE THERE'S A PLACE WHERE NEITHER ONE OF US HAS TO PRETEND.
FINGERS CROSSED, ANYWAY...

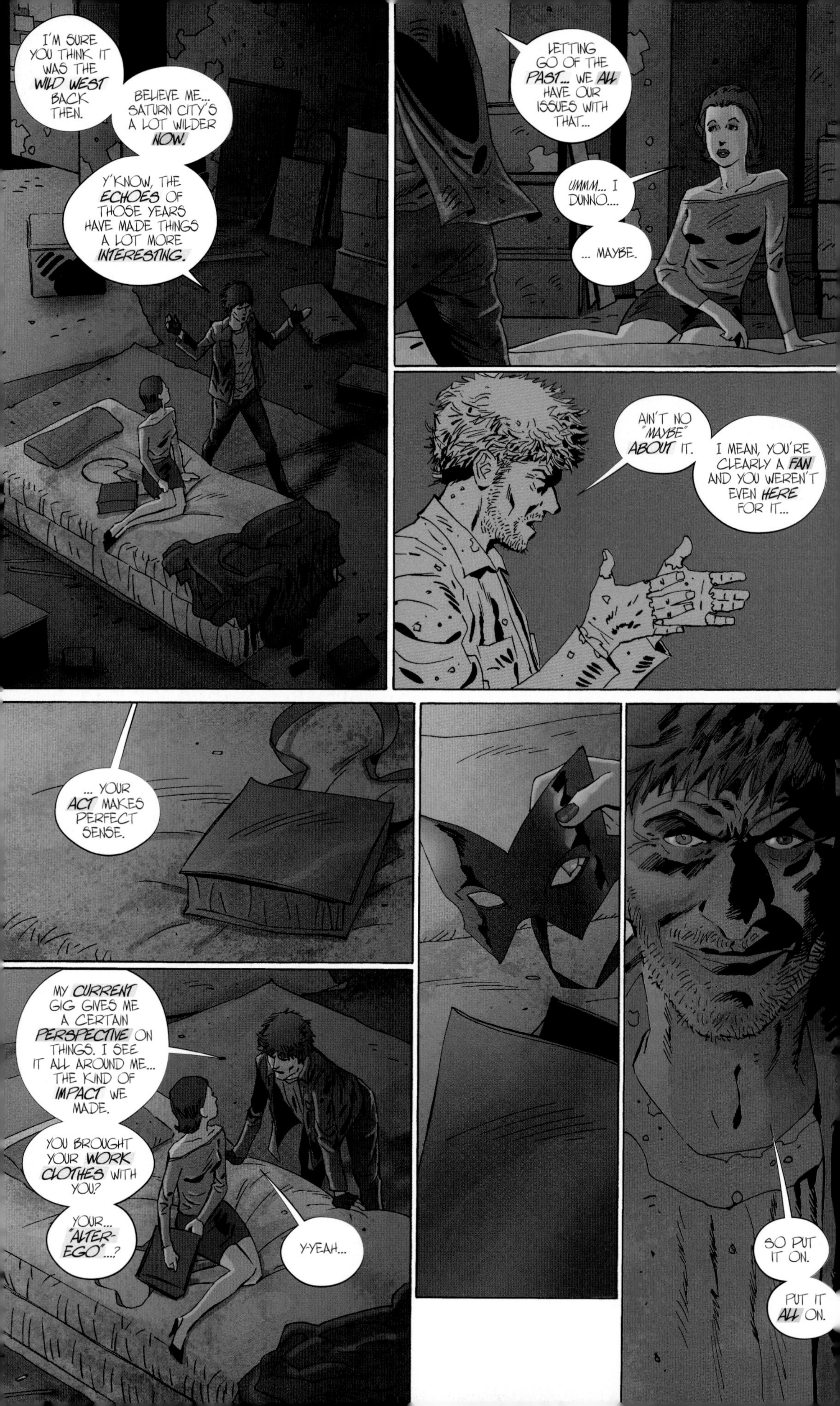
I'M SURE YOU THINK IT WAS THE WILD WEST BACK THEN.
BELIEVE ME... SATURN CITY'S A LOT WILDER NOW.
Y'KNOW, THE ECHOES OF THOSE YEARS HAVE MADE THINGS A LOT MORE INTERESTING.
LETTING GO OF THE PAST... WE ALL HAVE OUR ISSUES WITH THAT...
UMMM... I DUNNO....
... MAYBE.
AIN'T NO "MAYBE" ABOUT IT.
I MEAN, YOU'RE CLEARLY A FAN AND YOU WEREN'T EVEN HERE FOR IT...
... YOUR ACT MAKES PERFECT SENSE.
MY CURRENT GIG GIVES ME A CERTAIN PERSPECTIVE ON THINGS. I SEE IT ALL AROUND ME... THE KIND OF IMPACT WE MADE.
YOU BROUGHT YOUR WORK CLOTHES WITH YOU?
YOUR... "ALTER-EGO"...?
Y-YEAH...
SO PUT IT ON.
PUT IT ALL ON.

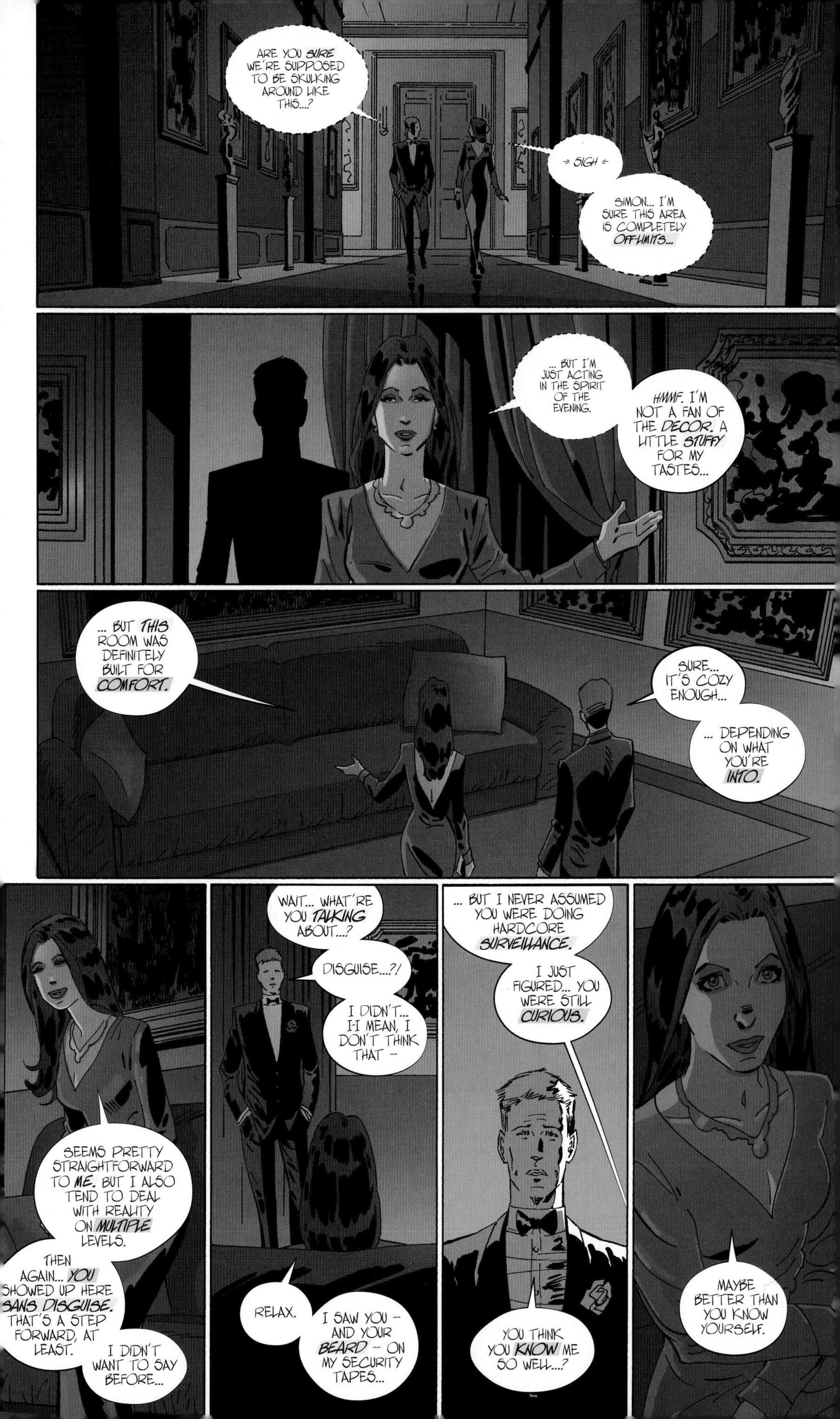

ARE YOU SURE WE'RE SUPPOSED TO BE SKULKING AROUND LIKE THIS...?
SIGH
SIMON... I'M SURE THIS AREA IS COMPLETELY OFF-LIMITS...
... BUT I'M JUST ACTING IN THE SPIRIT OF THE EVENING.
HMMF. I'M NOT A FAN OF THE DECOR. A LITTLE STUFFY FOR MY TASTES...
... BUT THIS ROOM WAS DEFINITELY BUILT FOR COMFORT.
SURE... IT'S COZY ENOUGH...
... DEPENDING ON WHAT YOU'RE INTO.
SEEMS PRETTY STRAIGHTFORWARD TO ME. BUT I ALSO TEND TO DEAL WITH REALITY ON MULTIPLE LEVELS.
THEN AGAIN... YOU SHOWED UP HERE SANS DISGUISE. THAT'S A STEP FORWARD, AT LEAST.
I DIDN'T WANT TO SAY BEFORE...
WAIT... WHAT'RE YOU TALKING ABOUT...?
DISGUISE...?!
I DIDN'T... I-I MEAN, I DON'T THINK THAT --
RELAX.
I SAW YOU -- AND YOUR BEARD -- ON MY SECURITY TAPES...
... BUT I NEVER ASSUMED YOU WERE DOING HARDCORE SURVEILLANCE.
I JUST FIGURED... YOU WERE STILL CURIOUS.
YOU THINK YOU KNOW ME SO WELL...?
MAYBE BETTER THAN YOU KNOW YOURSELF.

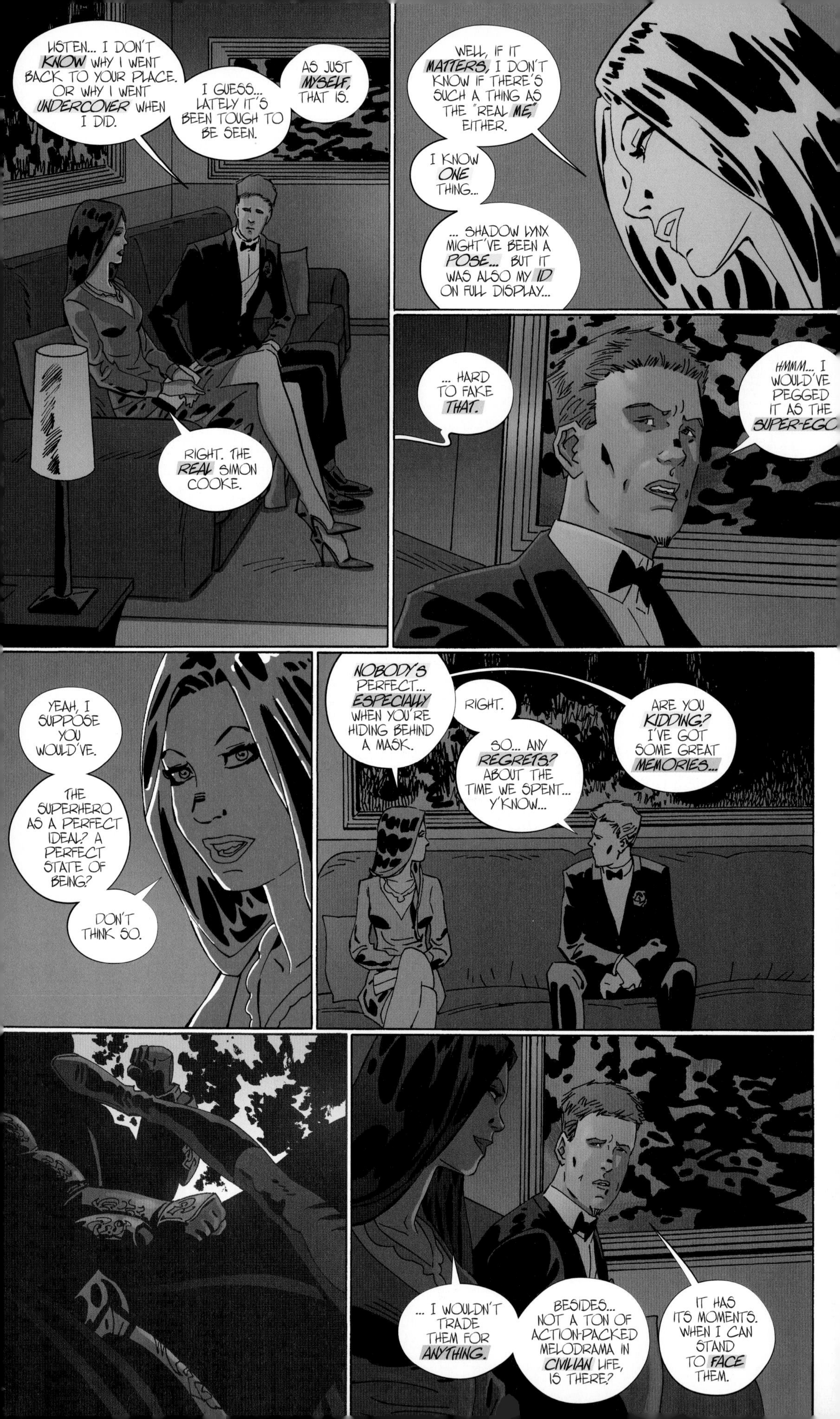
LISTEN... I DON'T KNOW WHY I WENT BACK TO YOUR PLACE. OR WHY I WENT UNDERCOVER WHEN I DID.
I GUESS... LATELY IT'S BEEN TOUGH TO BE SEEN.
AS JUST MYSELF, THAT IS.
RIGHT. THE REAL SIMON COOKE.
WELL, IF IT MATTERS, I DON'T KNOW IF THERE'S SUCH A THING AS THE "REAL ME," EITHER.
I KNOW ONE THING...
... SHADOW LYNX MIGHT'VE BEEN A POSE... BUT IT WAS ALSO MY ID ON FULL DISPLAY...
... HARD TO FAKE THAT.
HMMM... I WOULD'VE PEGGED IT AS THE SUPER-EGO.
YEAH, I SUPPOSE YOU WOULD'VE.
THE SUPERHERO AS A PERFECT IDEAL? A PERFECT STATE OF BEING?
DON'T THINK SO.
NOBODY'S PERFECT... ESPECIALLY WHEN YOU'RE HIDING BEHIND A MASK.
RIGHT.
SO... ANY REGRETS? ABOUT THE TIME WE SPENT... Y'KNOW...
ARE YOU KIDDING? I'VE GOT SOME GREAT MEMORIES...
... I WOULDN'T TRADE THEM FOR ANYTHING.
BESIDES... NOT A TON OF ACTION-PACKED MELODRAMA IN CIVILIAN LIFE, IS THERE?
IT HAS ITS MOMENTS. WHEN I CAN STAND TO FACE THEM.

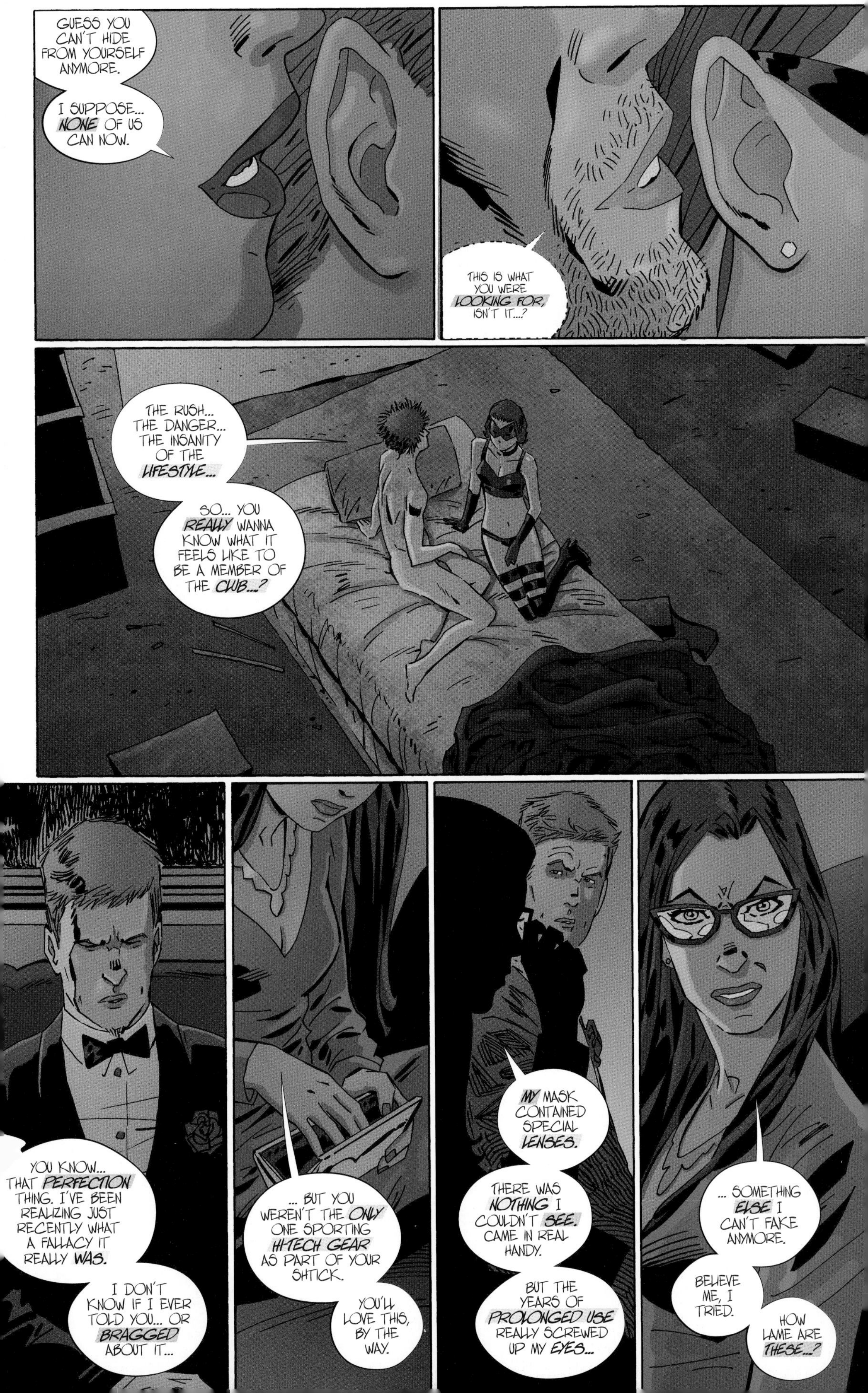
GUESS YOU CAN'T HIDE FROM YOURSELF ANYMORE.
I SUPPOSE... NONE OF US CAN NOW.
THIS IS WHAT YOU WERE LOOKING FOR, ISN'T IT...?
THE RUSH... THE DANGER... THE INSANITY OF THE LIFESTYLE...
SO... YOU REALLY WANNA KNOW WHAT IT FEELS LIKE TO BE A MEMBER OF THE CLUB...?
YOU KNOW... THAT PERFECTION THING. I'VE BEEN REALIZING JUST RECENTLY WHAT A FALLACY IT REALLY WAS.
I DON'T KNOW IF I EVER TOLD YOU... OR BRAGGED ABOUT IT...
... BUT YOU WEREN'T THE ONLY ONE SPORTING HI-TECH GEAR AS PART OF YOUR SHTICK.
YOU'LL LOVE THIS, BY THE WAY.
MY MASK CONTAINED SPECIAL LENSES.
THERE WAS NOTHING I COULDN'T SEE. CAME IN REAL HANDY.
BUT THE YEARS OF PROLONGED USE REALLY SCREWED UP MY EYES...
... SOMETHING ELSE I CAN'T FAKE ANYMORE.
BELIEVE ME, I TRIED.
HOW LAME ARE THESE...?

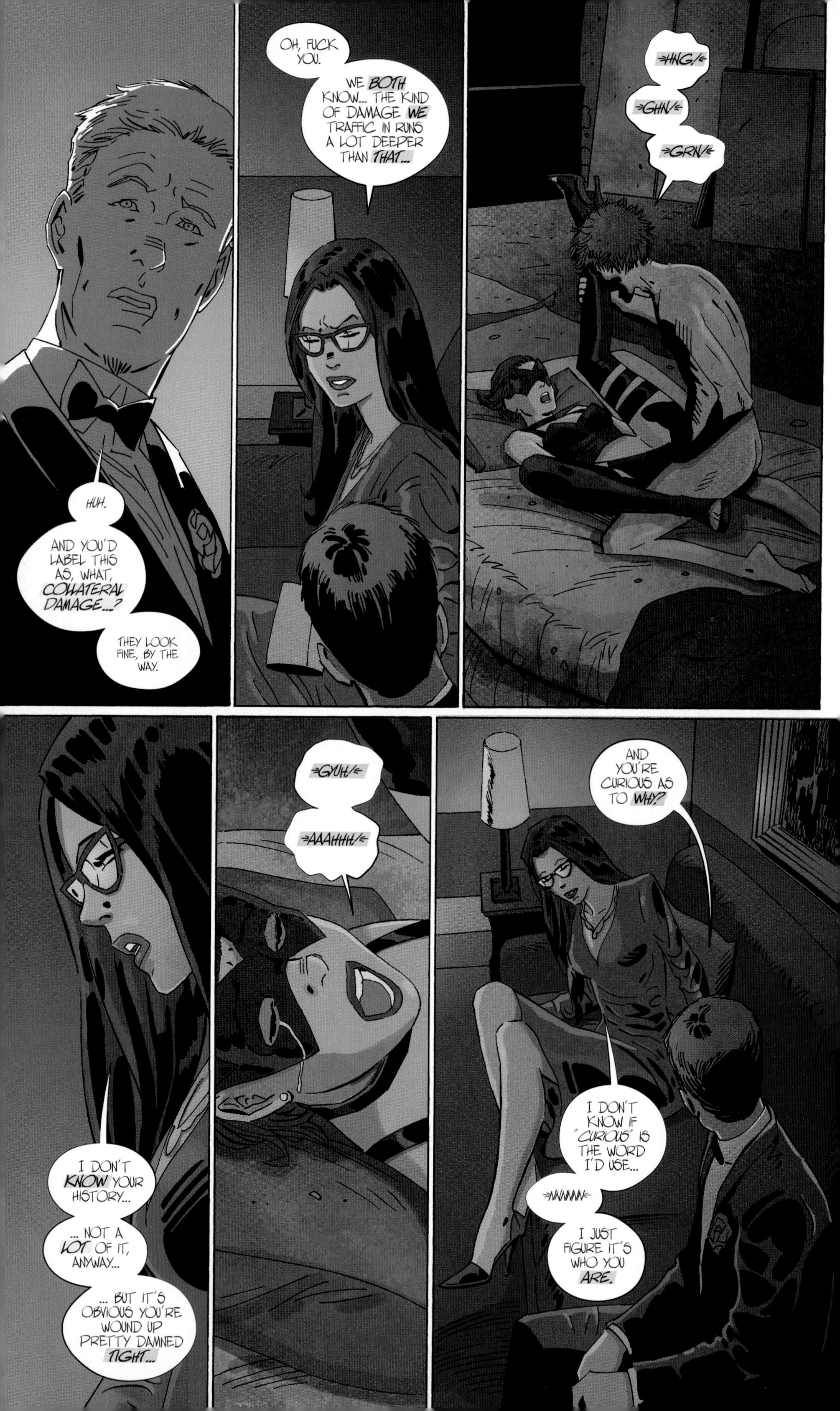

HUH.
AND YOU'D LABEL THIS AS, WHAT, COLLATERAL DAMAGE...?
THEY LOOK FINE, BY THE WAY.
OH, FUCK YOU.
WE BOTH KNOW... THE KIND OF DAMAGE WE TRAFFIC IN RUNS A LOT DEEPER THAN THAT...
HNG!
GHN!
GRN!
I DON'T KNOW YOUR HISTORY...
... NOT A LOT OF IT, ANYWAY...
... BUT IT'S OBVIOUS YOU'RE WOUND UP PRETTY DAMNED TIGHT...
GYUH!
AAAHHH!
AND YOU'RE CURIOUS AS TO WHY?
I DON'T KNOW IF "CURIOUS" IS THE WORD I'D USE...
NNNNNN
I JUST FIGURE IT'S WHO YOU ARE.

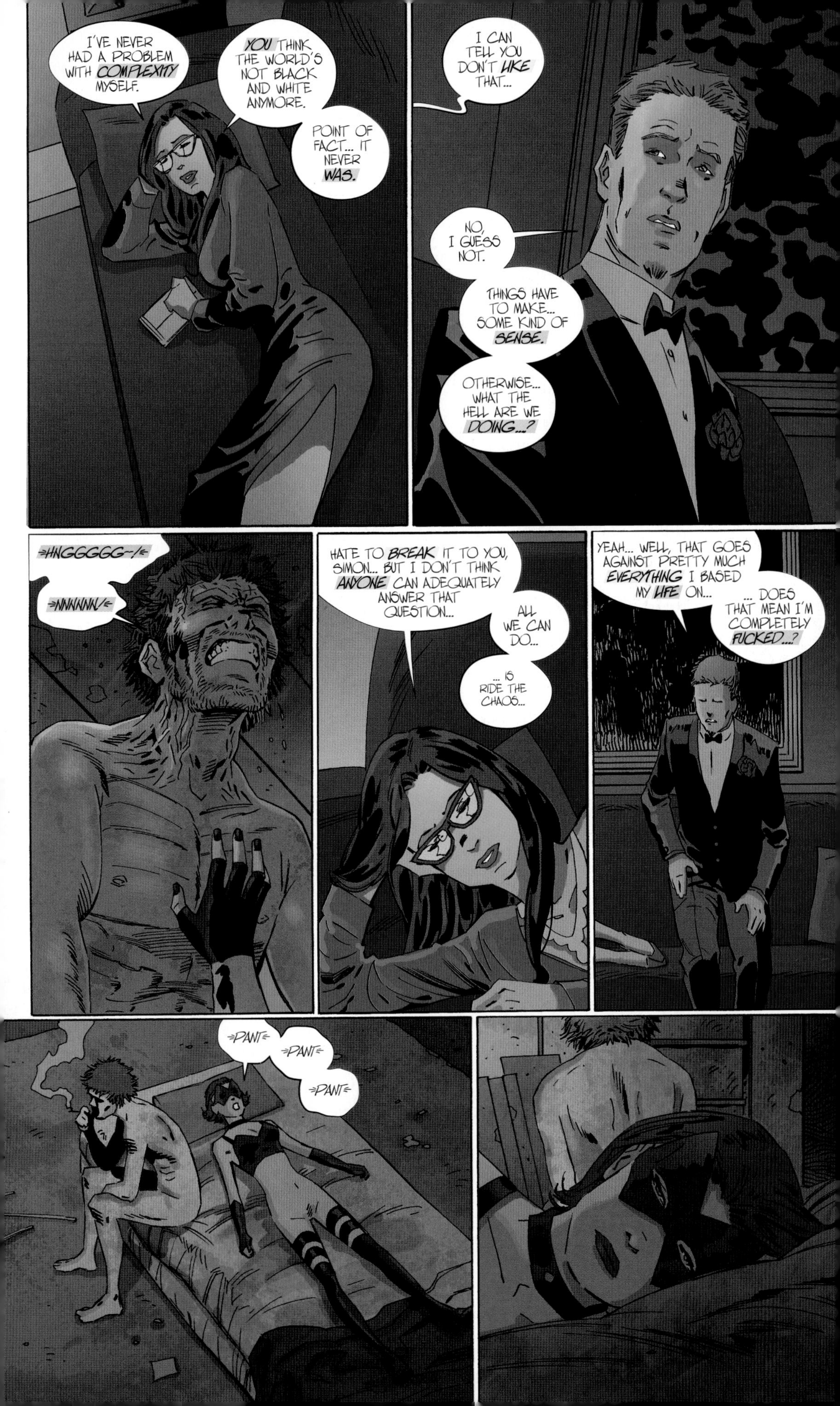
I'VE NEVER HAD A PROBLEM WITH COMPLEXITY MYSELF.
YOU THINK THE WORLD'S NOT BLACK AND WHITE ANYMORE.
POINT OF FACT... IT NEVER WAS.
I CAN TELL YOU DON'T LIKE THAT...
NO, I GUESS NOT.
THINGS HAVE TO MAKE... SOME KIND OF SENSE.
OTHERWISE... WHAT THE HELL ARE WE DOING...?
HNGGGGG~!
NNNNNN!
HATE TO BREAK IT TO YOU, SIMON... BUT I DON'T THINK ANYONE CAN ADEQUATELY ANSWER THAT QUESTION...
ALL WE CAN DO...
... IS RIDE THE CHAOS...
YEAH... WELL, THAT GOES AGAINST PRETTY MUCH EVERYTHING I BASED MY LIFE ON...
... DOES THAT MEAN I'M COMPLETELY FUCKED...?
PANT
PANT
PANT

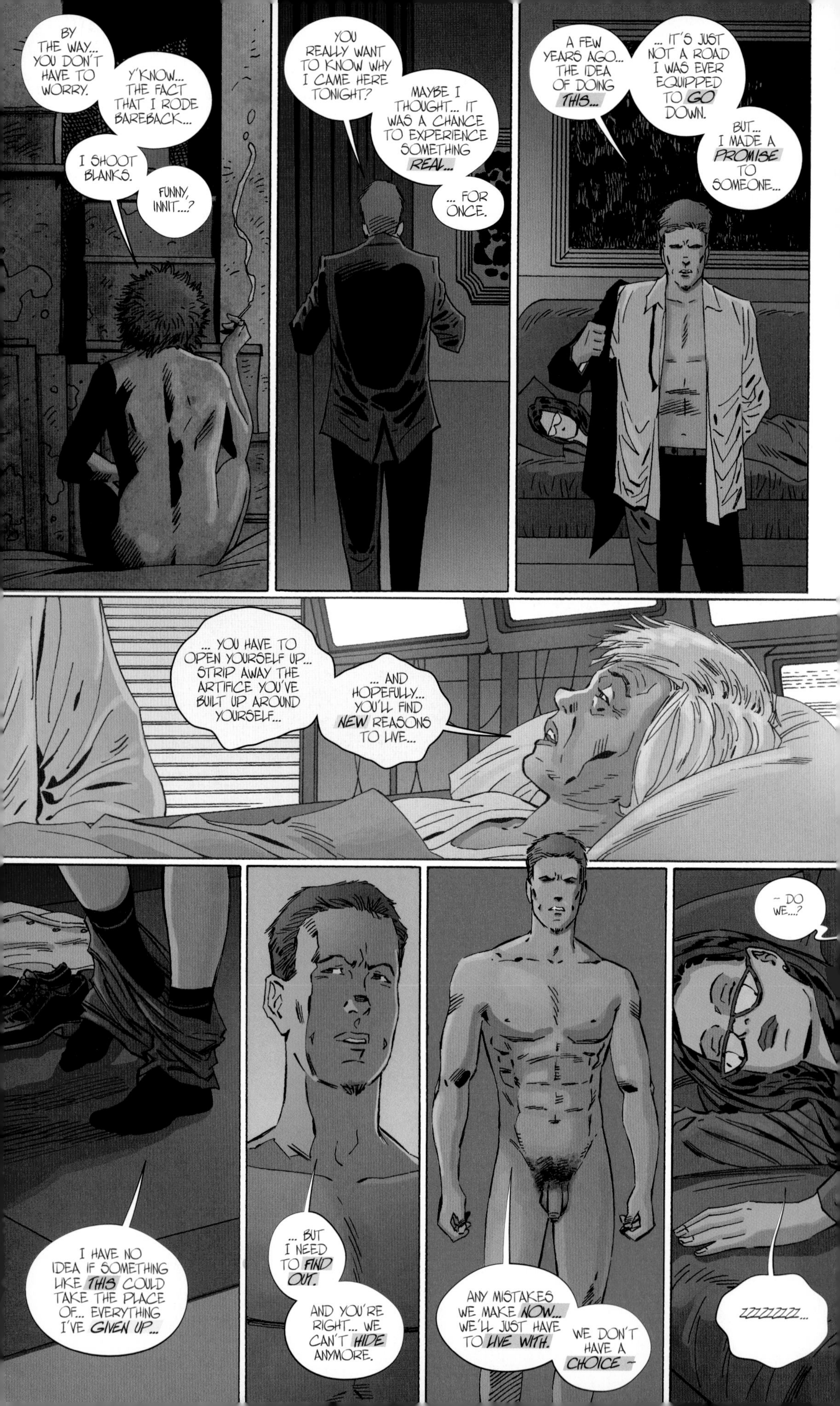

BY THE WAY... YOU DON'T HAVE TO WORRY.
Y'KNOW... THE FACT THAT I RODE BAREBACK...
I SHOOT BLANKS.
FUNNY, INNIT...?
YOU REALLY WANT TO KNOW WHY I CAME HERE TONIGHT?
MAYBE I THOUGHT... IT WAS A CHANCE TO EXPERIENCE SOMETHING REAL...
... FOR ONCE.
A FEW YEARS AGO... THE IDEA OF DOING THIS...
... IT'S JUST NOT A ROAD I WAS EVER EQUIPPED TO GO DOWN.
BUT... I MADE A PROMISE TO SOMEONE...
... YOU HAVE TO OPEN YOURSELF UP... STRIP AWAY THE ARTIFICE YOU'VE BUILT UP AROUND YOURSELF...
... AND HOPEFULLY... YOU'LL FIND NEW REASONS TO LIVE...
I HAVE NO IDEA IF SOMETHING LIKE THIS COULD TAKE THE PLACE OF... EVERYTHING I'VE GIVEN UP...
... BUT I NEED TO FIND OUT.
AND YOU'RE RIGHT... WE CAN'T HIDE ANYMORE.
ANY MISTAKES WE MAKE NOW... WE'LL JUST HAVE TO LIVE WITH.
WE DON'T HAVE A CHOICE --
-- DO WE...?
ZZZZZZZZ...

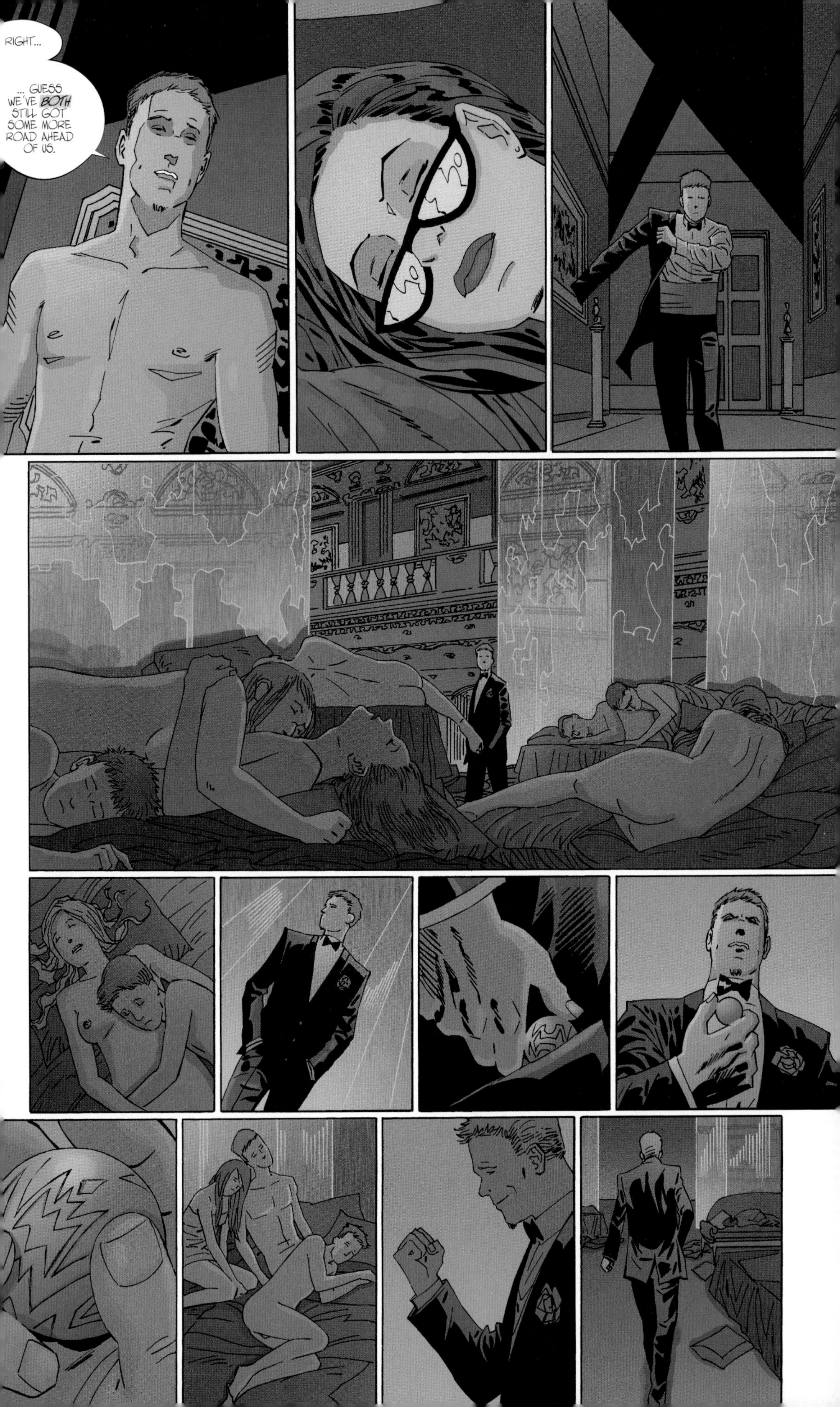
RIGHT...
... GUESS WE'VE BOTH STILL GOT SOME MORE ROAD AHEAD OF US.

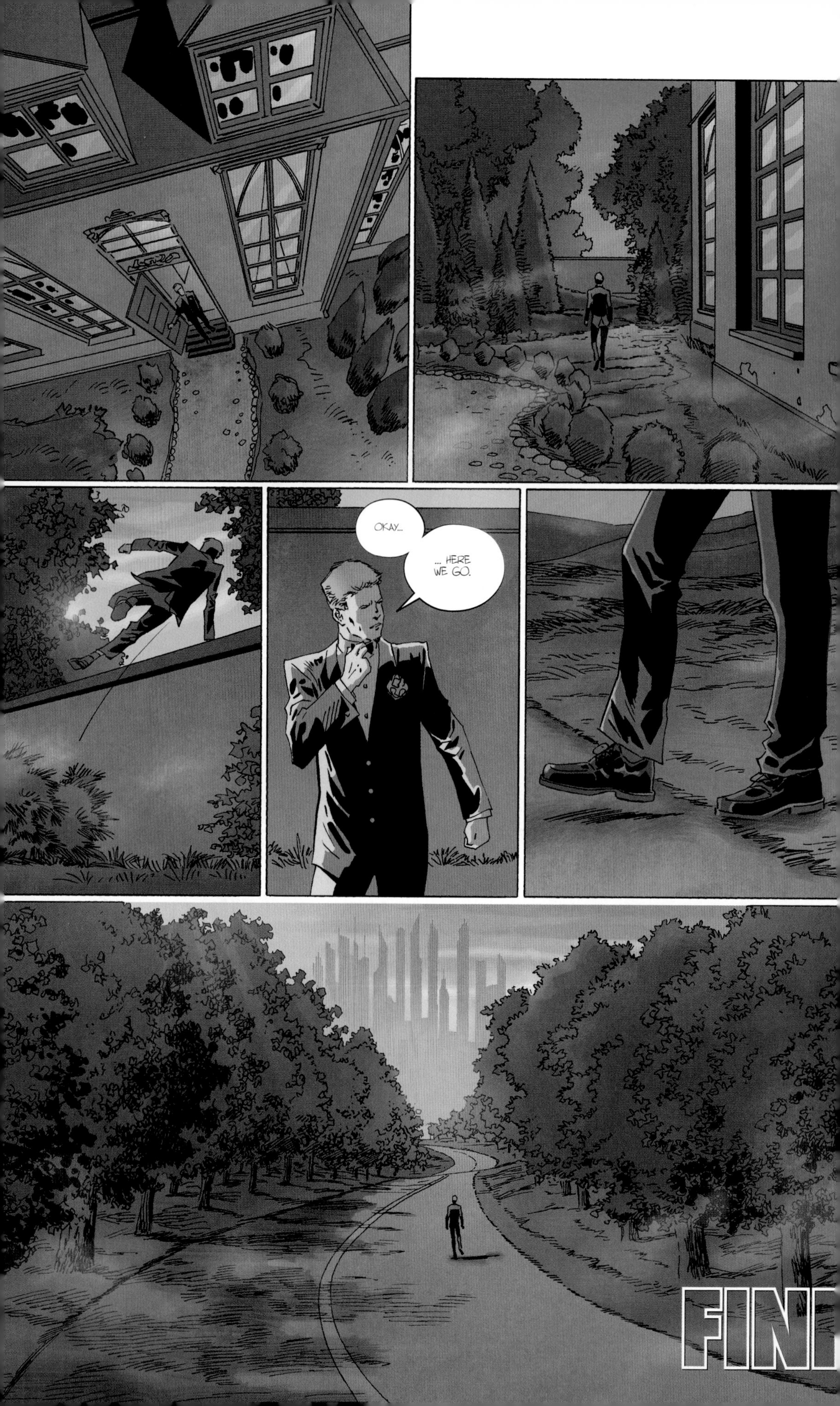

OKAY...
... HERE WE GO.
FIN

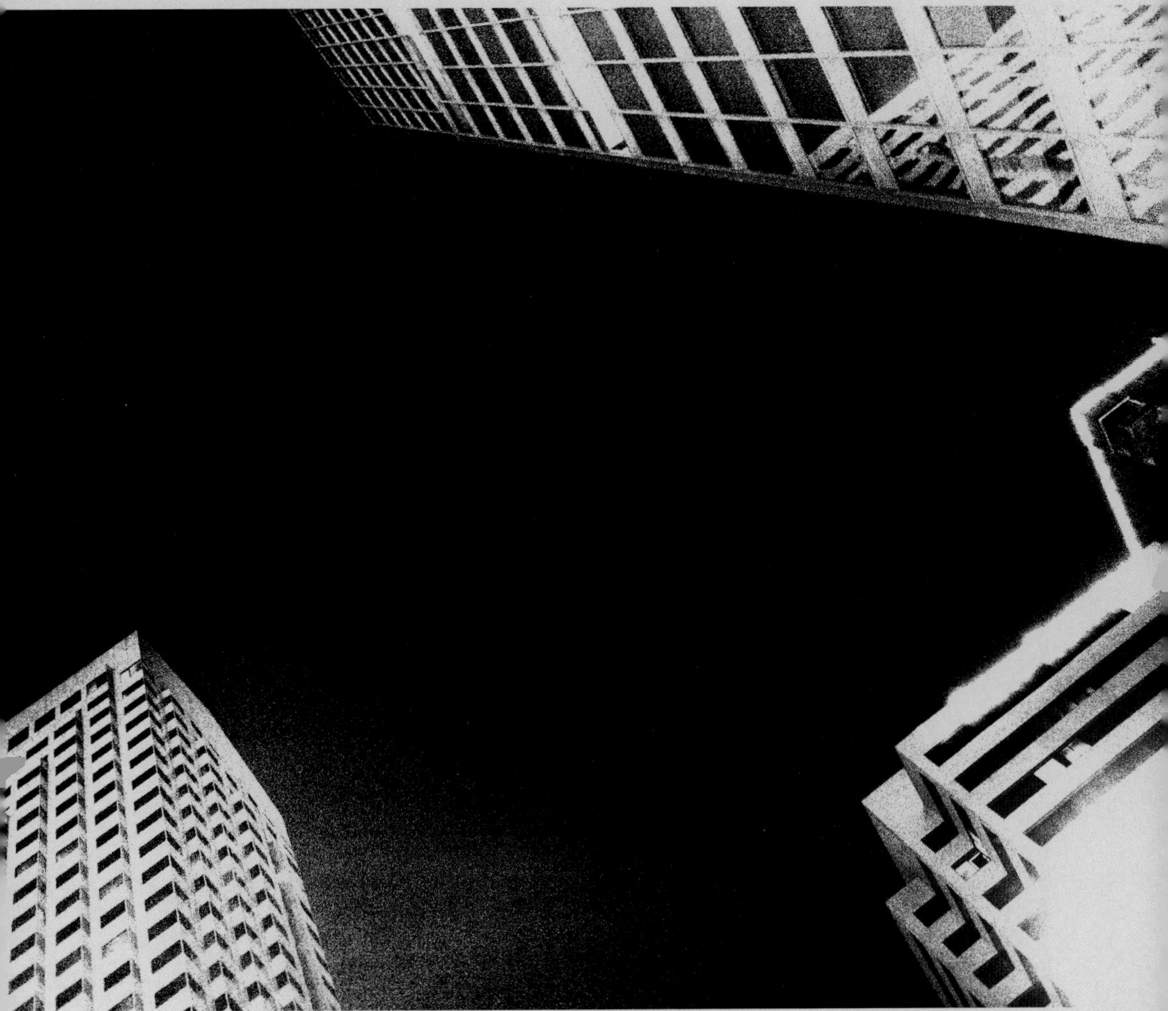

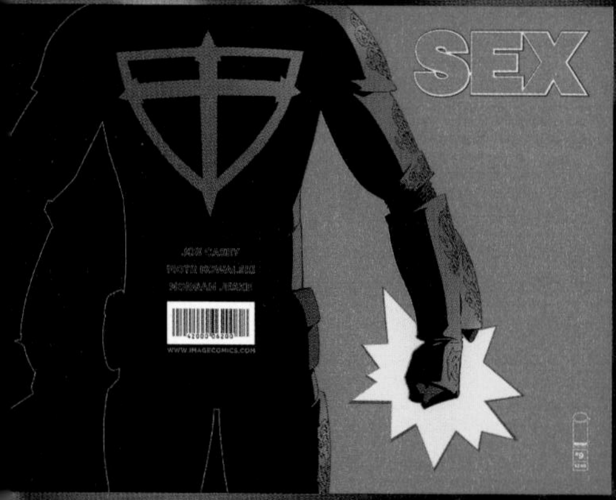
SEX
JOE CASEY
PIOTR KOWALSKI

SEX #9 - DECEMBER 2013

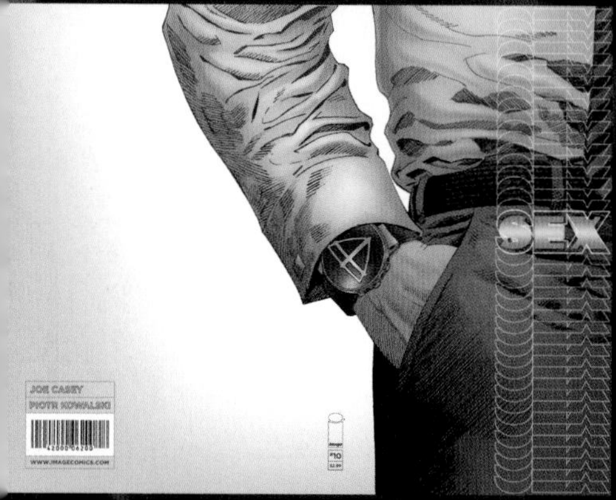
SEX
JOE CASEY
PIOTR KOWALSKI

SEX #10 - JANUARY 2014

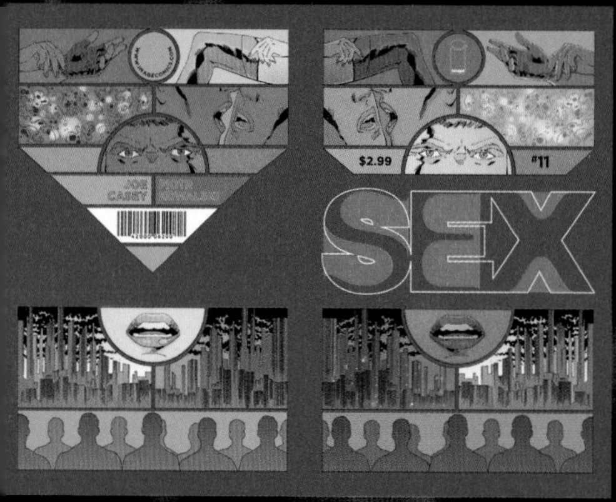
$2.99
#11
SEX

SEX #11 - FEBRUARY 2014

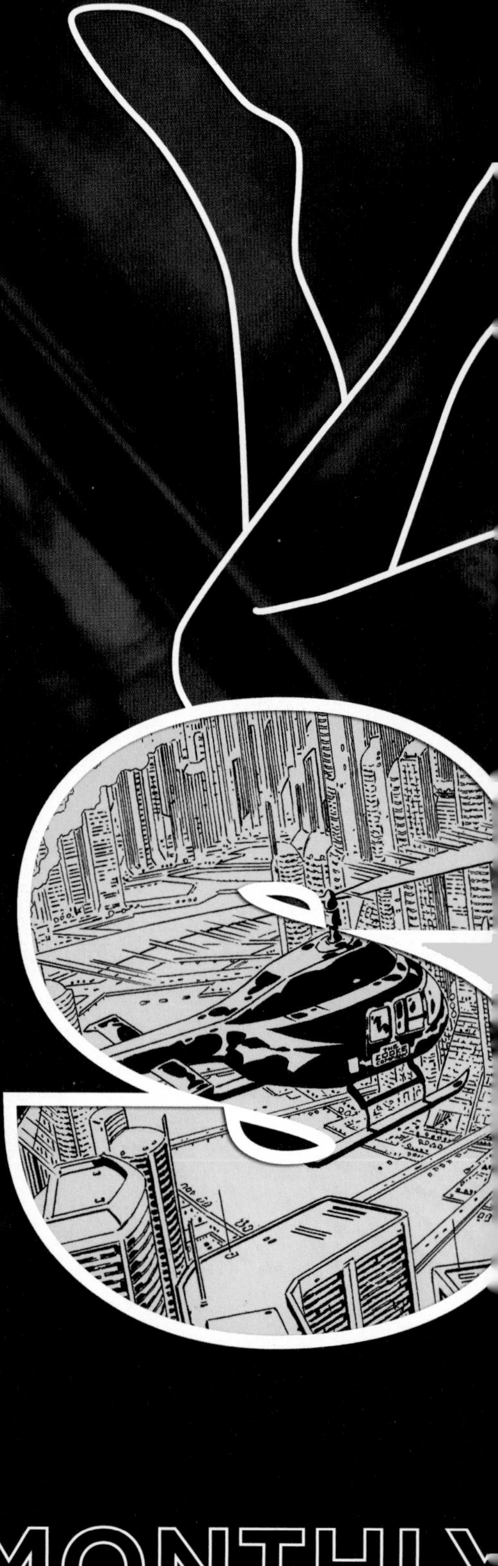

THE MONTHLY

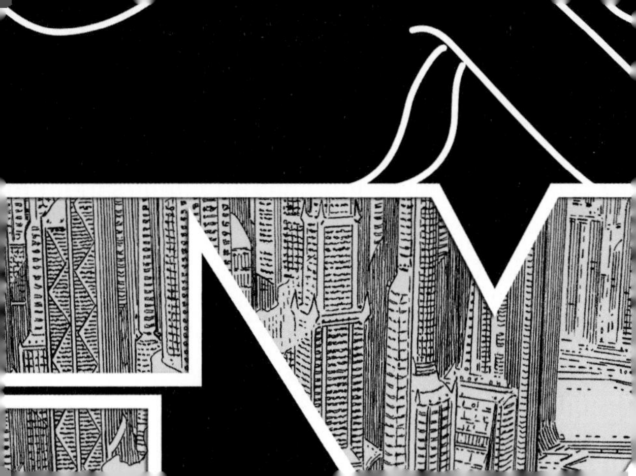

HOW TO ANNOUNCE A NEW SERIES

There are so many ways to go with a book title SEX, but the direct approach turned out to be th best approach. What seemed coy at first glance turned out to be as blatant an announcement as Image Comics has ever attempted (or ever will attempt). When in doubt -- and there was neve any doubt -- just be honest...

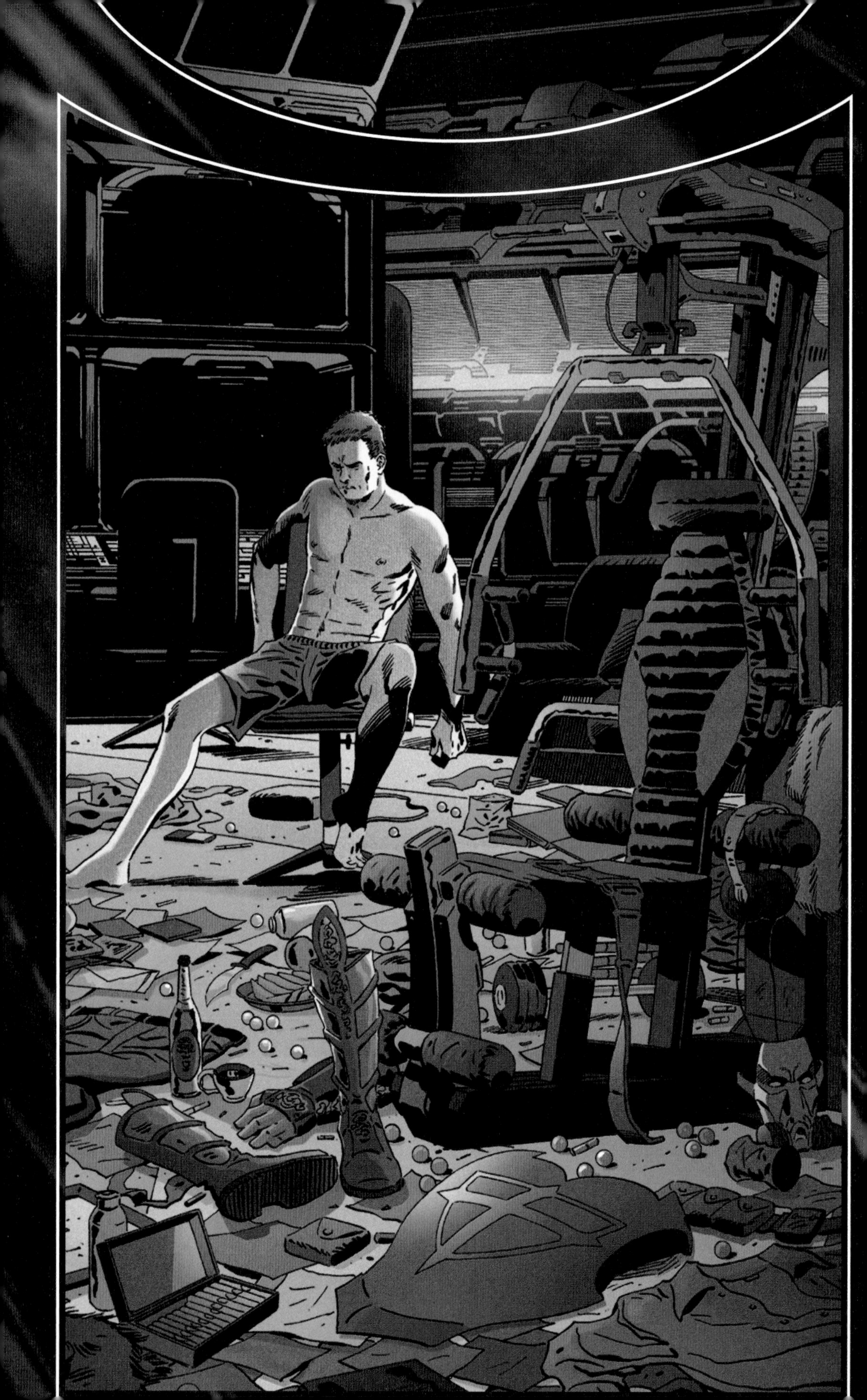

OTHER WORKS BY JOE CASEY

CODEFLESH
(WITH CHARLIE ADLARD)

ROCK BOTTOM
JOE CASEY CHARLIE ADLARD

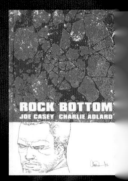

ROCK BOTTOM
(WITH CHARLIE ADLARD)

KRASH BASTARDS
JOE CASEY 1 AXEL #13

KRASH BASTARDS
(WITH AXEL 13)

NIXON'S PALS

NIXON'S PALS
(WITH CHRIS BURNHAM)

OFFICER DOWNE
BIGGER BETTER BASTARD EDITION

OFFICER DOWNE
(WITH CHRIS BURNHAM)

JOE CASEY & ANDY SURIANO
CHARLATAN BALL

CHARLATAN BALL
(WITH ANDY SURIANO)

DOC BIZARRE M.D.
JOE CASEY ANDY SURIANO

DOC BIZARRE, M.D.
(WITH ANDY SURIANO)

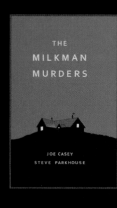

THE
MILKMAN
MURDERS
JOE CASEY
STEVE PARKHOUSE

THE MILKMAN MURDERS
(WITH STEVE PARKHOUSE)

FULL
MOON
FEVER
CASEY
GERARD
COUCEIRO

FULL MOON FEVER
(WITH CALEB GERARD/
DAMIAN COUCEIRO)

BUTCHER
BAKER
THE RIGHTEOUS
MAKER
JOE
CASEY
MIKE
HUDDLESTON

BUTCHER BAKER
THE RIGHTEOUS MAKER
(WITH MIKE HUDDLESTON)

THE
BOUNCE
1
JOE CASEY
DAVID MESSINA

THE BOUNCE
(WITH DAVID MESSINA)

GØDLAND
VOLUME ONE
"HELLO, COSMIC!"
JOE CASEY • TOM SCIOLI

GØDLAND
(WITH TOM SCIOLI)